THE RESTORATION AND ORGANIC DEVELOPMENT OF THE ROMAN RITE

T&T Clark Studies in **Fundamental Liturgy** offer cutting-edge scholarship from all disciplines related to liturgical study. The books in the series seek to reintegrate biblical, patristic, historical, dogmatic and philosophical questions with liturgical study in ways faithful and sympathetic to classical liturgical enquiry. Volumes in the series include monographs, translations of recent texts and edited collections around very specific themes. This series is an initiative of the Society of St Catherine of Siena intended as an encouragement to the renewal of the intellectual apostolate of the Catholic Church.

Edited by
Laurence Paul Hemming
Susan Frank Parsons

Forthcoming titles in the series:

THE RESTORATION AND ORGANIC DEVELOPMENT OF THE ROMAN RITE

László Dobszay

With an Introduction and edited by
Laurence Paul Hemming

t&t clark

Published by T&T Clark International
A Continuum Imprint
The Tower Building   80 Maiden Lane
11 York Road   Suite 704, New York
London SE1 7NX   NY 10038

www.continuumbooks.com

Copyright © László Dobszay, 2010

László Dobszay has asserted his right under the Copyright, Designs and Patents Act, 1988, to be identified as the Author of this work.

British Library Cataloguing-in-Publication Data
A catalogue record for this book is available from the British Library

ISBN: HB: 978-0-567-03385-7
          PB: 978-0-567-03386-4

Typeset by Pindar NZ, Auckland, New Zealand

CONTENTS

CONTENTS

To Father Robert A. Skeris

ACKNOWLEDGEMENTS

First and foremost I wish to thank Msgr Robert A. Skeris, who originally encouraged me to present my thoughts about the sacred Liturgy to the English-speaking world, and who later corrected and published several of my articles on sacred music and the liturgy as a volume in the series *Musicae Sacrae Meletemata* (*The Bugnini-Liturgy and the Reform of the Reform*). He has continued to assist me over a period of more than two decades with friendly advice and help. As a sign of gratitude I have dedicated this volume to him.

I would also like to express my sincere gratitude to Father Ervin Alácsi for making, with great care and delicacy, the first revision of this text as it emerged from its Hungarian original.

I owe special thanks to my friend Laurence Hemming, who encouraged publication of this book, and who edited and improved the text over long months, and worked so closely with the publisher to ensure its completion. My thanks go also to Thomas Kraft, Publishing Editor at T&T Clark, and the Revd Nick Fawcett, for their care in preparing this book for actual publication.

But above all I wish to express my gratitude to those great masters, alive and dead, who taught me everything I know and think about what St Benedict so rightly calls the *Opus Dei*. I still feel even now, and with the same keenness, the truth of the remark made to me by my first teacher in liturgy, Francis Xaver Szunyogh, OSB: 'All that I have done is no greater than the size of my fingernail, and yet it is enough that I should have made even so modest a mark.' Should I receive even the slightest approval from these great masters in looking upon my work, I should be more than satisfied.

László Dobszay

FOREWORD
Laurence Paul Hemming

The twentieth century, from beginning to end, witnessed an entire reform of the worship of the Catholic Church. Commencing in 1903, the reform finally ended in 2001 with the publication of the last of the revised liturgical books, the *Martyrologium Romanum*.[1] In his first book to be published in English, *The Bugnini-Liturgy and the Reform of the Reform*, László Dobszay laid out for those Catholics who were accustomed to think that liturgical reform started in 1965 (and so after the Second Vatican Council) the fact and significance of the far-reaching alterations to the Breviary and Calendar made in 1911. That same book drew attention to the sweeping changes that had been made to the rites of Holy Week (and by inclusion, the celebration of Pentecost) between 1951, 1955 and 1962. This earlier book also explained the meaning of the Catholic Church's ancient ('Gregorian') chant and the significance of its almost complete disappearance by the end of a century that had begun with a papal call for its restoration,[2] the very initiative in 1903 that had ushered in the century-long liturgical upheaval.

In this reform the Catholic Church recast, and so remade from beginning to end, the form, content and character of her every act of worship and her every liturgical book.[3] No corner was left untouched, nothing was left unscrutinized, so much so that one might even say that what scraps remained unaltered were edited by omission. Even where there was no reform in the actual structure or ritual content of a rite, the texts of the prayers were invariably and substantially edited, and the accompanying chants pared away.

In no small way was this a restoration of a kind, necessitated by a complex situation that arose on the basis of perhaps five full centuries of dramatic

---

[1] *Martyrologium Romanum* (2001). An English edition is in preparation.
[2] Pope St Pius X, Motu Proprio of 22 November 1903, *Tra le Sollecitudini* in *Acta Sanctæ Sedis*, vol. 36, pp. 329–39. The Latin text is at pp. 387–95 of the same volume.
[3] At least in the West. The Catholic rites of the East have remained largely untouched by this process. One after another of the forms of the Roman Rite have disappeared – with the possible exception of the Carthusian Rite, all the rites of the religious orders have fallen into desuetude: Dominican; Praemonstratentian; Carmelite; and the varieties of Roman Use to be found among the Benedictines and the Cistercians. The attempt to revive Diocesan uses, as at Braga, flowered and then fell. Nor was the reform confined to the Roman Rite – the Ambrosian and the Mozarabic Rites have both been extensively revised. The Papal Rite, and the vestiges of the Old Roman Rite in customs of the Roman basilicas, have disappeared.

change across Western Europe as a whole: the end of medieval Christendom; the Reformation; the eclipse of feudal rights (fundamental to the way decisions were made about actual and daily church life, decisions all too often concerned with the liturgical practices of dioceses, religious houses, or religious orders); the relegation of religion to the private sphere (epitomized in the concordat that Napoleon forced upon Pope Pius VII in 1801, which said that if the Catholic religion was to be the faith of the majority of Frenchmen it was nevertheless no longer the religion of the French State, a decision that was to be extended to every country that fell under Napoleonic influence or rule); the philosophical proclamation of the 'death of God'; and the rise (and then fall) of Communism; to name but a few. The ecclesial effects of these transformations, especially on the place of chant in the life of the Church (which was never simply the music to be found in hymnaries and antiphonals, but rather the concentrated and sedimented activity of scholas, communities with long histories and carefully nurtured skills),[4] are touched upon and hinted at throughout this book. The re-edition of a book that will appear later in the series of which this book is the first, Geoffrey Hull's *The Banished Heart*, will lay out those effects in far greater detail. That is not the work of this important text, which concentrates on two other things: the requirements for change in the liturgy; and the place and role of the Church's ancient practice of chant in its living practice of worship.

The editors of the series in which this book appears believe that László Dobszay has made here a fundamental and remarkable departure for future debate concerning the Sacred Liturgy of the Catholic Church, the importance of which cannot be underestimated; one that opens up quite new possibilities on the basis of Pope Benedict XVI's Motu Proprio *Summorum Pontificum* of July 2007.[5] In this it heralds the preparations needed for a restoration yet to come. László Dobszay's anglophone work, falling as it does into the broad category of the 'reform of the reform' of the Roman liturgy, and filled as it is with careful, if often passionate, arguments for liturgical adaptation and change, nevertheless sits uneasily in the existing shape of any of the present debates. Liturgical purists of any stamp – and so including those irrevocably wedded to the 'reform of the reform' – will find little comfort here. This book calls for something quite other, and altogether greater, than has been heard hitherto – something which emerges from and gives shape to the very reform made possible by Benedict XVI, and not just by his Motu Proprio. This begs the question of how this book should be read, and in what context. Does it, as would seem most superficially to be the case, simply announce itself as yet one voice among the many 'expert opinions' claiming to have the 'one' solution to the liturgical crisis of the contemporary Church? Voices like these inevitably machinate for the actual dissolution of the integrity of the liturgy of the Western Church in their very clamouring for its restoration. Crying for authenticity, they instigate, invent or restore, practices and

---

[4] A relic of this survives in some Anglican cathedral churches with their regular, in cases daily, singing of Evensong, supported by choir schools – some of quite ancient foundation.

[5] Benedict XVI, Motu Proprio of July 2007, *Summorum Pontificum*, in *Acta Apostolicae Sedis*, vol. 99, pp. 777–81.

habits that have the effect of introducing *another* style, *another* universal form, which then merely takes up its place alongside all the rest. In the very name of unity they fracture the living whole given in each and every liturgical event.

To the contrary, any reader who spends even a short time with this work will quickly discover the gentle, quite reticent tone with which it speaks, marked by generosity and humility, and the tentative character of much that it proposes. If the last century has been filled with the shrill desire – lay and clerical alike – to lay transforming hands on the levers of the ancient and sacred liturgy of the Catholic Church, László Dobszay's is not one of them.

How then should this book be read?

To answer this question one might well recall that in 1953, into the middle of the theological debates of the last century (debates that swirled around an already unfolding liturgical reform), Fr Henri de Lubac introduced the enigmatic phrase 'it is Church that makes the Eucharist, but the Eucharist also makes the Church'.[6] De Lubac goes so far as to say of the Church and the Eucharist that 'each stands to the other, one would say, in reciprocal causality'.[7] It is a telling phrase, not untypical of de Lubac, with his energy for capturing the essence of the interpretative moment, distilling it into an at once immediately intelligible and at the same time elusive formulation. It might therefore seem overly interpretative to draw attention to the way in which de Lubac places the Church's making of the Eucharist first in the order of reciprocity, if it were not for the fact that his work *Corpus Mysticum*, on the Holy Eucharist, of some years earlier had sought to establish precisely the reverse, corrective, thought: that it is the Eucharist that makes the Church. Here he had stressed, in a careful exegesis, that 'strictly speaking, therefore, the Eucharist *makes* the Church'.[8] Why a corrective, and against whom is de Lubac arguing? The phrase 'the Eucharist makes the Church' was stressed in opposition to what de Lubac calls 'the sociological order' of the ecclesial body, and so the argument then current that it is the group that has assembled in order 'to become in all reality the body of Christ', who 'make' the Church.[9] De Lubac is formally opposed to the idea that the sociological order, the assembled body (he speaks repeatedly of the 'people of God', an idea that received ecclesial recognition only at the Second Vatican Council) can in any sense 'make' the Church.[10] For him, it is the exercise of priesthood that makes the Church, inasmuch as it is the priesthood that confects the Eucharist. If, as

[6] Cardinal Henri De Lubac, SJ (1953), *Méditations sur L'Église*, p. 113: 'C'est l'Église qui fait l'Eucharistie, mais c'est aussi l'Eucharistie qui fait l'Église.' English translation by M. Mason (1956), *The Splendour of the Church*; cf. pp. 92–108.

[7] De Lubac (1953), *Méditations sur l'Église*, p. 113: 'De l'une à l'autre, on peut dire que la causalité est réciproque.'

[8] Cardinal Henri De Lubac, SJ, (1949), *Corpus mysticum: l'Eucharistie et l'Église au moyen age*, p. 104: 'A la lettre, donc, l'Eucharistie *fait* l'Église' (author's italics). English translation by G. Simmonds, CJ, R. Price and C. Stephens (ed. L. P. Hemming and S. F. Parsons) as *Corpus Mysticum: The Eucharist and the Church in the Middle Ages*; see pp. 83–88.

[9] De Lubac (1949), *Corpus mysticum*, p. 103: 'L'ordre sociologique [...] devenir en toute réalité corps du Christ.'

[10] Cf. Vatican Council II, Dogmatic Constitution on the Church *Lumen Gentium* of November 1964, Chapter 2, *De populo Dei* (*Concerning the people of God*), §§9–17 *et passim* in N. Tanner, SJ (1990), *Decrees of the Ecumenical Councils*, vol. 2, pp. 855–62.

he argues, the 'people of God is a "cultic community"' and at one and the same time a priestly one,[11] 'nevertheless this priesthood of the Christian people is not concerned with the liturgical life of the Church. It has no direct relation with the confection of the Eucharist.'[12] The idea appears first in his formula, and is then corrected, only because the understanding the formula represents had already taken hold. In the minds of many who were arguing for liturgical reform, any assembly of the baptized was a social manifestation of the Church, such that, in coming together ('gathering'), they therefore 'made' the Church, and so brought it into being.

In both the works in which one or both halves of this formula appears, de Lubac is at pains to stress that 'in the strictest sense Eucharist *makes the Church*',[13] all as a corrective to any idea that the laity, the Christian community, or even the 'people of God' in any sense 'make' what makes the Church. Between the years 1944 (the publication of the first edition of *Corpus Mysticum*) and 1953 (*The Splendour of the Church*) de Lubac had clearly intensified his efforts to correct the view that the merely assembled Christian people 'made' the Church: the later work draws on, comments on, and extends the understanding of the earlier (and in explicit dialogue with it) in precisely this issue.[14] It would not be wrong to say, therefore, that the formula 'the Church makes the Eucharist: the Eucharist makes the Church' is announced precisely to challenge and set aside the understanding toward which it most obviously seems to point. The priority of the first half of the formula ('the Church makes the Eucharist') announces precisely what de Lubac seeks through his exegesis then to disavow.

Fr Paul McPartlan, commenting on de Lubac's formula, draws attention to the fact that from the moment the formula appeared, so self-evident did it seem to a swathe of theological commentators that the French Jesuit Fr Bernard Sesboüé 'says that he saw the celebrated double principle coined by de Lubac . . . quoted here and there as a patristic formula!'[15] If de Lubac's rebuttal of the claims of the 'sociological order' are quite clear, nevertheless a particular understanding of the priority he accords priesthood in the 'making' of the Church manifests itself in Pope Pius XII's use of the phrase *ex opere operantis Ecclesiæ*, introduced in his 1947 encyclical letter on the sacred liturgy *Mediator Dei*. Pius XII had spoken of the 'prayers and sacred ceremonies . . . "sacramentals" and the other rites which

---

[11] De Lubac (1953), *Méditations sur l'Église*, p. 127: 'le Peuple de Dieu est une "communauté cultuelle"'.

[12] De Lubac (1953), *Méditations sur l'Église*, p. 117: 'Mais ce sacerdoce du peuple chrétien ne concerne pas la vie liturgique de l'Église. Il n'a pas de rapport direct à la confection de l'Eucharistie.'

[13] De Lubac (1953), *Méditations sur l'Église*, p. 129: 'Au sens le plus strict, l'Eucharistie *fait l'Église*' – in the later text we have moved from 'strictly speaking' to 'in the strictest sense', and the scope of de Lubac's italics are extended.

[14] De Lubac specifically references *Corpus Mysticum* on this question in *Méditations sur l'Église* (cf. p. 129), noting 'L'Église est alors véritablement "corpus Christi effecta"' and adding in an accompanying note 'Textes dans *Corpus Mysticum*, 2ᵉ ed. p. 103 et pp. 197–202. [The Church is indeed veritably the effected body of Christ – supporting texts in *Corpus Mysticum*, p. 88 and pp. 175–80.]'

[15] P. McPartlan (1993), *The Eucharist Makes the Church: Henri de Lubac and John Zizioulas in Dialogue*, p. xv, citing B. Sesboüé, *Eucharistie: deux générations de travaux*, in *Études*, no. 335, p. 101.

FOREWORD

have been instituted by the hierarchy of the Church',[16] as things formally distinct from those things (really, the sacraments alone) instituted by Christ himself for the worship of the Church. The suggestion was that there were many things in the worship of the Church that had been fashioned by the Church alone, and introduced by its hierarchical activity in tradition, over which (through the juridical oversight of the papacy) the Church as an institution (a fact of a sociological order if ever there was one) had ultimate control. In reality, this distinction between the work of Christ (*ex opere operato*) and the work of the hierarchy (*ex opere operantis ecclesiæ*) was an innovation, itself reflecting a quite changed understanding of the history and origins of Christian worship.

In 2003 Pope John Paul II referred to de Lubac's formula in a significant way, appearing to repeat it, but in effect reinforcing exactly the understanding that de Lubac sought earnestly to correct, in saying 'the Eucharist builds the Church and the Church makes the Eucharist'.[17] The distinction between building and making is further reinforced in the Latin text by the priority in each case of the word 'Church' in the formula as it is given in the (definitive) Latin text. For the central ambiguity in de Lubac's formula is the meaning of the word 'Church'. Is the Church the assembly of the people of God, coming together to undertake a work, the work of the Sacred Liturgy? This understanding is precisely the one that has prevailed since the Second Vatican Council, fortified by Fr Henri de Certeau's interpretations of de Lubac's work, especially *Corpus Mysticum*,[18] and yet we have already seen it ruled out by de Lubac. Or is the Church a work of the priesthood, inasmuch as the priests make (confect) what *makes* the Church? And if this is so, to what extent is this making their own, and to what extent is it only a making given in the image and pattern of Christ? Or is *all* the work done (*operatus*), the very making in question, properly and solely that of Christ, of whom, the Second Vatican Council had affirmed, the Church is something akin to a sacrament, such that the Church is in the image and pattern of Christ, and therefore not that the image and pattern of Christ appears in the reality and activity of the Church. This means that the Church's being the sign of Christ is given in the very effecting of the sign (the Church) in its being given.[19] Could it be that, central to the question of liturgical theology, and the Sacred Liturgy as such, is Christology, such that all failures in liturgical understanding are failings in the order of knowing and understanding who the Christ himself is, as failings in understanding of the very 'how it is' that He gives Himself to be known among men?

In truth, in none of de Lubac's attempts at correction, nor in the priority of

---

[16] Pius XII, Encyclical Letter *Mediator Dei* of November 1947 in *Acta Apostolicæ Sedis*, vol. 14, pp. 521–95; p. 532: 'precibus sacrisque cærimoniis . . . de "Sacramentalibus" ac de ceteris ritibus . . . quæ ab Ecclesiastica insituta sunt Hierarchia'.
[17] John Paul II, Encyclical Letter *Ecclesia de Eucharistia* of April 203 in *Acta Apostolicæ Sedis*, vol. 95, pp. 433–75; p. 451 [§26]: 'Ecclesiam ædificat Eucharistia et Ecclesia Eucharistiam efficit.'
[18] Cf. H. de Certeau SJ (1987), *La fable mystique*.
[19] Cf. *Lumen Gentium*, §1. 'Cum autem ecclesia sit in Christo veluti sacramentum seu signum et instrumentum intimæ cum Deo unionis totiusque generis humani untitatis.' ['Since the Church is in Christ in the manner of a sacrament or sign and instrument of the intimate union of God with the whole of the unity of the human race.']

the Church 'making the Eucharist' that de Lubac seeks to correct, is any formal clarification ever given to the meaning of the term 'making' (French *faire*, Latin *facere*, *efficere*). Precisely the runaway success of the formula, and its pitfall, is the obscurity of meaning concealed in its articulation. For even if we were to accept, with de Lubac, that it is the institutional, hierarchical, priesthood that 'makes' the Eucharist (and so precisely not the assembly who have come together as 'people of God'), *even* here, in what sense is the verb 'to make' employed in the making of the Church? Is it the *human* activity (the effecting of what they have been taught to will, for and on behalf of God) of priests which makes the Church, or is it that they are human instruments of a divine activity, such that their very will must already be cancelled for the sake of undertaking a work which is not theirs, and which has been effected already, but whose effects they make present in skilfully and intelligently fulfilling a divine command? Or is the priesthood divided, as Pius XII suggests, into effecting those things which are of divine command, and those things that accompany and surround those divine institutions, through the manifestation of willed human superadditions?

This question goes right to the heart of the way in which this book is to be read. For if László Dobszay is certainly not laying claim to any lay manipulation of the sacred liturgy for the sake of a 'better' experience of the worship of the 'people of God', could he, nevertheless, be seeking to place in the hands of the hierarchy, and above all the ministerial priesthood, an improved set of 'tools' to 'improve' the efficaciousness of liturgical practice? Is what is laid out here simply a restoration of the Roman Rite as a further activity of 'making', such that he has a better plan of production than any reform yet instituted or envisaged, and such that this book simply poses (alongside all other similar, if yet competing, claims) the 'making' of the Church's worship as that means by which it 'makes' the Eucharist? If the people of God make the Eucharist, or even if it is just the priests, were we to put into their hands a better means of making (a better form of the liturgy – whatever 'better' means here), would we not better equip and teach them for the Eucharist they have been called upon to make? And is this not the dilemma with *all* liturgical reform – that it subordinates the work of the sacred to merely human intentions and planning, however *well* intentioned, or however highly trained? And what of that which is not known or adequately understood in the origins of Christian worship, such that some essential act or ritual of making whose meaning and effects are now forgotten, but without which the rites cannot be efficacious – what of this forgotten thing whenever it is left out and erased? What then to make of it all?

At the origins of modernity lies another not less troublesome formula crucial to understanding this question of making. In a key text, St Thomas Aquinas notes that 'natural things from which our intellect gets its knowledge (*scientia*) measure our intellect, as is said in Book X of [Aristotle's] *Metaphysics*: but these things are themselves measured by the divine intellect, in which are all created things, just as all works of art find their origin in the intellect of the artificer'.[20] When

---

[20] Aquinas, *Quæstiones Disputatæ: de Veritate*, Q. 1, art 2, corp.: 'quod res naturales, ex quibus intellectus noster scientiam accipit, mensurant intellectum nostru, ut dicitur X *Metaphysicis*: sed

'making' is understood to be the willed action of an agent subject, then a certain metaphysical structure of intentionality comes into play, even if that agent subject is said to be the creator God himself. In all perfect making, the maker decides in advance what is to be made, and then executes the plan of that making for the sake of the idea to which the thing made then conforms. The things of nature, as Aquinas describes them here, are *intended* to be as they are in the mind of God. As so intended, they produce in the perceiving human intellect an understanding which, when true, corresponds to the truth God intended for them. Indeed, and conversely, for Aquinas, the truth of a thing is given when the human mind comes to know what God already *intended* to be known in the knowing of that thing. This is the original meaning of the formula that 'truth is the adequation of intellect to thing'. St Thomas spells this out in full when he says:

> The first coordination of being to the intellect is in the correspondence of the intellect to a being, or what is called the adequation of thing and intellect: and in this formula the formal condition of the true is completed. This is therefore what truth adds to being, namely the conformity, or adequation, of thing and intellect.[21]

What has been so often overlooked in this formula is that what is at issue is conformity of thing not to the human intellect, but to the divine. The thing lets the human mind be coordinated to the divine, and when that coordination is fulfilled the human mind comes to know what the divine mind already knew to be true. There is here potential for a misunderstanding: we must take care to note that while in this understanding the human mind is perfected by the thing, inasmuch as the thing is 'natural', there is perfection only in the order of natural knowing, and not in the order of salvation. The human mind, in knowing the natural truth of things (what God intended in them to be true) is not ordinarily thereby saved by what it perceives to be true. Truth and grace are distinct in the order of the knowledge of the natural. It is precisely in the liturgical order that the natural and the supernatural come to be distinguished.[22] In the natural order, in the contemplation of a Eucharistic host it is precisely not true that this thing before me is a disc of bread: it has supernaturally been revealed in and through the actions of the Sacred Liturgy that what appears to be natural bread is in fact

---

sunt mensuratæ ab intellectu divino, in quo sunt omnia creata, sicut omnia artificiata in intellectu artificis'.

[21] *De Veritate*, Q. 1, a. 1, corp.: 'Prima ergo comparatio entis ad intellectum ut ens intellectui correspondeat: quæ quidem correspondentia, adæquatio rei et intellectus dicitur; et in hoc formaliter ratio veri perficitur. Hoc est ergo quod addit verum supra ens, scilicet conformitatem, sive adæquationem rei et intellectus.'

[22] My use of the terms *natural* and *supernatural* here is not developed on the basis of de Lubac's own, but is entirely noetic: it arises on the basis first, of a distinction between the human intellect and what God may be said to know as proper to Himself; and second, on a distinction between that knowing, which is ordered directly to the redemption of man (in revelation) and that knowing, which is not directly so ordered. See for de Lubac's mature view of the supernatural his *Le mystère du surnaturel* in *Théologie 64: Études publiées sous la direction de la Faculté de Théologie S. J. de Lyon-Fourvière* (Paris, Aubier, 1965). Translated by Rosemary Sheed as *The Mystery of the Supernatural* (New York, Crossroads, 1998).

the body and blood, soul and divinity, of the Lord. If we did not know that this thing had been transubstantiated by divine decision and liturgically, we could mistake it for other than it really is.[23]

In any Christian understanding this formula for divine truth is unproblematic until human, and not divine, prior intentionality is in question. St Thomas speaks of the way in which the human, the natural, and the divine are all related to each other by means of the verb 'to measure'. (At one point he goes so far as to argue that the word 'mind', *mens*, is itself taken from the verb *mensurando*, 'measuring'.[24]) St Thomas says that 'the divine intellect, therefore measures, and is not measured; a natural thing both measures and is measured; but our intellect is measured, and measures only artefacts, not natural things'.[25] Although by 'natural' St Thomas means all those things that God intends, and although I have sounded a note of caution here, in fact this can extend to including the means of our salvation. In this sense what is to us strictly speaking 'supernatural' has in St Thomas's formula here the same status as the natural. The supernatural, as that which alone is divinely revealed (in Christ) and not otherwise available to the human intellect, nevertheless *also* 'measures' the human intellect and conforms it to the divine mind, but this time the conformity has the additional power to save the intellect it conforms. Yet *all* things are revealed in Christ – both the 'natural' and the 'supernatural'. In this sense creation is also *naturally* in the manner of a sacrament and instrumental sign of Christ: St Athanasius says of Christ the divine Word (glossing the phrase *per quem omnia facta sunt* – 'through whom all things were made' of the Nicene Creed), 'the Word of the Father is Himself divine, that all things that are owe their being to His will and power, and that it is through Him that the Father gives order to creation, and by Him that all things are moved, and through Him that they receive their being'.[26] Inasmuch as it is in Christ that all natural things are given, so too are all things pertaining to human salvation, and so all supernatural things, both before and after the Incarnation. By ancient tradition it is the Word of God who is the Presence in the Jerusalem Temple; it is the Word whom Moses encounters in the burning bush and on Mount Sinaï, and from whom he receives the Law; it is the Word who walks and speaks with Adam in Eden.

If all natural things are encountered in and as nature itself – 'the natural world', the encounter with the supernatural things of God is entirely liturgical.[27] This is as true of the liturgy (and sacraments) of the old dispensation as it is of

---

[23] It is for this reason that the sacred species must never be separated from the liturgical context: it resides in a tabernacle fitted for the purpose in a Church, at an altar; it can only be touched by one ordained and wearing a stole and appropriate dress; in must be kept in a vessel of suitable design and quality, and covered with a veil; it must be accompanied by a light and, when moved, by a bell or clapper.

[24] *De Veritate*, Q. 10, a. 1, resp.: 'Dicendum quod nomen mentis a mensurando est sumptum.'

[25] *De Veritate*, Q. 1, a. 2, resp.: 'Sic ergo intellectus divinus est mensurans non mensuratus; res autem naturalis, mensurans et mensurata; sed intellectus noster est mensuratus, non mensurans quidem res naturales, sed artificiales tantum.'

[26] St Athanasius (1939), *De incarnatione*, ed. F. L. Cross, §38, l. 7–11: καὶ περὶ τῆς θειότητος τοῦ Λόγου τοῦ Πατρός καὶ τῆς εἰς πάντα προνοίας καὶ δυνάμεως αὐτοῦ. καὶ ὅτι ὁ ἀγαθὸς Πατὴρ τούτῳ τὰ πάντα διακοσμεῖ καὶ τὰ τάυτα ὑπ' αὐτοῦ κινεῖται καὶ ἐν αὐτᾷ ζωοποιεῖται.

[27] As all four Gospels are at pains to stress, what reveals Jesus to be the Divine Son of God in every

the new. The Sacred Liturgy is the instrumental means – the sign as such and the constellation of signs, wherein the Word reveals and *effects* the supernatural understanding of salvation to mankind. The revealing is an effecting, it is the making (creating) of us. We can only consider this point in outline here, but it has been explained in full elsewhere.[28] The Liturgy is how Christ comes to be known and continues to be revealed in the midst of, and through, the natural world. The sanctuary – ritually the Holy of Holies – is a midpoint, between heaven and earth, between the natural and the supernatural realm. It shows how the two are related (for humanity), it is made of natural material, and yet it intends, and reveals the supernatural, and what is found therein is nothing of (non-divine) nature. It is in this sense that the sanctuary is sacred – although made of natural materials (how else could it be made, since it is made by the hands of men), it is a reserved place, such that only the supernatural is visible and to be encountered within it. Yet the whole fabric is required for this visibility to be effected: an essential part of the fabric is not just the stones or marble of the sanctuary, but also the practices, the texts and the actions that belong within. Since the passion of the Lord, since the rending of the Temple veil, the supernatural it reveals can be visible to the eyes of all the faithful.

For St Thomas, the human mind is measured by natural things. It cannot intend, and so make, anything natural: everything the human mind makes is a matter of artifice. As an artifice it would be (for St Thomas) 'true' inasmuch as it conformed to what that human mind had planned for it. Inasmuch as the Sacred Liturgy has been a thing of human manufacture and production – even if safeguarded in the hands of the priesthood and its guarantor, the papacy, nevertheless, it remains an artefact. However, inasmuch as the Sacred Liturgy is divinely revealed, it falls under the scope of what St Thomas understands by the natural, as what is by nature proper to the divine mind and is capable of 'measuring', which means here, redeeming, the human mind.

Is the Sacred Liturgy largely a human artefact (as Pius XII had suggested), or is it that class of 'natural' thing that is 'natural' to God and 'supernatural' to man? For priesthood, correctly understood – indeed understood from its very origins – is the effecting of divine things at human hands. Priesthood, strictly speaking, is only properly exercised in the Holy of Holies, in the Sanctuary of the Lord, where its human signification is essentially different. For the Sanctuary is (ritually and symbolically) outside time and beyond (earthly, 'humanly natural') place: its time is God's (eternity), and its place is heaven. The priest effects the things of God, but he does not make them – or rather, we might say, priesthood is the one instance where human hands may make something that is natural to God, and supernatural to man, because the priest does not act through his own will, but alone effects what is known to be the will of God. Inasmuch as priesthood 'makes' the things of God, above all the Eucharist, it does not produce them,

---

case refers us to the relation between the Word and the Jerusalem Temple, culminating in the Lord's claim 'destroy this Temple and in three days I will raise it up' (Jn 2.19).

[28] See Hemming, L. P., *Worship as a Revelation* (London: Burns & Oates/Continuum, 2008).

but, because the priest fulfils ordinances that only God has ordained, he effects at human hands what God alone makes, or, we would more properly say, creates.

This distracts and unravels the entirely productive, 'poietic', sense of 'making' that we moderns otherwise immediately hear in de Lubac's formula – even as he himself understood it as a corrective to an increasing trend in the development of Catholic theology of the twentieth century. As a thought that takes hold and grips the theological thinking of that time, even more so does it now, such that theology, insofar as it is overcome by the modern sense of making and fashioning – that all things are essentially constructs, artefacts to be grasped by the human will and at its disposal – is now as much dominated by the modern understanding of making as every other discourse and body of knowledge.

This book is written into the midst of that situation. It is written with an inherent sensitivity to the catastrophe implicit in the saturation of contemporary thinking with 'making' and construction, and so with an instrumental under-standing of all production, such that even God's creating is instrumentalized to human reason (because the real meaning of priesthood is now only rarely adequately understood). The Sacred Liturgy of the Catholic Church has above all become the site of the most tragic manufacture: a productive 'making' in the most extreme sense of the word. The 1911 liturgical reforms of St Pius X began with the justification that the liturgy be reorganized for the sake of human concerns: the justification for the reforms after the Second Vatican Council was that the ancient liturgy of the Catholic Church needed to be adjusted to 'the requirements of our modern age'.[29] The things of God were refashioned in man's image. The then Joseph Cardinal Ratzinger wrote of (especially the postconciliar) liturgical reform: 'What happened after the Council was . . . fabricated liturgy. We abandoned the organic, living process of growth and development over the centuries, and replaced it – as in a manufacturing process – with a fabrication, a banal on-the-spot product.'[30] In the same place Ratzinger describes this situation as 'a devastation',[31] and elsewhere spoke of himself as gazing on what had hap-pened to the liturgy as on the ruination of all that had been hoped for.[32] It is this situation, and not any situation of mere making, that this book addresses.

Nevertheless, and whatever else may be the case, as is pointed out in this book several times, the present liturgical situation of the Catholic Church is normative for the overwhelming majority of Catholics, now two, or perhaps more, genera-tions from the Second Vatican Council, and several generations from the papacy

---

[29] Cf. Pope St Pius X (1911), *Divino afflatu*, in *Acta Apostolicæ Sedis*, vol. 3, pp. 633–37, especially the phrase concerning the liturgy, 'ut clero . . . non maius imponoretur onus' (that the burden for the clergy might not be any heavier); Vatican Council II, Dogmatic Constitution on the Sacred Liturgy, *Sacrosanctum Concilium* (1963), §1: 'Ad nostræ ætatis necessitates.'

[30] Cardinal Joseph Ratzinger (1992), *Preface* to Klaus Gamber, *La Réforme Liturgique en ques-tion*, p. 6 f.: 'Ce qui s'est passé après le Concile . . . on a mis une liturgie fabriquée. On est sorti du processus vivant de croissance et de devenir pour entrer dans la fabrication. On n'a plus voulu continuer le devenir et la maturation organiques du vivant à travers les siècles, et on les a remplacés – à la manière de la production technique – par une fabrication, produit banal de l'instant.'

[31] Ratzinger (1992), *Preface*, p. 6: 'une dévastation'.

[32] Cardinal Joseph Ratzinger (2005), *Preface* in Alcuin Reid (2005), *The Organic Development of the Liturgy*, p. 11.

of St Pius X. The reform László Dobszay proposes is, therefore, not so much the reform of the reform that actually took place, as the (organic) reform, which had long been discussed in the nineteenth century, and which the fathers of the Second Vatican Council had thought themselves to be approving.

Such a reform is a way back (an un-making), a return, not simply to a former age, but rather to how the ancient forms of the Roman Rite might once again speak, and so unfold their truth, in the present age. What is invited here is a journey of understanding, not by one man, nor by the clergy and the priesthood alone, but one that needs to be undertaken by the whole Church. Such a journey is not a simple mental act of understanding, but rather an intrinsic insertion of souls into the very spirit of the Sacred Liturgy, through a whole range of means and discourses – all the elements that comprise the sacred rites (revelation, scripture, dogma, tradition, ritual, music), in order to disclose all over again the real meaning of the word 'Church'. For what is implicit in St Thomas Aquinas's use of the word 'natural' (as that which is natural to God but supernatural to man) is nevertheless able to be revealed to humanity, and in fact is so revealed in the person of the Word, the Christ. Liturgy is Christological from beginning to end.

Humanity is, by the means of salvation to be taken up (the very *ad superiorem* of the super-natural) into the divine nature, to be divinized, by a means supernatural to man but natural to God. To share the supernatural life of God becomes man's final end and true nature. In this life the means by which this superorientation of man, beyond himself and into the divine life, takes place is the Sacred Liturgy. It is for this reason, as László Dobszay well understands and makes clear in this book, the liturgy is not something made by man, but is the very *making* – the completion of the creation – of man. As something entirely supernatural, and whose meaning is entirely revealed, it is the means by which creation is again taken up into the active creativity of God and refashioned into that one (in) whom it was first called to be. Here the meaning of priesthood can be fully understood. Priesthood, properly understood, effects and repeats at their proper times the supernatural itself, as those rites revealed by God to man which take him up into the divine life. It is for this reason that every rite is foreordained in its structure and its content by God. Every human intrusion into this revealed character of liturgy intrudes into the capacity of the liturgy to undertake the work that it is, which makes of man a heavenly being, one fit for the society of God and his Divine Son.

We are required to ask whether de Lubac was not to a certain extent the victim of the very objectification that he sought to correct and overcome, both in the writing of the book *Corpus Mysticum* and in the formula 'The Church makes the Eucharist: the Eucharist makes the Church'. For this formula only makes sense once the Holy Eucharist has become the foremost object of the liturgical action, reducing the rest of the Sacred Liturgy (the eternal hymn of praise to the most high God in the greater offices of Matins, Lauds and Vespers, and the sanctification of daily life in the little hours from Prime to Compline, and the rites surrounding the other sacraments) to so many ceremonies and texts. While the Eucharist is indeed both the summit and the centre of all liturgical action, nevertheless the Eucharist can never be understood, which means never adequately interiorized in the soul, without the efficacy of the whole panoply of the liturgical cursus whose centre it is. The texts of the Eucharistic liturgy echo and resonate throughout the rest of the daily round of the liturgy – above all in the offices, the hours of the Church: Matins, Lauds and Vespers especially; but also at Prime, Terce, Sext, None and Compline. Without this continuing cycle of chant: praise, sanctification and litany; the Eucharist can never fully be understood – which means never be fully appropriated by the human intellect. The explanatory texts of the Holy Eucharist above all are to be *sung*. It is no accident, therefore, that the one to explain this – the author of the book for which this Preface is only the introduction – is first and foremost an exemplary student of the Church's sacred chant.

Even in pre-Christian antiquity it was well understood that music, above all sacred music, set man in proportion to the heavens and coordinated him to a sacred rhythm and meaning that was cosmic in its breadth. This was prefigured in the Pythagorean roots of the understanding of music as intrinsically ordered to the unity and singularity of the cosmos, as an earthly expression of a divine realm and order. That Christian liturgy was first sung and only later merely recited shows the extent to which Christian worship took up the insights of antiquity, to complete and fulfil them. The liturgical voice is *essentially* seraphic – it exchanges the praises of God 'alter ad alterum',[33] from one to the other, in the earthly vision of the descending New Jerusalem (the sacred liturgy enacted in the sanctuary of a church), proclaiming in a voice that echoes through the whole canopy of heaven the glory and majesty of that triune One whose praises are sung. Whenever the Church sings, she *is taken up* into this eternal chant of the divine praises, and *is made* audibly the heavenly sanctuary in which man, fulfilled and replete in God, is to have his proper abode. Deprived of song, the Sacred Liturgy can only gesture towards its true meaning and work. The restoration of the Roman Rite will therefore be effected in and through the restoration of the understanding of its seraphic voice, a voice which in lifting men into the company of the angels (prefigured in Sacred Scripture at both the resurrection and the ascension of the Lord),[34] proclaims the completion of creation, and so fulfils the end toward which creation is ordered and for which the created order was indeed made.

Our Lady of Sorrows in Lent, 2009

---

[33] Cf. Isa. 6.3, describing the vision of God in the Temple. The two seraphim before the Lord in the Temple 'cried one to another, and said "Holy, holy, holy, the Lord God of hosts, all the earth is full of his glory"'. This text forms the basis for the words of the eighth Responsory at Matins in the weeks after Pentecost.
[34] Cf. Jn 20.12; Acts 1.10-11.

INTRODUCTION

This book is an absurdity.

It is absurd, first, because now is not the time to start making changes again in the liturgy; people – priests and faithful alike – are fed up with innovations and debates. For each generation one shock is enough. There are always those who will say that whatever the liturgy is, or is not, only one thing really suffices: to follow the approved liturgy with due devotion and observance.

Secondly, this book is absurd in the sense that the shaping of the liturgy is not the task of any individual. The laws of the Church – and rightly so – do not follow the proposals of individual men; it is the task of the prelates – and foremost among them, the Holy Father – to take ultimate responsibility for considering these problems.

And it is absurd because these pages are written by a layman living in an isolated country far from the mainstream. His voice does not even reach the centre, where things really happen. Let the hermit be silent and pray.

There is a history behind why – after long reluctance – I decided to write this book. When, in 2003, my papers, previously published in 'Sacred Music', were collected in one book as *The Bugnini-Liturgy and the Reform of the Reform*, I felt (and later learned conclusively from people's reactions) that to speak in *general* terms runs the risk of being misunderstood or misinterpreted. When I stated that there *is* a way out of the present-day crisis of the liturgy, and – full of apprehensions – pointed to a few directions, some commentators attributed certain ideas to me that I had never entertained. On the other hand, others may have considered my scribings to be simply a collection of general guidelines without any thought concerning the concrete steps that need to be undertaken.

Five years ago, when I presented my book to Joseph Cardinal Ratzinger, then Prefect of the Congregation for the Doctrine of the Faith, he pointed to the title and asked me: What do you mean by 'the Reform of the Reform'? In the short time available I could say hardly more than that I understood there to have been a 'break' in the liturgy, an interruption of the continuous development of the Roman Rite; in fact, a new rite of essentially Neo-Gallican type had been introduced. If we are to be returned only to 1962, the task is not simply to restore that state of the liturgy, but to implement the reform of the Roman Rite that was clearly desired at that time, but that got lost in various committees. I supposed then that to try to encapsulate this in a very brief formulation of a few moments would hardly have made sense, and if I had not been sitting face to face with so highly intelligent a person, one who had been dealing with these problems for decades, I would have been very much ashamed of being unable to say anything more concrete.

This book therefore strives to illustrate what was actually behind what I was able to say only very briefly in that meeting. I intend no more than to show that a reform in this sense *is* possible. I do not delude myself with the hope that these 'proposals' will be heard by anybody; and still less that they will play any role in the future. My only wish is to make more comprehensible what I wrote in my first venture into English, and to leave this earthly life knowing that I have clarified my position for anyone who might have an interest in what people are thinking when they address themselves to liturgical problems in this periphery of Christian Europe. This book, then, is a message in a bottle and testament from a scholar who has been studying, ruminating and meditating on these liturgical questions for most of his life.

Today we are not in the same place that we were in 2003. Since then the keenly anticipated Motu Proprio *Summorum Pontificum* has been promulgated, permitting the celebration of the classical Roman Rite throughout the whole Church. Numerous studies and articles of great erudition and deep speculation are published on this topic nearly every day all over the world; frequently, and, inevitably, these writings contradict each other. They ponder, mostly from a *theological* or *pastoral* viewpoint, what has happened and what is happening (or what ought to happen). There have also been contributions of historical interest, discussing the arguments, considerations and debates that prepared the introduction of new liturgical books and new regulations after the Council.

As I mentioned, however, in my previous book, relatively few works have analysed the liturgy *as a liturgy*. The liturgy has its own life, its own laws of evolution; it also has its 'illogical' or 'alogical' elements, and perhaps it is precisely due to these that the liturgy shows itself to be a living organism. As such, the liturgy is not a specified body of dogmatic statements, nor is it a source of pastoral efficiency. As far as theology is concerned, in the subtle texture of the liturgy the *lex credendi* is undoubtedly a determining factor, and the 'sacris erudiri' an excellent goal to attain. As to the pastoral viewpoint: the specific condition and aptitudes of individuals and communities taking part in the liturgy cannot be left out of consideration. But there is even more at stake than that. The *Opus Dei* in full is a complexity of spiritual, psychological, historical, cultural and artistic factors, all of which have their proper function in transmitting the full essence of the liturgy, akin to the physical realities used in the administration of sacraments and sacramentals. The liturgy stands before the faithful as something not made by man. It is God's own activity and a living form of and for the Church. The anonymous character of the liturgy was not intended as a device simply to conceal its actual authors (in fact, pious tradition at times preserved the name of the supposed authority behind a rite or parts of it). It is meant rather to emphasize that the liturgy cannot be fabricated. It appears before our eyes as a living reality, an organism. One receives it not only out of mere obedience towards the laws and regulations of the Church, but as 'the tradition of our ancestors'.

For this reason changes in the history of the liturgy are not so much results of arbitrary interventions into its life, but rather the consequences or manifestations of its living presence in the day-to-day practice of men. In the everyday use of the liturgy sometimes there may emerge the necessity for slight 'improvement', or for adaptation according to the exigencies of time. But these changes are to be integrated into a continuous tradition. As we know, the Council Fathers intended nothing more than *this* kind of liturgical reform.

In the first part of this book I cannot bypass discussion of some points that arise in international discourse today. I do try, however, to keep discussion of abstract principles to a minimum. This is made all the more possible since I wish to say very little about theological and pastoral themes; only adding where necessary to my previous book, and relative to recent events.

On the other hand, the reader will find that I have written more extensively about some typically *liturgical* matters, surveying the parts of the liturgy one by one. When writing my first book I felt somewhat forced into a *critical* analysis of the Neo-Roman liturgy. This book aims to provide definite answers to the questions and doubts that arose from that work; I am able now to focus on what might happen in the future. Though I have to return to some points of my book on the *Bugnini-Liturgy* – and I apologize for any unavoidable repetitions – I do so only in a cursory way, referring anyone seeking fuller details to the relevant chapter of my first book.

Though the material in Part I of this book is apparently arranged chronologically, it is not intended as a history of modern liturgy; such a way of organizing simply offered an effective way of presenting the main issues. Since the book as a whole is an explanation of a *standpoint* rather than a scientific survey, bibliographical references are kept to a minimum.

PART I

1

WHAT IS THE 'ROMAN RITE'?

The word 'rite' is not unequivocal; its use without clarifying its meaning in a given context gives rise to misunderstandings. Sometimes we label as 'rites' single elements of a ceremony, rubrics of a cultic activity: when to kneel down, when to use the sign of the Cross, how to go over from right to left, how or when to recite this or that text, and so on. In this context 'rite' only means a 'rule' to be followed in a cultic setting.[1]

When we speak of the 'Tridentine Rite' or 'Dominican Rite', we refer to the system of a *full* liturgical order. In this sense a 'rite' is the content, the entire fixed material, of the liturgy. It is more than the sum of single elements; rather, it is their complexity in an organic structure. The single parts mutually suppose and indicate each other; they are in line with a common conception, a unitary style. This cohesion is the result not of some kind of engineering process, but of a continually cultivated, controlled tradition, always improved according to necessity.

There are rites attached to historical epochs, like that of the ancient Roman basilicas (the Old Roman Rite), the post-Tridentine, or the post-Vatican era. There are also rites pertaining to individual communities, like those of religious orders (Praemonstratensians, Cistercians, etc.), of the papal court (*Ritus Curiae*) or – much less known nowadays – of medieval dioceses (e.g. Paris, Mainz, Salisbury, Prague, etc.). Though the community adheres to its proper rite, the single rites are not sharply and permanently separated.[2] A rite might develop in the course of history without losing its continuity and essential content. It may have received new elements, while other elements may have been forgotten. The various rites were frequently influenced by other rites; sometimes one rite was changed into another: for instance, the *Ritus Curiae* became the basis of the Tridentine Rite; the Paulite order took over the Esztergom Rite and adapted it to their own usage. Stability and 'liquidity' can both be equally present in the life of a rite. For example, monks under the Rule of St Benedict generally followed their common, if specific, monastic customs, yet individual monasteries also had

---

[1] Some points of this chapter are explained in a more detailed way in László Dobszay (2008a), 'What Does the "Roman Rite" Denominate?'
[2] 'Rites are not rigidly fenced off from each other. There is exchange and cross-fertilization between them': Joseph Ratzinger (2000), *The Spirit of the Liturgy*, p. 164.

distinctive traditions. For what follows it therefore becomes necessary to make the notion of the *Roman Rite* more precise.

The analysis of particular rites manifests that they are not all separate and independent formations; some of them are members of what we may call ritual families, either because they are descendants of a common rite, or because they were amalgamated as a result of particular historical circumstances. It would be false to conceive of this process as the separation of a parent liturgy by a creative expansion into sub-rites, or as a historical break caused by negligence, or, for that matter, as a purposeful, calculated secession. It is entirely possible that the parent rite itself was not formally canonized in all details and homogeneous in all parts, but rather a composition of some common, as it were, *obligatory elements*, and some *options*, leaving place for local decisions and development in less important, peripheral aspects. On this basis, particular traditions could have emerged, more or less canonical, which shared all the essential features, but added a number of local decisions through accretion or by deciding on certain options.

In this sense we can regard the Roman Rite as an amalgamation or parent rite of different local traditions. When the Western half of Europe received the Roman Rite, this rite was a composite of fixed and optional (or even free) elements. Their ranking reflected some kind of conceptual 'hierarchy' within these components. Thus dioceses and religious orders formed their proper rite on the basis of a common heritage, and so they canonized their proper rite to the extent they thought necessary. Though the ancient Roman Rite had also been regulated by papal resolutions, the norm was intrinsically the liturgical life of the rite itself, which means the way it was celebrated in the city of Rome, and respectively, in other given bishoprics. Continuity of practice and tradition was a force even stronger than legal determination. As for legal determination, it was enough to say: keep yourself to the usual liturgy, the received liturgical tradition of your church!

For the Roman Rite, taken in this sense, no exact time of origin can be ascertained. What is surely documented is that its essential elements survived in a continuous tradition from the earliest liturgical books (eighth–ninth centuries) up to the twentieth century. All this time it was faithfully preserved in its identity, but also *augmented*, that is (as we like to say today), it developed organically. Concerning certain parts of the Mass there are even earlier witnesses, and the structure of the Divine Office in St Benedict's time (early sixth century) was identical to what we see in the liturgical books three centuries later, or, in fact, what was preserved until the beginning of the twentieth century.

This means that we have formal evidence that the Roman liturgy lived and developed organically in its essential content over at least 1,500 years (and from this we can safely presume its origins are yet more ancient). This is, however, not a continuity that pertains to every single component. More strictly speaking, the phrase 'Roman Rite' should be used more like a collective term: it refers to the essential unity of the ancient Roman liturgy as it lived in many particular liturgies of dioceses and religious orders,[3] as well as in the *Ritus Curiae*, or what became

---

[3] Cf. Alcuin Reid (2005), *The Organic Development of the Liturgy*, pp. 19–30.

the 'Tridentine' Rite. With this common term we refer to the historical coherence and dependence of individual rites on a common parent liturgy. Though the particular traditions frequently named themselves 'rites' (*Ritus Romanae Curiae, Ritus Ecclesiae Sarisburiensis*,[4] etc.), any misunderstanding can be avoided much more easily if these are referred to as *Uses* within the Roman *Rite*. According to this improved phraseology, we can say, for example, that the Tridentine *Use* (or the Use of Pius V) is a form or part of the Roman *Rite*.

Does this mean that *all* Latin liturgies of the past centuries can be labelled 'Roman'? Not at all: first, the Roman Rite was originally the liturgy of the city of Rome, which later spread across the continent of Europe, and then to the whole world. But before this expansion it coexisted with other rites, not quite independent from, but neither identical with, the Roman Rite. Some features connected these rites with each other but they had their proper, fixed structures and peculiar style. Drawing well-adaptable borderlines: the wider environment of the Roman Rite was the community of *Old Latin Rites*. Among them the best known is the Rite of Milan (*Ambrosian*), the *Beneventan* Rite (Southern Italy), the quite distinctive *Mozarabic* and the enigmatic *Gallican* Rite. Remnants of earlier rites can be guessed at through some curious items recorded in Central- and Northern-Italian sources. Concerning the Office, some historical evidence has also survived of other rites from Italy and ancient Gaul.[5] In spite of some common features, they cannot be considered as points of convergence within a fluid process. They all had their proper logic and sets of rules, their style and a continuous life. The Roman Rite in this respect is *one*, surely the most balanced and classical one, among the Old Latin rites, which aptly became later almost the only rite of Latin Christianity.

The case is quite different with the formations *after* the Roman Rite had been generally established; these originated from attempts at subsequent reform. The creators of reform-rites were familiar with the Roman Rite, they grew up in it, but became discontented, and wanted to 'improve' it; or they composed new structures for replacing some parts or the whole of the Roman tradition.

There were theoreticians in the field of the Roman Rite as early as the Middle Ages who were discontented with what they experienced in their environment; they proposed modifications, sometimes even significant modifications. It suffices for now to refer to one example: that of Amalarius.[6] These reformers differed, however, from 'modern' ones in three respects: they never laid hands on the essential elements of the rite; their proposals were – in comparison with the entirety of the rite – few in number; and in most cases they did not want to 'improve' the rite, but rather to effect a 'return' from 'disturbed' or 'corrupted'

---

[4] An exemplary case is the Sarum Use, the only one where detailed study is possible in modern transcription (cf. Nicholas Sandon (1984), *The Use of Salisbury*, vol. 1: *The Ordinary of the Mass*; vol. 3: *The Holy Week*). I will later refer repeatedly to this edition, mainly in chapters 20 and 21 of Part II.

[5] Suitbert Bäumer (1895), *Geschichte des Breviers*, pp. 143–62. (Bäumer's book, though surely outdated in some details, is the most informative description of the history of Roman Office.) See also Robert F. Taft, SJ (1986), *The Liturgy of the Hours in East and West*, pp. 93–163.

[6] *Lexikon für Theologie und Kirche*, vol. 2: esp. pp. 147–48; 'Amalarius of Metz', in David Hiley (1993), *Western Plainchant – A Handbook*, pp. 569–71.

forms to the 'pristine' practice of Rome. Other liturgical experts undertook no more than what we would really call an editorial task: they found confusions, divergent practices and uncertainties, and wished to offer their assistance by improving some elements of the rite. First of all, it was in the early Middle Ages (after the transfer to the new Frankish environment) that such rearrangement became truly urgent (e.g. the reforms under Alcuin and Benedict of Anian). A third kind of liturgist excelled in augmentation: by virtue of a commission or of their own volition, they composed new offices, new hymns and additional liturgical material for new feasts, which then found perhaps wider, perhaps more limited, reception.[7] Needless to say, none of these reform activities disturbed the continuity of the Roman tradition.

It was different at the end of the Middle Ages. By then, not only the adequate nature of *some elements* was subjected to criticism, but large portions – indeed, almost the whole of – the Roman Rite were criticized. Many criticisms and proposals remained only written in theoretical treatises, but one of them was actually implemented and introduced in the Church; the so-called Quiñonez Breviary (1534), which nearly overturned the order, structure and material of the Roman Office.[8]

In the following centuries diocesan rites flourished (mainly in France) that selected certain items from the Roman Rite and the local traditions in an eclectic manner, and supplemented them with hundreds of their own inventions.[9] This was not an extension of the situation of the Middle Ages when new compositions (e.g. rhymed offices) were created for new feasts, or poetic commentaries (tropes) were added to the old material. No: here the tradition and fabric of the Roman liturgy itself was laid aside for the sake of completely new material. Plans for producing a brand new 'Roman' liturgy were prepared by the condemned Pistoia Synod and Scipio de Ricci.[10]

The three characteristic features of these reform-rites may be summed up as follows:

(a) They were the expression of individual, voluntaristic ideas. This was the case even when they received the approval of the local bishop or (as in case of the Quiñonez Breviary) of the Holy See itself.[11]
(b) They were not rites that evolved over long periods and developed through an ongoing process of minor changes, but were the result of hasty work at a writing desk.

---

[7] E.g. Stephen of Lüttich, Fulbert of Chartres, St Thomas Aquinas.
[8] Bäumer (1895), *Geschichte des Breviers*, pp. 383–409. Reid (2005), *The Organic Development of the Liturgy*, pp. 32–41, 49–54, 57.
[9] Bäumer (1895), *Geschichte des Breviers*, pp. 531–62.
[10] Cf. *Mediator Dei* (1947), Encyclical of Pope Pius XII on the Sacred Liturgy, §64; John B. Parsons (2003), 'A Reform of the Reform?', pp. 215–17, 220–21; Reid (2005), *The Organic Development of the Liturgy*, pp. 52–60.
[11] On the sharp criticisms made by Dominicus Soto, Martin de Azpilkueta and John Arze see Bäumer (1895), *Geschichte des Breviers*, pp. 403–05. According to the interesting distinction made by Arze: this reform-breviary was, though authorized, illegitimate (citation in Reid (2005), *The Organic Development of the Liturgy*, pp. 37–38).

(c) They exuded a detectable odour of insensitivity or downright contempt for the tradition. They could not properly appreciate the importance of tradition in liturgical life. Even if the authors did not declare it (as their descendants did at the end of the twentieth century), they were convinced that the liturgy ought not to preserve the past, but rather was to serve the requirements of their own age, and they behaved as if the two were mutually exclusive.

The different fabrications sprang from the same spiritual root. With regard to their historical determinants, they can be included in the category of 'reform-liturgies'. The Quiñonez Breviary was inspired by the ideology of humanism; the French (Neo-Gallican) reform-liturgies were vehicles for expressing opposition to Rome; in some of the later rites the spirit of Jansenism or of the coming Enlightenment was at work.

There is one thing, however, that is common to all: they cannot be called 'Roman'. They are not particular liturgies *within* the Roman Rite in the same sense as, for instance, the Dominican, Carthusian, Curial, Tridentine, Bamberg and Uppsala Rites were (to name but a few). Though they adopted some things from the 'outdated' Roman Rite, and were different in the extent to which they distanced themselves from it, the material of the rite itself and the spirit of their composition exclude them from the family of the *Roman* Rite.

Let us now sum up what has been said for the sake of drawing some conclusions. If we were able to compare all the liturgical Uses of the East and West, we would find a number of *common* elements that may be called the *basic common layer of the Christian liturgy*.[12] A part of this clearly goes back to the Holy Scriptures and Christ himself. Others parts come from the common treasury of the apostolic era and the religious life of the second to fourth centuries.

There are other features responsible for the differentiation between the liturgical traditions of the Eastern and Latin churches. In the positive sense: the rites of the Latin church (or better, Latin churches) contain common elements that might be the result of the same basic traditions and their constant interrelationship. Within the widest circle of *Christian* rites, this narrower circle can be labelled as *Old Latin* rites.

Within this sphere again, proper liturgical traditions of single *regions* might exist (as can be deduced from extant remnants). The most important of those seems to be the Western Mediterranean. One may suppose that the intensive theological, homiletical and liturgical activity of Northern Africa played an important role here, all the more since the liturgy here was celebrated in Latin at a time when Greek was still accepted in Rome. In this region, however, it was Rome that formed the most characteristic, more or less fixed, rite, and transmitted it through a variety of ecclesiastical institutions (the papal chapel, the clergy of the basilicas, the scholas and, later, urban monasticism), and took hold of it more and more

---

[12] These could be listed from Taft, SJ (1986), *The Liturgy of the Hours*, Parts I and II. See also the survey in Louis Duchesne (1903), *Christian Worship: Its Origin and Evolution*; 2nd edn 1927, pp. 11–45.

self-consciously as her 'proper' liturgy. It is hardly possible to assign just one period for the date of its birth, but we are probably not in great error if we assume that the second half of the fourth century and the subsequent one, or one and a half centuries were of decisive importance. At the beginning of this period this liturgy was probably in an embryonic state; but its development went on continuously until it received its canonical, classical form by the seventh century.

When in the eighth century the Transalpine regions of Europe made the rite and chant of Rome their own, an accretion of material started; but that was only an expansion of the material that already existed. This change required a new codification or, rather, a series of subsequent codifications. The consequence of this geographical expansion was that decisions were made not by a centralized power, but by the competent local authorities determining how they actually were to live this tradition. It was in this manner that the Rites (Uses) of (arch)dioceses and religious orders gradually emerged.

The Papal Court – departing from the liturgy of the great basilicas – developed a proper Use based on Central Italian customs.[13] Later public opinion began to regard this Use as identical with the liturgy of the pope and Rome, so the Curial Use gained great respect, even though in the Middle Ages it hardly influenced any of the other Uses. It grew significantly in importance, however, when Rome wished to surmount the troubles caused by the Reformation and Humanism by returning to an ideal 'purity of the rite'. Thus after the Council of Trent the Curial Rite became regarded simply as *the* Roman Rite.[14]

We have both to narrow and, at the same time, broaden the meaning of the term 'Tridentine Rite'. The Tridentine Rite does not 'formally' exist; it is simply one sub-type or Use of the Roman Rite. On the other hand, the Tridentine Rite is not *identical* with the Roman Rite; it is rather less than that greater whole, since the Roman Rite includes also the liturgy of the Roman basilicas, as well as the particular usages of the medieval episcopal sees and religious orders.[15]

We have to ask two more questions. One is: how can one define the *contents* of the Roman Rite? The task – in spite of its complexity – is not too problematic. If all liturgies developed upon the basis of the Roman Rite were to be collected and analysed, what is *common* in them could be defined as the most important content of the Roman Rite. If all the proper material accumulated in the sister-liturgies were added to this common core, a second circle could be drawn, wider than the inner one, which includes elements on different levels of importance. Just an example: the five antiphons of the Lauds on the First Sunday of Advent (not only the pieces but also their liturgical assignments) belong surely to the inner circle; a similar case is, for example, the Advent Alleluias *Excita* and *Ostende*.[16]

---

[13] Josef Andreas Jungmann, SJ (1958), *Missarum Sollemnia. Eine Genetische Erklärung der Römischen Messe*, vol. 1, pp. 133–35; Bäumer (1895), *Geschichte des Breviers*, pp. 315–18.
[14] Jungmann (1958), *Missarum Sollemnia*, vol. 1, pp. 174–86; Reid (2005), *The Organic Development of the Liturgy*, pp. 38–44; Bäumer (1895), *Geschichte des Breviers*, pp. 416–57.
[15] Cf. Dobszay (2008a), 'What Does the "Roman Rite" Denominate?', pp. 57–66.
[16] *Antiphonale Missarum Sextuplex* (1935), Nr 1a, 4; Max Lütolf (ed.) (1987), *Das Graduale von Santa Cecilia in Trastevere (Cod. Bodmer 74)*, p. 66; *Monumenta Monodica Medii Aevi*, vol. 2,

To the second, outer circle belong (again, for example) the two Alleluias of the Second Sunday of Advent (*Laetatus sum, Rex noster adveniet*), which were used alternatively in different dioceses. (From the Frankish period onwards, the Alleluia *Laetatus sum* became the property of a wider environment, while the *Rex noster* only of a narrower one.[17]) Also to this (outer) circle belong the private prayers of the priest during the Offertory, or, let us say, the Office cycle of St Nicholas. Some important, but not integral, parts of the liturgy may have dropped from the Rite in the course of centuries. For instance, the Offertory verses are present both in Old Roman and early Gregorian sources (such that they can properly be said to be part of the 'inner circle'), but their use was discontinued after the twelfth century.[18]

What have we learned from this historical survey? Terms like 'Roman Rite', 'Roman Mass', 'Tridentine Rite', etc. should be used more carefully, in a more nuanced way than hitherto. If we wish to refer to the antiquity of the traditional Roman Mass, we cannot adapt this term – without differentiation – to the 'Tridentine Rite', and still less to its younger editions (e.g. the 1911 Breviary or the 1962 Missal). On the other hand, to think that the Tridentine Mass is a sixteenth-century historical product would be to forget that it is but one form of the much older Roman Mass.[19]

It would be more reasonable to create a new convention in the use of terms. The phrase 'Classical Roman Rite' or 'traditional Roman Rite' should mean the totality of the tradition, which is at least 1,500 years old. The term 'Roman Rite' has the same scope, but one has to include in this all the diocesan and religious liturgies, not just this or that edition of a Missal. (The habit of referring to the 1962 Mass simply as '*the* Latin Mass' is a deceptive looseness of idiom.) The term 'Tridentine Rite/Use', just as the 'Dominican Rite/Use' or other ritual usages, describes merely one variant of the Roman Rite. The term 'Roman Rite' has also another, canonical or legal meaning, but we will speak of this later.

Our historical retrospective offers one even more serious lesson. When we discuss the contemporary liturgical order, we must distinguish between the *universal* features of the Roman Rite, stable in time and place, on the one hand, and *accretions* or *additions*, on the other.[20] It is not possible to speak with the *same* veneration and concern; for example, of the prayers at the foot of the altar when compared with the Canon of the Roman Mass, or: the preservation of the feast of the Visitation of the Holy Virgin as opposed to the feast of the Ascension.

   Die Gesänge des altrömishcen Graduale Vat. lat. 5319 p. 629; László Dobszay (2001), *A római mise énekrendje* [The Order of the Chants in the Roman Mass], pp. 8–9.

[17] *Antiphonale Missarum Sextuplex* (1935), Nr 2; Dobszay (2001), *A római mise énekrendje*, pp. 8–9. For the *Alleluia Rex noster* see *Missale Notatum Strigoniense ante 1341 in Posonio*, fol. 2v; recorded also in the Old Roman Gradual, see Lütolf (ed.) (1987), *Das Graduale von Santa Cecilia in Trastvere*, fol. 4.

[18] Jungmann (1958), *Missarum Sollemnia*, vol. 2, pp. 36–37. Adrian Fortescue (1912), *The Mass: A Study of the Roman Liturgy*, 4th edn, 2005, pp. 304–05, mentions that Durandus, the great liturgist of his age, drew attention to the disappearance of the verses but did not approve of it.

[19] Dobszay (2003), *The Bugnini-Liturgy and the Reform of the Reform*, pp. 151–53; Cf. Thomas M. Kocik (2003), *The Reform of the Reform? A Liturgical Debate: Reform or Return*, p. 26.

[20] 'First and Second Order Elements' in John Parsons' terminology: Parsons (2003), 'A Reform of the Reform?', pp. 235–37.

This is not 'archaism' or 'antiquarianism', and I am not saying that the more recent elements of the liturgy merit no respect or protection. But if some actual changes are to be deliberated, the weight of a late addition is not the same as that of the more stable elements.

The Roman Rite lived in an abundant richness of Rites or Uses up to the sixteenth century, but for the last 400 years its liturgical life (apart from some religious orders) has been practically reduced to just one (Tridentine) form. In the meanwhile, however, the entire secular and ecclesiastical environment has undergone significant changes.

2

THE LITURGICAL MOVEMENT

One of the most promising phenomena in recent church history was the Liturgical Movement, which started in the mid-nineteenth century.[1] It was called to life by several developments, and for the following discussion it will be useful to list some of these.

1. The Liturgical Movement – at least in the case of its most eminent members – began as a reaction against the Neo-Gallican reform-liturgies that proliferated throughout the dioceses of France. Dom Prosper Guéranger recognized, and helped others to realize, how alien the message of these fabricated liturgies are to the Roman Rite and its genuine tradition (whose importance was then still unquestioned within the Catholic Church); how rootless and how scanty they were in comparison to the rich treasury of that venerable rite.[2]

2. Some distortions in popular piety and religious practice also inspired a turn towards the liturgy. Without a doubt, in the dogmas, moral norms, liturgical teaching of the Church there was nothing contrary to the apostolic legacy, and Christ's promise of indefectibility to the Church defended the Christian religion against doctrinal aberrations. Yet, in the area of religious practice some kind of disturbance, an unsteadiness in the equilibrium, could be observed. The growing number of spiritual 'schools', the shift of peripheral elements to the centre, a one-sided didactical or emotional approach, the ever-increasing popularity of devotional practices dating from the time of the *Devotio Moderna*, Catholic Humanism, elements in the style of the Baroque and the growth of Romanticism resulted in a degree of fragmentation. A unifying conception was needed to reset the focus on the most important facts of the faith and sacramental life of the Church, and one which allowed all the aspects of religious life to be organized around this common centre. This was meant to provide a reminder of the need to follow a proper hierarchy of values: some values, however real and precious they may be, are secondary or derivative by their very nature. Many excellent thinkers of the Church saw that the religious ideas of the new times, albeit valuable in themselves,

---

[1] For a comprehensive description of the history of the movement (with a wide selection of relevant literature), see Alcuin Reid (2005), *The Organic Development of the Liturgy*, chapter 2.

[2] Reid (2005), *The Organic Development of the Liturgy*, pp. 56–60.

actually obscured – certainly not in the official doctrine, but in the common perception – the most ancient and fundamental truths, and ended up weakening public adherence to the most appropriate forms of religious observance. In short, there was a need to return to the sources: '*ad fontes!*'[3] Three sources were opened for those minds who wanted to recover the faded treasures of tradition: Sacred Scripture, the liturgy, and the patristic heritage. The men who began to argue these positions were right in thinking that this tradition cannot be a secret garden offering its delights only to experts. Its vital power must be shared with the whole Church, and so include all the communities of the clergy and the faithful.[4]

3. This kind of rediscovery was not an isolated phenomenon, specific to the Catholic Church. Similar movements appeared also in Protestant communities, especially in Anglicanism and Lutheranism. Furthermore, even in various areas of secular intellectual life, ancient and nearly forgotten values were once again in demand. The idea seemed to be more and more acceptable that the wisdom of the Graeco-Roman world, Roman Law, scholastic philosophy, the culture of the Middle Ages, ancient folk traditions, the neglected music of the medieval, renaissance or baroque periods, for instance, did not need to be relegated to a museum of outdated relics of merely historical interest. These were living realities, able to enrich our life today, and sources of regeneration and inspiration to creativity. 'Return to the forerunners and this will be a real progress!' said Verdi, who really cannot be accused of a backward, old-fashioned mentality. History does not run on linear tracks leading only forwards. This approach gained momentum precisely in an age when the opposite trend was also hard at work in the societies of Europe and the West: the repudiation of the past and the plunging of traditions into oblivion were likewise fashionable at the time. No doubt, there were also examples of an infertile archaism (e.g. the Palestrina imitations by the composers of the Cecilian movement), but where the turn towards original sources mobilized considerable spiritual energies, and where the tiresome path of learning and practice was followed, memorable and great results arose in the nineteenth and twentieth centuries.

'Renewal from the sources' or 'going back to the roots' means, of course, something different in the fields of secular culture and religious life. In the former this renewal is but one of the possibilities of a ceaselessly changing life, one of the moments confirming, completing, negating each other, which emerge and merge again. In the area of religion – and mainly of the Christian religion, founded by God himself who appeared at a given point in human history – renewal based on its most fundamental traditions is like the development of a living organism with respect to its genetic code.

4. The liturgical renewal movement was also necessitated by the inner state of the liturgy itself. The Church taught and practised the liturgy in the continuity of the apostolic tradition. But the attitude of Christian communities towards the

---

[3] On 'ressourcement' see Thomas M. Kocik (2009), 'The Reform of the Reform in Broad Context'.
[4] Reid (2005), *The Organic Development of the Liturgy*, pp. 73, 78–80.

liturgy and the way they lived it was certainly in need of some kind of renovation. In the actual performance of the liturgy in the eighteenth to nineteenth
centuries a poignant polarization could be observed: the duality of magnificent
(sometimes downright theatrical) celebrations and, simultaneously, seriously
reduced average practice. The liturgical formation of the faithful was limited
to catechetical issues (e.g. about the meaning of the Holy Mass), or themes of
faith and morals explained from liturgical texts. (A good example of this is
the otherwise excellent and truly edifying didactic book by L. Goffine, which
was used by a number of generations.[5]) The Liturgical Movement suggested a
simple way forward: '*sacris erudiri*' – let us learn the liturgy from the liturgy
itself! Let us examine the liturgical texts and customs, thus getting nearer
to the essence of the liturgy! Let us *do* the liturgy in all its possible fullness;
let us have frequent recourse to the sacraments, let us follow the liturgical
seasons, the Divine Office, the rubrics, the chants! In doing so, community
and individual alike will be more and more imbued with the *sacred*, the most
important aspect of our religion – and not only through doctrinal formulation,
but by virtue of the actions themselves.

St Pius X's utterances justified and took up the intentions of the pioneers; and
thus multiplied their effectiveness in the Church.[6] How the liturgical life evolved
in many forms, and gave life to the early twentieth-century Catholic renaissance,
is an area yet deserving of serious historical study. The rich theological, liturgical
and spiritual literature that resulted was both the output of, and inspiration for,
the renewal. We can make mention of some names at this point only for the sake
of presenting more clearly the directions of the movement as a whole.

Dom Prosper Guéranger[7] urged the restitution of the historical Roman Rite
in his homeland, and the arduous study of the rite also helped him to rediscover
some Pre-Tridentine relics, the fruits of which appeared in his many-volumed
work, part study, part devotional manual, on the liturgical year. Guéranger
emphasized the special situation and responsibility of the monastic communities
in this regard, as they are obliged to celebrate the liturgy in its entirety and to
immerse themselves deeply in its spirit – for the good of their souls and the benefit
of the whole Church.

This challenge was well represented by the example of the monasteries of
Beuron and Maria Laach. We owe thanks to Maurus Wolter, Archabbot of Beuron,
for reviving in contemporary form the ancient way of interpreting the Psalter,[8]
which he also introduced in the training of novices. If only this early Christian
method of understanding the Psalms had spread more widely (at least among

---

[5] Leonard Goffine (1690), *Handpostille oder Christkatholische Unterrichtungen auf alle Sonn und
Feyer-tagen des ganzen Jahrs*.

[6] Pius X, *Tra le solicitudini* (1903), *Sacra Tridentina Synodus* (1905), *Quam singulari* (1910).

[7] His most influential work are the *Institutions liturgiques* (Paris: I, 1840; II, 1841; III, 1851);
L'Année liturgique (Paris, 1841–1901). On his activity directed toward the restoration of
the Gregorian Chant, see Pierre Combe, OSB (2003), *The Restoration of Gregorian Chant*,
pp. 11–22.

[8] Maurus Wolter, OSB: *Psallite Sapienter, 'Psalliret weise!'. Erklärung der Psalmen im Geiste des
betrachtenden Gebets und der Liturgie*, vols 1–4 (Freiburg im Bresisgau: Herder, 1891–1907).

the clergy), it could well have prevented much incomprehension and mistaken judgement in the twentieth century.

The *Magna Carta* of the movement was Romano Guardini's book *The Spirit of the Liturgy*.[9] It is not by chance that the then Cardinal Ratzinger adapted the title of this work for his own book on the liturgy.[10] Another influential work was his *Signs of the Liturgy*, a basic work – in spite of its modest size – of liturgical pedagogy.[11] Guardini was not, in fact, a liturgical expert; he was a philosopher who demonstrated that the liturgy corresponds to the deepest requirements and desires of the religious psyche. He did not explain the liturgy, but reflected on its intrinsic value and essential nature. In this respect, his worthy companion was Dietrich von Hildebrandt[12] and – in the field of 'art and liturgy' – Ildefons Herwegen[13] of the monastery of Maria Laach.

Dom Columba Marmion's two masterpieces[14] are usually categorized as spiritual, and not liturgical, literature. Yet the Blessed Abbot was, in fact, the modern Doctor of liturgical life. He revealed how one can build up an integral Christian life based on the principal truths of the faith and the liturgy. His work is a sure guidebook of Christian life; puts an end to its fragmentation; unfolds the fullness of dogma, ethics, asceticism and piety out of one single central experience: the mysteries contemplated in the liturgy.

What Maurus Wolter did for an authentic understanding of the psalms, Odo Casel and his school (the writers of the *Archiv für Liturgiewissenschaft*)[15] did for the understanding of liturgical texts in the Roman Rite (orations, Canon). He published in his journal a long series of articles that examined strenuously, word for word, the prayers of the Church; and surveyed the largest possible number of sources from Christian and pagan antiquity in order to achieve an exact understanding of the words and the meaning intended by their authors. Behind this painstaking philological exercise lay the intention to understand the manner and content of the thinking. Casel's partial studies are summarized in the genial context of his 'mystery-theology'.[16] This does not mean that his many philological findings were fashioned into a general system: he contemplated, rather, everything under the appearance of mystery, according to the same vision that determined the liturgical consciousness of Christian Antiquity, and that has been made manifest in all its prayers and expressions. His partial studies functioned like a prism, diffusing the single beam of the mysterium into many rays of light. At first it is perhaps shocking, but surely worthy of note, what an important role the study of certain aspects of pagan antiquity played in Casel's interpretation. Yet this was not some form of syncretism. When an ancient Christian author wanted to manifest his

---

9   Romano Guardini (1918), *Vom Geist der Liturgie*.
10 Romano Guardini (1922), *Von Heiligen Zeichen*.
11 Cardinal Joseph Ratzinger (2000), *The Spirit of the Liturgy*.
12 Dietrich von Hildebrand (1943), *Liturgy and Personality*.
13 Ildefons Herwegen, OSB (1955), *Liturgy's Inner Beauty*.
14 Columba Marmion, OSB (1924), *Christ in His Mysteries*; (1925), *Christ the Life of the Soul*.
15 *Jahrbuch für Liturgiewissenschaft Maria Laach* (Abt-Herwegen-Institut), 1921–1941.
16 Odo Casel, OSB (1922), *Die Liturgie als Mysterienfeier*; (1932), *Das christliche Kult-Mysterium*; (1941), *Das christliche Festmysterium*. For a critical summary, see Theodor Klauser (1969), *A Short History of the Western Liturgy*, pp. 24–30.

faith, he necessarily used the words and notions current at the time that were apt to express his thoughts on the highest level of religious experiences. If we study these words in their proper context, the Christian liturgy and its texts will not be 'paganized', instead, we will be able to attain to a deeper understanding of their true Christian content. This also applies to the term 'mystery' itself. Perhaps I am not off the mark if in this approach I see more than merely a hermeneutical tool. There is a sharp contrast, of course, between paganism and the Christian doctrine of Salvation. However, considering Christianity in the broader context of human history, a history Casel held to be fully under the power of Divine Providence, it is right to recognize in Christian cult the fulfilment of the most genuine desires of mankind, its search for truth and God, and to appreciate some of the elements and formulas which expressed this desire. In earlier times theologians were, perhaps, afraid that this recognition would somehow diminish the authenticity of Christianity. On the other hand, in the eyes of modern man – unwilling to ban the totality of pagan civilization along with its religious culture and the best of its human ambitions – this fact may rather increase respect for Christian cult.[17]

The thought of the authors mentioned above (notwithstanding the ones we do not have space to mention[18]) was transmitted to the multitude of priests and faithful by literary products great both in quantity and quality. Beyond strictly liturgical writings and explanations, I am thinking of their influence on the texts and commentaries to be found in numerous missals and other prayer books, and the spiritual literature, lectures, retreats and above all, the liturgical events themselves, celebrated with the utmost care and devotion. I do not think anybody has ever tried to survey how deep and broad was the impact of the movement between 1920 and 1960, or studied the extent to which these resulted in a deepening of understanding or merely remained on the surface as words and actions alone.

In speaking of these tireless efforts to popularize the liturgy, one cannot leave unmentioned the name of Pius Parsch. His books communicated to the faithful on a high level all that could be learnt from the masters of the 'great movement'; his church in Klosterneuburg became the point of reference for many churches aiming at liturgical education.[19] After 70 years we now perceive in his activity some small signs of unbalance which, unsympathetically evaluated, could suggest false conclusions. The idea of a 'folk liturgy' could be transformed from 'the folk in the liturgy' to 'liturgy for the folks', or simply 'liturgy in folk-style'. But the interpretation of the liturgy as presented in Parsch's books is fully in accord with the authentic spirit of the movement. There is nothing written in his works that could be interpreted as an intention to adjust the liturgy to the real or presumed demands of the people – instead of (his undoubted intention) raising people up to the liturgy.

This is the key problem with the whole movement of the liturgical renewal and its relationship to the 1970s. For the fathers of the movement the motivating

---

[17] Cf. Reid (2005), *The Organic Development of the Liturgy*, pp. 119–22.
[18] Reid (2005), *The Organic Development of the Liturgy*, pp. 8–124.
[19] Reid (2005), *The Organic Development of the Liturgy*, pp. 110–15. The most important works are Pius Parsch (1935), *Meßerklärung im Geiste der liturgischen Erneuerung*, and (1953), *The Church's Year of Grace*.

impulse was the enthralling attraction of the *existing* liturgy.[20] They recognized day by day the perfection of the Roman Rite in its full and complex reality. For them the liturgy was that given 'whole', in which doctrine, culture, form, beauty, dramatic quality, psychological impact and, above all, immersion in the presence of God appeared to them as an indissoluble perfection. Their whole endeavour was to understand and live through with ever-greater intensity this *donated* reality. They celebrated, meditated, prayed and studied the texts, visible signs, actions, style and language – which carry the inner reality of the liturgy like the sacramental signs carry the grace. This is a sensitive texture, and if one thread is pulled out, the whole may be unstitched.

For them this discovery was, first of all, their inner experience. Like the man in Matthew's Gospel,[21] they really appreciated the pearl of great price they found, and they gave everything they had for it. It was precisely this joy that led them to encourage and teach the whole Church, every single community and individual to search the same in the sure hope of finding it. The pastoral-pedagogical side was not the motive of their activity but its consequence.

We fully misapprehend the Liturgical Movement if we do not recognize this basic emotion of admiration and fascination evoked by the Roman Rite in its very essence. The real concern was not what should be changed in the liturgy or where: they fell deeply in love with the very liturgy that was actually celebrated in the Church. They knew the history of the liturgy and surely knew that this liturgy was not eternal in all its elements. They commented on the age of this or that part of the rite; on the historical context of a prayer or ceremony. If they had been asked, certainly they would have agreed that changes would eventually happen in the future; probably they would even have named certain areas where such a change could be favourable to the liturgy.[22] But this knowledge left intact their adherence to what they recognized as the Roman Rite.

Still less would they have been inclined to see the liturgy as a mere framework to be filled up with inventions of a priest, a congregation (or a subcommittee), or even by the Church hierarchy itself. The Mass is not an *occasion*, a gathering advertised on the notice board of church gates – with prayers and chants to be defined later. The liturgy for them was not the occasion of worship, but the act of worship itself, as had been happening for long centuries: the very texts, pericopes, chants and gestures of which it was actually and historically comprised.

They could not even understand the late twentieth-century slogan: 'not the man for the liturgy but the liturgy for the man'. They always kept the liturgy before their eyes, and they wanted to serve just that, knowing that if man serves the liturgy, then liturgy will also serve the man.

Already before the Council the liturgical activity of Pope Pius XII showed that

---

[20] John P. Parsons (2003), 'A Reform of the Reform?', p. 213. Cf. Reid (2005), *The Organic Development of the Liturgy*, pp. 80–81; James Hitchcock (2006), 'Liturgy and Ritual'.
[21] Matt. 13.44-46.
[22] Reid (2005), *The Organic Development of the Liturgy*, pp. 78–85. Only modest proposals appeared in the 1930s for a reform within the Movement; more demanding voices sounded later (never approaching, however, the changes realized in the late 1960s); see Reid (2005), chapter 2 and pp. 305–08.

the preservation of the identity of the Roman Rite and the introduction of necessary changes are not opposed to each other. The encyclical *Mediator Dei*[23] was not only the confirmation of the results of the movement, but also a warning against exaggerations or errors that appeared during its spread. When the pope expressed his disapproval of liturgical archaism, he implicitly admitted the legitimacy of historical changes. The encyclical stood up against the demand to return to the conditions of Christian antiquity and the elimination of all liturgical developments of more recent centuries. His words were also a declaration that these changes did not offend the continuity of the Roman Rite, and that, in the future, changes could also occur without harming that continuity.[24]

Pius XII presented a model for these changes when he reformed the order of Holy Week.[25] Half a century later we can see that not all of these changes were fortunate (this will be discussed later, in the chapter on Holy Week). However, the reform was for the benefit of the Church and, in its essence, was in harmony with the tradition of the Roman Rite. Not so with another innovation. It seems the pope had a weakness *vis-à-vis* some of his aggressive advisers, and introduced (true, only for *ad libitum* use) a new translation (made in the Institute led by Cardinal Augustin Bea, SJ) of the Psalter that heavily injured the continuity of the Roman Rite at an essential point.[26] This example shows that though single elements of the liturgy may be studied (with regard either to their inner logic or to their expedience) the changes suggested after the analysis may be fortunate or ill-advised from a liturgical or practical perspective. Accordingly, one may agree with these changes or criticize them in the appropriate tone. But these kinds of changes do not result in the transformation of the rite; they do not cut off the continuous line of tradition; and still less do they serve to justify any concession to the 'spirit of the age' or contemporary ideological trends.

---

[23] Pius XII, *Mediator Dei* in *Acta Apostolicae Sedis*, vol. 39 (1947), pp. 521–93.
[24] The encyclical is compared with the *Sacrosanctum Concilium* in Aidan Nichols, OP (2000), 'A Tale of Two Documents', pp. 9–27.
[25] *Ordo Hebdomade Sanctae Instauratus.* Cf. Reid (2005), *The Organic Development of the Liturgy*, pp. 172–81 and 219–34.
[26] Cf. *Acta Apostolicae Sedis*, vol. 37 (1945), p. 65.

3

IN THE NAME OF THE COUNCIL

The Second Vatican Council was expected – with good reason – to fulfil the best aspirations of the 100-year-old Liturgical Movement. In fact, if we read the theological paragraphs of *Sacrosanctum Concilium*,[1] we find there a reflection of the thoughts, approach and style of the great predecessors of the movement itself; the vision of the liturgical life of the Church is, in substantial outline, in harmony with their ideals. The guiding ideas were: the celebration of the liturgy as worthily and fully as possible; and the renewal of the life of the Church, of individual communities and of the faithful through a deeper attachment to the liturgy. These are in their essence identical with the aims of the Liturgical Movement.

A great body of scholarly literature has dealt with how the declaration of the Council took shape, what was in the schemes, how they were modified, what opinions and intentions (sometimes contradictory to each other) were voiced during the discussions, and how individual interventions refined or developed the text until it became definite and accepted by a great majority.[2] It is not the aim of this book to evaluate or give an account of this background information; we wish rather to turn our attention to the Constitution itself.

The Constitution was intended to make actual liturgical practice more fruitful in the life of the Church. It wanted to make the Roman Rite itself more effective, as it was celebrated in the Church in the time of the Council. The Council Fathers did not plan to create a 'new liturgy'. Had such a thing been suggested, the proposal would have been voted down with a sweeping majority. Due respect for the identity of the rite and the ideal of an organic development are principles clearly perceptible in the Constitution. The document takes account of some changes, and sets up clear norms for them:

> That sound tradition may be retained, and yet the way remains open to
> legitimate progress. Careful investigation is always to be made into each

---

[1] Second Vatican Council, Dogmatic Constitution on the Sacred Liturgy, *Sacrosanctum Concilium* of 4 December 1963, in *Sacrosanctum Œcumenicum Concilium Vaticanum II: Constitutiones; Decreta; Declarationes*, Vatican, Libreria Editrice Vaticana, 1993, pp. 3–60: translated by Norman Tanner (1990) in *Decrees of the Ecumenical Councils*, 2 vols, vol. 2, pp. 820–43.

[2] For documentation of the process, see Annibale Bugnini (1990), *The Reform of the Liturgy 1948–1975*; Carlo Braga and Annibale Bugnini (2000), *Documenta ad Instaurationem Liturgiam Spectantia (1903–1965)*.

part of the liturgy which is to be revised. This investigation should be theological, historical and pastoral. Also the general laws governing the structure and meaning of the liturgy must be studied in conjunction with the experience derived from recent liturgical reforms and from the indults conceded to various places. Finally, there must be no innovations unless the good of the Church genuinely and certainly requires them; and care must be taken that any new forms adopted should in some way grow organically from forms already existing.[3]

Three points are obvious from this statement. It speaks, first, about changes that are quantitatively and qualitatively *small* in comparison to the fullness of the rite. The method of 'little steps' is the guarantee that the continuity of tradition will be kept, while, at the same time, making room for modifications that do not compromise the rite, but help to set forth its essence more clearly. Secondly, a norm is given for the changes. The direction should be determined not by superficial slogans, by a false modernization, or the will of innovation.[4] Changes should be for the 'genuine and certain good of the Church' and duly justified by careful investigation. In order to preserve a continuity of tradition, this investigation must cover also the history of the liturgy. The third observation cannot be read out of the text itself, but is a consequence of the previous two: the Council did not propose a speedy process producing a quite new liturgy in the space of only a few years. It made possible some slight changes immediately (like the 1965 modifications in the *Ordo Missae*); but these gradual and minor changes would only produce what later and in retrospect may be called a 'reform' of the rite over a longer historical period.

The changes described in concrete terms by the Constitution were not conse-quences of 'progressive' theological developments. They were either intended to help the improvement of the liturgy (e.g. the restitution of the texts of the psalms and hymns), or they were of a pastoral nature assisting a better understanding (using the vernacular in *some* parts) or serving practical purposes (abbreviations, simplifications). Most of the provisions are not concrete; instead, they assign a general direction for the changes. For instance, paragraph 51 ('The treasures of the Bible are to be opened up more lavishly, so that richer fare may be provided for the faithful at the table of God's word; in this way a more representative por-tion of the Holy Scriptures will be read to the people in the course of a prescribed number of years')[5] could have been implemented in several different ways; the three-year system is but one of several possible arrangements.

Since the changes outlined in the Constitution are not doctrinal declarations,

---

[3] *Sacrosanctum Concilium* (1963), §23: 'Ut sana traditio retineatur et tamen via legitimae progres-sioni aperiatur, de singulis Liturgiae partibus recognoscendis accurata investigatio theologica, historica, pastoralis semper praecedat. Insuper considerentur cum leges generales structurae et mentis Liturgiae, tum experientia ex recentiore instauratione liturgica et ex indultis passim concessis promanans. Innovationes, demum, ne fiant nisi vera et certa utilitas Ecclesiae id exigat, et adhibita cautela ut novae formae ex formis iam exstantibus organice quodammodo crescant.'

[4] Klaus Gamber (2002), *The Modern Rite*, pp. 62–63, 72–75.

[5] *Sacrosanctum Concilium* (1963), §51: 'Quo ditior mensa verbi Dei paretur fidelibus, thesauri

they can be criticized with due respect on the basis of appropriate knowledge.[6] After a thorough analysis one may conclude that there are rules which assist 'the genuine good of the Church' and so are favourable in our times (e.g. limited use of the vernacular), while there are also unnecessary and harmful elements (e.g. the abolition of Prime in the Divine Office),[7] and again, there are other proposals, which may be either beneficial or detrimental depending on the way of implementation (e.g. the rearrangement of the system of readings in the Mass[8]). I am of the opinion that in the present state of affairs such cautious deliberation is only reasonable – accompanied, of course, by due obedience in practice.

For most priests and faithful, however, the 'liturgy of the Council' means not the Constitution itself, but the complexity of the new books and regulations that originated in the workshop of the '*Consilium*' (with Archbishop Bugnini as secretary) and its subcommittees set up after the Council. The outcome of their work was introduced into the life of the Church through mandatory papal directives. No one has either any reason or, indeed, any right to question the orthodoxy of the new liturgy, and nobody may withdraw himself from the duty of following these rules – neither those who are enthusiastic devotees of the new rite, nor those who have genuine and heartfelt criticisms of it.

There is again a great deal of literature on the work of the committees, their debates, and their internal processes. These are irrelevant for this book; I do not want to pass judgement on the *process* of this reform, nor comment on the stories often circulated about obscure and hidden agendas that drove the reform.[9] We have to confront ourselves with the fruits of this tree.

It has already been admitted a number of times and in rather broad circles that the liturgy promulgated under the name of Paul VI is not an improvement of the Roman Rite, but a new liturgy incorporating some elements of that noble rite. It was precisely Cardinal Ratzinger who spoke in the most forthright manner about the *break* that occurred in the continuous development of the liturgy of Rome.[10] Later we have to return to this judgement of this highly respected Cardinal Prefect, now become pope.

---

biblici largius aperiantur, ita ut, intra *praestitutum annorum spatium*, praestantior pars Scripturarum Sanctarum populo legatur.'

[6] 'I think one must frankly say that, while the doctrinal sections of Sacrosanctum Concilium ought to be regarded, along with all teaching on faith and morals by general councils, as sacrosanct . . . the bishops enjoyed no assistance of the Holy Spirit – even negatively – in matters of the aesthetics of ritual': Aidan Nichols (2003), 'Salutary Dissatisfaction: An English view of Reforming the Reform', pp. 206). Cf. John B. Parsons (2003), 'A Reform of the Reform?', pp. 248.

[7] *Sacrosanctum Concilium* (1963), §89/d.

[8] *Sacrosanctum Concilium* (1963), §51.

[9] Parsons (2003), 'A Reform of the Reform?', pp. 250–51. He writes, moreover: '. . . a binding, sacral, non-vernacular and theocentric liturgical ethos enshrined in ancient tradition must be replaced by an option-filled, secularizing, vernacular, and anthropocentric approach, reflecting the aspirations and tastes of the human spirit in the present day. The authority of the Roman Church and her historic liturgy had to be taken out of the way . . . It is the entry of this *Zeitgeist* into the temple of God, through the window thrown open by John XXIII, that is the fundamental driving force behind the liturgical revolution.'

[10] Cardinal Ratzinger in the introduction to Klaus Gamber (1992), *La Réforme Liturgique en Question*, p. 8. 'After the Council . . . in the place of Liturgy as the fruit of development came fabricated Liturgy. We abandoned the organic, living process of growth and development over centuries, and replaced it – as in a manufacturing process – with a fabrication, a banal

It was the object of my earlier book to point to the evidence of this break in many parts of the Holy Liturgy[11] (and I will return to some of the evidence in Part II of this work). It is enough now to state that the change – both in the attitude towards, and the actual material of, the liturgy – was so great that the 'Pauline Rite' (or, if we name it after its architect: the Bugnini-Liturgy) cannot be regarded as the late twentieth-century form of the *Roman* Rite. (We will return later to the meaning of Pope Benedict XVI's formula: 'one rite, two forms'.) Looking for its place in the history of the liturgy, it can be identified principally as the successor of the Neo-Gallican rites that flourished in the seventeenth to nineteenth century.[12] It is reminiscent of them not only in its shape but also in its threefold inspiration: it is voluntaristic, artificially fabricated and anti-traditional.[13]

Caution is required not only with the use of the attribute 'Roman' but also with the epithet 'Conciliar'. Although this liturgy was introduced and propagated as the creation of the Council, if its content is compared with the actual Constitution *Sacrosanctum Concilium*, it can hardly be labelled as 'the liturgy of the Council'.[14] The Constitution spoke in general terms, which permitted different interpretations. Recently a good number of papers have discussed these questions: whether or not the committee followed, in fact, the directions of the Council; whether or not Paul VI himself – who was in contact with the liturgy only as a celebrant – gave serious consideration to the documents put in front of him. The *Consilium* and its Secretary possessed the means to put the pope under some kind of psychological pressure. I say this not out of irreverence, but only to underscore my opinion: the signature of the pope, taken in itself, does

---

on-the-spot product' (from the explanatory letter accompanying the Motu Proprio *Summorum Pontificum*). 'In the history of the liturgy there is growth and progress, but no rupture. What earlier generations held as sacred, remains sacred and great for us too, and it cannot be all of a sudden entirely forbidden or even considered harmful' (*Discourse to the Roman Curia*, 22 December 2005, *Acta Apostolicae Sedis*, Vatican, vol. 98 (2006), pp. 44–45). Cf. Laurence Paul Hemming (2008), *The Liturgical Subject*, p. 5. 'The hermeneutic of discontinuity risks ending in a split between the preconciliar Church and the post-conciliar Church. It asserts that the texts of the Council as such do not yet express the true spirit of the Council.'

[11] László Dobszay (2003), *The Bugnini-Liturgy and the Reform of the Reform*, pp. 5–17, 23–24, 58–68, 86–88, 122–33.

[12] In John P. Parsons' interpretation ('A Reform of the Reform?', 2003, pp. 214–15) the direct motives of the Bugnini-Liturgy were similar to those of the heretical 1794 Synod of Pistoia and the activity of Scipio de Ricci, condemned by the papal bull *Auctorem Fidei*. Cf. Hemming (2008), *The Liturgical Subject*, p. 5.

[13] Gamber (2002), *The Modern Rite*, pp. 44. The discourse preparing such a turn became louder in the 15-year period before the Council. See Alcuin Reid (2005), *The Organic Development of the Liturgy*, chapter 3.

[14] Parsons (2003), 'A Reform of the Reform?', pp. 229–30: 'The Council Fathers did not authorize the introduction of alternatives to the Roman Canon as the sole Eucharistic Prayer; yet many have been introduced. The Council Fathers did not authorize the destruction of the immemorial Roman lectionary; yet it was destroyed. The Council Fathers did not authorize a recasting of the annual cycle of Sundays or any change to the very anicent Sunday Collects; yet both these changes were made . . . The Council Fathers did not authorize the abandonment or tendentious alteration of over 80 percent of the orations . . . yet this momentous step was taken. The truth is that the Fathers of the Second Vatican Council assumed that the great Roman rite as known to history would be maintained in all its essentials and would continue to be the principal form of the celebration of the Catholic Eucharist. In this they were deceived. The historic Roman rite was suppressed de facto.' Cf. Cardinal Alfons Stickler (1999), 'Recollections of a Vatican II Peritus'; Thomas M. Kocik (2003), *The Reform of the Reform*, p. 39.

not suffice to prove that the new liturgical books and norms properly express the intentions of the Second Vatican Council.[15] As I said earlier, our obligatory attitude of obedience does not exclude the freedom to reconsider the appropriateness of given (practical) points in the Constitution. This is all the more true for the documents promulgated around 1970.

The reception of these documents was determined basically by two sentiments: respectful obedience due to the papal approval and enthusiasm towards the Council. Joyful acceptance was, however, not quite unanimous. This was the period when the debate started between the two wings representing theological tendencies – usually referred to by the (rather inane) labels 'progressive' and 'conservative'. The two 'parties' in themselves were hardly homogeneous.

Those who were not happy with the 'new liturgy' can be categorized roughly according to three major tendencies:

The first tendency can be called theological criticism. Its objection was fed mostly by the famous Ottaviani-intervention.[16] Here we largely find learned theologians whose criticisms needed to be taken seriously; they confronted the new ideas with the doctrines of the classical schools of theology.[17]

The second tendency might be called cultural criticism. Some were afraid that, along with Latin, the old ceremonial, and sacred music (as part of the cultural heritage of the Church), the gravity and mystical power of Catholic cult itself would perish. They supposed – rightly I might add – that if the Church abrogates in its cult the alliance between religion and culture, this would have a negative effect on the overall life of the Church.[18]

The third direction can be called psychological criticism. It represented the aversion of the ordinary faithful (and a part of the clergy) to something that cut them off from beloved forms of worship that for so long enriched them with

---

[15] Recently a vivid discourse developed concerning the limitations of papal authority over the liturgy. According to Pope Benedict XVI in his Homily for the Mass of Possession of the Chair of the Bishop of Rome, 7 May 2005: 'The Pope is not an absolute monarch whose thoughts and desires are law. On the contrary: the Pope's ministry is a guarantee of obedience to Christ and to his Word'. Cf. Ratzinger (2005), Preface to Reid (2005), *The Organic Development of the Liturgy*, pp. 10–11. Reid (2005), *The Organic Development of the Liturgy*, pp. 37–8 and 249.

[16] A. Ottaviani and A. Bacci (1992), *A Short Critical Study of the New Order of Mass*, pp. 27–55.

[17] Michael Davies (1976), *Liturgical Revolution – Volume I*, (1980), *Liturgical Revolution – Volume III*, (1991), *Mass Facing the People*, (1992), *Liturgical Time Bombs in Vatican II*, and (1997), *Sanctuary and the Second Vatican Council*; Klaus Gamber (1992), *La Réforme Liturgique en Question*; Dietrich von Hildebrand (1993), *The Devastated Vineyard*; Josef Pieper (1991), *In Search of the Sacred: Contributions to an Answer*; Romano Amerio (1997), *La veillée pascale dans l'Église Latine* and (1999), *Iota Unum*; Aidan Nichols (1996), *Looking at the Liturgy*; James Hitchcock (1994), *The Recovery of the Sacred* and (2006), 'Liturgy and Ritual'; James F. Wathen, SJ (1971), *The Great Sacrilege*; Didier Bonneterre (2002), *The Liturgical Movement*; Robert A. Skeris (1994), *Crux et Cithara*; Alcuin Reid (2006), 'Looking Again at the Liturgical Reform'.

[18] On a broader field of cultural philosophy see Dietrich von Hildebrand (1967), *Trojan Horse in the City of God*. Alcuin Reid (2005), *The Organic Development of the Liturgy*, p. 286, speaks in term of 'historical arrogance' and Mgr Peter J. Elliott (2003) of some kind of liturgical Maoism ('A Question of Ceremonial', p. 266): 'The Roman liturgy has thus become prey to predators with their own obsession. A few proponents of liturgical Maoism are still promoting further simplification . . .'

spiritual goods. They were deprived of their missalettes, the Communion rail, the customary tranquil order of the nave, quiet devotion and worthy solitude. They were annoyed by a constant 'agitation' of the faithful, incessant prodding to some kind of activity and ceaseless didacticism. Here is not the right place to examine how much of this 'nostalgia' was really justified. For many people these things made it very difficult to accept the new liturgy.

The more populous body of those who accepted the 'conciliar liturgy' can also be divided into three main groups:

The first is that of minimalists. They sought – knowingly or instinctually – how the new forms could be integrated into the old context with the least effort. The turn to the vernacular caused them no problem. These were they who dragged the credence-table into the middle of the sanctuary and made of it an altar. The chants of the Propers (and in some places also the Ordinary) were replaced by folk songs. Once this was achieved, they were done with the 'reform'.

The second group comprised the obedient: their motto was '*Roma locuta, causa finita*'. They received and assented to the changes of the liturgy with the long-accustomed obedience of the clergy, and realized the requirements of the new rubrics without any extra endeavour and with the discipline acquired during the reign of old rubrics. In the mid-1960s a priest explained to me with great conviction how much the pre-Lenten period (of Septuagesima, etc.) revealed the wisdom and psychological sensitivity of the Church. Two years later the same priest argued with the same persuasion how good it was that the Church had deleted this unnecessary and burdensome institution from the calendar.

The third group was that of the 'creatives'.[19] The introduction of the new liturgy gave them wings. They understood, or presumed to understand, the 'spirit of the Council', and year by year went further in producing individual rites that were introduced in parallel to or even against the law. They constituted, in fact, a virtual group: an innovation by one priest appeared soon in another church. These innovations were sometimes no more than mere 'mannerisms', for example, to place the two candles neatly to one corner of the altar. Sometimes more was at stake: mannerisms offending the spirit of the liturgy (preaching while walking up and down; shaking the hands of all the faithful in every pew at the Peace; agitating the faithful or a group of them to raise their voice freely during the Mass, etc.). Then a gradual escalation followed and they turned to the texts, structure, rubrics and gestures of the Mass. A priest comes to my mind who once explained to me that he preferred to pray with his own words in the liturgy, because in ancient times the fixed prayers had also been composed *ad libitum*. These men put together a list of the 'conciliar ideas' that should form the liturgy: up-to-dateness, accommodation to the character and needs of a congregation, social sensitivity, missionary élan, etc.; and under these headings they shaped or let teams shape the rite.[20] A friend of mine reported that in a monastery the monks were really proud that all the prayers and chants of the Good Friday celebration were composed by different members of their community, and so

---

[19] Cf. Gamber (2002), *The Modern Rite*, pp. 10–11.
[20] Gamber (2002), *The Modern Rite*, p. 11.

they would thereby participate in producing the liturgy. Some innovations, widespread in these groups, became so general that finally the wider Church accepted them almost universally (demolition of Communion rails, distribution of the Communion in the hand,[21] etc.).

Innovations of this type cannot, of course, be justified from the Council, not even on the terms of the documents issued around 1970. The innovators were quick to advance the justification: 'life has transcended the Council', indeed, they went beyond the Council concerning language (the nearly total disappearance of Latin), musical standards and the setting of, at least, some barriers to reform. But in spite of this, the innovations were not independent from the Council or what happened after it. Before the Council the priest mentioned above would have never been able to arrogate to himself the right to celebrate the Mass using his own words. This only became possible because confidence in the stability of the Church's liturgy had been shaken by the very reforms themselves (not to mention the fact that the priest above would have been unable to perform this creative gesture, since his Latin was not good enough to improvise such a text; he only became capable of speaking in his own voice in the context of the innate laxity of the vernacular).

This situation was also true in a broader sense. The 1970 documents generated a new psychological atmosphere. The clergy and the congregations entrusted to their care gained the impression that almost everything could change in the Church from one day to the next. The liturgy came to depend on the decisions of human persons (committees, or even the pope), and if rules exist, they are merely legal niceties, and do not spring from a deep adherence to liturgical norms. The liturgy is a 'formality' that can change as time proceeds, provided that the 'eternal' truths of the Church are not harmed. The 'eternal' truths, at the same time, should be expressed in a modern language. After the reform was implemented, some priests began to say that the vernacular translations had made it clear that the trouble was not with Latin *per se*, but with what was being said in Latin. The vernacular reveals for them at once that the texts themselves had become outworn.

It only a question of time before the 'eternal' validity of just about everything became doubtful – be it a dogmatic or a moral truth.[22] A dark cloud of doubt enveloped everything – as we all experienced at the time. Finally, many even asked the question: 'what is Christianity after all?' It is not an exaggeration to refer to this situation as a collapse. I repeat: the motivation of doubts and negation in this case was not taken up through any rational argumentation. The situation was unlike that of the great heresies of the past, which emerged as a result of some real theological speculation or question. For this reason the heresies of today's

---

[21] Gamber (2002), *The Modern Rite*, pp. 59–68.
[22] Cardinal Joseph Ratzinger said in an interview: 'A community is calling its very being into question when it suddenly declares that what until now was its holiest and highest possession is strictly forbidden and when it makes the longing for it seem downright indecent. Can it be trusted any more about anything else? Won't it proscribe again tomorrow what it prescribes today?' (quoted in Kocik (2003), *The Reform of the Reform*, p. 90). Cf. Gamber (2002), *The Modern Rite*, p. 11; Parsons (2003), 'A Reform of the Reform?', pp. 226–27.

Catholicism have not even been properly formulated or openly declared; and the Church has shown no real zeal in recognizing, identifying and censuring them. The motivation was rather psychological; it would be interesting to analyse its elements (loss of the sense of stability, activism, a 'profit-oriented' approach to religion, the appearance of an anthropocentric mentality and relativism, to name but a few examples). A direct consequence of these events was the massive desertion of men from the priesthood. This latter had, of course, also a theological reason. If the ontological-sacramental dimension of the priestly order and the sense of what had formally been understood to be an indelible character grow dim, the priest becomes a social worker in the service of men, and there remains nothing to link him to his own priesthood; since he can fulfill the 'service of men' just as well, perhaps even better, as a layman.

These manifestations of the crisis in the life of the Church are ultimately the consequence of the liturgical reform. The 'disintegration' of the liturgy (as Cardinal Ratzinger put it[23]) led to the disintegration of the Church, as seen in the state of its theology and moral order. The expected pastoral benefits were never realized, as is clear from the rapid decrease in church attendance and priestly vocations.[24] The disintegration of the liturgy became manifest on three levels: the disintegration of its *apprehension*, of its *material* and of its *style*. The Catholic liturgy once *had* a style – this vanished: liturgical styles are now as numerous as church buildings themselves.

The Church (on the level of papal, hierarchical and official utterances) had only one answer to this. The actual cause of the difficulties was seen in the excesses of the conservative and progressive parties, and thus the only medicine offered was obedience towards the liturgy enacted by and after the Council. But here we have a difficulty with this judgement, in its seeking a *'via media'*. The majority of the 'conservatives' deviated from the conciliar liturgy only in their rhetoric. Only small groups of them became liturgically 'conservative' in actual practice, and most of them did so only on the basis of legal indults. Fragmentation was the result of the innovations by the so-called 'progressives'.

The Church proved to be weak in enforcing due obedience in liturgical matters. There was a fear that if a recalcitrant priest were to be rebuked, the lack of priests would increase; in fact, liturgical abuses were nearly never punished.

But there is still a bigger problem with the 'medicine' that was proposed.

---

[23] Cardinal Joseph Ratzinger (1998), *Milestones; Memoirs 1927–77*, p. 148: 'I am convinced that the crisis in the Church that we are experiencing today is to a large extent due to the disintegration of the liturgy'. Cf. Ratzinger (2000), *The Spirit of the Liturgy*, p. 82. See also the desperate description of the situation in Brian W. Harrison, OS (2003), 'The Postconciliar Eucharistic Liturgy', pp. 151–60, James Hitchcock (2006), *The Recovery of the Sacred*.

[24] James Lothian (2000), 'Novus ordo Missae'.

4

IS THE MEDICINE CALLED OBEDIENCE?

If we wish to examine calmly and patiently the problem of obedience, first we have to declare that the obligation of obedience cannot be called into question. *In practice* we keep ourselves within the liturgical directions of the Church – for the sake of preserving and defending liturgical discipline, and the hierarchical order and unity of the Church, but also because nobody (neither priest, nor layman, theologian or even liturgical expert) has a right of governance over the liturgy. Whatever is done against the rules of the Church cannot be regarded as the liturgy of the Church any more.

On the other hand, I do not think that the obligation to obedience prohibits thinking and deliberating in liturgical matters, provided that this is done with competence and according to due form.[1] The liturgy is, of course, not any matter for decision by referendum; a wanton and destructive discussion can never be opened over it. But in the past every change approved or ordered by the Church was first prepared in the mind of experts. When the popes introduced a new feast or mandated a change in the rite (as Pius XII did with the reform of Holy Week), they made specific reference to the requests of the bishops, priests, experts and various communities. If it were illegitimate to think and speak (with competence and due respect) on the liturgy and its possible changes, these petitions could never have been formulated, and the study and discussions that preceded these petitions would have been blameworthy.

Before launching an analysis of the problems concerning obedience, let me allude, by way of exception, to my personal experience. Not as if this memory were particularly pleasant for me, or as if I am in search of some justification, or much less as if I took any satisfaction in burdening anyone else with my own concerns. But I suppose this story can render more understandable the problems I want to speak of.

Some years ago two Hungarian bishops (one responsible for the liturgy, the other the head of the bishops' conference) reprimanded me for favouring the use of Latin, propagating Gregorian chant, rebuked my efforts to introduce the Introit and Communion antiphons to be sung at Mass instead of folk songs and also for expressing my scholarly opinion that the coordination of responsorial

---

[1]   John B. Parsons (2003), 'A Reform of the Reform?', p. 248.

psalmody to the Mass readings is false both from a historical and a pastoral perspective. I advocated the adoption of the one-year system of psalms, explicitly permitted in the official liturgical books. (Parenthetically, the accusations failed in the supposition that the promotion of one choice means the deletion of the other.) The bishops' letter had very unpleasant official consequences; it was circulated among the clergy who afterwards shunned me almost as if I were a leper, and whenever I said but one word, they attacked my writings in howling packs.

I add another experience. My students who enrolled in parish jobs complained that when they tried to develop musical life in a classical ecclesiastical direction and most in conformity with the traditions of the Church, they had to face serious, insoluble conflicts with their parish priest, who – referring to their pastoral intentions and the obligation of ecclesiastical obedience – rejected what in fact corresponded the most to the letter and spirit of liturgical law. These colleagues received no support either from committees set up for the promotion of sacred music, or from ecclesiastical superiors – who were often foremost in transgressing the rubrics.

Let us therefore study the question of obedience in light of these two experiences.

The first question is: *to whom* do we owe obedience in liturgical matters? I think that it is to the directions of the universal Church and the rubrics described in the liturgical documents. Furthermore, we owe obedience to the bishop; but we have seen that this obedience is not without its problems. What should we do when the instructions or recommendations of the universal Church seem to be in opposition to the bishop's will? And what can be done if somebody, while remaining within the legal prescriptions, aspires to do something better, but finds himself opposed by a dictatorial minimalism? And what can be done when individual priests or lay people work in complete accord with the letter and spirit of the relevant directives, or aim to improve things in a way *permitted* by the regulations – and yet by doing so they provoke the displeasure of their direct ecclesiastical superior? To whom do we then owe obedience?

The second question is: *in what* exactly do we owe obedience concerning liturgical matters? Whatever is prohibited by the Church must not be done, of course, and whatever is commanded by the Church, one is obliged to do. But consider the examples above. The liturgical Constitution *Sacrosanctum Concilium* says that Latin *must* be retained in the liturgy, while the vernacular *can* be given *some* place.[2] The later possibility was broadened after the Council: everything may be said in the vernacular. But the concession surely did not *proscribe* the use of Latin. Furthermore: Latin merits an eminent role in the liturgy, according to a *higher* legislation (the Constitution *Sacrosanctum Concilium* itself). For as long as things stand like this, can somebody be accused of disobedience if he, while

---

[2] Vatican Council II, Dogmatic Constitution on the Sacred Liturgy, *Sacrosanctum Concilium* (1963), §36: 'Linguae latinae usus, salvo particulari iure, in ritibus latinis servetur. Cum tamen, sive in Missa, sive in Sacramentorum administratione, sive in aliis Liturgiae partibus, haud raro linguae vernaculae usurpatio valde utilis apud populum exsistere possit, amplior locus ipsi tribui valeat, imprimis autem in lectionibus et admonitionibus, in nonnullis orationibus et cantibus, iuxta normas quae de hac re in sequentibus capitibus singillatim statuuntur.'

accepting the vernacular, wishes to give *some* place to the Latin – and more than *no* place at all? According to the Constitution on the Liturgy, Gregorian chant has pride of place in the Roman liturgy. This principle has not been abolished by later documents, even if actual ecclesiastical practice eliminated the Gregorian chant for the sake of folk hymns and pop songs. Can somebody be accused of disobedience if he asks that *some* role be given to chant (praised by highest authorities), even if less than to any other repertories actually used? The General Instruction of the Roman Missal in the relevant paragraph refers to the Introit and Communion chants as proper chants of liturgy,[3] and mentions possible substitutions only later, and as a minimal alternative. If this is so, is it reasonable for the bishops to criticize someone who makes realistic proposals for how the Introits and Communion can be sung in Latin and/or in the vernacular? The question concerning the responsorial psalm is a question of historical studies; the General Instruction of the Roman Missal makes clear that the one-year cycle is just as legal as the three-year system. Can anyone be blamed, therefore, if he argues for the one-year cycle (as given in the *Ordo Cantus Missae*[4]) – without denying the legality of the three-year system? When a choirmaster has been successful in teaching and adopting Gregorian chant in the practice of the schola and congregation (without displacing the folk hymn), can he be directed in the name of obedience to leave the 'outdated style' aside, to dissolve his schola, and give place to the more 'contemporaneous' pop music?

Obedience, yes, but in what? We spoke about three levels. The first is the level of the *rules* of the Church; in this obedience can be exacted both in the universal and local sphere. The second is the level of official *recommendations*; in this it would be strange to call it disobedience if somebody chose at every point what is more traditional, more ecclesiastical, and is recommended by law. The third level is in *thinking about* the liturgy. In this area both the recognition of the intellect of a Christian, and of the spirit of charity, demonstrate the right to explain unassumingly every well-grounded opinion that is justifiable both in terms of doctrine and ecclesiastical tradition.

Is the medicine called obedience?[5] It is not easy to answer this question.

It would be difficult to refute that it was partly the official Church itself that is responsible for generating disobedience. First, because the Church permitted its appointed committees to stretch far beyond the limits set by a higher statute (the Constitution *Sacrosanctum Concilium* of the Second Vatican Council itself), and what is more, at several points these committees enacted new regulations explicitly *against* the higher law. Who was disobedient first? Was it not the one who disregarded both the tradition and the Council's Constitution?[6] I suggested in my previous book that it were very audacious for the *Consilium* to have

---

[3] *General Instruction on the Roman Missal*, 2000, §48. 'Adhiberi potest sive antiphona cum suo psalmo in Graduali romano vel in Graduali simplici exstans . . .'
[4] *Ordo Cantus Missae* (1972). Cf. 'Institutio Generalis Missalis Romani' (= IGMR), Nr 61, in *Missale Romanum* (2002).
[5] Cf. Brian W. Harrison, OS (2003), 'The Postconciliar Eucharistic Liturgy', pp. 162–66.
[6] Thomas M. Kocik (2003), *The Reform of the Reform*, p. 72, quoting Michael Davis: 'Traditional Catholics are often accused of disobedience to the Council. There has indeed been disobedience to the Council, disobedience on a massive scale, but it has been on the part of those who took it

created a rite in the space of some few years that is so essentially different from the liturgy that has been celebrated for over one and a half millennia. But it is impudence indeed if it then declares the previous rite illegitimate, and banishes it in the name of its own construction.[7] By what moral authority could it thereby expect obedience from others?

Secondly, the reform itself generated this wave of disobedience, since it damaged the sense of stability that belongs to the proper exercise of faith, and, in some sense, belief in the superhuman and revelatory character of the liturgy itself. In the Old Testament all the rituals were proposed as something ordered directly by God. In the New Testament Church this appears to be true only for the foundation of the ritual. But the faithful in their communities have always accepted the liturgy and lived it as something received from above (even if not in exactly the same way as in the Old Testament), something in which to participate was, indeed, a great honour. This confidence declined after the Council, and this – confirmed by slogans – resulted in a wave of disobedience.

Thirdly, the official Church herself is responsible for the disobedience, since concrete cases of disobedience were hardly ever followed by concrete rebukes. In a paradoxical way, while individual innovations persisted without consequence, those who insisted on the preservation of ecclesiastical traditions were reproached! The innovators obviously transgressed the set confines of the law; the traditionally inclined, however, in most cases remained within those confines. Yet it was still considered the gravest of sins if from among the possibilities offered by the law they tried to choose the one that was the most appropriate to the traditions. Surely, sometimes they endeavoured to broaden the limitations, or tried to interpret the law in a sense most favourable to tradition. They did this in the conviction that if the universal Church tolerates the free creation of liturgies by monasteries, communities and individuals, the same right perhaps also belongs to those who, without wanting to transform the liturgy, strive to persevere in the rite they inherited, at least in this or that point. The two excesses were not of similar content and of comparable influence; yet in concrete cases it seemed it was always the 'traditionalists' who were reprimanded.

---

upon *themselves* to defy the Council's Liturgy Constitution and destroy the most venerable rite in Christendom, which it had commanded should be preserved and fostered in every way.'

[7] Klaus Gamber (2002), *The Modern Rite*, p. 14: 'All that is happening . . . is that an old rite, which despite many weaknesses has stood the test of centuries, is replaced by a new one which is yet to be tested'. He speaks (p. 82) – analysing the Easter Vigil rites – also of 'autocratically introducing new and untested material'. On the totalitarian and violent character of the Bugnini-reforms, see Parsons (2003), 'A Reform of the Reform?', p. 217. Going further, Parsons says, (p. 223): 'Bugnini shared Scipio de Ricci's conviction that Catholic worship had been in need of reform for many centuries, and shared also in the complacent conviction that he was just the man needed to reform it.' It is curious to see that Klauser (1969, *A Short History of the Western Liturgy*, pp. 58–69), the devoted reformer, still had the vision of new Roman liturgical books giving only a general frame for the local usage: 'as a result of the Second Vatican Council the centuries-old, cast-iron uniformity of liturgical books and prayers has been abandoned in favour of an attempt to make the liturgy correspond more closely to the needs of different people and different countries . . . in the future the liturgy will only be universally the same in respect of its fundamental principles, but will differ widely as to the manner in which it is put into practice.' In spite of this the reform has been realized with the most 'cast-iron uniformity of the liturgical books'. See also James Hitchcock (2006), 'Liturgy and Ritual'.

However, the most serious question is not this, but the following: is the new rite *worthy* of such obedience? What if there are, in fact, failures in the new rite? What should be done if the new rite, in fact, diminishes the sacrality, the mystery, the sense of transcendence so characteristic of the liturgy? One might, of course, say that the new rite can also be celebrated without harming these values and with the proper theocentric orientation (and this precisely is the true meaning of obedience!). People in general, however, do not think in abstract categories; their way of thinking is formed by their own actions. If norms are introduced that inspire a 'reinterpretation' of the meaning of the liturgy, people will be re-educated in their minds as they themselves follow these norms. If the rules that used to surround and defend the holiness of the host are relaxed, is it any wonder that the sense of the mystery of the Eucharist will at the same time be diminished?[8] If the system of pericopes is transformed in a way that a didactical aim is advanced to such prominence, this view of the pericopes will gain prevalence, and some communities or priests may draw unfavourable conclusions (e.g. free selection of readings) from this state of affairs.

All of this directs our attention to a problem that is rarely mentioned. In some cases obedience causes a conflict of conscience.[9] While one assumes with the best of intentions an attitude of obedience towards the Church, it is possible to find – with good reason and without rebellious inclinations – that the innovations have adverse effects on the Church and are hardly tolerable insofar as personal piety is concerned. This conflict frequently occurred precisely in those who were the most faithful to ecclesiastical doctrine and liturgical practice. In some cases they came to feel that their own Church has somehow deceived them: today, the Church denies them that which was taught only yesterday; while these individuals remained devoted, the Church laid aside her own teaching. No doubt, the Church should be consistent: if she expects something in the name of obedience, she has to justify it for the sake of the whole community. On the other hand – especially in the present-day situation – she has to consider very seriously what is the actual *content* of the rite or the elements of the rite in which she expects obedience. Surely, she must reject false, baseless and ignorant statements (as well as a kind of 'democratic outlook' in liturgical matters), but she should attend closely, with understanding and good will, to every well-founded criticism and reasonable proposal.

---

[8] Harrison (2003), 'The Postconciliar Eucharistic Liturgy', pp. 190–91.
[9] Cf. Kocik (2003), *The Reform of the Reform*, p. 90.

5

OBJECTIONS

As soon as the new liturgical books were published, some people began to voice their criticism of these books or, in more general terms, of the postconciliar reforms. It appeared first that these objections could simply be ignored, since they were only the reactions of an older generation, educated in the 'old liturgy' to which they felt somehow attached, so the motivation behind this criticism was no more than conservativism or nostalgia. If this is the case – or so many reasoned – this generation will either acquiesce to the changes or they will die out. But things turned out otherwise. As time went on, the criticism escalated and, to the surprise of all, young people became the most resolute representatives of this attitude of criticism, people who had not even known the 'old' liturgy. They grew up in the 'new' liturgy, and not infrequently they were rather assiduous in its service. Some kind of disappointment, or perhaps an encounter with the 'old' rite first awakened their interest, and later changed their attitude. Their criticism was linked, of course, with the positive wish for the restitution of the old liturgy, or for the radical improvement of the new one. In common parlance this mixture of criticisms and desires often crystallized under the label of 'the reform of the reform'.

Be that as it may, we are now only interested in the actual *content* of the criticism, or even in some particular points of it. The criticism – and the concomitant demands for change – appeared on three levels:

The first touched on the concepts and sentiments that had originally provoked the reforms or, in fact, those that the reform itself had provoked. These discussed primarily the changes in pastoral behaviour or in the psychological dispositions of the priests and of the faithful which, in the final analysis, also included theological connotations. The typical points analysed were the horizontality versus verticality of the liturgy; the relationship and importance of the external and internal aspects of active participation; or the right, as opposed to false, interpretation of inculturation (just for some examples). I rank in this group the critical analysis of the impact of the reforms: for example, the change of mentality, the meaning of priestly vocation and the practice of church attendance. These questions cannot be completely bypassed, but instead of a detailed discussion I direct the reader to the vast literature available on the matter.[1]

---

[1] Among the first people to indicate deep-seated objections was Cardinal Ratzinger himself, saying

31

I also intend to exclude from the following chapters the discussion of mainly disciplinary rules or customs, such as receiving Holy Communion in the hand, the shaking of hands as a sign of peace, penitential practices, etc. Some of these are based on official regulations; others were spread as a consequence of individual initiatives. An intermediate group is comprised of the innovations by private persons, more or less tolerated and accepted by the Church. Disciplinary observance is an essential part of liturgical life, but strictly speaking it does not belong to the rite.

Critical discussions of the reforms often touch upon two subjects of great importance: one is the question of the use of the Latin language and the other is celebration *ad orientem*, that is with people and priest facing the same way (east) towards the altar. Strictly speaking, these are not components of the rite but they are closely linked to it as formal traditions, and historically, with the fall of the rite, they themselves became 'endangered species'. These questions will be discussed in Part II, and I hope I will also be able to make some formal proposals and suggestions.

The criticism of the reforms confined itself – almost without exception – to the Order of Mass, and so failed to address changes to the Mass Propers and the Divine Office. This neglect is essentially a consequence of the situation that pertained before the Liturgical Movement. In the piety of the eighteenth and nineteenth centuries, prayers paraphrasing the Ordinary of the Mass were prepared to help people in their participation in the rite; very little attention was paid to the readings, and still less to the prayers and chants. In the same period the Divine Office ceased to be an integral part of the liturgy, if not in terms of theological reflection, surely insofar as daily practice was concerned. Even the public singing of Vespers was replaced in many churches by litanies, devotions and afternoon blessings. I am unaware of an in-depth analysis of the recent rearrangement of Holy Week.[2] The fact that criticism was limited to the arrangement of the Order of Mass indicates a certain superficiality; it even suggests there is at least some question about the credibility of the critique. Even though the changes in the Order of Mass (omissions of some gestures, substitutions for texts of secondary importance, abolition of duplications, etc.) were immediately perceptible, they in fact touch upon the essence of the rite much less than other elements of the liturgy, which were also substantially reformed.

The critique of the Order of Mass reflected only on two points that truly belong to the *material* of the rite. One is the abolition of the prayers at the foot of the altar; the second, the replacement of the offertory prayers. These two are akin in one respect: neither of them belongs in reality to the essential material of the Roman Rite. They are accessories completing the integral parts of the official

in the Preface to Alcuin Reid (2005), *The Organic Development of the Liturgy*: 'Anyone who, like me, was moved by this perception in the time of the Liturgical Movement on the eve of the Second Vatican Council can only stand, deeply sorrowing, before the ruins of the very things they were concerned for'. A good summary of the objections (worded in a popular tone) is given in Thomas M. Kocik (2003), *The Reform of the Reform*. Cf. Gamber (2002), *The Modern Rite*, p. 9.

2   Although there has been some scholarly discussion concerning aspects of the rites of the Triduum. See Robert Ameit (1999), *La veillée pascale dans l'Église Latine*.

liturgy with certain devotional elements, something we may actually consider the 'private matter' of the celebrant priest. In the Franco-Roman period a series of texts found their way into the Mass destined to express feelings of penitence, of the indignity of the priest, and these were included in order to give voice to the celebrant's personal devotion and piety. These prayers were adopted not only to express such emotions, but also to awaken them in the soul. The priest 'announced' in these prayers what he was about to do, and so beseeched God to accept his service. In addition to the two mentioned above, similar prayers are, for example, the '*Aufer a nobis*', '*Oramus te Domine*', '*Munda cor*', '*Placeat tibi*', the '*Orate fratres*' dialogue after the offertory, the prayers before the priest's Communion, the '*Panem caelestem . . . Domine non sum dignus*'. These prayers, of course, are very charming, suitable and excellent texts to form the priest's attitude or to instruct the faithful who read them. It is also true that these prayers assist in better understanding the individual items of the Mass, and they have the power to deepen, as well as explain, the theological force of the rite. However, they can be ranked only as belonging to the outer circle of the material of the Roman Rite. Their later origin, and thus limited historical validity, might be used as an argument when their omission or replacement is at stake. Their omission may be regretted, but it cannot be viewed as the most problematic point of the reforms. I return to these two set of prayers in Part II with consideration of their liturgical place; now I make do with remarks on their liturgico-theological meaning.

The omission of the prayers at the foot of the altar can be criticized – and not merely as the repudiation of a venerable custom – on the basis of the observation that in the new rite the expressions of penitence and humility on the part of the person (priest and faithful) entering into the liturgy were made poorer and so even defective. (It is said that the original plan of the reform was to begin the Mass, without Confiteor or any other penitential act, immediately with the Kyrie, and it is due to the personal intervention of Paul VI that the Confiteor has been retained.)

But there are several problems with this argument. The prayers at the foot of the altar are in fact the preparatory prayers of the priest, and not the beginning of the Mass of the faithful. In earlier times the priest had said them in the sacristy or on his way from the sacristy into the sanctuary.[3] There was no part of the Mass in the past that was designated to express the penitence of the faithful.[4] Recently, when the Confiteor was ranked among the prayers said aloud, the status of this 'private' element was changed to a public one.[5] This prayer had no tone or musical aspect in former times. This fact shows that it was not ranked among the public features of the rite. Let us add that there were several versions of the priest's prayers before Mass in the Middle Ages. It is not rare in the liturgy that

---

[3] Josef Andreas Jungmann, SJ (1958), *Missarum Sollemnia*, pp. 377–86; Adrian Fortescue (1912), *The Mass*, 4th edn 2005, pp. 225–8. Cf. Nicholas Sandon (1984), *The Use of Salisbury*, vol. 1, *The Ordinary of the Mass*, pp. 6–11.
[4] The *Confiteor* recited before the Holy Communion on the behalf of the faithful by the deacon or a server is of a different origin and is an insertion into the rite of Mass, a relic of when the rite of Communion was separate from the rite of Mass. The public act of penitence that preceeded the principal Mass on Sundays, the Asperges, will be discussed in Part II, pp. 218–20.
[5] Gamber (2002), *The Modern Rite*, p. 13.

one psalm verse is selected for a given occasion, which then, in later developments, draws the full psalm into becoming part of the rite. This is the case with Psalm 42, which found its way into the prayers at the foot of the altar because of a single verse ('I will go unto the altar of God'). The meaning of the full psalm is, of course, quite majestic, but it is connected to the beginning of the Mass only by the antiphon that is taken from this verse.

The omission of Psalm 42 from Mass for the Dead, and from Passion Sunday until Easter Day (and therefore at the beginning of the Good Friday liturgy, which begins only with the first Collect after the prostration) clearly manifests that these preparatory prayers are appended to the prayers for processing *to* the altar.

This does not mean that Psalm 42 and the subsequent prayers should or could not have been maintained as a private prayer of the priest. On the way to the altar he concludes the series of prayers said in the sacristy during the putting on of the vestments. These prayers lead the priest across from the extra-liturgical sphere of life into the realm of the sacred. In this sense the psalm and its antiphon has its precedents in the most ancient orders for the Mass: the pope, bishop or priest proceeding to the altar prayed silently while the Introit was sung. The function of the prostration on Good Friday is the same as the function of these preparatory prayers in Ordinary Time. But in spite of all these, the omission or abbreviation of the prayers at the foot of the altar is not the greatest loss of the reform. I will return to this question with a suggestion in Part II.

The case with the offertory prayers is not different. The criticisms of the changes to them were even more sharply made. It was said that their substitution means the negation or at least the deliberate obfuscation of the sacrificial character of the Mass.

The prayers themselves are, of course, fine and their deletion is a loss. In the new rite the offertory became too abbreviated, especially if the incensation is also omitted. In spite of this, the criticism is defective on several accounts.

These prayers do not belong to those parts of the Roman Rite that are destined to express the primary liturgical intention of the Church. They were placed on the lips of the celebrating priest in order to buoy up his attentiveness and to give him the proper disposition.[6] The prayers are not sung: the priest prays them silently – thus they should be regarded as private prayers.

The Offertory is primarily an act and not a prayer. Its essential momentum is placing the gifts on the altar, in the holy quadrant of the corporal; that is, transferring them to the sacral sphere, separating them from the noble but profane world of creatures. This intention is also expressed by their incensation and in a more solemn way by the 'Secret' prayer or prayer *'super oblata'*. This prayer is in fact the true offertory prayer; these are the 'preces' to which the liturgical texts make reference: 'Suscipe, quaesumus, Domine, *preces populi tui cum oblationibus* hostiarum' (Paschal Vigil); 'Placare . . . humilitatis nostrae *precibus*

---

[6] Jungmann (1958), *Missarum Sollemnia*, vol. 2, pp. 55–88. Fortescue (1912), *The Mass*, 4th edn 2005, pp. 304–08.

et hostiis' (Second Sunday of Advent); '*muneribus* nostris, quaesumus, Domine, *precibusque* susceptis' (Septuagesima),[7] and so forth.

The sacrificial nature of the Mass is not even the same as the intention made manifest in the private offertory prayers. The priest offers the bread as 'this immaculate host', the wine as 'chalice of salvation'; he asks God to receive 'this oblation'; he does not mention the act as a 'sacrifice' prior to the prayer 'In spiritu humilitatis' ('et sic fiat sacrificium nostrum', a phrase which is also retained in the new rite!).

On the other hand, the sacrificial character is abundantly clear from the true offertorial prayer, the Secret or prayer '*super oblata*'.[8] Just to name some examples, we find: 'Oblatum tibi sacrificium' (first Sunday after Epiphany); 'et ad sacrificium celebrandum . . . sanctificet' (third Sunday after Epiphany); 'Concede, quaesumus . . . ut huius sacrificii munus oblatum' (fourth Sunday after Epiphany); 'sacrificiis praesentibus, Domine . . .' (Thursday after Ash Wednesday).[9] The Secret prayer not only mentions the reality of sacrifice but offers a rich explanation of the essence of Eucharistic sacrifice, in a more conspicuous manner than any other ecclesiastical document, declaration or prayer. I can hardly understand why those who love the liturgy deal so little with these prayers, containing as they do the most eminent textual evidence of the sacramental theology of the Church. These prayers are the best possible points of departure for liturgical catechesis or meditations on the theology of the Mass.

But going further: the clearest expression of the sacramental character is found where it is the most appropriate: the Canon. 'Uti accepta habeas . . . haec sancta sacrificia'; 'offerimus praeclarae majestati tuae . . . hostiam puram, hostiam sanctam, hostiam immaculatam'; 'et accepta habere, sicuti accepta habere dignatus es . . . sacrificium Patriarchae nostri Abrahae, et quod tibi obtulit summus sacerdos Melchisedec: sanctum sacrificium, immaculatam hostiam'. And also in the new Canons: 'ut . . . oblatio munda offeratur momini tuo'; 'offerimus tibi, gratias referentes hoc sacrificium vivum et sanctum'; 'offerimus tibi eius Corpus et Sanguinem sacrificium tibi acceptabile et toti mundo salutare', etc.[10]

It might be said that the omission of the old offertory prayers is a liturgical or spiritual loss, but the change has no theological significance strictly speaking;

---

[7] 'Accept, we beseech Thee, O Lord, the prayers of Thy people together with the sacrifice . . .' 'Be appeased, we beseech Thee, O Lord, by the prayers and sacrifices of our humility . . .' 'Receive our offerings and prayers, we beseech Thee, O Lord . . .'

[8] Cf. Kocik (2003), *The Reform of the Reform*, p. 55. Parsons (2003), 'A Reform of the Reform?', p. 241.

[9] 'O Lord, may the Sacrifice we offer up to Thee . . .'; '. . . make them fit to celebrate this Sacrifice . . .'; 'Grant, we beseech Thee, almighty God, that the offering of the gifts of this Sacrifice . . .'; 'Look down favourably . . . on these Sacrifices . . .'; etc.

[10] '. . . to accept and bless this holy Victim without blemish . . .'; 'we . . . offer to Thy supreme Majesty . . . a pure Victim, a holy Victim, an unblemished Victim . . .'; 'to accept them, as Thou wert graciously pleased to accept . . . the sacrifice of our patriarch Abraham . . . a holy Sacrifice, a stainless Victim.' Also from Eucharistic Prayer 3: 'that . . . a pure sacrifice may be offered to your name'; 'we offer you in thanksgiving this holy and living sacrifice'. From Eucharistic Prayer 4: 'we offer you his Body and Blood, the sacrifice acceptable to you which brings salvation to the whole world . . .'

in itself it does not indicate a will to negate or conceal the sacrificial nature of the Mass.

These two examples illustrate that while the criticism of the reform is right and, to a great extent, acceptable on the level of principal questions and general practice, the theological questions that were actually raised were not always adequately based. In other words, a great defect of the criticism of the reform is that the liturgy is not measured *as a liturgy*, as a *sui generis* self-expression of the Church. The aspects most often discussed were not the most essential points of the Roman liturgy. To put this more sharply: careful and learned criticism of the liturgy – which could have made the criticism really effective – is still wanting (or started only in the most recent times)! I honour the theologians, philosophers, experts of sociology, etc., who dared to take a stand for the continuous traditions of the Roman Rite in so adverse an atmosphere, but where is the voice of those who are familiar with the liturgy in its details? Where are those to whom the liturgy means more than scholarship? Where are the Guéranger, the Guardini, and the Casel of today?

6

LEX CREDENDI

The theological aspect of criticism requires us to make an important diversion. This kind of argumentation clearly relies on a frequently cited formula – going back to St Augustine's disciple, St Prosper of Aquitaine: *legem credendi lex statuat supplicandi*, that is, 'let the law of prayer establish the law of faith'.[1] This sentence has a double meaning.

Prayer, in our case liturgical prayer (and liturgical custom), must be in concord with the dogmas of the Church. Not only in that they cannot be *contrary* to Christian teaching, but also inasmuch as they have to reflect the entirety of Christian doctrine, its inner coherence, order, proportions, equilibrium. Whatever is prominent in the hierarchy of Christian doctrine should also be prevalent in the practice of prayer; this is true, first of all, for the liturgy. Whatever is of secondary importance, let us say, peripheral in terms of doctrine, cannot be emphasized disproportionately in the liturgy. As Robert Taft has indicated: the liturgy as a whole cannot be Trinitarian, Christological, Mariological, Eucharistic, penitential or latreutic, since all these (and other elements of Christian doctrine) appear in the liturgy in a proportionate unity.[2] Guardini says just as much in the beginning of his book *The Spirit of the Liturgy*,[3] observing that this is the basic difference between liturgy and folk or private devotion; the latter may focus on certain themes favoured by a given age, spiritual school and religious group – the liturgy, on the other hand, is more universal.

Consequently (and this is the second aspect of Prosper's statement), the liturgy is a source of faith, a witness of the faith of the Church. Time and again, whenever a new dogma was announced (i.e. it was announced that a given truth was always believed and maintained as a sound and basic teaching of the Church), the Magisterium appealed to the liturgy as a pre-eminent proof-case, a safe point of reference. This is true not only for professional theologians, but also in the life of ordinary Christian people. As the Hungarian spiritual writer Fr Balázs Barsi put it at a conference: 'the Christian people believe what they pray'; that is, the average believer does not draw and learn the content of his faith primarily from dogmatic declarations, doctrinal books or theological courses, not even

---

[1] Laurence Paul Hemming (2008), *The Liturgical Subject*, p. 15.
[2] Robert F. Taft, SJ (1986), *The Liturgy of the Hours in East and West*, pp. 368–70.
[3] Romano Guardini (1918), *Vom Geist der Liturgie*, chapter 1.

from catechetical classes, but rather he learns it from the prayers, the words he hears and says in church. This fact, taken in itself, would be enough to justify the legislative control of the Church over the liturgy, as well as the vigilance she exerts over popular devotions and private prayers.

In spite of the validity of the principle 'lex orandi, lex credendi', there are some problems with the sense in which it is often used in our days. Though doctrine does indeed direct and control the liturgy and liturgical life (the 'lex supplicandi'), the liturgy itself is more than the *lex credendi*. Or, one may say, the *lex credendi* works in a quite peculiar and subtle way in the liturgy. The standard of doctrine is not enough for an understanding of the liturgy. It has its own laws: the *lex credendi* is only one, albeit indubitably eminent, component. In fact, the liturgy is so complex that it could hardly be described by the use of one single standard.

Let me give an extreme example to enable this to be comprehended. If somebody were mad enough to propose the transferring of the proclamation of the Gospel until after the consecration, no *theological* argument could really be made against it. Furthermore, the suggestion could be backed by a somewhat forced theological argumentation: 'In the consecration Christ begins his real presence, and then he feeds his faithful with his word (in the Gospel) and his Body (in Communion).' The reader has every right to be horrified; but at least it can be understood from this example that the sequence of the Gospel followed by the consecration is defined not by a theological norm, not by the *lex credendi*, but by some kind of *lex celebrandi*, which is nearly as strong as the former.[4] In this sentence I used the word 'lex' not in a legal or disciplinary sense but as a reference to an inner standard, a demand that cannot be violated, a standard or order which is given in the nature of the matter itself.

As the *lex credendi* regulates the 'lex supplicandi' and, therefore, the 'lex supplicandi' reveals the *lex credendi*, so the *tradition* establishes and, at the same time, embraces and reveals the 'lex celebrandi'.

Masterful minds of the liturgy tried to approach this 'lex celebrandi' in dozens of books and meditations (Romano Guardini, for instance, demonstrated some of these standards[5]). I would not even attempt to give a description to this *lex celebrandi*, since it would require unravelling a highly refined texture. However, the fact that the liturgy has its own inner character is true not only for the liturgy as a whole, but also for its individual parts and elements. There are elements that allow for some variants; the barrier of this variation is determined by the liturgy's inner system of regulation. Other elements belong to the identity of the individual rites. A deviation in this area is not against the logic of the liturgy in general, but would certainly harm the given rite. (This new aspect, the defence of the *style* of the Roman Rite, is stressed in a recent papal document; in this fact I see a significant change in comparison to the last three decades.[6])

---

[4] Similarly: the spirit of the liturgy is what required the placing of the Gospel in the last place among the readings of the Mass. Cf. Josef Andreas Jungmann, SJ (1958), *Missarum* Sollemnia, vol. 1, pp. 565–7.

[5] Guardini (1918), *Vom Geist der Liturgie*, chapters 3–7.

[6] *Liturgiam Authenticam*, 2001, §§40, pp. 57–58.

Instead of a detailed analysis it is enough to say that the liturgy is not a tool of religious instruction. The liturgical text is neither a catechism put into prayer, nor an illustration of such an instruction. When a homily says: 'the teaching of today's liturgy is . . .' it goes, in fact, against the spirit of the liturgy, since it treats the liturgy as if it were a school class with a principal 'theme' and a set of texts intended to explain this theme. In some sense, the liturgy has always the *same* 'teaching'. On the other hand, the liturgy is much more than a vehicle for teaching, and here I am not thinking only of the sacramental reality of the liturgy which is clearly beyond teaching. The liturgy places people in a *special situation of existence*. This medium is supra-personal, supra-communal, supra-natural, and eschatological. One blessing of the liturgy is that temporarily we can put aside our 'methodological' or rational way of thinking (without becoming inattentive). We forget ourselves and our direct duties, and we come under the influence of something higher. We find ourselves somehow taken out of this day-to-day world so that we are transported to a place (the vestibule of heaven) where we are given to experience the magnificence of simply standing in the presence of God. The liturgy no doubt requires a proper understanding (*rationabile obsequium*);[7] but it does not require a great intellectual, voluntary or emotional activity. Although it defines the rules of external active participation, it leaves – with a bit of discretion – the otherwise today over-manipulated human person to himself – in reality not to himself but to the inimitable intimacy of the divine mystery.[8] It is true that when the soul enters into the liturgy, or more precisely, when it is exposed to frequent celebrations of it, it becomes more learned in divine matters in the sense of tasting the divine. An ecclesial sense (*sensus ecclesiasticus*) is formed in us, we learn spiritual discipline, and our emotional sphere is imbued with piety. But all these are not the result of a direct and calculated didactical effort, moral lesson, or manipulated emotional influence. This effect is analogous to the impact of a great concert, a friendly talk, a beautiful excursion, or a true and loving conjugal act.

The liturgy cannot be reduced to the service of the *lex credendi* because when the 'ideas' drawn from the liturgy are translated into the language of catechesis, they step outside, so to speak, of their true sphere of influence, and then come to be spoken in a style alien to them. The liturgy is articulated, but it does not proceed like the articles in a treatise.[9] The liturgy uses the polished words of the intellect, but it is imbibed with poetical inspiration. The liturgy as a whole is an expression of well-balanced doctrine but at certain individual points it may express with exuberance and exaggeration one's joy, despair, hatred of sin or love of God and man. Hence the equilibrium is not created by some rigid pedantry. The liturgy has its proper vocabulary, grammar, rhythm and rhetoric, all of which exist in close association with the words of theology; the liturgy is never

---

[7] Rom. 12.1.
[8] Cardinal Joseph Ratzinger (2000), *The Spirit of the Liturgy*, pp. 171–77. Gamber (2002), *The Modern Rite*, pp. 56–57.
[9] I tried to make distinction between 'Sacramental Truth', Doctrinal Truth', 'Juridical Truth' and 'Liturgical Truth' of the Liturgy (László Dobszay (2003), *The Bugnini-Liturgy and the Reform of the Reform*, pp. 156–59).

opposed to doctrine but is certainly different from it. The liturgy also has its own dramaturgy, which was formed in the course of many centuries: to subvert it is a very dangerous experiment, indeed.

With respect to the *lex credendi*, the individual genres of the liturgy require different interpretations. The Gospel is indubitably a vehicle for Christian instruction but it fulfils that purpose very differently when we read it in a Bible study group or when it is sung in the liturgy. In the Mass the Gospel is in correlation with the Eucharist and the liturgical year; it acquires its actual (and mystical) meaning in that particular context. When we pray the psalms the elements of teaching appear to us in a lyrical setting, in the co-efficiency of mind, intellect, will and emotion. The Collects (Secret, Preface, Postcommunion) are the most direct expressions of the liturgical teaching of the Church. In them, however, the individual themes are coordinated by some kind of synoptical view: everything appears in close association with the matter of human salvation.

Tolstoy in his *War and Peace* speaks about the war of Russia against Napoleon. One of the most memorable scenes of the novel is the battle at Borodino. And yet, thinking of this piece of literature, there emerges some kind of *totality* in our memory: it is the texture of single human fates and overall human destiny, the joyful and painful wandering of peoples, nations, communities through time and space; desires, delusions, attractions, unreasonable alienations. All this appears not 'in general terms', not in an abstract way, but in the concreteness of living life. And so, though all that is written about campaigns and battles is true historically, what we read is not a book of history.

Yet another comparison comes to mind while speaking about the role of tradition in the 'lex celebrandi'. It is tradition that makes the liturgy a living organism and not an artificial *fabrication*. One can cut his hair and nails; one may medicate against illness; if he is seriously ill, an operation might be needed; in modern medicine, it may occur that one of his organs is replaced. But it is impossible to take out all his inner organs and replace them with new ones, and after all that to point at his figure and say: see, it is the same man.[10]

Let us suppose that in spite of all the efforts of those who oppose the reform, not a single case were to be found in the reformed liturgy where the *lex credendi* had been harmed. Even so, we can say with conviction, knowing the proper world of the liturgy, that this rite in its fullness and inspiration breathes an air *different* to that of the Roman Rite. As we have said, the reformed rite is reminiscent principally of the rites that originated in a climate characteristic of Jansenism, Gallicanism and the Enlightenment.

By all these I do not want to deny, of course, the principal importance of rationality in the liturgy. The Catholic liturgy is not an *ecstasy* or *hypnosis* – it is irradiated in its every moment by the serene light of divine reason. Inasmuch as it transmits Catholic doctrine, we have to strive to understand its teaching; the faithful should learn the words, signs and message of the liturgy. Yes, the content of the liturgy should be explained in liturgical catechesis with due tact, possibly without any abstraction from the concrete, visible elements of the liturgy.

[10] Cf. Alcuin Reid (2005), *The Organic Development of the Liturgy*, p. 308.

The content of the liturgy should be 'translated' to the language of the human mind, according to the capacity of those receiving it, which means, with due accommodation to the given community. But the liturgy is not equal with this explanation, with this teaching. Many were scandalized when I wrote in a short article that the symbolism and meaning of the Paschal Candle can and should be explained, but that the Paschal Candle is not identical with this explanation; the Paschal Candle is identical only with the Paschal Candle.

What is the most important conclusion of all that has so far been said? In the debate between the 'old' and the 'new' liturgy, their direct and indirect theological meaning *could* be analysed, but my argument is something different. We cannot avoid seeing the liturgy as a liturgy, according to the inner standards of the *lex* (or rather, the manner, the *ars*) *celebrandi*.

7

FROM 'ECCLESIA DEI' TO 'SUMMORUM PONTIFICUM'

What will be described in this chapter is now well known; however, a short summary is still needed in preparation for our conclusions.

The 'liturgy of the Council' (a Council which accepted the fact of pluralism) was introduced with a cruel standardization that remains without any precedent in Church history.[1] (Paradoxically, in reality this could not prevent the fragmentation of liturgical practice.) One exemption was, however, permitted by the pope: older priests who were not able to learn the new liturgy could keep the rite to which they had grown accustomed in their private masses and Office prayers. It was clear that this permission was destined to last only for a short and transitional time, almost as a gesture of mercy.

The reception of the new rites (*Novus Ordo*) did not happen without opposition. The first warning was Cardinal Ottaviani's intervention in which he was (to be) joined by other cardinals. The first critical comments soon appeared in print. There was only one prelate, Archbishop Lefebvre, who – with the support and at the instigation of his circle – decided to make a practical step. The seminary of Ecône – independent from any diocese and able to accept students from all over the world – began to educate the young priests-to-be in the old discipline, and the archbishop insisted on the previous standards of theological study, as well as on the 'Tridentine' liturgy. The reaction of Rome and the tendencies within this movement sharpened the conflict, the resistance escalated, and they sought a theoretical justification. The contention came to be formulated thus: Rome abandoned the apostolic tradition on more than one matter, and so others have been forced to become the defenders of this tradition. The attempts to make peace suffered shipwreck, and finally the movement went into something akin to schism. Proper institutions were created, a hierarchy, and all this outgrew the framework of Ecône. The movement became an independent organism under the name of the Society of St Pius X. Archbishop Lefebvre was first suspended, and then excommunicated, and eventually the institution found itself hierarchically outside formal Communion with the Catholic Church.

This series of events did not shock the whole of the Church, but the arguments

---

[1] John P. Parsons (2003), 'A Reform of the Reform?' p. 217.

of the Society of St Pius X – or at least some points among them – led many within the Church to reflect more closely on the issues. Since demands for the 'old' rite were also made by some groups loyal to the pope, the Sovereign Pontiff at the time, John Paul II, felt compelled to consider the pastoral responsibility involved: was the adherence of some to a venerable rite valid for long centuries a sufficient reason to call into question their loyalty to the Church?

The solution John Paul II came up with was the so-called indult (Quattuor abhinc annos, 1984, renewed and extended by the Motu Proprio *Ecclesia Dei adflicta* in 1988[2]) which made it possible for devotees of the classical Roman Rite to celebrate the Mass under certain restrictions according to the *Missale Romanum* of 1962, that is, the last Missal issued by Blessed John XXIII before the reform. The most important condition was that there must be an acknowledgement of the validity of the new liturgy and that the local bishop must give permission for any celebration of Mass according to the older books. This provision was the manifestation of the pope's pastoral concern, but there was also the hope that the indult would make the complaints of those disloyal to the pope irrelevant, leading them sooner or later back to the unity of the Church.

In fact, in many places in the world groups were organized which asked for and obtained the necessary permission, and, accordingly, in a few churches the Mass was celebrated monthly (in rare cases, even weekly) using the Missal of 1962. For their control and protection John Paul II set up a curial commission, while the indult-groups themselves created a network to strengthen and support each other with writings and information. The place and time where and when 'Latin Masses' (an erroneous label) were accessible came to be widely broadcast, mostly on the internet.

In spite of this, conditions remained adverse for those who adhered to the former rites because of three factors. At the time the indult was issued, already two decades had passed since the Council. During these decades a priestly generation reached the canonical age when they became eligible for episcopal preferment; a generation with the memory of their young enthusiasm back in the days of the Council; with minds formed by the slogans and practices spread in the name of the Council. They insisted now on the 'new' with the same emotional conservatism and nostalgia as their predecessors on the 'old'. As a result, the majority of the clergy and higher hierarchy became uninterested in, or expressly inimical to, the indult. The stigmatizing label of 'Lefebvrism', so easily made, added greatly to this feeling. Once these priests became bishops many of them resisted giving permission. The pope and cardinals responsible (such as Augustin Cardinal Meyer in his letter to the US bishops' conference) called repeatedly for respect to be shown to the faithful who longed for this form of the liturgy, and asked the bishops to be magnanimous in permitting the celebration of the old rite. In most cases the appeal remained ineffective. Many bishops responded, almost as a reaction of defiance, with total rejection, or with the malevolent

---

[2] See the Letter of the Congregation for Divine Worship and discipline of the Sacraments, *Quattuor abhinc annos* of 3 October 1984 in *Acta Apostolicae Sedis*, vol. 76 (1984), pp. 1088–89 and John Paul II, Motu Proprio *Ecclesia Dei* in *Acta Apostolicae Sedis*, vol. 80 (1988), pp. 1495–98.

qualification of these priests and faithful as 'integrists' or 'traditionalists'. This state of affairs induced sadness, despair, sometimes practical anticlericalism in those who wanted to live within the indult.

But the so-called traditionalist side was also discontented with the indult. Although initially they received it with gratitude as a temporary state of affairs; they longed for more. They were encouraged by the unexpected growth of the movement itself. They remained a minority in the Church, but a dynamically growing, often young, and very active minority. Their voice became purer, and they started to argue for the 'Latin Mass' in a more intelligent, realistic and even-tempered style; at times even in possession of respectable ecclesiastical learning. Concerning their loyalty to the Church and the pope there could be no question, the ignoble charge of separatism could not be made against them. What was even more surprising: the bulk of the movement was made up more and more by young people. Priests and lay people who earlier had never even heard of the preconciliar liturgy began to attend the 'old' mass and to share their experiences with others. The technical developments of our age (especially the internet) helped them considerably. It became impossible to say that the whole thing was but the nostalgia of old men. Still less because numerous books and treatises of young theologians raised arguments in favour of liturgical tradition and these arguments could not be rejected by mere slogans.

The third event was that some respectable clerical groups regularized their canonical situation. In other cases, communities, already in a proper canonical position, decided to follow the old rite. The Priestly Fraternity of St Peter, the Institute of Christ the King, some religious orders or their branches, adopted the 'old rite' as their own. They founded seminaries that prepared their candidates from the first year of their education for the celebration of the old Roman Rite. In some churches the congregations had access to the Mass in both rites. It caused a great stir when a large group of priests and lay people in Campos, Brazil returned from an irregular situation to full unity with the Church, and Rome set up a personal prelature for them. This meant they were taken out of ordinary episcopal jurisdiction and given a certain canonical independence as a guarantee of undisturbed existence.

These groups frequently asked the Holy See to extend the indult to the universal Church, putting an end to the situation in which the possibility of celebrating the liturgy in a form that had existed legally for many centuries was completely dependent on the good or bad will of the local bishop.

For them a series of utterances by the Prefect of the Congregation for the Doctrine of the Faith, a cardinal commanding great respect, Joseph Ratzinger, was a great consolation and source of strength.[3] In this case, since he was otherwise one of the most active theological experts at the Council, his voice of anxiety over the current state of the liturgy could not be disregarded by charging him of 'Lefebvrism' or a schismatic mentality. Ratzinger raised his voice, first of all, for the orthodox theological interpretation of the liturgy. He defended the essentially

---

[3] Good summaries of his words and deeds are Alcuin Reid (2009), 'The Liturgical Reform of Pope Benedict XVI' and Robert A. Skeris (2009), 'On the Theology of Worship and of its Music'.

theocentric, latreutic and eschatological nature of Christian worship, and rejected the activist approach of the 'pastoral liturgy'. He separated the question of the 'orientation of the altar' from the conciliar reforms; defended with great vigour the role of true art and sacred music in the liturgy, and attacked the degrading and profane trends in liturgical music.[4]

Two of his comments carried special weight. He was the first one who dared to announce that the postconciliar processes had led to a 'disintegration of the liturgy'[5] and, in the last resort, to the disintegration of the Church itself. There had been no one else in the hierarchy able and brave enough to say that the continuity of the Roman liturgy had been broken. His statements were not quite unequivocal. It was not clear if the judgement concerning the 'break' referred to the new rite or merely to its implementation by some. At any rate, these thoughts, repeated and propagated by many others, opened a new perspective in the discussion of the liturgy.

The election of Joseph Ratzinger to be the successor of John Paul II was a great joy for the whole Church. It was received with exceptional enthusiasm by those who expected the restitution of the classical Roman liturgy or, at least, the declaration of its equal status with the *Novus Ordo*. They were all conscious of the fact that in the present-day state of the Church the pope should do everything with the utmost caution in order to avoid turmoil and division in the life of Church. Hence it was well understood that he had to take into account the disintegration of theological understanding, the position of influential persons and the reactions of the secular media (that regularly portray church affairs with bias). Despite these difficulties, it was only logical to suppose that the Cardinal, who presented such an accurate diagnosis of the liturgical situation, would not tarry in administering the appropriate resolution now that he had become pope.

Three years after his election we can say that the pope acted with great wisdom, tact and circumspection, but that he remained faithful to his previous standpoint in every possible aspect. These years were full of impatient expectations but now, in hindsight, we have to acknowledge that for the careful preparation of such a momentous decision this period was not unduly protracted.

On 29 June 2007 the Motu Proprio *Summorum Pontificum* was promulgated by the Holy Father. The accompanying letter to the bishops was firm not only in calming their anxieties and explaining the pope's motivation, but also in laying out the formal theological position to the wider Church.

With great wisdom, however, he did not reduce the question of the liturgy to a debate merely about the two rites. Some months before the Motu Proprio was promulgated the pope had issued an apostolic exhortation (*Caritatis Sacramentum*)[6] which provided careful and authentic teaching on the liturgy, valid for both the old and the new forms. He corrected a series of theological errors and practical abuses, and gave guidance for the Catholic spirit and practice

---

[4] Cardinal Joseph Ratzinger (2000), *The Spirit of the Liturgy*, pp. 74–84, 136–56.
[5] The relevant statement of Cardinal Ratzinger is to be found in the *Preface* of Reid (2009), 'The Liturgical Reform of Pope Benedict XVI'.
[6] Benedict XVI (2007), *Caritatis Sacramentum*, Acta Apostolicae Sedis, vol. 99, pp. 105–80.

of the liturgy. A survey of the last few years proves that some kind of 'reversal' was in the air. The change could be felt first in *Liturgiam Authenticam,*[7] an instruction concerning liturgical language and translations. The instruction *Redemptionis Sacramentum* by the Congregation of Divine Worship[8] confirmed the overall view of the liturgy in the spirit of authentic tradition. These declarations left the conciliar reforms untouched, and, in so doing, they called attention to the fact that the *Novus Ordo* can also be celebrated in a worthy way; in this sense the implicit claim was being made that the distorted or at least one-sided pastoral interpretation (mentality and practice) of the post-1965 period should not be traced back to the will of the Second Vatican Council itself.

The *Novus Ordo* remains in its full integrity under the new Motu Proprio, too. Moreover, it is called the 'ordinary' form of celebration. Simultaneously, however, the document gave permission without limitations to celebrate the preconciliar liturgy as the 'extraordinary form' of the Roman Rite. The practical and disciplinary regulations need not concern us here. There are, however, two remarks in the Motu Proprio and the accompanying letter that require a detailed analysis. The vision of the 'mutual influence' between the two forms is the object of a subsequent chapter. First we have to deal with the formula: 'one rite, two forms'.

---

[7] (2001), *Authenticam Liturgiam, Acta Apostolicae Sedis*, vol. 93, pp. 685–726.
[8] *Redemptionis Sacramentum* (2004), *Acta Apostolicae Sedis*, pp. 549–601.

8

ONE RITE, TWO FORMS?

'One rite, two forms.' It would be irreverent to raise doubts about the formula used by the pope. But perhaps it is not disrespectful to elucidate and refine it with regard to the liturgical *facts*. We follow the method of St Thomas Aquinas: first we will oppose the formula, and then we give an interpretation that supports the papal thesis. During the discussion I will use simply the terms 'old' and 'new' liturgy in order not to waste time on defining our terms with meticulous precision.

First of all, a seeming contradiction emerges almost immediately. Cardinal Ratzinger in several of his writings complained of a rupture or break in the tradition of the Roman Rite, as well as of a definite departure from its organic development. If it is so, how can it be said that the 'old' and the 'new' are the same rite? Is there not a contradiction between the perspectives of Cardinal Ratzinger and Pope Benedict XVI?

In the first chapter I stated that the 'new' rite cannot be placed even in the wider sphere of the Roman Rite. Its place is in the company of the sixteenth- to nineteenth-century 'reform-liturgies', more precisely of the Neo-Gallican rites. This judgement depends, of course, on the definition of the term 'rite'. If one wishes to describe the Roman Rite and separate it from any other rite, it is not enough to examine the Order of Mass or some individual elements; all of its parts should be studied and weighed with regard to their weight and significance. If the principal elements of the Roman Rite are seen this way, its relationship to the 'new' liturgy can be surveyed with the following results:

In the *Ordo Missae* the difference between the two rites is relatively small. We have already spoken of additional elements (such as the preparatory and Offertory prayers). It is more important that the new liturgy gave up the utmost stability of the Roman Canon (now the 'first' Eucharistic Prayer) so that there are hardly negligible differences between the rank of Roman Canon and the new Eucharistic prayers.[1] One cannot ignore the fact that in addition to the three new texts added in 1970, there are also heterogeneous texts produced after 1969, like the so-called 'canons for children', which are simply incompatible with the

[1] Thomas M. Kocik (2003), *The Reform of the Reform*, pp. 87. Brian W. Harrison, OS (2003), 'The Postconciliar Eucharistic Liturgy', pp. 188.

spirit of the liturgy.[2] The question arises, to what extent do certain regulations for the *ars celebrandi*, the priest's gestures (e.g. signs of the Cross, genuflections, closed 'canonical' fingers, etc.) form an integral part of the classical Roman Rite, and this requires further historical and theological study. The introduction of 'prayers of the faithful' and the sign of peace among the faithful are undoubtedly an innovation compared to the preconciliar rite.

The changes in the *Mass Propers* are quantitatively and qualitatively more significant.[3] The traditional arrangement of pericopes (both in its liturgical function and concrete distribution) was deleted from the rite. The Sacramentary (the three principal orations of the Mass, the Collect, or 'Opening Prayer'; the Secret or 'Prayer over the Gifts'; and the Postcommunion, together with the Prefaces) has been totally transformed. Old prayers have been reintroduced (which is, of course, a gain); many texts were rephrased or replaced modifying the teaching of the liturgy (the Collects of Lent, for just one example). Many new texts have been added to the Mass. If this had occurred also in the past, it was never in such quantity, and never in the main body of the liturgy. The total rearrangement of the Sacramentary was a very radical change; the new distribution deleted the association between the given liturgical days and their prayers (which was in effect at least for 1,200 years). The same happened to the Prefaces: the number of Prefaces was increased to nearly ten times as many (justified by archaic sacramentaries), and so the traditional function of the Preface, and, moreover, its relationship to the system of the liturgy, was altered. In the Roman Mass – as crystallized in the Franco-Roman period and transmitted then as a tradition – the proper 'arrangement' was to proceed from many secreta prayers through few Prefaces to one single Canon. There was no Use within the Roman Rite that dared to change this. Since there was only a limited number of Prefaces, the priests and the faithful could easily become familiar with them, or even memorize them. This reassuring familiarity and ease in recognition is severely impaired if there are too many Prefaces. The third body of the Rite, the proper chant – as I described the process in my *Bugnini-Liturgy*[4] – practically ceased to be the part of the Proper; it ceased to live as a bearer of the liturgical message of the Mass.

The Roman Rite is incarnated more in the Propers than in the Order of Mass, which is more or less common with other rites outside the Roman one (e.g. with the Ambrosian Mass). The new Propers took over a number of elements from the old one. Yet the imported strengths hardly link the two rites, since the old system was not only modified, but practically demolished. It is unreasonable here to speak of continuity or organic development; and in most cases one cannot prove that the changes were, in fact, for the spiritual benefit of the Church.[5] The supporters of the old rite would far strengthen their case in criticizing the changes to the Proper rather than the Order of the Mass.[6] But in order to advance such a

---

[2] *Missale Romanum* (2002), pp. 1271–80.
[3] For these points see chapters 17–19 of Part II.
[4] Dobszay (2003), *The Bugnini-Liturgy and the Reform of the Reform*, pp. 86–92.
[5] *Sacrosanctum Concilium* (1963), §23.
[6] For example, Pristas (2002), 'Missale Romanum 1962 and 1970'; (2003a), 'The Orations of the Vatican II Missal'; (2003b), 'Theological Principles that Guided the Redaction of the Roman

criticism one would have to analyse the changes from a truly liturgical viewpoint, instead of merely a theological one.

The most prominent period of the Temporal Cycle is *Holy Week*. The importance of these days is the highest possible, since throughout the centuries it was protected from historical changes better than any other liturgical cycle, and so it preserved many elements from the most ancient usage of the Roman Rite, up to the twentieth century. The changes instituted by Pius XII[7] were significant only in the order of Palm Sunday, and – to a lesser extent – of Good Friday and the Paschal Vigil. In the former, the Frankish additions were omitted; in the Vigil service, the function of the Exsultet and the Litany became a little different in the context of the whole service. On the other days of Holy Week small textual changes were introduced (e.g. in the solemn prayers of Good Friday). Barely a decade later, the new rite brought radical innovations. I have written about this from a very critical aspect in my *Bugnini-Liturgy*,[8] and I shall return to it in Part II. As an example now it is enough to refer to the total rearrangement of the Paschal Vigil which, as a result, lost its dramatic proportions and structure, while its meaning and spiritual significance have been seriously harmed. In these cases, to speak of continuity or to speak about two forms of the *same* rite requires extreme good will.

The reform went still further in the case of the Divine Office. The three essential components of the Roman Office (the structure and proportions of the Hours, the principles of psalm distribution, and the stock material of the *Antiphonarium*) were rejected. Out of the stones of the demolished house a completely new edifice was built. Surely here, more than any other place in the liturgical edifice as a whole, we may accuse the architects of the new rite of total neglect for §23 of *Sacrosanctum Concilium*: this cruel mutilation could not be justified on the basis of any measured or gradual development; it was not based on any profound historical or spiritual study, and it was not for the genuine spiritual benefit of the Church. One cannot speak of continuity between the two rites in the matter of the Office at all. It is correct to refer to the new composition by a new name ('The Liturgy of the Hours'), without any reference to a (non-existing) 'Roman' character that might persist. The Roman Office, which had sustained some significant damages already in the reforms of Pius X, actually died in 1971.[9]

It may be, however, that the heaviest blow against the rite took place in the *ritual of the sacraments*. I am somewhat unfamiliar with this field, and so propose to pass over discussing the subject; but I cannot conceal my suspicion that here the reform could, in fact, also be attacked with theological arguments. If it is not the case that explicitly heterodox motives were mixed into the ritual, even so the way that teaching on the essence of the sacraments is manifested in these

---

Missal (1970)'; (2005), 'The Collects at Sunday Mass'; (2007), 'Post Vatican II Revision of the Lenten Collects'; (2009), 'Septuagesima and the Post-Vatican II Reform of the Sacred Liturgy'.
[7] The decree of the Sacred Congregation of Rites: *Maxima redemptionis nostrae mysteria* (1955, XI. 16), *Acta Apostolicae Sedis* (November 1955), vol. 47, pp. 838–47. Cf. Reid (2005), *The Organic Development of the Liturgy*, pp. 172–81 and 219–34.
[8] Dobszay (2003), *The Bugnini-Liturgy and the Reform of the Reform*, pp. 20–44.
[9] Dobszay (2003), *The Bugnini-Liturgy and the Reform of the Reform*, pp. 58–68.

services is such that what we have now is surely different from the substantive tradition of the Church.

In sum, (1) with regard to the full liturgy (and not only the Order of Mass) and (2) with regard to the liturgy not only as a doctrinal instruction but *as a liturgy* with its own spirit, inner standards, tradition and style: the *Novus Ordo* cannot be labelled a new form of the classical Roman Rite. There is no Use, no variant within the classical Roman Rite, which would be so different from the other ones than this. There are many points where even the Ambrosian Rite of Milan stands closer to the classical Roman Rite. To draw another analogy, the differences in the two liturgical orders are much greater than those between the liturgy of St John Chrysostom and St Basil the Great in the Byzantine Rite.

We must speak frankly: the real question is whether or not it is true that the Roman Church replaced her rite with a new one. In this respect the standpoint of Cardinal Ratzinger ('rupture') was more logical than the one of Benedict XVI ('one rite, two forms').

And yet we owe a great debt of gratitude to him for *Summorum Pontificum* and one has to defend the formula used in it. First, we have to accept the present-day historical motivation. Many were afraid of the consequences of 'bi-ritualism' in the Catholic Church. The formula wished to provide an answer to these anxieties.

But I think it is not correct to excuse its use only with tactical – or more nicely put, pastoral – intentions. The expression 'Roman Rite' can be interpreted as 'the rite living in the Roman Church'. Since the Roman Church has been using the *Novus Ordo* legally for the last 40 years, but the same Roman Church also used the classical rite legally for many centuries – and in the Motu Proprio she declared its legality once again – we may say that they are both rites of the Roman Church, even if their forms are different. The formula is true if it is considered a reference to liturgical law and everyday practice without regard to the content and material. The Roman Church has not been divided liturgically into two different churches. The whole Church follows the rite of Rome, using its legal forms while celebrating the holy liturgy.

Based on this interpretation and following the given historical and morphological standards, this book will deal with the classical Roman Rite and the *Novus Ordo* as if speaking of two different rites. On the other hand, we acknowledge that the formula given in the Motu Proprio is correct in a legal and pastoral sense.

This chapter, which might be thought to be passing an extremely negative judgement on the *Novus Ordo* (though it was intended to clarify its relationship to what is called the Roman Rite), should be closed with a complementary issue. *The conciliar and post-conciliar reforms were responses to rightful aspirations.* They wanted to answer a latent demand and they conveyed an inescapable truth. The supporters of the classical rite are in great error if they think that the next necessary step is to banish the *Novus Ordo* and to return simply to the 1962 (or still earlier) rite. This question will be raised once again in Chapter 10.

9

THE COEXISTENCE OF THE TWO RITES

The period of expectation, hesitation, debate, lament and rejection is over. Dating from the feast of the Exaltation of the Holy Cross (2007) the liturgy can be celebrated anywhere according to the classical Roman Rite, while the *Novus Ordo* is valid without any change. In other words: the two rites are forced to coexist. The anxieties of those who opposed a kind of 'bi-ritualism' will probably not end up being justified. The two rites will bring no division into the Church, the majority of the faithful will see in the situation a manifestation of the multifaceted nature of life. Those who regularly visit the *Novus Ordo* will sometimes go to the 'Latin Mass', impelled by curiosity (or because this Mass is celebrated at a time most appropriate to them on a given day). The supporters of the 'Latin Mass' will also frequently participate in the *Novus Ordo*. There will be groups insisting on following this or that form, like the religious orders in the past when they followed their proper Use. The new situation will bring peace: nobody will question the validity of this or that rite; everybody will regard them as the implementation of a sound plurality – often mentioned during the Council.

There is, however, a half-sentence in the Motu Proprio that has not been mentioned so far. The Holy Father hopes that there will be a fruitful mutual influence between the two rites (i.e. the two forms of the same rite). This may mean two different things. First, change and mutual influence in the way of liturgical life, approach, celebration, discipline, style of the liturgy and in the quality of pastoral provision. But it may also mean an influence in the area of the rubrics, the material of the rite, that is, the celebrated liturgy itself. In this chapter I concern myself only with the first kind of influence between the rites living side by side (I call them rites for the sake of brevity); the other type of mutual influence will be discussed in the next chapter.

How will (or should) the classical Roman Rite influence the celebration of the *Novus Ordo*? I think it will intensify its latreutic character and will temper the excesses of its 'propagandism'. It will bring to life again the conviction that we are delivering a service to God in the liturgy. It will weaken the shrillness of alien intentions imported into the liturgy: the direct didactical will; its intention to 'form a community', tempering the practices whose virtues were propagated under the pretext of wooing specific groups of people (for instance, the youth). Instead of the false interpretation of 'pastoral liturgy' and the methods proper to this approach, the liturgy will regulate pastoral activity as a real *fons et culmen*, which is to say, pastoral solicitude will prepare the faithful to fulfil their cultic obligation, which is derived from their baptism. The liturgy will act upon the people of God as a liturgy. It will not be merely an empty frame for pastoral experiments; it will be liberated from these kinds of direct 'aims', and it will exert its educational capacity as a consequential effect (Guardini: 'the liturgy has no aim but a meaning').[1]

The return of the classical Roman Rite will strengthen liturgical discipline in those who use the *Novus Ordo*. It will help priests and laity alike to recognize that the liturgy is not something created by them, but something to be received. They will recognize that if the priest faces the same direction as the people (at least in his mind), he is not separated from the people, but rather he is fulfilling a service before God for the sake of the people. In the major part of the Mass, his task is not to impress people. He simply has to perform his ecclesiastical duties, and by doing so he will complete and perfect the work done for the faithful entrusted to him. The priest will behave himself like a priest; he will not want to fraternize with the congregation during the liturgy, but to fulfil his task in the spirit of the Aaronic priesthood and the ecclesial order.

The example of the classical Roman Rite will serve also to change the *style* of the *Novus Ordo*. The liturgy will thereby regain its discrete objectivity. The priest and the congregation will not look for some kind of performance (as it were, a spiritual exhibition) – rather will they come to 'handle' holy things with the discretion – almost shyness – that is due to the mystery. The stewards of the *Novus Ordo* will recognize once again that although the Church is living in the world and the world around does have some influence on her cult, the liturgy is still a closed sanctuary; its sacrality should be saved and defended from the direct influence of the profane.

Certainly, the classical Roman Rite has the power to influence the *Novus Ordo* concerning such 'practical' matters as the wider use of the Latin, the cultivation of noble liturgical music (and the elimination of unworthy music), the dignified arrangement of cultic space, of the altar, and of the holy vessels; as well as the promotion of what the Holy Father has repeatedly urged be understood: the *beauty* of the ceremonies.[2] Paradoxically, the 'Latin Mass' will also influence the texts of liturgy in the vernacular, and it will assist with the implementation of *Liturgiam Authenticam* (which has not been taken seriously so far). All these things do not touch upon the content of the liturgy, and so they can be accomplished without the introduction of any change in the postconciliar liturgical books.

The classical Roman Rite will assist in rediscovering the role of liturgical assistants. The reading belongs to the lector, prepared for his work both in general terms and concretely before the Mass. He performs his duty in appropriate choir dress even if he happens to be a layman. The duties of the ministers

---

[1] Romano Guardini (1918), *Vom Geist der Liturgie*, chapter 5.
[2] *Sacramentum Caritatis* (2007), §35: 'Pulchritudo et Liturgia'. Other citations are collected in Robert A. Skeris (2009), 'On the Theology of Worship and of its Music' and Alcuin Reid (2009), 'The Liturgical Reform of Pope Benedict XVI'.

are accurately defined in the liturgical books. Regularly they are boys, which is important also for priestly vocations. Some admonitions, acclamations and acts properly belong to the deacon or subdeacon. I do not think it is appropriate if the chalice and paten – which in earlier times could not even be touched by anyone unless he was an ordained subdeacon – are brought to the altar by an 8-year-old little girl.[3] Nothing should or could be taken over from the duties and functions properly assigned to the priest (a layman, or a laywoman, cannot deliver a homily).[4] The external participation of the people should be defined according to the inner nature of the liturgy. In our age it is acceptable if members of the laity fulfil different liturgical roles in a formal capacity. But if this is to be the case, they must be well prepared, they have to accept the discipline of the rite, and during the Mass – while they are performing their service – their place is around the altar wearing appropriate liturgical vestments. (I once observed in an Anglican church that even the sanctuary lamps were lit and extinguished by a layman wearing a surplice.) The Liturgical Constitution speaks very strictly on the order of these services.[5] Liturgical roles have become muddled up in the confused situation after 1970, and on occasion priests have *even* started to call people out from the pews to perform functions. Often they passionately tried – with the zeal of activist pedagogy – to draw people beyond their proper roles into the liturgy (perhaps under the pretext of a false etymology, 'liturgy' being a service done *by* the people). I do not think it is wrong if lay people undertake some liturgical functions according to their capacity and state of life. It can be acceptable if those prepared and initiated are commissioned with some functions that were once reserved to the clerical state alone. But the abolition of the distinction between the nave and the sanctuary surely offends the dignity of the liturgy. I am sure that the well-organized order of celebration usual in the classical Roman Rite will have a good effect upon congregations following the *Novus Ordo*.

There is one more link between the two rites that I wish most emphatically to recommend to the celebrants of the *Novus Ordo*. The new rite in many cases offers more than one option for doing something; the celebrant and congregation are permitted to choose rather freely. Among these options in most cases there is one that is concordant with the classical rite, or stands nearest to it, or, at least, is not altogether dissonant with its spirit. If the celebrant of the *Novus Ordo* is conscious of the value of classical tradition, he will tend to choose this one out of all the possible variants. For instance, the Missal gives the option of taking the Introit and the Communion either from the *Graduale Romanum*, the *Graduale Simplex*, or from another suitable and approved chant.[6] No doubt,

---

[3] Klaus Gamber (2002), *The Modern Rite*, p. 60.
[4] Thomas M. Kocik (2003), *The Reform of the Reform*, p. 83.
[5] Vatican Council II, Dogmatic Constitution on the Sacred Liturgy, *Sacrosanctum Concilium* (1963), §§28–29: 'In celebrationibus liturgicis quisque, sive minister sive fidelis, munere suo fungens, solum et totum id agat, quod ad ipsum ex rei natura et normis liturgicis pertinet. Etiam ministrantes, lectores, commentatores et ii qui ad scholam cantorum pertinent, vero ministerio liturgico funguntur. Propterea munus suum tali sincera pietate et ordine exerceant, quae tantum ministerium decent quaeque populus Dei ab eis iure exigit'. Cf. *Redemptionis Sacramentum* (2004), §§43–47, pp. 554–60.
[6] 'Institutio Generalis Missalis Romani' (= IGMR), in *Missale Romanum* (2002), Nr. 48.

the first of these possibilities is the one most in harmony with the tradition of the rite. The living practice of the 'Latin Mass' will hopefully propel priests to choose an Introit or Communio with the text as it can be found in the *Graduale Romanum*. Another example: the 1970 Missal permits three forms for the Palm Sunday procession. One of these is similar to the Roman tradition as reformed by Pius XII. In my opinion, the best solution is for the priest to choose this one, because it is closest to the normal classical form. On Passion Sunday (Fifth Sunday of Lent) the crosses are traditionally veiled. The *Novus Ordo* agrees with this custom but permits its omission.[7] A community that learns from the Motu Proprio will not make use of this permission. The *Novus Ordo* allows Mass to be said either in Latin or in the vernacular. We can hope that after the Motu Proprio priests will not strive for the total elimination of Latin. It is not obligatory to read the Sequence on the feast of Corpus Christi,[8] but is it of any 'spiritual benefit' to omit it? Many more examples can be brought forward which may be summed up in one 'golden' rule or counsel: among the possibilities offered by the *Novus Ordo*, in every possible case choose the one which is nearer to, or identical with, the provision of the traditional Roman Rite.

But the followers of the 1962 Missal should not shut themselves off either from the influence of the *Novus Ordo*, its approach, intentions, or the manner of its celebration. After the conciliar reforms it would be impossible to return to a view that simply contents itself with the fact that the celebration was perfunctorily completed according to the minimum prescriptions of ecclesiastical law, and the 'ex opere operato' influence of the sacraments cannot be interpreted any more as a dispensation from the pastoral duty of offering real liturgical education to the people. No doubt, the *validity* of the liturgy does not depend on the number, activity, or devotion of those present; the reality of the sacrament is not a result of a common will or piety. But it is precisely the objective presence of the sacrament and the objective order of the full liturgy that demand an attentive, conscious, well-prepared participation from the priest, the servers and the congregation.

Under the pretext of active participation many unworthy things and even abuses took place in recent decades. Many claimed, and rightly, that active participation should be, first of all, an internal actuality: intention, devotion, spiritual attitude. In this sense, contemplation, attentive listening, silent adoration also belong to active participation. On the other hand, the Council demanded, and rightly, that everything by the nature of the liturgy pertaining to the people (for instance, responses to the priest) must be done with the real participation of the entire congregation.[9]

The reintroduction of the 'Old' Mass does not justify a return to a practice whereby the celebration of the liturgy pertains only to the priest, while the piety of the faithful is fed by extra-liturgical devotions, prayers, hymns and spiritual literature, which are all right in their place but independent in style, piety and

---

[7] *Missale Romanum* (2002), p. 255.
[8] *Lectionarium: Missale Romanum* (1971), vol. 2, p. 915. 'Haec sequentia ad libitum dicitur vel integra vel forma breviore . . .', in the new lectionary, vol. II, at the solemnity of Corporis et Sanguinis Christi.
[9] *Sacrosanctum Concilium* (1963), §30. Cf. Gamber (2002), *The Modern Rite*, pp. 51–57.

emotion from the liturgy itself. We have heard this claim so often, although mostly in a one-sided interpretation, that one is almost unwilling to reiterate it: the true fruit of the conciliar reforms was that it directed our attention to the relationship between the faithful and the liturgy. Not even the best celebration of the 1962 Missal permits neglect or diminution of the participation of the faithful. This is the most important enrichment that the classical Roman Rite has to gain from the *Novus Ordo*.

In the logical (and not in a chronological) order, the first step is lifelong preparation of the faithful for liturgical celebration. Knowledge of liturgical texts, signs and customs should be incorporated into elementary catechesis, not only in the form of instruction on the ceremonies, but throughout. It is not enough to speak *of* the liturgy; the liturgy *itself* has to be permitted to speak for itself. The very words used by the liturgy should be learnt, and the faithful should become familiar with the liturgy's vocabulary, style and mentality.

The second step is the preparation for actual participation. This means memorizing the liturgical texts, learning the basic melodies, at least, insofar as they pertain to the congregation and thus entering into the musical culture of Gregorian chant. After the 'Latin Mass' is reinstalled, this introduction has to include the most important Latin texts to be said or chanted by the assembly.[10]

The third step is actual participation *during* the celebration. I am not thinking of interruptions to the ceremony with long and frequent explanations, or disturbing the faithful in their quiet contemplation and adoration. But at a Mass celebrated fully in Latin the congregation should have access to translations of the texts; if the choir sings, let us say, a longer motet at points in the Mass, the faithful should understand what follows and why.

The methodology of this pastoral care is the topic of another study. For now it is enough to say that the celebration of the classical Roman Rite introduces obligations for the priest and his assistants, the musicians and so forth even more than in the *Novus Ordo*: to think of the people, to give them – without disturbing them – all the help necessary for both internal and external participation.

The Liturgical Movement of the last 100 years provided countless good examples of this work. This is not a new method. If next to an old rite church there is also a new rite parish, its very existence is an imperative for such attentiveness. If we have become sensitive to this matter, to a great extent this is due to the influence of the liturgical changes of the Council.

[10] *Sacrosanctum Concilium* (1963), §54.

10

MIXING THE RITES?

One of the most remarkable provisions of the new Motu Proprio is that it permits reading the Epistle and Gospel in the vernacular; and not immediately before the homily, but at their normal place, without the obligation of reading them also in Latin.[1] This is another type of influence: an element is taken over optionally from the *Novus Ordo* into the classical rite. The intention of bringing the two rites closer to each other is so obvious that there has been talk of using the new lectionary in the classical rite. Fortunately, this is not possible or permitted, but the direction is clear: over lengthy time the two rites may indeed come to influence each other not only in their spiritual attitude but also in their material. In the following I shall speak only about a one-way influence: that of the *Novus Ordo* upon the preconciliar rite.

What might be the *motivation* of such an influence?

As sharp as our criticism has sometimes been of some individual aspects of the *Novus Ordo*, one cannot deny that legitimate desires and rightful demands motivated some of the changes. All the more so, since these desires were in great part stimulated by the 100 year-old Liturgical Movement whose proposals were formulated exclusively in the perspective of the classical Roman Rite! Its representatives were sure that the liturgy must become a living agent in the life of the Church; it must influence the catechesis, piety and spirituality of individuals and communities far more profoundly. To reach this goal the liturgy had to become a public matter, far more than before. Surely, even in the past, believers received the grace conveyed by the liturgy; but the liturgy has other blessings beyond enabling the free gifts of grace. It forms the minds and emotions; it keeps religious life in proper balance, and corrects it where necessary; it is a source of pious experiences; it is an objective point of orientation; it is a divine source of inspiration for the spiritual life of individuals. These kinds of blessings, however, perhaps reached only a relatively limited group (let us say, probably those using missalettes), and affected the life of the greater majority of believers only through homilies, prayer books, retreats and catechesis. The spread of missalettes is one of the most favourable phenomena in modern piety;

---

[1] *Summorum Pontificum*, Art. 6, 'In Missis iuxta Missale B. Ioannis XXIII celebratis cum populo, Lectiones proclamari possunt etiam lingua vernacula, utendo editionibus ab Apostolica Sede recognitis.'

they became the main tools for people to join in the liturgy more intensively. But they reached only a few, and they transmitted the actual content of the liturgy in an indirect way: people could learn from them what the priest is doing or saying at the altar. The 'blessings' seem to reach people more abundantly if the liturgy itself fosters actual participation. We have already complained about how many anti-liturgical practices or even abuses have been justified by these two words ('active participation') found in *Sacrosanctum Concilium*, but this fact does not invalidate the desire expressed by them.

This means that the requirement of active participation was the formulation of a rightful desire, and the restoration of the Roman Rite cannot be authentic if it is unable to integrate this expectation. An exhortation to fervent and devoted involvement is certainly indispensable, but it is not enough. The rite itself should create its preconditions. As we said above: due preparation for the liturgy and the teaching of all the responses are such preconditions. The permission given by the Motu Proprio to announce the readings in the vernacular is yet another step. But can we not go even further?

In order to understand the liturgy the faithful should be able to follow it, which – in the case of the vast majority of people – is only possible if the vernacular is given a greater role. Using a missalette is a step in this direction, but it should be considered whether more can be done according to §§36 and 54 of the Constitution[2] – of course, with the guarantee of preserving the Latin. This is the theme of Chapter 13, in Part II.

The need for some simplification emerged as early as the heyday of the Liturgical Movement. Even such an eminent expert as Adrian Fortescue, with full respect for the discipline of the liturgy in its tiniest details, mentioned in his fundamental book certain elements which could, or perhaps should, be omitted or simplified.[3] The Constitution of the Council also declared that 'the rites should be distinguished by a noble simplicity; they should be short, clear, and unencumbered by useless repetitions . . .' and '. . . the rites are to be simplified, due care being taken to preserve their substance; elements which, with the passage of time, came to be duplicated, or were added with but little advantage, are now to be discarded . . .'[4] Let us have a look at the background to these statements.

There has been no liturgy, no rite in the history of religion that did not produce

---

[2] Vatican Council II, Dogmatic Constitution on the Sacred Liturgy, *Sacrosanctum Concilium* (1963), §36: 'Linguae latinae usus, salvo particulari iure, in Ritibus latinis servetur. Cum tamen, sive in Missa, sive in Sacramentorum administratione, sive in aliis Liturgiae partibus, haud raro linguae vernaculae usurpatio valde utilis apud populum exsistere possit, amplior locus ipsi tribui valeat, imprimis autem in lectionibus et admonitionibus, in nonnullis orationibus et cantibus, iuxta normas quae de hac re in sequentibus capitibus singillatim statuuntur'; (§54). 'Linguae vernaculae in Missis cum populo celebratis congruus locus tribui possit, praesertim in lectionibus et "oratione communi", ac, pro condicione locorum, etiam in partibus quae ad populum spectant, ad normam art. 36 huius Constitutionis. Provideatur tamen ut christifideles etiam lingua latina partes Ordinarii Missae quae ad ipsos spectant possint simul dicere vel cantare.'
[3] Adrian Fortescue (1917), *The Ceremonies of the Roman Rite Described*, 2nd edn 1932, p. xxiii.
[4] *Sacrosanctum Concilium* (1963), §34: 'Ritus nobili simplicitate fulgeant, sint brevitate perspicui et repetitiones inutiles evitent, sint fidelium captui accommodati, neque generatim multis indigeant explanationibus' (see also §50). Cf. Brian W. Harrison, OS (2003), 'The Postconciliar Eucharistic Liturgy', pp. 177–81.

a set of complicated rules for the texts, repetitions, style of delivery, gestures or postures to be used and adopted within it.[5] The liturgical 'informality' of some modern Protestant communities has never been a real characteristic of Christian cult. The Roman Rite we inherited, however, developed under the historical conditions of what we may call – for the sake of brevity and running the risk of oversimplification – a distinctly clerical culture. I have to describe it in rather secular terms: the implementation of liturgical standards for many centuries was the task of persons dedicated almost exclusively to this task, both because of their ordination and through their way of life. For liturgical service a professional ecclesiastical apparatus, vast financial resources, and ample time were always at its disposal. In the seventh and eighth centuries or in medieval cathedrals, the only job for a large number of priests, lower clergy and singers was the cultivation of the liturgy for long hours every day. City parish churches also had an average of eight to ten priests, persons in lower clerical orders and paid choristers; not to speak of the schools living alongside the church, which had a teaching schedule including all the daily services as well as the classes to prepare for them. In village parishes three or four pupils with their teaching master were able to maintain the liturgy on a level similar to the great cathedrals, except slightly simplified. The other great ambiance of the liturgy was the monastery. Their original destination was to maintain a 'school of the Lord's service'.[6] According to the Rule of St Benedict nothing should have preference (*nihil praeponetur*) to the liturgy (*Opus Dei*).[7] Even though monks in the Middle Ages turned more and more towards active, secular life, their fundamental obligation remained unchanged; there were always enough monks in the cloister to prevent the *Opus Dei* from being neglected.

This situation left its imprint also on the body of the rite, and it led to the prolongation of the liturgy, the multiplication of supplements and the overcomplication of the rubrics. It is true that the lengthiness of the services and the elaborateness of the rules of celebration are also characteristic of the Eastern rites but the Eastern communities (for historical reasons, or perhaps in keeping with the Eastern temperament) accepted, even desired this prolixity. Moreover, there the way of celebration was more flexible and could be better adapted to different local conditions, and it was not obligatory for the individual faithful to be present all the way through the liturgy.

In the Western Church the environment of the elaborate medieval liturgy changed during the fifteenth and sixteenth centuries. Though the aim of the Council of Trent was to purify and restore the liturgical life of the Church, the crisis started in that very period. The 'infrastructure' of the liturgy became weaker while the rite itself remained practically unchanged. The Tridentine reforms omitted some medieval appendices (additional small offices, inserted elements,

---

[5] That means, the anti-rubricistic trends of the reformers cannot even be justified from the perspective of cultural anthropology Cf. David Torevill (2000), *Losing the Sacred*, pp. 22–79, 146–69.

[6] St Benedict (1980), *The Rule of St. Benedict*, Prologue, p. 164: 'Constituenda est ergo a nobis Dominici schola servitii . . .'

[7] Ibid., chapter 43.

Sequences, Tropes), but the body of the rite was left exactly as it was in the customary order of the Use of the Curia. In some places the personal and financial infrastructure of the ritual remained in place for a while but in most churches a series of compromises took place. The most characteristic case is the history of the proper chants: in 90 per cent of the churches they were not actually chanted any more, and the rubrics allowed them to be prayed silently by the priest.

A chapter in Guardini's famous book is titled 'The Playfulness of the Liturgy'.[8] The liturgy – besides its many other features – is formally a kind of sacred game. The circumstances described above automatically multiplied the rules and tactics of this game. Though the use of ceremonies for long centuries may have resulted in a certain abrasion, as a whole it led rather to the expansion of the structure and the proliferation of texts and rubrics, which kept growing like the flora of a forest. This, beautiful in itself, produced more beauty. Many nuances may emerge in the continuity of a long life, which cannot be produced by a momentary creative process. This is, of course, only one dimension of the liturgy, since the living tradition and the hierarchy constantly tried to check this growth. However, the liturgical *life* of the past, which was much richer than today, resulted in a system of rules that became a little too difficult to coordinate with the conditions that were present. We would not like to turn the liturgy into a French garden with geometrically arranged bushes and alleys assigned by rulers, but a romantic English park also needs caretaking: the vegetation should sometimes be cut back; the paths are to be cleared.

One cannot deny that the Roman Rite was in need of such a revision and some slight simplifications in the middle of the twentieth century. We are speaking of no more than what has already happened in some parts of the rite (the calendar, the ranking of feasts, the ceremonial, the obligation for the Office; or, most recently, in the rite of Holy Week by Pius XII).

The content and basic forms of the liturgy are outside time; the liturgy is not time-conditioned, but many social and historical changes have left their trace on it not only recently but also in earlier times. A major social change of recent centuries has been the increasing division of labour, and social differentiation, the consequence of which was the impact of social differences present in schooling, culture and religion. This diversification had increasing effects in the conduct of life, the daily and weekly schedule, and habits of recreation. Ecclesiastical society has also been differentiated so much that the scope for uniformity in conduct and customs has gradually diminished. The decrease in priestly vocations forced most of the clergy to dedicate themselves exclusively to pastoral engagements, and even monks were required to staff parishes. They all became overburdened even in this specialized activity. As a consequence, from the nineteenth century onwards the so-called 'low mass' became increasingly the norm and there was a demand to diminish the liturgical obligations of priests; for example, to shorten considerably the daily portion of the Office. The Roman Rite, however, remained uniform and required the same from everybody. Alternatives, adjustments to

---

[8] Romano Guardini (1918), *Vom Geist der Liturgie*, chapter 5.

different local situations, were hardly permitted. The advantage of this was that it prevented the liturgy from fragmentation or disintegration.

In the twentieth century, these growing tensions demanded some resolution. This was, for instance, the primary motivation when Pius X abbreviated the Divine Office, or Pius XII the ceremonies of Holy Week. The Constitution *Sacrosanctum Concilium* foresaw a new distribution of the Psalter over more than one week in the Divine Office.[9] The 1970 Missal offered a longer and shorter form for many readings and even for full services (like Holy Week), and permitted the omission of entire sections of liturgical actions.

During the last one and a half centuries there were also legitimate demands to increase the pedagogical or didactic role of the liturgy for the congregation. The Catechism of the Council of Trent was a good foundation for religious instruction. Its interiorization, however, was undertaken mainly by prayers and meditations created in the Late Middle Ages, or during the baroque and romantic periods. In spite of the beauty of these texts and practices, there was an increasing desire to turn towards a tradition of more universal validity, something undoubtedly great in its authenticity and completeness, and more independent from the tastes of any particular age. The ordinary faithful aspired to the possibility of receiving more abundantly – through the appropriate channels of transmission – the theology and spirituality of the Bible, the Church Fathers, and – as the prominent field of religious life – the liturgy. Even as the conflict between the denominations became ever sharper, the worship of Protestant communities, heavily focused on the word, could have served as a stimulus to strengthen the teaching function of the liturgy.

The liturgical instruction of the faithful and the translations that became increasingly available represented important means in the fulfilment of this desire. This point confirms any argument favouring the more widespread use of the vernacular in (at least parts of) sacred worship. It became an established custom in many places to read the Epistle and Gospel for the day in the vernacular, before the homily also after they had been recited or sung in Latin by the celebrant (or, in solemn forms of the Mass, by the deacon). Even before the Council, Masses took place in which the texts of the chants or even of some priestly prayers were pronounced by a 'commentator'. This didactical intention might well have been the motivation behind the decision to provide three readings at Sunday Masses, with the inclusion of many more Old Testament texts, so that a larger portion of the Bible may be read to the faithful at Mass[10].

The same didactic tendency can be observed in some of the other reforms, too. By including a greater number of Prefaces, texts were introduced that had more of a didactic character; the replacement of some texts was with the express intention of introducing 'fresh' new ideas into the minds of modern believers.

---

[9] *Sacrosanctum Concilium* (1963), §91: 'Ut cursus Horarum, in art. 89 propositus, reapse observari possit, psalmi non amplius per unam hebdomadam, sed per longius temporis spatium distribuantur.'
[10] *Sacrosanctum Concilium* (1963), §§33–5, 51.

In the Office, a better selection of patristic sermons and a more abundant set of hymns were also meant to play an educational role.

By all this I do not intend to say that the postconciliar reforms were efficient and beneficial decisions. They caused damage and in their sum total they actually ruined the Roman Rite without fulfilling the didactic aims either. The point is that, despite the destructive effects, the underlying intentions were often essentially for the best of reasons.

All of this brings us to the present day. There are areas where the classical Roman Rite is in need of some revision or adaptation. The 1962 Missal incorporated the Holy Week service as it was rearranged by Pius XII – the question is whether this form is really the best one. Should we continue to carry with us the revision of the Psalter under Pius XII (which in Holy Week is not simply optional but canonized)? If the Church were to want to reintroduce the Divine Office or, at least, Vespers into the normal liturgical schedule of parishes (and not only in monasteries and cathedrals): are we certain that an invariable use of the Breviary of Pius X is the best arrangement for that? I do not wish to multiply examples: in Part II we shall speak of them more extensively.

If the motives mentioned so far call for some developments in the preconciliar liturgical books that are again authorized for us, then the history, implementation, and continuing presence of the new rite, in fact, compels us to think more carefully about it.

What does it mean when, in his Motu Proprio, Benedict XVI calls the *Novus Ordo* the 'ordinary' form, and the preconciliar liturgy the 'extraordinary one'? Should we feel in this some kind of depreciation of the latter? I think the only thing that the Holy Father was thinking of was – in addition to settling certain anxieties – that the *Novus Ordo* is actually the form celebrated in the vast majority of churches all over the world; compared to this, the celebration of the traditional rite will be, even after the general permission, so rare that it is nearly negligible, and hence 'extraordinary'. Let us not deceive ourselves: even if the traditional Mass were to be celebrated more frequently and in many more churches after 14 September 2007, it will not quickly convince enormous numbers of the faithful or the clergy that it is 'better', nor will it attract great flocks or entire parishes to switch over from the 'ordinary form'.

Let us imagine attending an average Sunday Mass in a village or in the city suburbs. The priest says the Mass according to the *Novus Ordo*, faithfully, and according to the rubrics, in the vernacular all the way through. Let us envision that the priest (or anybody else) proposes a return to the form permitted by the Motu Proprio from the following Sunday. The congregation will not notice the *real* differences between the rites, instead they will first observe that Mass is now completely in Latin, that the priest stands in front of the altar, and they have to take Communion on the tongue kneeling at the rail. Even if the changes are duly prepared and explained, most people in the congregation would probably be repelled, not only because most of them from their early childhood grew up in the *Novus Ordo* already, but also because they feel more at home in the vernacular medium, which they are able to follow in a direct way. To attain to the same kind of familiarity in the 'Latin Mass' would demand an incredible amount of work over a very long time.

What I am trying to illustrate is that what people immediately observe is not the real difference between the rites. They would not necessarily realize that a quite different Gospel text and different prayers are recited; they perhaps would not even realize it if these were be read in the vernacular. It is a myth that after the shift into the vernacular people became more receptive to the actual *content* of the prayers. If tests were to be conducted and those leaving the church after Mass (the priest included) were asked about the meaning of the prayers of the day, many would surely be unable to recall even their general theme (the priest included).

What congregations do know is the customs of celebration introduced together with the *Novus Ordo*, and they probably insist on those, too. In fact, this is the 'ordinary' form and although there are those who will visit the classical Roman Mass on exceptional, 'extraordinary' occasions, they will then return home having had a 'nice and interesting' experience.

Let us consider this with care. Is it worthwhile to link the fate of the Roman Rite – so valuable for those who love and understand it – with the actual *customs* that characterize its celebration? Would it not be better to improve the opportunities for the ongoing vitality and receptivity of the classical Roman Rite by intelligent and modest alterations, by adopting standards and practices that come closer at some points to the *Novus Ordo*?

My opinion is that it is a matter of life or death for the classical Roman Rite to embrace the desires, expectations and demands that clearly preceded the Council.[11] If this is not done, the classical rite will remain isolated; although it will survive, satisfying the spiritual desires of small groups, it will be there only to decorate extraordinary feasts, special occasions and certain kinds of meetings. In this situation it will not be able to heal the rupture! It will not reinstate proper continuity of liturgical tradition; the classical Roman Rite will remain *for ever* something 'extraordinary', and it will never become once again the 'ordinary' practice of the Church.

We are speaking of developments that would have the effect of *preserving* the identity of the classical Roman Rite, and that will increase the chances for the historic survival of the rite.

The Council when speaking of organic development actually meant the development *of the classical Roman Rite* – and not the *Novus Ordo*! Returning to the classical Roman Rite, and simultaneously recommencing again its slow, organic and tactful development, imposes upon us a double fidelity: fidelity to the classical Roman Rite and fidelity to the Council.

One point I have so far left unexplained. I have not argued for the *mixture* of

---

[11] Alcuin Reid (2005), *The Organic Development of the Liturgy*, p. 310, quotes the well-formulated sentences of Bouyer on the harmony between tradition and progress. Aidan Nichols (2003), 'Salutary Dissatisfaction', p. 203, explains: 'I believe that the answer lies in the convergence of the two rites, the classical and the modern'. Cf. John W. Mole, OMI (2001), 'Problema Idem Perduret', pp. 18–19.

the two rites. There are many proofs in the history of liturgy that rites could be and actually were influenced by a different rite. This process was in most cases for the benefit of the rite in question.[12] For example, a number of elements in the Ambrosian Rite can be regarded as imported from the Roman Rite. Consequently, it is not the devil's work if one rite adopts something from another.

But here I am only thinking of 'mixing' at very few points. We may suppose that the *Novus Ordo* was intended to satisfy the particular and proper desires I have identified as preceding the Council. Would it really be impossible to fulfil these aspirations also within the context of the classical Roman Rite, by its organic development and so without demolishing it?

Our real interest now lies in the question whether the reforms of the Council – in the sense of the Liturgical Constitution *Sacrosanctum Concilium* – could be implemented using the material taken from the classical Roman Rite. This question was the motif for the appeal in my earlier book, where I suggested we should return to 1962, not in order to stop there but rather to implement a badly conducted reform in a good way![13] If someone gets lost on a journey, the only solution is to go back to where the wrong turning was taken, and then set off anew in the right direction. This new path may at first seem similar to the previous one, but it differs from it exactly where it should; it has a completely new angle. The Motu Proprio did precisely that, it went back to the point of wrong turning.

Is there any reason to think about another reform in our days? Can the Church endure a new reform? Could such a revision improve the chances of the classical Roman Rite against the *Novus Ordo*? These are not questions of principle but of method. This is the topic of the following chapter.

---

12 Cardinal Joseph Ratzinger (2000), *The Spirit of the Liturgy*, p. 164: 'Rites are not rigidly fenced off from each other. There is exchange and cross-fertilization between them. The clearest example is in the case of the two great focal points of ritual development: Byzantium and Rome . . .'

13 László Dobszay (2003), *The Bugnini-Liturgy and the Reform of the Reform*, pp. 176–79. Explained in Dobszay (2009c), 'The Perspectives of an Organic Development'.

11

THE METHOD OF ORGANIC REFORM

If the classical Roman Rite were celebrated in the vernacular and with the priest facing the people, the abandonment of the *Novus Ordo* could be realized without any shock, perhaps unnoticed by the faithful. An outsider may suppose that the postconciliar reform liturgy is being celebrated – but, in fact, its actual content would be different! I say this not to recommend this sort of 'behind the scenes makeover'; I only wish to emphasize that the wide-ranging reception of the classical Roman Rite is not hindered by the innermost essence of the rite.

But if this 'innermost essence' is so hidden for people, what use is it to concern ourselves with the problem at all? Why should one expose the Church at large to the pain of yet more change? The world, and the Church within it, lives among serious troubles and tribulations: environmental problems, tensions between poor and rich regions, terrorism, cultural decadence, apostasy, divisions within the Church, lack of priests, the apathy of the youth – and now we should focus on the Introit chant or Gospel of the day, or whether the hymn should be sung at the beginning or in the middle of Vespers? Does it really matter which rite is celebrated?

None of the problems of the world or the Church should, of course, be overlooked or ignored, but the task of a scholarly expert in the liturgy is to seek a solution for the predicament of the liturgy. Among the troubles of the world and of the Church the matter of the liturgy is not so unimportant. First of all, the work of the liturgy is only, in one sense, to have an impact on those actually present at a particular celebration. One of the causes for the difficulties in the liturgy is precisely that this one function is grossly overemphasized. The liturgy is the 'fons et culmen'[1] of the very life of the Church. It is at the liturgy that the Church is principally the Church. In each liturgical action the Church continuously reveals and communicates her *universal* inner essence, and identifies herself with it again and again. The liturgy is where the Church gives herself completely to God, like the bride to the bridegroom. The liturgy expresses, in very proper and stylized language but in the most accurate way, who the Church is, what the Church is, what it is she believes, what it is she hopes for, whom it is she loves, how she draws supernatural life from her 'faith, hope and charity'. Furthermore, a 'church-family', in our case, the Latin-rite Roman Catholic Church, expresses,

---

[1] *Sacrosanctum Concilium* (1963), §10.

lives and confirms her self-identity in the liturgy. If this is the case, it is not at all an unimportant question which rite is the one used in which all this takes place. Seemingly insignificant differences in a rite may actually change our image of God and the image of the Church reflected in it. The liturgy has the function of an icon (representing the Holy), and icons require that a definite *canon* (standard) be followed both in their production and their interpretation. The liturgy, precisely because of its stylized nature, plays its role not in the clear formulation of dogmas, but in the particular and often symbolic moments of the order of celebration.

Furthermore, the great crowds of the faithful receive the message of the liturgy not all at once, and not in an intellectual way, but over the continuity of longer periods, and in great part instinctively. The believer does not analyse each individual moment and yet he unites himself with its meaning, not only through the exercise of reason, but with his whole existence. When he genuflects in front of the Blessed Sacrament, he most likely does not think explicitly of the dogma of the Real Presence, yet he 'memorizes' this dogma by means and use of his knee, and sublimates it into the spiritual sphere. Single elements of the rite over a long time, in the larger context of ecclesiastical life, and with some changes in external form, do actually influence the religious concepts of the whole Church, of particular churches, of communities and individuals. They have an effect on morality in general and on emotional and religious culture or one's attitude towards God and neighbour. Just as our physical deeds influence our entire existence, so the quality of our liturgical actions impacts on the existence of the whole Church.

But is the Church ready to undergo yet another change of such proportions?[2] She is not, but she would not even have to. Our liturgical life will be determined for many years, perhaps for many decades to come, by the coexistence (in the West) of two rites. The true reform of the classical Roman Rite needs studies, preparation, meditation, a ripening period of gestation. During this time the single 'reforms' together with their explanation may penetrate into common parlance and common thinking. Not only the reform but also the reception of the reforms necessitates a long preparation.

What is more important, however, is that *these* reforms do not need to be announced or introduced by a striking new papal message, encyclical, or Motu Proprio. Take the example of the only reform-issue of the recent Motu Proprio: the permission for vernacular readings in the classical Roman Rite appeared in one (almost appended) sentence. This permission might be, as it were, the germ of the reform process. When new feasts are added to the calendar of the Roman Rite, when the vernacular is given more space in the celebration of the old rite, when standards are announced promoting the use of Latin, when small changes are made in the priestly prayers (like the inclusion of new Prefaces in the

---

[2] I hope Klaus Gamber's pessimistic opinion – Gamber (2002), *The Modern Rite*, p. 44 – that 'the new missal will prevent, for the foreseeable future, a genuine and lasting reform of worship in the spirit of Vatican II' will prove mistaken. Cf. John P. Parsons (2003), 'A Reform of the Reform?', p. 227; Brian W. Harrison, OS (2003), 'The Postconciliar Eucharistic Liturgy, pp. 166–70; Thomas M. Kocik (2009), 'The Reform of the Reform in Broad Context'.

Missal), when some adjusted offices are proposed, when the local use of valuable old (pre-Tridentine) elements is granted, when new instructions for singing are issued, then these smaller changes will not be perceived as shocking events, yet overall, they will accomplish a rather extensive improvement. Taking them one by one, they are part of a normal and unexceptional process, but taking them in their sum, they will implement the desired reform. It is a mistake to forget that such ritual changes were also frequent in the past. If we were to examine the declarations of the old Congregation of Rites, we would find that in almost every decade some minor changes were introduced, these being good examples of 'organic development'. Part of the desired changes represent no more than options or permissions, to be introduced by the sound judgement of bishops or local pastors. It would not be disastrous if a new lectionary were to be published for weekdays in order to offer more biblical readings, so long as, on the other hand, it did not have the effect of weakening the traditional system of Sunday pericopes of the 1962 Missal.

So far I have spoken only of changes which modify or might modify the *traditional* Roman liturgy. No mention has been made of modifications in the *Novus Ordo*. In the previous chapter I spoke about the necessary changes within the conciliar liturgy under the influence of the classical rite with regard to the spiritual attitude or atmosphere of the celebration. Perhaps some small changes may also be introduced from time to time in the material of the new rite, under responsible direction. In the rite itself, however, I do not expect or propose any significant change.

I would suggest the following process for the implementation of desirable changes: Let the two rites live peacefully side by side; so that the Church offers them both to the faithful in order to enrich them spiritually. A process of continuous and organic development of the classical Roman Rite, however, puts an end to the psychological advantage of the *Novus Ordo*. The faithful start to feel themselves at home in the classical rite just as much as in the postconciliar liturgy. In the meantime, they will start discovering the things that attract them to the old rite. And so, though the two rites will not be mixed, it will become less and less reasonable to call one 'ordinary' and the other 'extraordinary'. What follows later depends on Divine Providence and the wisdom of the Church. Maybe the classical Roman Rite, having adopted all the standards of the postconciliar liturgy and being more faithful to the will of the Council Fathers, will eventually make the *Novus Ordo* unnecessary. Then the unity of the rites, and continuity of liturgical tradition, will have been restored.

In other words: from now on I do not advocate the expression 'Reform of the Reform'. I do not think that the content of the postconciliar reform liturgy can really be reformed. It is enough there to filter out the abuses and extremes, and to shepherd its practices back to that more in keeping with ecclesial tradition – remaining all the while within the sphere of the rite.

On the other hand, the inner revision of the classical Roman Rite requires hard work and the improvement of its life conditions. Dedicated work is needed to preserve and enhance the vitality of the rite, and to render it a source of life for the whole Church, equal with, or more potent than, the *Novus Ordo*.

For those who believe in the higher quality of the classical Roman Rite, the aim of the following years is not the Reform of the Reform, but the Renovation of the Roman Rite and its organic development.

What does that mean in actual details? This is the theme of Part II.

PART II

INTRODUCTION TO PART II

As an introduction to Part II, I must repeat the warning I gave at the beginning of this book. If I criticized the *Novus Ordo* for being forced upon the Roman Church by the will of one man or the group around him – it would likewise be much too audacious for me to make a proposal for the renovation of the Roman Rite. In the following I will only use the word 'proposal' for sake of brevity. My intention is no more than to illustrate the thesis that the reforms planned by the Council *can* be implemented within the classical Roman Rite without abandoning it for the sake of the manufacture of a new rite. The corrections of the rite required by the life of the Church and by outside conditions can be accomplished so that the body of the traditional liturgy is preserved. In other words: an answer can be given to the 'true desires' of the preconciliar era *within* the boundaries of the classical rite. At some points, these proposals may seem to be even more radical than the postconciliar reforms, but their purpose is to revitalize the classical tradition.

To make the presentation easier, I will submit these 'proposals' in a descriptive manner: something has been done hitherto in such and such a way, henceforth it could change to be done so and so. I ask the reader not to see any pretension in this; my only intention is to make this book, as the essence of my proposal, shorter and easier to understand.

Insofar as necessary, I will try to justify the 'proposals'. The argument will only become complete, however, if it is compared with the postconciliar reforms, and respectively, with their critique. Since this was more or less presented in my previous book, I will only give a short summary of the facts and arguments with references to the appropriate section of that book.

12

RITUS, USUS, CONSUETUDO, OPTIO

In order to begin, let us consider the example of the Liturgy of the Hours. The reason for its restructuring was obviously to diminish the burden on the priests engaged in pastoral work.[1] The number of daily psalms in the Tridentine Use of the Roman Rite (the Breviary of Pius V) was 41 (praying the lengthy Psalm 118 in 11 divisions). In the reform of Pius X this number seemed to change to 35 but, most of them being divisions, the actual quantity was much less than in the Breviary of Pius V. Finally, the number of daily psalms in the postconciliar Liturgy of the Hours was reduced to 14, again a significant portion of them divisions of average length. This was only possible because the whole Psalter was now distributed over a four-week period, and some psalms were omitted altogether.

What exactly happened? The portions were measured against those whose conditions of life permit only a limited possibility for fulfilling their requirement to say the Office. The 'minimal-Office' became the standard for the whole Roman liturgy. Needless to say, the Roman Office, as a result, practically ceased to exist. As I have already explained,[2] with this arrangement all the essential elements of the Roman Office disappeared. I will analyse this process later; now I wished to illustrate the method of the reform with one example: all liturgical communities, living under very different conditions, were brought down to the same level, the lowest one. This resulted in the destruction of the Roman Rite.

Could there have been another solution? I think so. While preserving the Roman Rite nearly unchanged, some rules could be created for communities and individuals – living under different conditions – for a different mode and measure of celebrating the *same* rite. If so, the Roman liturgy as the rite of the Roman Church survives in its full integrity, but single communities have the option to participate in it differently. This is a method not unknown in liturgical tradition. In the Eastern churches it is the general practice. There are analogies also in the Western church: priests are at present obliged to pray the full Office,

---

[1] Pope St Pius X (1911), *Divino afflatu*, in *Acta Apostolicæ Sedis*, vol. 3, p. 636: '. . . revocaretur consuetudo vetus recitandi per hebdomadam totum Psalterium, ita tamen ut clero, in sacri ministerii vinea ob imminutum operariorum numerum jam gravius laboranti, non majus imponeretur onus' ['. . . ancient custom of reciting the whole psalter within the week might be restored as far as possible, but in such a way that the burden should not be made any heavier for the clergy, whose labors in the vineyard of the sacred ministry are now increased owing to the diminution in the number of labourers'].

[2] László Dobszay (2003), *The Bugnini-Liturgy and the Reform of the Reform*, pp. 58–68.

lay people may say only parts of it (without obligation, unless they are in vows) according to their abilities. In the final years of the Office as it existed before 1970 an instruction was issued that permitted some abbreviation for priests engaged in pastoral care.[3] The rite itself was not changed in these cases: on the contrary, these rules of adaptation made it possible to keep the rite intact.

Let us now turn our attention to another phenomenon. The reforms of the Council of Trent established one form of the Roman liturgical books, and these books finally obtained general acceptance. The Council of Trent itself, however, did not abolish the individual Uses of the Roman Rite, and several religious orders, in fact, preserved their proper Use. Some dioceses also persisted in the use of their proper traditions because they were not independent rites, but merely variants of the same Roman Rite.[4]

In the time of the Second Vatican Council the opportunity would have been there to retain or restore these rites. The Council itself acknowledged the rights of local traditions to exist within the broader Roman Rite. It would, in fact, be a scandal if this provision were limited to the cults of pagan tribes and denied to the ancient Catholic traditions (e.g. Sarum, Mainz, Paris (etc.) Uses) which are integral parts of the Roman Rite and were legitimately followed over many centuries.[5] However, the reform that started under the aegis of pluralism ended in an exaggerated dictatorship of uniformity; these ambitions were stifled,[6] or they were realized only in limited ways in the life of some religious orders, involving greater or lesser degrees of compromise.

A new development of recent decades is that those struggling for the right of the Roman Rite to exist started to take note of these other Uses, too. On the internet especially, information has been gathered in several places about the old monastic and diocesan liturgies, and several times this has promoted publications discussing these Uses.[7] In Hungary some elements of Holy Week according to

---

[3] Cf. John XIII, *Codex Rubricarum* (1960).

[4] When we speak of a Dominican or Carthusian (etc.) rite, as I discussed earlier, this is an inexact term employed merely for the sake of brevity.

[5] Vatican Council II, Dogmatic Constitution on the Sacred Liturgy, *Sacrosanctum Concilium* (1963), §§37–38: 'Ecclesia, in iis quae fidem aut bonum totius communitatis non tangunt, rigidam unius tenoris formam ne in Liturgia quidem imponere cupit; quinimmo, variarum gentium populorumque animi ornamenta ac dotes colit et provehit; quidquid vero in populorum moribus indissolubili vinculo superstitionibus erroribusque non adstipulatur, benevole perpendit ac, si potest, sartum tectumque servat, immo quandoque in ipsam Liturgiam admittit, dummodo cum rationibus veri et authentici spiritus liturgici congruat. Servata substantiali unitate Ritus romani, legitimis varietatibus et aptationibus ad diversos coetus, regiones, populos, praesertim in Missionibus, locus relinquatur, etiam cum libri liturgici recognoscuntur; et hoc in structura rituum et in rubricis instituendis opportune prae oculis habeatur'. Cf. Miklós István Földváry (2009), 'The Variants of the Roman Rite'; Sven Conrad, FSSP (2009), 'Die innere Logik eines Ritus als Maßstab liturgischer Entwicklung'.

[6] A Mass was celebrated in 1964 according to the old Paris (Notre Dame) rite; an experiment 20 years later to restore the Sarum rite was, however, disallowed by Rome – see Alcuin Reid (2005), *The Organic Development of the Liturgy*, p. 130. Excepting some special occasions or special churches, it is unthinkable to restore a local Use in its entirety.

[7] First of all, in internet discussions developed by various liturgical web sites, which have regularly provided detailed descriptions of the Use of the Dominican, Carthusian and other religious Orders.

the ancient Use of Esztergom have been incorporated into the Folk Hymnal as optional variants; in Office books printed for lay people (who are not obliged to pray the Office) some structural devices and items have also been taken over from the Esztergom Use.[8]

As I have already made clear: these Uses are variants of the Roman Rite, and in many cases even better variants than the Tridentine Use which, being the descendant of a respected tradition, namely, the simplified Use of papal officials (*Usus Curiae*), did not observe the public liturgy of the Church (the tradition of the basilicas of Rome), and comprised only a small portion of the precious legacy of the Franco-Roman rite. These monastic and diocesan Uses also preserved a number of ancient elements that the Curial and, consequently, the Tridentine Use ceased to observe. One of these is the Baptismal Vespers of the Paschal Octave ('*Gloriosum Officium*') with its origins in the Basilica of St John Lateran.[9]

In the Middle Ages the members of different religious orders or secular churches jealously guarded their privileges to have a proper liturgy as a symbol and guarantee of their self-identity. 'The choir makes the monk' – said the old dictum, and we may add: *this* choir makes *this* (kind of) monk. The Praemonstratensians would understand their being Praemonstratensians first of all through their distinct liturgy. The Agram (Zagreb) diocese insisted on its own liturgy up to the end of the eighteenth century: the canons of the cathedral regarded this use as preserving their own identity.[10] This fact did not separate anybody from unity with Rome; neither objectively, as the liturgy of the Praemonstratenisans and the diocese of Zagreb were identical in essence with the Roman liturgy, nor subjectively, as they received the Roman liturgy from the hands of their own order or chapter. The fidelity of the order or diocesan chapter to the Roman tradition was a guarantee for their members that they belong to Rome *through their own Use*.

After the Tridentine Use was introduced in the dioceses and orders, their particular feasts and commemorations became no more than a mere addition to the calendar. Their patrons appeared in the appendices, mostly with 'Common' material. It was a very rare occurrence if their proper offices ('Historiae') and sequences were kept or revived.

During the renovation of the Roman Rite it would be plausible to reconsider the position of these particular Uses. Why would it be troublesome if in one or two churches assigned for that task the liturgy were regularly celebrated according to the traditional local Use in order to nourish and make visible (and audible – many of these uses have distinct musical traditions in their chant) the precious heritage that they represent, strengthening self-awareness in the local church, and displaying a kind of model for the daily practice of other churches? It would have a very beneficial effect if one or two churches in Rome were commissioned to celebrate the Old Roman Rite of the Major Basilicas – similar to

---

[8] Cf. *Éneklő Egyház* (The Singing Church). Budapest (Szent István Társulat), 1986, pp. 1389–454.
[9] See below in Chapter 21, sub-section VI.
[10] Cf. Nándor Knauz (1865), 'A magyar egyház részi szokásai. I: A római rítus behozatala', pp. 401–13.

the liturgy in its particularities in the Church of San Ambroggio in Milan with its Ambrosian Rite, or in Toledo with the Mozarabic Rite.

If a revised edition of these ancient Uses were available, they could be used also in a wider circle on particular solemn occasions. To accomplish this, no new reform would be needed; it would be enough to get a favourable answer from Rome to a request from the local bishop or the superior of a religious order.

But I am thinking of something more than that. In the scheme below, the Uses appear as one level of *adapting* the Roman Rite. The following 'proposal' exemplifies the coordination of these levels in a descriptive form:

1. The highest level is the *Rite*, the most comprehensive and common standard of worship, including the whole and all its details. The point of departure is the preconciliar form of the classical Roman Rite, as the latest, valid expression of the continuous liturgical tradition of the Roman Church. In this rite, however, the reforms planned by the Council are gradually introduced in order to fulfil the 'rightful desires' summed up by the Constitution *Sacrosanctum Concilium*,[11] and to adapt the liturgy to our own time in a way and measure that leaves the identity of the rite intact.

   It would be useful if the system were not to be fixed down to the last detail. The rite itself may contain optional variants (e.g. the 4-responsories and 12-readings system for Easter Vigil,[12] or reading the Epistle either in Latin or in the vernacular); but points may also be designated where local tradition can be included (for instance, additional Sequences).

   At certain points the rite may determine only the framework, giving way to legislation on the lower level for more precise arrangement. For instance, the early antiphonaries accurately and uniformly fixed the text and placement of some antiphons (like at Lauds on the ancient solemnities); but at other points offered a repertory, a set, leaving their assignation to the particular leaders of the liturgy. These antiphonaries give all the antiphons of a week in one list without assignation to the individual days. At some points the liturgical books explicitly allowed the supplementation of the more basic liturgical material (for instance, the use of the Proper Office of a saint, instead of being taken from the common offices).

2. Particular traditions can appear on the second level, which is that of the local or particular *Usus*. Formally they might be included as an appendix to the Roman Rite, like the local feasts in the books today but larger in size and quantity. Some examples to aid comprehension: individual offices, antiphons, responsories missing in the stock material of the Roman Rite; traditional alleluias of the local Use; valuable prayers that disappeared after 1570, and so forth. A small part of them could be used as substitutes for the stock material. Again an example: in the majority of medieval Uses, during the Triduum Sacrum Lauds was closed by the chant *Kyrie Puerorum* (instead of

---

[11] Especially *Sacrosanctum Concilium* (1963), §§21, 33, 37.
[12] See below in Chapter 21, sub-section V.

Psalm 50 + *Christus factus est*).[13] This precious Litany is very appropriate in a public celebration and is worth reinstating.

Such additions need a fixed place in the Order, and so some particularities of arrangement may belong to the Use. For example, in the majority of medieval churches different Sequences were chanted on each day of the Paschal Octave. If one or more of them were reintroduced somewhere (like the beautiful sequence *Mundi renovatio* by Adam of St Victor[14]), their relationship to the *Victimae paschali* should be defined (let us say that in a given Use the *Mundi renovatio* is prayed instead of the *Victimae* on Tuesday and Thursday of that week; or this Sequence closes the Octave on the following Sunday).

There are *structural* devices that give place to the tradition not only at one particular point but in the entirety of the rite. Again, one example: in the Tridentine Breviary the antiphons for Lauds are mostly anticipated in the First Vespers of the feast. Many of the medieval dioceses, however, assigned one remarkable antiphon to be sung 'super psalmos', or over all five psalms of First Vespers (for instance the antiphon *Veni Sancte* in First Vespers of Pentecost).[15] This practice, characteristic of almost all feasts, has its own integrity and beauty.

The Propers of a Use might then be published in the appendix of the Roman books or in separate booklets. But it is not unrealistic to think of more. The discontinuation of earlier Uses after the Tridentine reform was the result of not only idealistic motives. The printing of books according to the use of particular churches required a lot of work and large sums of money. When the local churches stopped printing their own liturgical books, they wanted not only to display their loyalty to Rome, but also to save money by purchasing the cheaper Roman ones. Today, however, it is much easier and cheaper to print an antiphonary for Paris, Salisbury, Mainz or Prague. A viable method of production is possible whereby all appendices, substitutions and the distribution of the material in the whole of the Use is presented in a well-conceived structure to be given by the superior of the order or by the archbishop as a proper (possibly bilingual) book into the hands of the priests and lay people of the order or archdiocese.

There need be no fear that such books might disrupt the unity of the Roman liturgy. The differences would make up less than one-tenth of the full material, and the ancient and continuously used (essential) parts of the Rite would be untouched. In legal terms, the legitimate authority (traditionally the cathedral chapter with the approval of the bishop; the superior or legislative body according to the Rule of the given order) guarantees that the proper Use is identical with the Roman Rite. As a further guarantee – differently from the Middle Ages – the approval of Rome could be required. In fact, this way nothing *new* would find its way into the Rite, rather the common

---

[13] See below in Chapter 21, sub-section II.
[14] *Analecta Hymnica medii aevi*, vol. 54, p. 254.
[15] *Corpus Antiphonalium Officii* (1965–79), vol. 3, Nr. 5327.

treasury of the Rite would appear more abundantly before the eyes of the universal Church.

3. The third level is the *Consuetudo*. One of the most valuable liturgical sources in the Middle Ages was the Ordinary Book (also known as Consuetudinary (Customary) of cathedrals, city parishes, monasteries. The Ordinary Book described the precise way that the ceremonies recorded in the liturgical books and directions were to be undertaken at the given location. The Consuetudinaries were valid within the context of a more general system of arrangement; but their editors were persons or legislative bodies with specified authority in the liturgy (bishop, abbot, chapter and convent).

The Use, or even the Rite itself, left some freedom for choices, additions and the stabilizing factors of celebration. Frequently, the Customary does not exceed the localized sphere of adaptation. For example: it defines what places and what altars should be visited during a procession; who should be the celebrant and who are the assistants during the ceremonies on the feasts of a given rank. These kinds of Ordinary books would be very useful also in our times: parish churches are often unable to standardize and stabilize their particular local customs because of the mobility of the clergy. The result is that the order of celebration has to be 'figured out' over and over again, which takes away a lot of time and energy that could otherwise be spent on technical and spiritual preparation.

It is even more important that the Ordinary Book also regulates the *material* of the liturgy in a given community – of course, within the framework of the higher regulations. Again, for example, the rite (or Use) defines what kind of abbreviation of the full form of Office is legal. Let us say that the full Psalter can be prayed in the period of one, two or eventually four weeks. The Customary of a given religious order decides which system is more suitable to the more contemplative or more active life of the order (or to the different types of communities within their congregation). Another example: the Antiphonary permits that the psalms of an Hour be prayed either with one antiphon for each psalm, or all of the psalms under one antiphon. The Customary makes the choice according to the condition (for instance, the size and level of musical expertise) of the institution. Yet another example: the rite permits the use of the vernacular (besides or along with the Latin) in given items – the Customary determines the distribution of languages for a given community or a given celebration. Or: the psalm between the readings of the Mass (Gradual) can be sung either in its melismatic tune (with two verses) or in a responsorial recitation (with slightly longer selection from the psalm). It is good if one community adapts regularly one of the two methods (and uses the other one only as an exception).[16] On some liturgical days the tradition offers two possible Gospel texts (earlier this was determined on the regional level) or a shorter/longer form of them. If the rite wanted to prevent this traditional heritage from being consigned to oblivion, it may allow a

---

[16] The two systems also live side by side in the *Novus Ordo* as can be seen from the *Ordo Cantus Missae*, the *Graduale Simplex* and the Lectionary.

choice between them; then a diocese or monastery decides which one of them will be taken up in their Ordinary.

The number of such local rules might be rather high concerning the way of *realization*; the formation of the *structure* (e.g. the rhythm of progress in the Psalter) touches upon an extensive area of the liturgy, and greatly helps the community to integrate the liturgy into its regular schedule of life. The choices offered in the *material* for the lower level are, of course, nearly negligible in quantity, at least, in relation to the full liturgy, and they do not change the essential parts of the liturgy.

4. Finally, the fourth level is that of *Optio*. These concern certain choices between possible devices given by the rite, Use or even Customary; but here choices are offered to smaller local communities or to individual persons. It is obvious that such options may be given mainly in the Office and especially for those who are not obliged to pray it in full. Again some examples: a lay person reading the Office may pray or omit some Hours, and may alter the number of psalms. A small community celebrating Vespers once a week might be free as to which vesperal psalms from the given set will be taken at particular occasions. Another community prays the Vigil seven or eight times a year, but they decide on which days, with how many Nocturns, choosing which psalms of the given set are sung, how long the readings are to be. Since they are not obliged to any of these, they can decide with some freedom – without causing harm, of course, to the general standards of the rite.

These indults of adaptation, I repeat, do not touch upon the rite but only upon the mode of participation. The rite is the whole, while a given community may take a smaller or bigger part of it according to the rubrics or permission of their own rules set within the extent of higher legislation. This system is not designed to introduce disorder into the rite; just the opposite, it is meant to consolidate it and to confirm general respect for the rite on every level of adaptation. There is no need to destroy the entire rite in order to adapt it to celebration among more modest conditions. The local Ordinary Book can be composed in such a way that the rite itself remains unharmed.

Now, if we return to the problem presented at the beginning of this chapter, it will be clear that the adjustments to different living conditions could have been done without giving up the standards of the traditional Roman Office. All these will be clearer when we speak about the individual parts of the liturgy. We are going to describe the *rite* (sometimes with references to the local or particular *Uses*) and some alternative variants will be qualified with the terms *ex consuetudine* (according to custom) or *ex optione* (according to choice).

13

THE LANGUAGE OF THE LITURGY

I. Non solum sed etiam

The biggest obstacle to the *practical* renovation of the liturgy is the question of the Latin language.[1] Once at a meeting of a group of priests – though all sympathetic to the classical Roman liturgical tradition – one among them declared, to general applause, that he would never return to the old rite because he could not 'linguistically' abandon the flock entrusted to him. These priests were afraid that the meaning of the liturgy would not be able to reach the faithful (or that it would do so only in fragments), and also the dialogical character of the liturgy would inevitably be compromised – a feature present from the most ancient times on, and present even nowadays in the liturgy of the Eastern churches. This was all said with reference to the Mass; what would be the judgement of these priests regarding the Office?! How many priests or congregations are ready to turn (return) to the Latin breviary?

It would be too easy as a way out to suggest that people can learn the few Latin texts pertaining to the congregation, and beyond that, the rest of the liturgy can be followed from the hand-missals. This way is, of course, already to some extent well-trodden; generations grew up using missalettes and became familiar with the liturgy like this. But two points cannot be neglected: for many people, actually using bilingual missals is not easy. Moreover, if the Mass is followed from a missalette, it becomes possible to understand what the liturgy is about, but paradoxically not from an experience of the liturgy itself. The liturgy in this case does not speak directly. The situation is like 'listening' to a music broadcast with the mute button on, while reading the score, and thus knowing more or less accurately that the orchestra is playing now this or that bar.

The rite is not identical to the language it is in.[2] The classical Roman Rite would be able to retain its full identity if it were celebrated in the vernacular. But

---

[1] Klaus Gamber (2002), *The Modern Rite*, p. 13: 'Among the current reforms . . . there are entirely positive aspects to the use of the vernacular'. Concerning the question of the use of the vernacular at the Council, see Johannes Overath (1983), 'The Liturgical and Musical Innovations of the Second Vatican Council', pp. 172–77.

[2] Cf. László Dobszay (2003), *The Bugnini-Liturgy and the Reform of the Reform*, pp. 168–76.

are these two demands – to preserve the traditional Latin, and to give abundant place to the vernacular – irreconcilable?[3] We should perhaps first consider the arguments in favour of both.

The primary argument for celebration in Latin in the classical Roman Rite is liturgical law itself. The law today stipulates the use of Latin for the celebration of the Roman Mass and for the recitation of the Divine Office according to the 1962 books.

The second argument is consideration for the express will of the Council. In spite of the few concessions given to the vernacular, it declares that the language of the Roman Rite remains Latin[4].

The third argument is that of preservation of uniformity in the Church. Fifty years ago a Catholic entering a Catholic church in any part of the word could feel at home because the Latin liturgy he found there was identical to that experienced in his own country. Latin manifests that the liturgy is the worship of the whole Church and not merely of particular or local communities. Though a great part of the congregation does not necessarily understand it, the validity and efficacy of the liturgy does not depend on this understanding; and the faithful are able to reap the fruits of what is offered by the priest.

The fourth argument is that the Latin creates, as it were, a protective veil by linguistic means around these most holy mysteries. This supposedly 'dead' language, unknown to most people and far from everyday parlance, has the capacity to inspire a deeper respect for the mystical reality of the liturgy than their everyday language.

I think that the most convincing argument is actually a fifth one: the treasures of the Roman liturgy came into being in this language. Latin is the home of the classical Roman rite. This is the only language, precisely because it is a 'dead' language, that preserves perfectly and enduringly the content of the liturgy in its unchanged and unchangeable meaning. In fact, no equivalent translation can really be made of those texts which are most typically Roman. Nevertheless, the liturgy speaks not only to those present; it pervades the whole life of the Church through multiple channels, through theology, catechesis, the spiritual life and so on. It is of crucial importance that the texts, with their exact meaning and strict formulation, should be found not only in the liturgical books but also in the living reality of ecclesiastical life, and in its actual voice.

Latin unites us not only in space but also in time. The citations from, and references to, the liturgical texts are present in the works of the Church Fathers and many spiritual writers, as well as in the prayers and meditations of the saints. Priests and a lay people who have a high level of theological formation but do not know the Latin liturgy extremely well (which means now they are not familiar with the Latin texts), surely cut themselves off from the historical records of the Church's life. Not to know the vocabulary used, or the sentences referred to, means not being able to recognize their context and origin in the theological and spiritual literature of the tradition itself. Perhaps one cause of theological

---

[3] Cf. Gamber (2002), *The Modern Rite*, pp. 35–40.
[4] *Sacrosanctum Concilium* (1963), §36.

laxity in recent decades has been the rejection of proper terminology, precise formulation, and linguistic discipline that is concomitant with a true formation in liturgical Latin. Had a formation of this character been deeply rooted in the Catholic mind of clergy and laity alike, not even a tenth of the false doctrines currently circulating could have arisen. This doctrinal collapse would have been impossible if what came to be said especially had been worded in Latin, or, at least, if it had been measured against the Latin textual tradition – which means above all the liturgical one.

Let us now look also at the arguments in favour of the vernacular:[5]

First, the Motu Proprio that 're-established' the classical Roman Rite has already provided the option of using the vernacular in reading the Epistle and Gospel at Mass.

The same Council that stipulated the preservation of Latin, also thought it useful to pray and sing at *some times* and in *some parts* (the readings, chants, prayers) in the vernacular.[6]

The universality of Latin is a weighty argument for its retention. But the question of universality is, first of all, a matter of *content*. We all celebrate essentially the same liturgy (in lawful variants). The vernacular, in some sense, even favours this universality: the same content can be transmitted more effectively and securely into the minds of priests and the greater masses of the faithful.

The rite is not identical to the language in which it is received. The Roman liturgy was originally in Greek; a move into Latin took place not earlier than the third or fourth centuries. In the Eastern churches, the language has changed many times (for instance, from Greek to Armenian, Georgian, Russian, Serbian, Romanian, Bulgarian and so forth), while the rite itself remained unchanged, and perhaps even more faithful to its essential identity than in the sphere of Latin rites.

Without doubt, ancient religions in the course of their long history of transmission all developed for themselves a sacred language that was not identical with the everyday parlance. Every language is made up of various linguistic layers, and each layer has its own special vocabulary, grammatical customs and style. This is also true for the language of cult. History bears witness, however, that this sacred language specific to cultic use also was able to come into being within the context of the vernacular (Old Slavonic would be a case in point). The necessary precondition for this to occur is a well-disciplined and regulated cultic use of a language for a rather long period of time. The use of vernacular does not mean automatically the language of the street. This means that if the standards for translations are correct and the sacral traditions of each language are adapted accordingly, sacred 'sub-languages' were able to be produced over a given time on the basis of a contemporary tongue.

[5] Concerning the preconciliar history of 'vernacularism' (mostly limited to the readings), see Alcuin Reid (2005), *The Organic Development of the Liturgy*, pp. 101, 111–12, 125, 133, 199, 239, 270. He refers (p. 235), however, to the results of a worldwide consulation of the episcopate: 'a desire for the use of the vernacular was expresseed by no more than 17.9%'.

[6] Vatican Council II, Dogmatic Constitution on the Sacred Liturgy, *Sacrosanctum Concilium* (1963), §§36.2 and 54.

One cannot deny that a significant part of the Latin liturgical texts are not able to be translated with absolute precision. With due effort, however, translation is able to approximate to the original (not on the basis of the 1976 instruction,[7] of course, but by a strict application of the norms proposed in the Vatican document *Liturgiam Authenticam*). The proprieties of a theological and liturgical style can even enrich modern, demotic languages. Moreover, there are other texts of the Roman Rite (first of all, passages and excerpts from the Bible) which cause far fewer difficulties for translation.

The close connection between the Latin liturgical texts and other fields of religious life is also true for the vernacular. A vernacular liturgy, if it follows strict standards, may beneficially influence the language of catechesis, homiletics, theological reflection and spirituality.

We are aware that by means of the vernacular liturgy liturgical meaning can reach the minds of the faithful *directly*. The liturgical texts teach them, admonish them, form their conscience and their religious mentality, instruct them in the right expression of religious truths, and present them with the Church's prayer to which they unite themselves with their 'Amen'.

Can the benefits of both Latin and the vernacular be preserved and combined? In my opinion, they *can* be. The question should be studied on three levels. How much place should be given to the vernacular? How can Latin be preserved as the language of the Roman liturgy? What are the standards that need to be adopted for appropriate translations?

II. *Latin and Vernacular in the Traditional Roman Liturgy*

Let this be established as a principle: the language of the Roman liturgy is Latin. Everything is in Latin, except what is permitted by liturgical law to be announced *also* in the vernacular. In today's situation the following parts *can* also be in the vernacular in the classical Roman Rite:

(a) According to the Motu Proprio, the Epistle and Gospel of the Mass can be read or sung in the vernacular.
(b) Even before the Council the congregation or the choir were permitted in specified circumstances to sing in the vernacular during the Mass. This was possible because the priest prayed the liturgical texts at the altar in Latin, and so the requirements of liturgical law were fulfilled. The difference is that the liturgical chants themselves were not to be sung in the vernacular. Today it is not forbidden to sing the Introit, Communion, or the items of the Ordinary of the Mass in the language of the people. If in the meantime the priest reads them in Latin, both liturgical tradition and pastoral needs can be satisfied.
(c) Already before the Council some lay people (individually or in groups) prayed some of the hours of the Office in the vernacular. Since the Liturgical

---

[7] S. Congr. pro Cultu Divino, Letter to the Presidents of Conferences of Bishops '*De linguis vulgaribus in S. Liturgiam inducendis*', of 5 June 1976: *Notitiae* 12 (1976), pp. 300–02, §§20–56.

Constitution urged people to join the Office,[8] I am of the view that this earlier custom could be interpreted more widely: the vernacular can be used in any form of the Office that is predominantly for the laity – what we might call (and is called in other languages) the 'folk office'. Perhaps it is too audacious to suggest that, by extending an existing permission, when the priest celebrates one of the Offices together with a congregation, he is not obliged to pray the same Office again in Latin. (It would also be a good stimulus to the priest to introduce the celebration of Office in their parishes.)

(d) It is a centuries-old practice that several of the sacraments (or larger parts of their ritual) can be administered in the vernacular.

New permissions are necessary (within the framework of the Roman Rite) for the following steps, that is, to extend §36 of the Constitution *Sacrosanctum Concilium* to the old rite:

(a) If the liturgical chants of the Mass are sung in accurate translation, the priest might then omit reading them in Latin.

(b) Perhaps it could be considered whether permission might be granted to pray the Preface, the Pater Noster and the Embolism (the prayer immediately after the Pater Noster) either in Latin or in the vernacular.

(c) The Divine Office is the best means of introducing priests to the daily use and proper comprehension of, at least, liturgical Latin. Surely, candidates for the priesthood have to be prepared for this in seminary. Since, however, they lack the proper training once received in more formal secondary schools, this level cannot be achieved if the 'bridge' built by an adequate use of the vernacular is missing. Accordingly, perhaps priests could be permitted to keep the (partly) vernacular Office for five years after their ordination and then begin using the Latin gradually (first the stable parts: the Magnificat, Benedictus, then the psalms and hymns, and finally the readings). Those who are unable to understand the patristic texts in Latin could read them in the vernacular even after the five-year period is over.

(d) The sacraments could be administered either in Latin or in the vernacular, perhaps with certain reservations. (For instance it is more appropriate always to read the exorcisms in Latin.)

This means that within the classical Roman Rite the following parts would best remain permanently and exclusively in Latin.

(a) The Collect, Secret ('Prayer over the Gifts'), and Postcommunion of the Mass.

(b) The Canon of the Mass.

---

[8] *Sacrosanctum Concilium* (1963), §100: 'Curent animarum pastores ut Horae praecipuae, praesertim Vesperae, diebus dominicis et festis solemnioribus, in ecclesia communiter celebrentur. Commendatur ut et ipsi laici recitent Officium divinum, vel cum sacerdotibus, vel inter se congregati, quin immo unusquisque solus.'

(c) The private prayers of the celebrant (at the foot of the altar, the offertory prayers, the prayers of preparation for Communion).
(d) The Office, if priests pray it privately (starting from the fifth year after their ordination).
(e) The exorcisms during the administration of those sacraments that have them.

At least the Collects, Secrets and Postcommunions, and the Canon of the Mass, should be placed in the hands of the people in a faithful translation. It would be even better if they were to get the full liturgy in bilingual editions, in books similar to the hand-missals of former periods. It may be advisable to include vernecular translations also in the ceremonial books used by the clergy, in order to provide them with the means to assist the faithful for whom they provide sacraments and sacramentals with better comprehension and an improved communication of the meaning of what is done.

The widest use of the vernacular here outlined would not, of course, be obligatory. It would not even be recommended for every situation; these wider permissions simply set a boundary for those cases where the vernacular might, sometimes, be most widely used. It is far more desirable that these parts are prayed sometimes in Latin and sometimes in the vernacular, according to local conditions. This leads to our next question: what kind of 'ramparts' should be built around the Latin language in order to ensure its preservation of use?

(a) Alongside the more extended permissions I have suggested, the Church would need to declare once again the primacy of Latin in her liturgy, and with force. To exhibit the importance of Latin more clearly, Masses celebrated with large gatherings of people, comprised of different nations (for instance, papal Masses), should be fully in Latin. Multilingual Masses have only an emblematic meaning; when one part is read in German, only the Germans understand it, and for the Germans all the other parts read in English, French, Italian, etc. might just as well be in Latin: so also *mutatis mutandis* for all the other native speakers present.
(b) In seminaries across the full period of preparation of candidates for Orders the Latin language needs to be taught intensively, and a major part of the liturgy, along with other prayers and devotions, should be celebrated in Latin. In this way young men could prepare themselves by acquiring good pronunciation, learning the grammatical structures, commiting many texts to memory and forming an emotional link to this classical language. For the larger part of the week (at least for four days) the 'official' Mass of the seminary should of necessity be celebrated in Latin. Since the Office is prayed by both beginners and those more advanced all together, the vernacular could, let us say, be permitted for three days (with some Latin parts), and the Office would be in Latin for the rest of the week (perhaps with some parts in the vernacular). For the sake of familiarity, the two systems should be complementary: whatever is in the vernacular during the Latin Office, would be in Latin during the vernacular one.

(c) In all churches where minimally three Masses are celebrated on a Sunday, one of them should be entirely in Latin (optionally with the readings repeated in the vernacular before the homily). If possible, the Sunday Latin Mass of a parish church should be, at the very least, a Latin *Missa Cantata*.

(d) In cathedrals and the monastic churches (of men) the Masses of the classical Roman Rite should be in Latin, with the exception of one morning Mass in the vernacular and one evening Mass partly in the vernacular.

(e) Priests from the fifth year after their ordination would be required to pray the full Office in Latin (from a bilingual breviary), except for the patristic readings, which can be read in the vernacular by those unable to attain the necessary level of comprehension.

(f) At large gatherings, conferences, and retreats of priests, the Mass and Office should always be celebrated in Latin.

(g) It is *laudable* if communities of lay people pray at least a part of the Office in Latin; at conventions, retreats, courses and so forth, at least some parts of the Mass and Office Hours should be in Latin.

III. *Standards for Translation*

The concessions for the use of the vernacular within the classical Roman Rite are appropriate only if the translations used are duly approved by church authorities, and, in terms of their inner content, only if they correspond to the requirements of the liturgical texts. The miserable translations produced in many countries after the Council are simply inappropriate for the traditions of the Roman liturgy (in spite of having received ecclesiastical approval!), and are unfit either to be used in the rite or to play a complementary role (interpretation, missalettes and so forth). The first task is to put an end to the exclusively *legal* function of ecclesiastical approvals, and before granting any such approval, the translation's conformity to all the proper requirements must be ascertained. The standards for this process should be, of course, those set by *Liturgiam Authenticam*.

What are these requirements? The following remarks will refer first of all to the material of the Sacramentary (i.e. collections of prayers).

(a) The first requirement is that of utmost accuracy. The first pillar of precision is the consistent use of words. A given Latin word should be translated always with the same vernacular word, except if the context requires that it have another meaning or nuance of meaning. The selected word should render the original *intention* perfectly (which does not mean, of course, the substitution of a *commentary* for the *translation*). The translator should understand the sense of the word in the context of its origin, including its cultural and theological significations. It is especially important when the most typical and most difficult texts of the Roman liturgy are to be translated; and these are those that originated in the patristic age. A great proportion of the classical texts (like the Roman Canon) come from this period. An average dictionary is insufficient to allow them to be properly understood; appeal to specialist and scholarly dictionaries is required. Since it would be impossible to expect all local churches to have highly trained experts in the linguistics of Christian Antiquity, it would be the task of the appropriate Roman dicastery to engage with the best scholars so that good commentaries on these texts could then be published and made available to translators.[9]

Sometimes it occurs that a specified Latin word has no exact counterpart in a recipient language, or the selected word has a secondary meaning that deflects the attention from the actual message. For instance, the word 'devotio' as used by Christian Antiquity has no equivalent in many languages, or its meaning has been modified (in the case of English, to mean fervour, piety). Then, but only then, the use of a two- or three-word phrase (with circumscription) could be permitted, since only *this* expression can transmit the precise sense of the *one* Latin word.

It is also necessary to take into consideration the particular features of the recipient language – an examination needs to be made what is the word normally used for the given concept in catechesis, common ecclesiastical parlance and technical theological definitions.

(b) Precise translations also require the analysis of both the context and the preservation of linguistic associations in the original. The liturgy does not use a dry schoolbook language and its artistic value is not the product of individual fantasy. Liturgical texts are consistent in transmitting a particular imagery together with the ideas that originally influenced and characterized them. This context can be determined by an analysis of the full text. For instance, when the first half of a Collect expresses its religious meaning by means of terms taken from medicine, horticulture, military affairs or sport, the terminology is probably preserved as the Collect continues to its conclusion. In such cases it is necessary to examine whether the other words (in the second half of the text) ought also to be interpreted in the light of the given associations. The edifice of the sentence is often built on correlative words. For example, the following words in the Collect of the Wednesday in the Ember Days of September are selected as a sequence of concepts consistently applied: *fragilitas nostra – sua conditione atteritur // tua clementia – reparetur*.[10] This example also demonstrates the importance of parallel grammatical phrases (*sua conditione – tua clementia*).

When accuracy of this kind is neglected, the translation often falls flat, ending up in banalities expressing itself in general terms and pious verbiage.

(c) The third level of accuracy is that of precise grammatical structure. The grammatical arrangement of the texts of the classical Roman Rite has an artistic, rhetorical and rhythmic function that makes the text more easily perceptible, increases its effect and serves its elevatedness. Accuracy also has an intellectual function; it reveals the correlation between thoughts, the subordinated and parallel aspects of the ideas seeking expression. The *precise*

---

[9]   With the use of the rich legacy of such scholars as Christine Mohrmann, Odo Casel or the Hungarian László Mezey, and others.

[10]   . . . our *weakness* – by its substance is *falling* into ruin / may be *restored* – by Thy *clemency*.

order in which things are said is not accidental, and establishes a centrally important aspect of the overall meaning. Because the order of the words in a sentence is less prefixed in Latin than in English, it is possible to convey secondary meanings in Latin through a specific word order that is adjunct to, and enhances, the meaning disclosed by the grammatical forms. Latin grammar, unusually, provides the means for two opposite tendencies: articulation and holding the statement together. The text has a little stop after each clause consisting of three or four words, which is a part of the thought and is understandable in itself. On the other hand, by its grammatical structure the clause becomes part of a more complex thought. To give an example: *Custodi, Domine, quaesumus, Ecclesiam tuam* – Defend Thy Church, we beseech Thee, O Lord (the fundamental deprecation), *proptiatione perpetua* – with unceasing favour (the 'how' of the protection), *et quia sine te labitur humana mortalitas* – and because apart from Thee falls the human mortality (why one needs this protection), *tuis semper auxiliis* – by Thy permanent help (an instrumental case, common to the following parallel expressions), *et abstrahatur a noxiis, et ad salutaria dirigatur* – it may be ever both withdrawn from harms and also guided to the things of salvation: (*et* – *et*: of the indication of a parallelism); *abstrahatur* – *dirigatur* (withdrawn – guided); *a noxiis* – *ad salutaria* (from harms – and things of salvation: from and to). The translator must attempt, as much as possible, to relay structures like these and their inner coherency into the recipient language.

(d) The use of compound sentences is also a feature of the particular identity of Roman style. One compound thought is expressed in one compound sentence. Except for some rare, quite exceptional cases, such sentences must not be broken up, else the thought itself falls apart, and the result is an intermittent, stuttering manner of speech. Attention is also required, of course, to keep the sentence acoustically and intellectually graspable. Ponderous words, and short but structurally important words (prepositions, implicit or explicit phrases), should be carefully arranged and well balanced. The sentence also needs some kind of nearly imperceptible rhythm, a harmonious flow; it should start from a point and, making a turn, it should arrive at the end just at the right moment.

(e) The instruction *Liturgiam Authenticam* called attention also to the importance of stylistic fidelity, which is to say that the style of the Roman prayers should be preserved (§57). The sentence must not be flattened either in the selection of words or in its structure or rhythm. It cannot be vulgar; the ceremonious style of sacred speech should be retained. No doubt there is something a bit artificial in this, but it is for the sake of the rite: it suggests that now something solemn, something set apart, is being pronounced.

So far I have spoken mainly of the translation of the prayers or Prefaces. Liturgical texts have several genres, all with different linguistic patterns. The biblical citations speak in much simpler, almost everyday, language. In most cases the thoughts (and sentences) are shorter, or the size grows by supplementation so that new elements are appended to what preceded; the vocabulary is reduced.

The psalms have the quiet rhythm of personal communication; it is only the double construction known as *parallelismus membrorum* that generates order in what is said. The frequent use of 'meus, meum, tui', as the constant dialogical conversation between the psalmist and God, helps this quiet flow of the poetry. This is not concise phrasing; rather it reveals a slow stream of thoughts springing from the depths of the heart.

The Gospels function at times stylistically like folk tales. The narrative style of an archaic poetic form shapes the meaning. The narrator speaks the events as they come to mind, he takes no particular care to colour what is said in dramatic words and synonyms. Stylization of this kind is far from the world of the Gospels. The sentences often start with 'And'; a typical stylistic trait of narration as it is found in oral cultures.[11] Utterances are introduced by stereotypical formulas: said, asked, answered and so on. The mannerisms of modern novels (for instance, inserting reference to the speaker only in the middle of a sentence, or just leaving it to the end) are quite alien from this biblical style. When the text is not read with the *eyes*, but it is pronounced in the context of orality, it is necessary to know, before the sentence actually begins, who it is that is about to speak. Such formulas as 'Jesus answered' only have an ancillary function; the translator's fancies of indulging in ever-changing linguistic dress make nothing but trouble. When Albert Lord analysed the archaic Serbian epics, he found that in these orally transmitted epics the style of the use of formulas is consistent. If the hero is to get up on his horse, this is related 15 or 20 times with exactly the same words.[12] This style itself reveals the origin of the Gospels! The style itself also has something to say, actually teaches the message through its very form of communication, hence it is necessary to remain faithful to it.

Three objections are usually deployed to criticize these principles; these very objections probably influenced the authors of the 1976 Instruction of the Congregation of Rites, at least implicitly:

(a) 'Servile translations fail to adapt the text to the spirit of the language into which it is to be translated.' There are, of course, extreme cases when a given language is unable to resolve a problem posed for it by a particular Latin expression or construction. But I cannot conceal that behind this objection there is a degree of ignorance. It regards individual languages as closed entities that are themselves incapable of any change. In fact, the history of languages shows that the influence of other languages often led to development, enriching the vocabulary, grammar and stylistic capacity of the language being influenced. When we transplant a text from a foreign language, new capacities are discovered in our own language; potential that could never be realized without this intervention. Figures taken over from foreign languages often introduce felicitious and pleasing nuances into a

---

[11] Leo Treitler (1985), 'Oral and Literate Style in the Regional Transmission of Tropes', (with reference to Walter Ong, who compared the Douay translation with that of the New American Bible), pp. 172–74.

[12] Albert B. Lord (1964), *The Singer of Tales*, pp. 30–67.

given language. They enrich its rational content, but still more, they extend its limitations with respect to *style*. The elliptical character of a compound sentence (if clearly perceptible) may, in fact, suggest a stylistic meaning. Language is never monolithic: in it there are many linguistic layers living in degrees of harmony. When a language develops its religious or cultic stratum – sometimes under the influence of other languages – this is a gain for that language, and even secular literature may profit from it. The Vulgate itself emerged by realizing new capacities within the Latin language because of the need to translate precisely the original Hebrew and Greek texts.

(b) A second objection can be expressed as follows: 'It is not the words that should be translated. If the message of the Latin text is grasped, its essence can be communicated using the characteristic expressions of the new linguistic medium.' This principle is called 'dynamic equivalence'. Often aimed at cultic communication, this is, however, not even true in the case of secular translations. Translators, as much as possible, strive to preserve and express not only the 'meaning' but also the structural and stylistic features of the original. 'Dynamic equivalence' definitely cannot be adapted to the religious sphere, and most especially to liturgical language. The liturgy is not an abstract, disembodied spiritual entity, but a spiritual entity incorporated in a physical body. In the case of language: a spiritual entity appears *as* a set of words. If its material stability is taken away, the whole system becomes fluid. The principle of 'dynamic equivalence' inexorably leads to the swamp of relativism and subjectivity. However, there is not even any need for it: the vast majority of the texts – with slight compromises – can be translated in a very precise manner. In the exceptional cases of certain expressions the problem should be solved in only those specificities, without fabricating an artificial method out of extraordinary cases.

(c) The third objection against making accurate translations takes the form of an accusation of archaism. In fact, a precise translation – and primarily, in the case of the Bible – sometimes requires archaic linguistic forms. This is all the more so when the translation is based on an old biblical translation of considerable reputation (an English example would be the Douay-Rheims Bible), the use of which which might be preferable in many respects. These translations, made in the sixteenth and seventeenth centuries, are in most cases very accurate, and produced a biblical style of a very high level. To create such a translation in our day is almost impossible; it would be a *creatio ex nihilo*. Not all 'archaisms' should be estimated as the same level. Whether God is addressed with 'Thou' or 'You' is indeed a stylistic question. But, let us say, the use of a variety of forms of the past tense has an impact on the way the content is understood. The 'archaic' perfect in some languages belongs to the means of expression. In some sentences the 'archaic' perfect places the reader into the distant past, or the 'time' before time. The same is true for cases where Christ or the Father pronounces something of universal meaning. The aversion to passive verbal forms – even in languages where this form is in everyday use in literature or conversation – is quite unintelligent. The passive form can only very rarely be replaced by the active, since here the actor (subject) of the sentence is deliberately not given or indicated. The passive form often means: this or that happened by the will of God, by the decision of God. In other cases the acting persons are simply left indeterminate. Again, sometimes behind the same event we find different persons contributing to it differently. 'In qua nocte *tradebatur*' (in that night in which he was betrayed) expresses many things: it refers to those assaulting Christ, to the decision of the Redeemer himself, and also to the will of the Father. The use of subordinate clauses also repulses some people, whereas it is often used in common parlance. It is quite incomprehensible to understand why it should have to be eliminated from sacral language. A simple case is: *Deus qui* = *God who*. In most languages there is no need to avoid this construction; its omission may destroy the structure of the sentence. The formula *Deus qui* also has a theological sense: it is a reference to one particular attribute or deed of God, which is the basis of our particular petition or deprecation. It is nearly ridiculous when it is replaced by 'God, you . . .' as if we wished to inform God about one of his attributes or deeds. For most languages it is simply not correct that this use is an archaism or is alien to the character of the language itself. The most that can be said is that archaisms of this type are elements of a literary and religious linguistic layer of the language itself – highly appropriate to the context of cultic worship.

In summary we can state that, with prudent deliberation, the use of Latin could be extended across the Church. The 'linguistic veil', however, can often be lifted, provided that the translations are precise, and nearly on the same level as the Latin itself.

Saying this, we might possibly placate the priest to whom I referred in the opening of this chapter: the Latin liturgy can be restored without harm to the genuine desires of the Second Vatican Council: and in this particular case, without doing away with a more abundant use of the vernacular.

14

AD ORIENTEM

The other neuralgic point of the entire liturgical reform is the direction (orientation) of the celebration of Mass, and so of the altar itself. Again, this is not something directly connected with the reform that was specified. Neither the Council, nor any individual instruction of the Church, ever decreed that altars be turned '*versus populum*' (for celebration with the priest facing to the congregation). It is obligatory neither in the classical Roman Rite nor in the New Rite.[1] Since a detailed discussion of the topic is available in Fr Uwe Michael Lang's book (*Turning Towards the Lord*),[2] which may be complemented with several writings of Joseph Cardinal Ratzinger,[3] there is no need here to repeat the arguments. A short summary of the facts:

- Liturgical law does not make obligatory celebration *versus populum* (in fact it does not specify the direction of celebration at all).
- In historical retrospection both orientations were possible in the Church from the very beginning; the prevailing (in fact almost universal) situation was that both the priest and the congregation prayed regularly turning towards the east.
- Turning towards the east was justified in the tradition by biblical and

[1] Response of Jorge A. Cardinal Medina Estévez, Cardinal Prefect of the Congregation for Divine Worship, 25 September 2000, Prot. Nr. 2086/00/L. The English translation of the *General Instruction of the Roman Missal* has a mendacious translation regarding the position of the celebrant at the altar. The Latin says (*General Instruction on the Roman Missal*, §299): 'Altare maius extruatur a pariete seiunctum, ut facile circumiri et in eo celebratio versus populum peragi possit, quod expedit ubicumque possibile sit [The altar should be built apart from the wall, in such a way that it is possible to walk around it easily, which is desirable wherever possible so that Mass may be celebrated at it facing the people].' The English translation has altered the reference of 'which is desirable wherever possible' to suggest that wherever possible what is desirable is not the separatedness from the wall, so that Mass *may* be celebrated facing the people, but that *it is desirable wherever possible that Mass should be celebrated facing the people*. The English translation of the General Instruction of the Roman Missal (Third Typical Edition, 2002, International Committee on English in the Liturgy), §299: 'The altar should be built apart from the wall, in such a way that it is possible to walk around it easily and that Mass can be celebrated at it facing the people, which is desirable wherever possible.'
[2] Uwe Michael Lang (2004), *Turning Towards the Lord*. Cf. Thomas M. Kocik (2003), *The Reform of the Reform*, pp. 80–81.
[3] Cardinal Joseph Ratzinger (2000), *The Spirit of the Liturgy*, pp. 62–84; also introduction to Lang (2004), *Turning Towards the Lord*, pp. 9–12.

theological motives, as well as by the eschatological orientation of the liturgy.

- It manifests more clearly the sacrificial character of the Mass.[4]
- In a pastoral perspective, this tradition expresses that priest and the congregation face the *same* direction while praying, turning towards the symbolic direction of the Lord's presence and future coming.

I. What is the Problem?

In the aftermath of the Second Vatican Council, there was, however, a practical argument and also a point of reference in support of celebrations facing the people.

The basic argument was simply to end the practice of the priest 'turning his back to the people'. The argument ran that the people should have a clear view of everything happening at the altar. The new direction was to link people more intimately to the ceremonies and to the priest.

The advocates of the new orientation also found a point of reference in the experiments conducted by the early Liturgical Movement. The movement itself had strong links to the ancient traditions of the City of Rome. Since in the great basilicas of Rome celebration facing the people was the general practice (because the basilicas themselves faced west, not east, so that in order to face east the pope turned in to the body of the building), many supposed that this had been the original and authentic tradition, and the Liturgical Movement had to return to that. Pius XII in his encyclical *Mediator Dei* criticized the one-sidedness of this argument, and called it a manifestation of extreme archaism.[5]

After the Council, however, many priests were (mistakenly) convinced that the new direction had become mandatory, and justified because it was only a return to Rome's ancient practice. At this point one priest began to learn from his neighbour that the 'rearrangement' of the sanctuary had become not only obligatory but was also a crucial 'conciliar' gesture.

Setting aside, therefore, the archaeological aspect of the question (which is summed up perfectly in Fr Lang's book), we need now to determine the impact of this change on the liturgy, and on the liturgical behaviour of priests and *congregations*.

In most older churches a reasonable rearrangement of the sanctuary was nearly impossible. The sanctuary was built intentionally so that the altar faced the apse (or was even more often attached to the east wall), and was placed on a rather high platform (with three or five, and sometimes seven steps ascending to it), and the sanctuary was spacious enough to give place to the assistants for the solemn forms of the liturgy. Following postconciliar fashions, most often a

---

[4] Uwe Michael Lang (2009), 'Once Again'.
[5] *Mediator Dei* 1947: §62. For the theological implications of the orientation see, for example, Louis Bouyer (1967), *Liturgy and Architecture*; Michael Davies (1991), *Mass Facing the People*; Klaus Gamber (2002), *The Modern Rite*, pp. 15–33, 43; Laurence Paul Hemming (2008), *The Liturgical Subject*, p. 11.

second altar was put into the middle or even the outer end of the sanctuary (either newly built or just a simple table; often what had previously been the credence table was dragged into the centre of the sanctuary); a lectern for reading was set up on one side or both sides of the altar; seats for the celebrant and servers were placed in a central position, often on the platform of the old altar or in front of its steps. Frequently the sanctuary became so cramped that it became difficult to find a place for the assistants in the available space. If the rearrangement was undertaken in a small church, there remained only narrow passages (a few feet in width) allowing for movement inside the sanctuary. To save space, the new altar has often been put on a one-step platform, or no platform was constructed at all. Completely contrary to the original intention, the congregation lost any proper view of the altar. The figure of the priest was now at the same height as the heads of the people in the pews. Use of a legilium or ambo severed contact between the congregation and the reader or the preaching priest . Formerly the congregation could understand the preacher well as he was standing at a good height, preaching from a pulpit. The people could read the text from the lips of the priest, and could be helped by visible gestures, whereas now the microphone remains the only tool for bringing the words nearer (in most cases without success)[6] to the assembly.

The real loss in these rearrangements, however, arose as a result of a trans-formation in the priests' mentality. In losing contact with the sacred area of the church the priest's attention has come to be focused rather on the assembly. No fixed direction remained for his eyes: the Cross (if there even was one on the altar) was too low and put aside; if he raised his gaze higher, he beheld only a choir loft or an organ-gallery. Eventually the priest stopped trying to raise his eyes higher: rather he tried to face the congregation. This change had the effect of modifying his entire attitude. The change of physical direction became a change in psychological orientation. He began to say the Mass not *for* (*pro*) but *to* or *at* the people. He began trying to influence what had become for him an audience, through gestures: head or eye movements during the holiest parts of the Mass; the priest became a president, or rather an actor or media-man for the assembly. This 'direct contact' was often accompanied with fraternizing manners. This psychological change became all the more exaggerated when he went down among the people during the Mass, or in other churches called the people up to stand around the altar. Paradoxically, a liturgy that was often blamed for being overly clerical had been transformed into a one-man show.

I am not sure what the exact order of cause and effect in this process actually is. The direct consequence of advocating a 'pastoral liturgy' was that the liturgy was adjusted to the community, instead of lifting the community up to the level of the liturgy. It could be that this change of emphasis caused the change in the

---

[6] Gamber (2002), *The Modern Rite*, pp. 52–53: 'The ears of modern people are often "soaked" all day long with voices from one loudspeaker or another . . . A direct form of address is in all circumstances more natural, and thus more effective in influencing people. Microphones should therefore only be used in churches when this seems to be absolutely necessary. The "missa cantata" which used to be performed, and the old-fashioned pulpits, made a loudspeaker system unnecessary in most cases.'

position of the altar and in the behaviour of the priest. But it might well have been the other way around: the rearrangement of the sanctuary (even done with good will) transformed the liturgical ethos in general and the liturgical mentality of the priests in particular. The priest surely mentally *imagined* but did not *experience* in his innermost being what it actually means to step up to the throne of the Most High God, to bring there prayer and the sacrifice of God's people in the name of Christ. The typical manners and concerns of a community leader or even a schoolteacher were now uppermost in his mind.

This change could not have taken place without the change in orientation of the altars. A priest who stands and acts with his 'back to the people' remains alone. Like the high priest of the Jewish temple, he enters the Holy of Holies and steps behind the veil, into the space of intimate intercourse with the Lord. '*Solus* intrat canonem' (he alone enters the canon).[7] If the priest were not holding – almost desperately – on to a false illusion of unity with his people, he would be inspired to resolve his solitude through his official-personal communication with God.

The turning around of the altars, celebration *versus populum*, was not commanded by the Council. In practice, however, the new rite and the new position of the altar are closely associated. We may say that changing back to the original direction will have a beneficial effect. Indeed the very fact that the bulk of the clergy protests with intense emotions against this return shows its serious *necessity*; the principal motivation behind the protest is not pastoral care of the faithful, but the psychological distress of the priest.

II. What is the Solution?

The Holy Father, while still a Cardinal, gave an indication as to the essence of the solution.[8] The priest standing either behind or before the altar should always turn towards God in his soul. The Cardinal also said that this spiritual direction is expressed and supported if a 'virtual East' is set up, towards which the priest can naturally allow his gaze to be drawn. If there is some necessity to celebrate facing the people, a Cross could be hung from on high, or a tall crucifix be placed in the middle of the altar, so that the priest may direct his eyes on it while celebrating Mass.

Uwe Lang proposed another solution: he suggested that the first part of the Mass might be celebrated in a dialogical form between the priest (or assistants) and the congregation. During this part the priest might stand or sit at the chair, turning towards the people when he addresses them. At the Offertory he goes up to the altar, says the solemn prayers and offers the sacrifice to God, turning – together with the people – to the east. (The expression 'with his back to the people' really must be laid aside.) Then, when the fruits of the sacrifice are to be

---

[7] *Ordo Romanus I*, §88.
[8] Ratzinger (2000), *The Spirit of the Liturgy*, pp. 82–84.

distributed, he turns again to the people and brings the Body of the Lord down from the mount of the altar.[9]

Is it really necessary for the people to see what is happening on the altar? The priest of the Eastern church acts behind the closed altar screen (iconostasis), 'in' the altar during the most important part.[10] In Christian Antiquity (not in the Middle Ages!) the altar was surrounded with drapes to be closed during the most holy action, and the Canon was not heard since it was pronounced in a low tone by the priest (again, not only in the Middle Ages!).[11] There are, in fact, only a few things to be seen in the action of the Canon; the holy Bread and the Chalice are raised after the consecration. How do people participate in this part of the Mass? First of all, they are taught to offer themselves as a living sacrifice and to unite their own offerings with the oblation of Christ and the Church.[12] Secondly, they have to follow the main moments of the Eucharistic action, and address their devoted prayers in the same direction (the commemoration of the living, of the dead, the offering of the sacrifice). Thirdly, if they wish, they can follow the words of the priest by reading the hand-missals or the distributed booklets. Fourthly, while it is certainly not necessary it is instructive to see that the priest not only says prayers but also performs certain actions: he bows, extends and closes his arms, makes the sign of the Cross, etc. These gestures, however, can be followed also while standing behind the priest, if the altar is built on a high platform.

I wish to complete the question of direction with one more element. As we have seen, the priest turns towards the people when he has something to tell them (greetings, admonitions, blessings, the homily, etc.). He turns to the physical or symbolic east when, as the servant of the Church and representative of Christ the *Mediator*, he brings prayers and the sacrifice of the Church before God. There is, however, also a third direction, common during the Office: here community and priest form a kind of circle, thus imitating the community gathering in the 'upper room' of the Jerusalem house and waiting for the advent of the Holy Spirit.[13] This is the direction of quiet community prayer, of meditation and praise. The choir sits or stands in stalls facing each other, then turns towards the altar when their adoration is emphasized (at the mention of the Saviour's name) or the focus is on the action of the priest (the Collect).

The Mass also has such moments, for instance, the Gloria. In the solemn form of the Mass the priest sits at the sedile, while the choir and congregation sing the Gloria. The position of the sedile corresponds to this symbolism: the priest is sitting neither facing the people as a president, nor facing the altar; his direction is the same as that of those in the choir. In these moments the priest forms, as

---

[9] Lang (2004), *Turning Towards the Lord*, pp. 122. Cf. Gamber (2002), *The Modern Rite*, pp. 15–34; Brian W. Harrison, OS (2003), 'The Postconciliar Eucharistic Liturgy', pp. 192–93.

[10] It is worth mentioning that the celebrant changes his position during the Holy Liturgy according to the meaning of a given part: sometime he sits in the sanctuary hidden behind the altar; sometimes he goes to the preparatory altar; then he comes before the iconostasis to the 'holy peninsula'; and, of course, he stands before the altar facing toward East during the Canon (Anaphora).

[11] Adrian Fortescue (1912), *The Mass*, 4th edn 2005, pp. 325–28.

[12] *Sacrosanctum Concilium* (1963), §48.

[13] Acts 1.13.

it were, a part of the community; with St Augustine's words: 'For you a bishop, with you a Christian'.[14]

And now let us survey the Order of Mass with respect to orientation. The priest approaches the altar, prays in front of it, and honours it with incense. The Gloria is sung 'in choir', which is defined by the position of the sedile. In the Collect, the celebrant brings the solemn deprecation of the Church to God; consequently, he turns to the symbolic east together with the congregation. The reading of the Epistle and Gospel may take place towards the faithful (there is another method with its proper history and symbolism but I suggest postponing discussion of it until later), the interlectionary chant (Gradual) is sung or listened to again 'in choir'. The homily is addressed, of course, to the faithful. The Creed is a case of its own, and therefore, I will discuss it later. The offertory, Canon and the Pater Noster are prayed, of course, at the altar, turned to literal or symbolic east (toward God). The distribution of Holy Communion is done in the opposite direction. The Postcommunion is again a prayer directed to God. The closing parts are recited with face to the people (except the private prayer known as the *Placeat*).

With this arrangement every single moment is understood through its natural orientation, which means that there is no need to define the liturgical position of the priest with one overall decision.

All this, however, necessitates a proper layout for the church building itself.

III. The Church and Its Furniture

The first point to consider is the overall *structure* of the church building.[15] Mostly it is defined as a building consisting of a sanctuary and a nave. From a historical and functional point of view it is more correct to speak of four units within the body of the edifice. The heart or head of the church, the focus of every activity is, of course, the sanctuary, with the altar standing – as the focus of every action – in the axis. The sanctuary is considerably higher than other parts of the building, and its isolated position is stressed by means of various architectural features (Rood, Communion rail).

The next part, the choir, is rarely mentioned. Here the church has a wider section perpendicular to the main axis, stressed – if not by a *solid* cross-nave – at least by some immediately apparent visual element. This is the place for the singers, but also for the clergy, and other assistants who participate with some immediate activity in the liturgy. According to the classical arrangement, this is furnished with stalls facing each other at the south and north. This direction

[14] St Augustine, Sermon 340, 1: in *Patrologia Latina*, vol. 38, col. 1483: 'Vobis enim sum episcopus, vobiscum sum christianus. Illud est nomen officii, hoc gratiae; illud periculi est, hoc salutis [*For you I am a bishop, along with you I am a Christian*. The name "bishop" signifies duties, the name "Christian" signifies the received grace. To be "bishop" suggests danger for me, to be "Christian" suggests salvation]'. Cf. *Lumen Gentium*, §32.
[15] Cf. Miklós István Földváry (2002), 'Istenünk tornácaiban, and (2003), 'A kultikus tér szervezése a kereszténységben'.

is not contrary to the main direction (west–east). Those sitting here may turn to each other (during the psalmody) or make a half-turn to the altar according to what is demanded by the liturgy. In the middle of the choir there is a large enough space; this is a continuation of the 'holy space' of the sanctuary along the longitude of the church, towards the nave and the entrance. In the Mass, and still more outside the Mass, some actions take place in this 'holy peninsula'. Some items are sung here, even at the halfway point of the longitudinal axis, in the middle of the choir. The processions leave and enter here; some blessings are given here, and the empty place between the stalls has a special function during the Office. It is perhaps a good thing if those present at weekday Masses are allowed to sit here, nearer to the sanctuary.

Then the nave follows which is the proper place for the greater assembly of the faithful. It is fitting if the middle 'corridor' reserved for the liturgy continues here, that is, the pews are not in one block, in the middle of the nave, but along the line of the stalls in two symmetrically positioned rows leaving a wide enough space in between.

The additional side- and foregrounds are not without their own significance. These provide space for those who can join the worship only for a shorter time, or want to remain nearer to the entrance (perhaps if they have little children with them), or if they wish to pray alone. Here is also the proper space for the baptismal Font and the confessionals.

What about the altar? The first requirement is that it should be rather high. In churches of average size at least three steps should be required between the floor of the sanctuary and the platform of the altar. The altar should be wide enough: this is necessary for the liturgical functions performed at it. But it is also interesting to note that in large churches everything appears reduced in size at greater distance; if the altar is too small, it becomes visually insignificant. The rules for the obligatory number and symmetrical position of the candles should be reintroduced. The candles have the function of surrounding the priest and the oblation, setting luminous columns to the right and left. The candle cannot be lower than the head of the priest. It is quite absurd when the candles are turned into a trinket: small candlesticks placed at one end of the altar (why?), balanced by flowers or a similarly insignificant little cross on the other end. The cross should stand or hang high enough so that the priest can look up to it.[16]

It is a beautiful custom, and one worth restoring, to build a ciborium or baldacchino above the altar. It covers the table with saving care, stressing its dignity. It is really strange on those occasions when there is a canopy above the throne of the bishop, but there is none above the earthly throne of the Lord.

For the covers of the altar there are respectable prescriptions often neglected in our day. These support the appropriate respect for the altar, and give a dignified appearance to it. The linen should hang all the way down to the floor at each end; the front of the altar is vested with a panel of coloured brocade (frontal).

Now we have arrived at the question of the direction of the altar. In churches built in the baroque or romantic periods, and in most of the medieval churches,

---

[16] As can be seen during all Masses celebrated by Benedict XVI in recent times.

an altar turned towards the apse is more appropriate and should be retained or restored; an altar facing the people, which disturbs the view of the sanctuary, should be taken away. In some medieval and in most modern churches the altar can be constructed so that the priest may walk right around it, and the Mass may be celebrated on either side. The necessary precondition for building this kind of altar is to have enough space on both sides of the platform for the movement of a greater number of assistants.

When an altar facing the people is constructed, it should be shaped so that it is not inferior in its general impression and dignity to an altar oriented toward the apse. It should be placed high, with a ciborum above if possible, with tall candlesticks and a tall Cross on the altar (this is the arrangement of the main altar of St Peter's in Rome!) The altar Cross and at least four, but preferably six, candles raise a wall in front of the priest, not only to conceal him from the people but also to conceal the people from his eyes; to bind his attention and direct it toward the holy action. Such an altar could effectively eliminate the problems we discussed above concerning the celebration *versus populum*.

The Council said nothing about taking away the rails of the sanctuary. Again this was an arbitrary decision of some priests that became a superficial fashion. The altar rail has two advantages. It gives due protection and honour to the sanctuary, but it also makes it possible for the faithful to kneel down at the Lord's table, instead of taking the Host almost in mid-air, while the communicant is forced into permanent motion and can find no repose and calm while kneeling at the altar.

If the size of the sanctuary is not already sufficiently reduced by the presence of two altars, then a place is found at its corner for the ambo, far from the altar. As the example of ancient basilicas shows, the ambo can be brought forward from the sanctuary to the 'holy peninsula', that is, into the choir. The elevated pulpits of baroque churches made it easy for the people to look at the priest, and added good acoustics (a well-chosen place with a sounding-board behind and above).[17] These unused pulpits in churches make for a dismal sight. There is no reason why they could not be used at least on special occasions. Wherever the ambo is now to be set up, at least four or five steps should lead up to it so that the priest can be clearly seen and heard while delivering the homily.

The baptismal Font is rarely now located in the most appropriate or proper place in many churches. The ideal arrangement, of course, is that of a separate Baptistery, or at least an enclosed space near the entrance to the church. The administration of baptism requires its own space; and we should not lose sight of the eminent function it has in the celebration of the Paschal Vigil or (potentially) the Great Baptismal Vespers during the Octave of Easter.

To sum up, it is desirable to celebrate the classical Roman Rite (and also the *Novus Ordo*) *ad orientem* – towards the east – respectively, turned towards

---

[17] In medieval churches in England the Epistle was often recited from the high rood-loft. Cf. Nicholas Sandon (1984), *The Use of Salisbury*, vol. 1, *The Ordinary of the Mass*, p. 16. On the lectern and pulpit in its historical variants see Miklós István Földváry (2008), 'The Lectern in Liturgical Culture', pp. 14–20.

the same direction as the assembly. If this is simply impossible, an altar facing the people should be somewhat set apart, raised to an appropriate height, and providing the celebrant a focal point for a common transcendental orientation of priest and people alike, rather than 'face-to-face'. Moreover, special care should be afforded to nurturing and conserving a cast of mind in every priest that is '*versus Deum*', turned toward God.

15

THE DIVINE OFFICE

There is no area of the liturgy where the Bugnini-reforms wrought so much damage as in the Divine Office: they left almost no stone untouched.

The Office is a principal part of the liturgy. In earlier times it belonged to the regular schedule of worship in each church, just like the Mass, and lay people joined in the celebration of at least some of the Hours. While the Mass is primarily an action, with additional words and chants, in the Office the words and chants, the sung prayer, *is* the liturgy that is accompanied by only a few actions. The Office provides a more abundant time and opportunity to immerse the mind in the things of God and in the mysteries of the liturgical season. The Office is not only adoration of God, but is also an effective means of forming a liturgical consciousness. The Mass mostly contemplates the work of salvation as a single comprehensive reality; the prism of the Office unfolds it in its manifold colour.

The Office also has an important pastoral role: through it the faithful familiarize themselves with the attitude, style and mentality of the liturgy much more easily in its actual practice than through wordy explanations. The Mass is celebrated by the service of the priest; the faithful *join* in. In the Office, however, the assembly itself is the visible subject of prayer representing the real subject: the entire Church. Since the validity of the Mass is based on a priestly 'office' or service, many aliturgical elements made their way into the pious practices in the congregation during the Mass without harm to its validity. Every pastoral-liturgical reform's main concern has been to improve an *already existing* practice. The Office defines this practice nearly automatically (psalms, biblical passages, church hymns, canticles). Also those who begin to celebrate the Office need not look for substitutions, but are able to pray the Office itself. The Office allows the congregation to perform a *liturgical* act of full spiritual significance even without a priest or deacon. Furthermore, by means of the Office the individual believer can know himself to be conjoined to the official prayer of the universal Church.

What was said in Part I of this book is particularly true for the Office. The Roman Office is something whole, and developed organically on an ancient foundation.[1] This uniform tradition became, however, the proper tradition of

---

[1] Of the huge scholarly literature on the history and theology of the Office, two summarizing works stand out. For historical reflections concerning the Roman Office I know of no better reference

dioceses or ecclesiastical provinces which enjoyed a fair amount of freedom in shaping and determining the particular details on their own authority. The identity of the Uses was manifest, first of all, in their Office; but all of these Uses represented the Roman rite in its proper character.

I have already dealt in detail with the principal moments of the history of the Office and with the *Liturgia Horarum* in my *Bugnini-Liturgy*.[2] It is sufficient now to begin the sub-divisions of this chapter with a short summary, and then my 'proposal' for the Office can be explained.

I. The Number and Structure of the Hours

The three constitutive elements of the Roman Office are: (a) the number and structure of Hours; (b) the distribution of the Psalter (which is the basis for the determination of the character of an Hour); and (c) the Antiphonary. Two more flexible components can be added to these: the Hymnal and the Lectionary.

The Office was not born in an instant, according to a pre-existent comprehensive design. The various Hours each have their separate histories which left traces on the nature of the given Hour. From earliest times, morning and evening prayers (Lauds, Vespers) were the corner-stones of common prayer, an institution of the general religious practice of mankind. It was a custom or rather a rule from the early Christian period that the day should not be allowed to pass without elevating the soul to the Lord. The soul was to have brief moments of recollection regularly (every third hour) dedicating a few minutes to God and to commemorating the remarkable events of salvation history (the descent of the Holy Ghost, the crucifixion, the Lord's death: *Tertia, Sexta, Nona*). Originally these stations, like milestones for the day, might have been short personal devotions without being 'liturgical' in the strict sense;[3] later – with the inclusion of short psalmody – they became proper liturgical services. Following Christ's admonition (keep awake and pray)[4] from time to time a longer vigil was celebrated by the early Christians, mainly on the nights preceding greater solemnities and the commemorative days of the death of martyrs and the other faithful (Vigils, later called Matins). Finally, for Christians who lived in stable communities a short prayer was needed to sanctify the minutes before starting work and before going to sleep (Prime, Compline). St Benedict observed that this number of Hours corresponded well to the admonition of David: 'Septies in die laudem dixi tibi' ('Seven times a day do I praise thee'; Ps. 118.164), and

---

- despite some obsolete details – than Suitbert Bäumer (1895), *Geschichte des Breviers*. For a wider perspective (includng the duality of the 'cathedral' and 'monastic' office, and their mutual influences) see Robert F. Taft (1986), *The Liturgy of the Hours in East and West*, pp. 31–190, 211–13, 297–317, which, however, hardly dealt with the Roman Office. Other short survey summaries include László Dobszay (1997), 'Offizium' and James McKinnon (2000b), 'The Origins of the Western Office'

[2] László Dobszay (2003), *The Bugnini-Liturgy and the Reform of the Reform*, pp. 45–84.

[3] Bäumer (1895), *Geschichte des Breviers*, pp. 43–50; Taft (1986), *The Liturgy of the Hours in East and West*, pp. 18–19.

[4] Matt. 24.42; 25.13; Mk 13.35-37.

also 'Media nocte surgebam ad confitendum tibi' ('At midnight I will rise to give thanks unto thee'; Ps. 118.62).[5]

The structure of the Hours is in harmony with their origin and character. Lauds and Vespers are of moderate length (about 30 minutes); they are solemnly celebrated, well-articulated prayers, mainly of praise. The Vigil (Matins) uses the quiet time of the night for much longer psalmody and meditation on readings (60–90 minutes). On the other hand, the three daytime or 'little' Hours were very short (8–10 minutes), and since they were nearly always the same in content, they could be recited from memory even while at work. Such also were the Prime and Compline, a little longer but practically unchanging, which made it easy to fulfil their function.

This structure of the Hours is accurately recorded in the Rule of St Benedict (from the beginning of the sixth century).[6] It is certain, however, that Benedict adopted an *earlier*, already fixed, usage of Rome, and adjusted it to the life of his monks. This system lived on with some minor variations until the end of the twentieth century. The stock material of the liturgy did not require any adjustment to the changing times: the Hours were celebrated this way in late Antiquity, among the vicissitudes of the Great Migration in Europe, in the cultural environment of the Middle Ages, in the Church of the Renaissance and the Baroque era.

The Second Vatican Council envisioned only three modifications. The rite itself did not change by the Council's concession that only one Little Hour need be obligatory.[7] The structure of the Office was more influenced by the abolition of the hour of Prime.[8] Those who originally proposed it were perhaps insensible towards the sharply different nature of the two morning prayers (Lauds: the sanctification of the dawn of the cosmos; an essentially dogmatic meaning; Prime: the beginning of the personal working day, with essentially a moral aspect). Perhaps it was thought that no one ever has the time to pray two Hours of the Church in the morning. The third innovation is more radical: the Matins left its character as Vigil.[9]

These few instructions of the Constitution *Sacrosanctum Concilium* that would seem to call for a certain careful reconsideration. If the Office of Prime is omitted from the cycle of prayer of the Church, a very old (at least 1,500 years old) element of the Roman liturgy vanishes without a trace, and – as will be argued later the traditional order of the distribution of the psalms is at the same

---

[5] '. . . septenarius sacratus numerus a nobis sic implebitur, si Matutini (= Laudum), Primae, Tertiae, Sextae, Nonae, Vesperae, Completoriique tempore nostrae servitutis officia persolvamus, quia de his Horis diurnis dixit Propheta: Septies in die laudem dixi tibi. Nam de nocturnis Vigiliis idem ipse Propheta ait: Media nocete surgebam ad confitendum tibi'.

[6] St Benedict (1980), *The Rule of St. Benedict*, chapter 16, p. 210, chapters 18–19, pp. 212–16.

[7] Vatican Council II, Dogmatic Constitution on the Sacred Liturgy, *Sacrosanctum Concilium* (1963), §§89/e: 'In choro, Horae minores Tertia, Sexta, Nona serventur. Extra chorum e tribus unam seligere licet, diei tempori magis congruentem.'

[8] *Sacrosanctum Concilium* (1963), §89/d: 'Hora Prima supprimatur.'

[9] *Sacrosanctum Concilium* (1963), §89/c: 'Hora quae Matutinum vocatur, quamvis in choro indolem nocturnae laudis retineat, ita accommodetur ut qualibet diei hora recitari possit, et e psalmis paucioribus lectionibusque longioribus constet.'

time upset.[10] I think that Prime could be restored, if not as obligatory then as an Hour that can regularly be prayed – 'as custom sees fit' – at least on Sundays (Psalm 117) and on Mondays as an invocation of heavenly blessings for the working week.

The essential changes in the number and structure of the Hours are not productions of the Council, but of the *Consilium* headed by Archbishop Bugnini. Practically, the system of the Little Hours as a series of stations punctuating the working day ceased to exist. The Council changed only the obligation but the *Consilium* contracted the three Hours into a single middle hour, *hora media*. Although psalms were given also for observing the two suppressed Hours, the overemphasis on the midday hour has led practically to their disappearance. The vigil-character of Matins has been lost along with its spiritual content; it was replaced by the Office of Readings, which may be read at any time during the day.

The change in the structure of the Hours is more significant. Earlier the arrangement and length of the Hours mirrored their origin and function in daily life. The Hours in the reformed *Liturgy of the Hours* were revised and are of nearly equal length: three psalms or psalm-divisions are provided for each (with only one, or by exception two, for Compline). The opening of the long Vigil-Office, the Invitatory Psalm (94) was separated from this Hour (its function having clearly been misunderstood). The dramaturgy, artistic constitution and psychological dynamism of Lauds and Vespers have been crippled by transposing the Hymn – without any acceptable reason – to the beginning of the Hours, and so the solemn Hours are almost indistinguishable in the structure to the Little Hours.[11] The Chapter is replaced in all Hours by a 'brief reading' of a quite different genre.[12] The structure of the Little Hours was adapted inasmuch as the three psalms in the single (usually midday) hour were lengthened. The order of the short responsory in the secular course was modelled according to that to be found in the monastic Office (which is structured with short responsories in Lauds and Vespers, and no responsory in the Little Hours). This latter does not represent major damage, but it has broken with a very ancient tradition without any necessity.

What were the motives for these changes? Sometimes they were the products of mere rationalization, or a kind of mechanical standardization quite contrary to the tradition (as in the case of the transposition of the hymns, and the Invitatory); but the main goal was to shorten the Office. The change required a total reordering of the psalmody, and consequently, the transformation of the Antiphonary.

This could be avoided if another principle had been adopted. Accordingly, the Roman Office would remain untouched in its fullness (only with few, quite

---

[10] Commenting on this, John P. Parsons (2003), 'A Reform of the Reform?', pp. 248–49, writes: 'It is false to assert that a Catholic is logically bound to agree with the prudential judgments a council may make on any subject . . . Is it *de fide* that God wanted the Hour of Prime suppressed from January 1964?'

[11] Cf. Dobszay (2003), *The Bugnini-Liturgy and the Reform of the Reform*, pp. 14–19.

[12] The *Chapter* was called, in fact, *lectio brevis* in the Rule of St Benedict, but was recited solemnly by the celebrant and not a lector.

reasonable changes). Specific rules for those bound to say the Office could, however, be introduced that establish which parts of the whole are obligatory for them. The rite defines the possible choices; the portion to be actually accomplished should be prescribed in the customaries (for communities obliged to the Office) or decided according to the specified choices (by those not obliged).

The restored structure of the Office might well have been as follows:

Vigils/Matins

Invitatory, and hymn (according to use)[13]

On Sundays and feast days: three Nocturns each with three psalms and three readings

On weekdays: one Nocturn with twelve/six/three psalms* and three readings

On Sundays and feast days: *Te Deum*

Conclusion (Collect and the versicle *Benedicamus*)

*NB. The number of psalms is regulated by the number three, but the multiplier of the number changes (following custom or choice) according to the life conditions of the individuals or communities. Communities of the contemplative life preserve the traditional number of twelve; in general custom six is advised; in folk Vigils and in communities in extraordinary circumstances the number of psalms can be three.

NB. According to local arrangement (according to choice) a Vigil should also be celebrated on eight to ten feasts of the year in parish churches. For some of those obliged to the Office a dispensation could be offered from having to pray Matins every day (three to four days in the week – meaning Sundays, feasts and one or two weekdays).

Lauds:

Introduction (*versiculus sacerdotalis*,[14] *Deus in adjutorium*)

Five psalms

Chapter

Hymn and versicle

Benedictus

(*Preces*), Collect, any commemoration, conclusion

---

[13] Originally this Hour had no hymn at all. St Benedict introduced a hymn in the monastic Vigils, but in most dioceses it was not accepted, clearly because the Invitatory was considered of sufficient importance alone for starting the Hour. Cf. László Dobszay (2004), 'The Liturgical Position of the Hymn in the Medieval Office', pp. 9–22.

[14] Lauds was introduced in many medieval Uses by a guiding verse, intoned by the celebrant (*versiculus sacerdotalis*); for example, on Sunday: 'v. Haec est dies quam fecit Dominus. r. Exsultemus et laetemur in ea [This is the day which the Lord hath made. Let us rejoice and be glad in it].'

The number of psalms could be reduced in reasonable cases (according to custom or choice) to three.

Prime:

Introduction

Hymn

Four short psalm divisions

Chapter, short responsory, versicle

Closing prayer

Prime need not be obligatory except on Sundays and on one weekday (as ordered by custom).

The 'Officium Capituli' (recitation of the Martyrology, distribution and blessing of chores, reading from the Rule of the community, reading from the Necrology) could be attached to the Prime (or Lauds if Prime is not said) *ad libitum*; its single parts can be fulfilled or omitted according to local use.

Tierce, Sext, None:

Introduction

Hymn

Three short, unchanged psalms/divisions

Chapter, short responsory, versicle, closing prayer

It is laudable to keep all three Hours but according to the Constitution *Sacrosanctum Concilium* only one of them is obligatory.[15]

In private use during the week all parts after the psalms may be replaced simply by a *Pater Noster*.

Vespers:

(Before, *ad libitum*: a short lucernarium)

Introduction

Five psalms

Chapter

(*On Sundays, feastdays, extraordinary celebrations ad libitum*: short responsory or 'responsorium prolixum')[16]

---

[15] *Sacrosanctum Concilium* (1963), §89/e.

[16] A good example is given in the Appendix of the *Antiphonale Monasticum*: 'Relinquitur arbitrio cujuscumque Congregationis, in Vesperis I Festorum solemnium, juxta morem antiquum, recitare seu canere in Choro post Capitulum, loco R. brevis Responsoria prolixa consueta et approbata [It is left to the decision of the individual congregations – according to an ancient custom – to

Hymn and versicle

Magnificat

(*Preces*), Collect, commemorations, (blessing), conclusion

(Marian antiphon)

The number of psalms can be reduced (according to custom or choice) to three.

Compline:

Introductory parts (short reading, *Confiteor*, versicles *Converte* and *Deus in adjutorium*)

Three or four psalms/divisions

Hymn

Chapter (and short responsory)

Versicle

Nunc dimittis

Closing prayer and blessing

For the psalms see the next subdivision of this chapter.

An old custom in this hour is to sing the hymn immediately after the psalms; but the hymn and Chapter can be exchanged according to custom.

In earlier times whether the short responsory was added to the Chapter depended on local Use. (In some places this was limited to the Lenten season.) This item can be regulated also in our time by the *Use* or according to custom.

General remarks:
In the Folk Office and in the private Offices of lay people, the psalms of an Hour can be replaced by other ones taken from another day.

Instead of the Chapters given in the Office book, other appropriate biblical passages can be used.

In principle, the Collects should be taken from the daily Mass. In addition, however, the Office book may contain other texts for general use.

These principles can be adapted to local circumstances: the basis is always, however, the full Roman Office; the common texts are used, albeit in different arrangements in accordance with a (monastic or religious) rule, a permission or a concession.

recite or sing on the first Vespers of a solemn feast (after the Chapter) a long responsory instead of a short one].'

II. *The Distribution of the Psalms*

The quality of the Hours greatly defines how many and which psalms are assigned to them. One of the most stable and characteristic features of the traditional Roman Office was its customary psalm distribution.

This system rested on two principles: the first was that in principle the full Psalter was covered in the cycle of the hours of one week. The second was an opportune combination of two very ancient arrangements, namely:

(a) Selected, almost invariable psalms were assigned to be repeated each day. This is the heritage of the cathedrals and parish churches of Christian Antiquity. This method facilitated widespread participation of the laity and fixed the proper character of every single Hour. To the first, third and fifth place in the psalmody of *Lauds* invariable psalms were assigned from very ancient times: Psalm 50 (or on Sundays and feast days Psalm 92 instead); Psalm 62, that is, the psalm of the morning (with 66 attached to it as a single entity); and finally Psalms 148 + 149 + 150 again as a single unit, in an arrangement dating all the way back to the Old Testament.[17] Seven psalms were selected for the second place of the psalmody; these spoke of the morning, the advancing light, and the reception of God's blessings. These were distributed among the single days of the week (starting from Sunday: Psalms 99, 5, 42, 64, 89, 142, 91). In the fourth place the canticle of the three young men (*Benedicite*) was prayed on Sundays, and six other canticles on weekdays. In the *Little Hours* the longest Psalm, 118, was recited each day in 11 divisions across all four hours from Prime to None. The three psalms of *Compline* spoke about the protection of God at night (Psalms 4, 90, 133), and they were completed with a short section from Psalm 30 with the dying words of the Lord ('Into your hands, O Lord, I commend my spirit').

(b) Adopted from an old monastic tradition, all the other psalms were read in the numerical order of the Psalter, which is to say, in the order given by God in Holy Scripture. This is known as the *psalmodia currens*. At Vigils they proceeded from Psalm 1 to 108 (omitting those psalms used elsewhere in the Offices other than at Vigils and Vespers); in Vespers from Psalm 109 to 147 (again, skipping those found elsewhere).

The Roman Office forged one consistent system out of the two-fold tradition. The daily Hours had great stability; the evening and night Hours were dedicated to the deeper meditation on the psalms (*Nocte surgentes vigilemus omnes semper in psalmis meditemur . . .*).[18]

This system remained untouched with slight modifications until the beginning of the twentieth century. St Benedict made minor changes in order to adjust the system to the daily schedule of his monks. The Benedictine arrangement

---

[17] Robert F. Taft, SJ (1986), *The Liturgy of the Hours in East and West*, pp. 79, 83, 89, 97, 118, 129, 133, *et passim*. Alcuin Reid (2005), *The Organic Development of the Liturgy*, pp. 77–78.
[18] Hymn in the Sunday Vigils. G. M. Dreves and C. Blume (1909), vol. 2, p. 396.

warrants closer examination on one particular point, the transformation of the Little Hours. In Psalm 118, instead of the 11 longer (16-verse) divisions of the secular Office, he introduced 22 smaller (8-verse) divisions (following the order of the Hebrew alphabet). Four small divisions were placed in Prime, the rest (18 divisions) was distributed for two days (2 × 3 × 3 makes 18). From Tuesday to Saturday, however, the nine 'gradual' psalms were assigned to the three Little Hours (Psalms 119–21, 122–4, 125–7). The psalm expressing the submission of our lives to God's law (118) was used for two days; in the remaining five days of the week the very short gradual psalms were prayed, which reveal nine different aspects of Christian life and are very fitting to the Little Hours.

After 1,500 years of uninterrupted history, the psalm-system of the Roman Church was seen as burdensome. The clergy, immersed in manifold duties (often secular ones), were troubled by this large quantity of prayer, and sought a reduction in its daily weight. At the beginning of the twentieth century a committee was set up, and it worked out the desired reduction. It became clear that, for the result desired, the two chief principles (full Psalter each week and combination of stable psalms and *psalmodia currens*) could no longer be maintained together. The committee decided to retain the first and to drop the second principle. The Breviary issued in 1911 under the name of St Pius X put an end to the tradition of invariable psalms in the Office. About half of the *psalmodia currens* was transposed from Matins to the Little Hours. Longer psalms were split into shorter divisions. One of the main elements of the Roman Office, namely the set of selected psalms which, as it were, controlled the daily course and had been prayed from very ancient times, lost its function. But the other element, the *psalmodia currens* was also effectively terminated, since the transposed psalms broke the effect of continuity in the progress through the Psalter.

Not even this reduction was adequate for the clergy, however, and they pressed the Second Vatican Council for further abbreviations. As a result, the second principle, that is, the weekly full Psalter, was also abandoned. The guideline given by Liturgical Constitution *Sacrosanctum Concilium* was (without specifying the method of implementation) that the psalms be distributed in a way that the priests cover the entire Psalter in a period longer than a week.[19]

The committee in charge effected a radical transformation. They not only reduced the psalm-portions assigned to the days of the week, but also rearranged the Psalter making the psalmody of equal length in each Hour. Every Hour was apportioned three psalms, or more correctly, three psalm-divisions. The full Psalter was to be covered over a period of four weeks (with the omission of some psalms altogether). A few psalms occur twice in the new distribution, in one function on a given week, and in another in the next. The point of division (at Psalms 108/109) disappeared: the psalms found their place in the daily four + one (the hour of Compline) Hours of the four weeks (4 × 7 × 4 = 112 Hours in total) without any obvious reason, jumping back and forth within the Psalter. For

---

[19] *Sacrosanctum Concilium* (1963), §91.

example, the psalms to be prayed in the Lauds of the second week are (without the canticle in the second place):

Sunday:	117,	150,
Monday:	41,	18a,
Tuesday:	42,	64,
Wednesday:	76,	96,
Thursday:	79,	80,
Friday:	50,	147,
Saturday:	91,	8.

By this arrangement the order of the psalmody of the classical Roman Rite totally disappeared. The traditional Office and the Liturgy of the Hours cannot be called two forms of the same rite: the two have so very little in common.

But could it have been done otherwise? Could the Roman Office be saved in a way that a multitude of people living very different lives is also taken into consideration under the one system of the Office? Was it necessary to respond to the request for reduction by reducing the Office to the lowest possible denominator for all?

I think it could be – or, in the hope of a better future, will be – possible to find a solution. *The Roman Office must be restored in its original integrity, making only a few, genuinely necessary modifications. On the other hand, the opportunity has to be provided for people and communities in different circumstances to use it differently.*

The Church needs some communities of priests and monks who keep the complete Roman Office in practice and in living memory. Regulated options and abbreviations could, however, be offered to others who may pray the full Psalter over a longer time (two or more weeks) in accordance with the provision of the Council. This several-week system could be adopted, first of all, in the *psalmodia currens*. (True, the distribution over more than one week is a novelty in the Roman Rite, but this is actually the arrangement, for instance, in the Ambrosian Rite, where the daily psalms are the same each week, while the *psalmodia currens* is completed at Matins over a two-week period.[20])

Options for abbreviation could also be given in the other Hours, with care taken to ensure that each psalm is read in the course of a longer period. In the case of those obliged to the Office, the legitimate superior could settle the details of implementation (by laying down what is customary). Those who are not obliged to the Office would receive full freedom of the various options, while remaining within the general framework of the Roman Office.

However individual believers or communities undertake the Office, the Roman tradition must be able in some sense to stand before their eyes in its fullness. They should all be aware that even if they themselves can only fulfil the lesser, this lesser is actually a part of something greater, something full, and whatever is missing, '*Ecclesia supplet*', is supplied on their behalf by the Church, elsewhere.

---

[20] Terence Bailey (1994), *Antiphon and Psalm in the Ambrosian Office*, pp. 158–66.

In this sense the following 'proposal' is arranged according to three schemes:

(A) *Greater Form (Forma plenior)*: The original form of the Roman Office, celebrated by specified communities.
(B) *Common Form (Forma Communis)*: A form, followed by most of those who are obliged to the Office, which retains the essential arrangement of the order of psalmody with some concessions.
(C) *Briefer Form (Forma breviour)*: An abbreviated form with three psalms following the model of the Liturgy of the Hours. With due permission of the superiors this can be adopted by some of those who are obliged to the Office (according to custom), and regularly by those who are not obliged (parish churches, secular communities, individual believers: according to choice).

The books (except the books of the Folk Office) should be edited so that the *Greater Form* appears as a point of reference. Rubrics and typography could assist in exhibiting the possibilities for adaptation.

Here is the 'proposal' according to the three different forms (A–B–C):

Lauds
(A)
1. Psalm 50 or (on Sundays, feast days, Eastertide): 92
2. The daily psalm (from Sunday to Saturday): 99, 5, 42, 64, 89, 142, 91
3. Psalms 62 + 66 linked
4. The daily canticle (from Sunday to Saturday): *Benedicite, Confitebor, Ego dixi, Exsultavit, Cantemus, Domine audivi, Audite caeli*
5. The Psalms of Praise ('Laudes' in the strict sense): 148 + 149 + 150.

(B)
1. Psalm 50/92
2. Daily psalm
3. Psalms 62 and 66 in daily alternation
4. Daily canticle
5. 'Laudes': On Sundays: 148 + 149 + 150; on weekdays: one of them alternatively.

(C)
One of the psalms given in points 1–2–3 can be chosen, with an admonition of care to pray each of them eventually.

On Lenten Sundays: Psalm 50 in the first place and Psalm 117 in the second.
In Forms (B) and (C) on Saturday – because of the length of the canticle – Psalm 50 and Psalms 62/66 are omitted, and the canticle is divided in three.

Prime:
(A)

1. Initial psalm (From Sunday to Friday; on Saturday none): 53, 23, 24, 25, 22, 21
2. Psalm 117 (only on Sundays)
3. Psalm 118, larger divisions i–ii.

(B)
Sunday: Psalm 117 divided in four

Monday (and *ad libitum* on other weekdays): Psalm 118, smaller divisions i–v (4 × 8 verses).

(C)
Sunday: Psalm 117 divided in four

Weekdays: Psalm 118, *one* of the smaller divisions i–iv.

Tierce, Sext, None:
(A)
Psalm 118, three larger divisions in each Hour.

(B)
Sunday and Saturday: Psalm 118, three and three smaller divisions in each Hour

Weekdays: 119–21 / 122–4 / 125–7 (the system of St Benedict).

(C)
Three smaller divisions from Psalm 118, *or:*
119–21 / 122–4 / 125–7.

If Psalm 118 is prayed regularly in the Little Hours, the gradual psalms (119–27) should be put back into Vespers.

Compline:
(A)
Psalms 4; 30.1-6; 90; 133.

(B)
In alternation: Psalms 4; 30.1-6; 133/90.

(C)
Psalm 90.

This way the full tradition of the Roman Office is preserved; every psalm remains in its original place. Yet in form (B) Lauds is 20–30 verses shorter, the psalm portions of the Little Hours are reduced to half of the original; in form (C) Lauds is about one-third of the original size.

All the rest of the Psalter is arranged according to the Roman principle in the Vigils (Matins) and Vespers, proceeding according to the system of *psalmodia currens*. Psalms 1–108 are prayed at Matins, Psalms 109–47 at Vespers.

Vigils (Matins):
(A)
Sunday: 4 + 4 + 4 + 3 + 3 = 18 psalms

Feasts: 3 × 3 psalms

Weekdays: 12 psalms

(B)
Sunday: 3 × 3 psalms (1, 2, 3 / 8, 10, 18 / 19, 20, 23)

Feasts: 3 × 3 psalms

Weekdays: 12 or 6 or 3 (shorter) psalms/psalm divisions

(C)
6 or 3 psalms

The longer psalms are divided; the psalms and psalm divisions (marked in the note with /) are gathered in groups of three (48 × 3 psalms/divisions).[21] The community (according to custom) or the individual person (according to choice) may take four or two or one group ('ternio') each day; accordingly, they recite the whole Psalter in two weeks (the 'Ambrosian' system of Milan), or four weeks (as in the *Liturgia Horarum*), or in exceptional cases eight weeks (abbreviated system). Lay communities and parish churches (C-form) may freely choose any of the 'ternios' (one or two groups: three or six psalms).

Vespers:
(A)
Psalms 109–47 (five psalms per day). The daily portions are:

Sunday: 109–13;
Monday: 114–16, 119–20;

---

[21] These are:

1. 6, 7/1–2	13. 33/1, 2, 3	25. 59, 60, 61	37. 83, 84, 85
2. 9/1–3; 14	14 34/1, 2; 35	26. 63, 65/1, 2	38. 86, 87/1, 2
3. 11, 12, 13	15. 36/1, 2, 3	27. 67/1, 2, 3	39. 88/1, 2, 3
4. 14, 15, 16	16. 37/1, 2; 38	28. 68/1, 2, 3	40. 93, 95, 96
5. 17/1, 2, 3	17. 39/1, 2; 40	29. 69, 70/1, 2	41. 97, 98, 100
6. 17/4, 5, 6	18. 41, 43/1, 2	30. 71, 72/1, 2	42. 101/1, 2, 3
7. 21/1, 2, 3	19. 44/1, 2; 45	31. 73/1, 2; 74	43. 103/1, 2, 3
8. 22, 24/1, 2	20. 46, 47, 48	32. 75, 76/1, 2	44. 104/1, 2, 3
9. 25, 26/1,2	21. 49/1, 2, 3	33. 77/1, 2, 3	45. 105/1, 2, 3
10. 27, 28, 29	22. 51, 52, 53	34. 77/4, 5, 6	46. 106/1, 2, 3
11. 30/1, 2, 3	23. 54/1, 2; 55	35. 78, 79/1, 2	47. 102/1, 2; 107
12. 31, 32/1, 2	24. 56, 57, 58	36. 80, 81, 82	48. 108/1, 2, 3

Tuesday: 121–5;
Wednesday: 126–30;
Thursday: 131–2, 134–6;
Friday: 137–41;
Saturday: 143–7

(B)
The nine gradual psalms are transferred to the Little Hours; the longer psalms are divided:

Sunday: 109–12 + 113.1-8;
Monday: 113/second and third divisions, 114–16;
Tuesday: 128–32;
Wednesday: 134 divided in two and 135 divided in three;
Thursday: 136–7 and 138 divided in three;
Friday: 139–41 and 143 divided in two;
Saturday: 144 divided in two and 145–7

(C)
The system of *psalmodia currens* is preserved, but the whole series is distributed to two (not full) weeks:

Week A–B
Sunday: 109–11
Monday: 112 and 113 divided in two;

Week A:
Tuesday: 114–16;
Wednesday: 128–30;
Thursday: 131, 132, 134;
Friday: 135 divided in two and 136;

Week B:
Tuesday: 137 and 138 divided in two;
Wednesday: 139 divided in two, and 140;
Thursday: 141 and 143 divided in two;
Friday: 144 divided in three;

Week A–B:
Saturday: 145–7

In form (C) the original psalms of Sunday Vespers are prayed each week distributed across Sunday and Monday. In addition, the three principal psalms of Saturday are kept each week on the same day. The other psalms are read in a two-week rotation; 114–136 on week A and Psalms 137–144 on week B.

In sum: the daily Hours roughly preserve their specific, invariable psalmody; the quiet flow of the *psalmodia currens* remained at Matins and Vespers. Communities and private individuals can use the Roman arrangement according to their mode of life, that is, the tradition and demands on time are able to be harmonized.

III. The Antiphonarium

First, we need to summarize the historical background for the current state of the antiphonary. When the Roman Office emerged in the fourth and fifth centuries, the repertory of the antiphons and responsories was probably very limited, the melodies were kept in a closed musical style, and the different texts were mostly adapted to a few model-melodies. The antiphons of the weekly Psalter, of some solemnities (Christmas, Epiphany, Ascension), a small Common of Saints (feasts of apostles, martyrs, virgins, with a single formula for each) and a few proper antiphons for individual saints, were enough to sustain the whole year. (In Eastertide the melodies of Ordinary Time were sung, with the word 'alleluia' instead of the usual texts.) In my estimation the whole cursus was no more than about 400 items performed on only 10–15 melodies.[22] During the major part of the year the responsories took their text from the Psalter (*Responsoria de Psalmista*);[23] if the responsories of solemnities and the Common of Saints are added to it, the result is about 150–200; in their musical form they are also adaptations to between eight and ten melodies. In an age of oral transmission this might be a very realistic way of singing the full Office over the continuous sequence of the year.

The material grew in the following two or three centuries: partly with new texts adapted to the same models, partly by developing new models but always remaining in the same style. The Office or Office-sections (e.g. Lauds) for Advent, Lent, and the feasts of some further saints belong to this period and stratum of development. The continuous use of this repertory already required regular instruction, learning and regular recital.[24]

This is all the more true for the great and rapid accretion of the ninth to eleventh centuries.[25] Not only did the quantity of new material cause difficulties (new antiphons, responsories added to existing feasts, a more varied elaboration

---

[22] A rough estimation: *Psalter*: Sunday Vigils and Vespers: 14; Monday–Saturday Vigils, Lauds and Vespers: 17 for each = 102. *Christmas* Vigils and Vespers: 18. *Epiphany* Vigils: 9. *Triduum Sacrum* Vigils: 9 for each + a common Vespers = 32. *Ascension* Vigils: 9. *Commune apostolorum, martyrum, virginum*: Vigils and Vespers: 14 for each = 42. Proper of Saints (Agnes, John the Baptist, Laurence, etc.) Vigils: 9 per each and some with only 5 Lauds-antiphons = approximately 80. All together: 316 that could be completed with about 80 single antiphons for some liturgical days. For the model melodies see the following categories in *Monumenta Monodica Medii Aevi*, vol. V: 1/A–D, 2/A, 3/A, 4/A–B, 5A (?), 6A, 7/A–B, 8/A–C (D?). Cf. Edward Charles Nowacki (1980), *Studies on the Office Antiphons of the Old Roman Manuscripts*; David Hiley (1993), *Western Plainchant – A Handbook*, pp. 91–2; László Dobszay (2009b), 'Short Remarks about the Antiphons of Christmas Vespers'.

[23] R. Le Roux (1963), 'Les Répons de Psalmis pour les Matines, de l'Épiphanie à la Septuagésime'; László Dobszay (2002b), *Responsoria de Psalmista*.

[24] The number of antiphons in the most archaic Gregorian antiphonary (Albi 44, ninth century) is 1152; of the responsories is 627 (there are some short lacunae in the manuscript). See John A. Emerson (2002), *Albi, Bibliothèque Municipale Rochegude, Manuscript 44*, pp. 344–67.

[25] The late tenth- (or early eleventh-) century Hartker Antiphonary (Paléographie Musical,

of Ordinary Time and not least the multiplication of the saints' feasts), but the tunes also became more and more individual, and stylistically divergent. Learning longer tunes one by one necessitated regular training over several hours of a day. Thus the medieval repertory was created, comprised of 2,000–3,000 antiphons and about 1,000 melismatic responsories. New pieces were added to this repertory right up until the end of the Middle Ages, mainly material in honour of the new saints, in the 'modern' musical style of the period.

It is paradoxical that while the accumulating repertory required the presence of many well-trained singers, the requisite institutional background began to waste away from the time of the late Middle Ages. After the sixteenth century the antiphonary (or rather only some Hours of it) were sung only in some monasteries and cathedrals. This decline weakened the knowledge of the chant, which eventually led to further reductions. The texts of the antiphonary came to be merely read or recited in most churches. The period between the sixteenth and twentieth centuries witnessed the death of a great liturgical and musical culture.

Did the Second Vatican Council have a proposal to turn this process around? The Constitution spoke (without any effect) in generalities on the setting up of musical institutes and choirs,[26] but did not go into the depth of the problem; nor did the *Concilium*. Instead, the revisers of the liturgical books came to a most mournful conclusion: they published an office book without music. But no melodies *could* in fact be provided in the new books, since the changes in structure and arrangement of the Office made it difficult or even impossible to use the old treasury. The majority of antiphons and responsories published in the Liturgy of the Hours have no proper melody at all.

No effort was exerted to rebuild either the culture of chanting or its institutional background. Nowadays the Office is almost entirely prayed in prose. Wherever it is sung, people are forced to accommodate themselves to painful experimentation: in some monasteries new melodies were composed (with disastrous barbarisms) or old antiphons and texts are substituted for the new ones. The result is that the Liturgy of the Hours and the chant lists or choir books are in disharmony and disarray.[27] In an age when some people make exaggerated attempts to reconstruct the 'authentic' sound in performing Gregorian chant, nobody seems to care that the primary authenticity of the tunes, their liturgical context, has been allowed to perish.

Is it possible to restore, at least partially, the culture of the *sung* Office? I think the solution is identical to what I have already suggested in this book repeatedly: a return to the integrity of the classical Roman Rite, while making *its use* more flexible.

What does the 'Roman Rite' mean in this context? It means neither the sum total of the antiphons and responsories included in the Liturgy of the Hours nor

Deuxième Série I, *Antiphonaire de Hartker, Manuscrits de Saint-Gall 390–391*) contains more than 2000 antiphons and 800 responsories.

[26] *Sacrosanctum Concilium* (1963), §§113, 114.

[27] The antiphons in a new antiphonary (*Liber Antiphonarius pro diurnis horis*, 2 vols (Solesmis, 2005–06) differ in important ways from those presented in the *Liturgia Horarum*.

of the Breviary of St Pius X; nor the repertory of the Tridentine Rite, nor even the medieval Uses. Instead, first and foremost it means *the stock material of the Antiphonarium*. In the most ancient times people could manage with a limited repertory for the entire year; similarly in our day a repertory could be recommended that would be suitable in terms of quantity and composition for regular use in most communities. This would be possible if greater place were given in this stock material to the pieces modelled on the old style, which would be easier to learn and deploy in daily practice.

This does not mean that the inherited great repertory would be curtailed; it could even be enriched by a number of forgotten pieces, sung at one time in local Uses. If a defined minimal core is given as a common base of diverse usages, this core could then be augmented just as the inherited stock material was augmented after the eighth century.

My proposal here is made in two parts; one concerns the composition of the antiphonary, the other its use. I will start the discussion, however, with the second.

Let us suppose we have an average size collection (with 600–800 antiphons and 300–400 responsories) that contains mostly older, relatively simple model melodies. A congregation of average capacity, if it were praying the Office regularly, could make use of this repertory without difficulties. What would they need to do, if this repertory exceeded their capacity? (For instance, in a house of only a few monks lacking musically trained members; or a praying community of lay people; or a small congregation in a parish church; or a community of priests without musical preparation.) Here I describe various methods:

By Cantors. The antiphons can be sung, instead of by the full congregation, by one or more cantors. This would represent the recovery of an old Roman practice, where the cantor sings the major part of the piece, and the assembly joins in at the last phrase (which, in most cases, is easier after the tonality has been established).[28]

With one single antiphon over all psalms. The number of antiphons that needs to be learned can be reduced if one single antiphon is set over all the psalms of an Hour, repeated once at the end of each psalm, which was a regular custom during the Middle Ages (called *antiphona sola super psalmos*).

Through the week. One of the antiphons is selected, and sung over the whole week in the same position (e.g. to the Magnificat).

For an entire season. One antiphon is assigned for the psalms and another to the canticle of a given Hour for the whole liturgical season (say, for Advent) or for a certain period of it (say, for a two-week period in Lent), and does not change. This method is recommended, for example, in parish communities.

Ferially. The Office, or a part of it, is sung with the ordinary antiphons;[29] the proper texts of the liturgical day appear only in the recited items (the

---

[28] Cf. Edward Charles Nowacki (1990), 'The Performance of Office Antiphons in Twelfth-century Rome'.
[29] In the oldest manuscript this is typical in the great part of year, Advent, Lent, etc. included.

Chapter or Readings) and in the hymn and one antiphon (to the Benedictus or Magnificat).

From the Common or Proper if required. The feast of a saint is sung with antiphons taken from the frequently used Common Office, and only a few antiphons need come from the Proper (in addition to the reading, Collect, perhaps the hymn). We have many examples of this system in the past practice of the Church.

Would it not be a loss to omit the proper items or the antiphons, responsories of a given day or week? There is no need to put them aside; they can be saved by the reintroduction of an older method:

A 'Verse before Repetition' – 'Versus ad repetendum'. In some communities the antiphons and responsories are nowadays simply recited in psalm tones. This way the musical contrast between the antiphon and the psalm is lost. But if one antiphon is set above the whole series of psalms (as suggested above), and the omitted text is recited as a *'versus ad repetendum'* at the end of the given psalm (before the return of the single antiphon) both the proper text and the musical contrast would be saved.[30] (This method was used in the medieval Office of St Paul and St Laurence.)

The substitution of the Common Office for the Proper texts can also be adapted in the case of responsories. Another possibility is to recite its text in the form of a short responsory. In such a case a part of the responsory should be transposed to the verse. This device saves the nature of the genre better than if it is simply recited in a psalm tone or *recto tono* (although as a last resort, even this could be acceptable).[31]

Another method could be adopted from the edition of the oldest Gregorian manuscripts. In the Old Roman Antiphonary and the ninth- and tenth-century choir books, the chants at the 'strong' positions of the liturgy are fixed precisely, but the rest is given in lists of set texts, leaving it up to superiors (and the consuetudinaries or customaries) to determine the exact place of the single items. Which are the 'strong' positions? Examination of the manuscripts reveals that these are the antiphons for the psalms of Lauds, which in most cases are repeated at Second Vespers. The Benedictus and Magnificat antiphons are frequently replaced by

---

[30] One example for the Lauds of martyrs: Antiphona sola super psalmos: Qui mihi ministrat, me sequatur, et ubi ego sum, illic sit et minister meus. Psalmus 92. Doxologia. Versus (in tono psalmi): Qui me confessus fuerit coram hominibus * confitebor et ego eum coram Patre meo. Antiphona: Qui mihi . . . – Psalmus 99. Doxologia. Versus: Qui sequitur me, non ambulabat in tenebris * sed habebit lumen vitae, dicit Dominus. Antiphona: Qui mihi . . . – Psalmus 62. Doxologia. Versus: Si quis mihi ministraverit + honorificabit eum Pater meus * qui est in caelis, dicit Dominus. Antiphona: Qui mihi . . . – Canticum. Doxologia. Antiphona: Qui mihi ministrat . . . – Psalmus 148–150. Doxologia. Versus: Volo Pater, ut ubi ego sum * illic sit et minister meus. Antiphona: Qui mihi ministrat.

[31] Again an example from the Office of Martyrs: The original text of the responsory is as follows: R) Justum deduxit Dominus per vias rectas, et ostendit illi regnum Dei, et dedit illi scientiam sanctorum: * Honestavit illum in laboribus, et complevit labores illius. V) Immortalis est enim memoria illius, quoniam apud Deum nota est, et apud homines. * Honestavit. – Distribution for performing as a responsorium breve: Justum deduxit Dominus per vias rectas, * et ostendit illi regnum Dei. V/1. Et dedit illi scientiam sanctorum, + honestavit illum in laboribus, * et complevit labores illius. * ET OSTENDIT . . . V/2. Immortalis est enim memoria illius + quoniam apud Deum nota est * et apud homines. * ET OSTENDIT . . . R) Justum deduxit Dominus . . .

other items; the antiphons for Matins are fixed on great solemnities, but chosen according to local use on other days, sometimes they are taken over from other parts of the daily or weekly cursus. See the note below for an example from the ninth-century antiphonary of Albi.[32]

It would therefore be quite consistent with the practices of the classical Roman Rite to present the antiphonary in a comprehensive distribution which – within strict limitations – can be adapted to specific liturgical situations. Individual items could more or less simply be selected out of 'set-lists' (and, if necessary, repeated during the week), following a specific local Use or custom.

So far I have spoken mainly about possible concessions that can be made in fulfilling and completing the Offices. Where liturgical life is intensive and when good singers are available, instead of a more reduced celebration, actually it is more desirable to augment the repertory. The quite noble obligation here is to keep alive a treasury accumulated across the course of long centuries. For that purpose a *Complementary Antiphonary* is required, making available an additional abundance of Propers, for example, additional Propers for the feasts of saints. The old rubrics here gain a new meaning: 'vel historia propria per totum si habes'[33] 'or, if they are available, the full cycle of the proper of the saint' – we may add: 'et si vales', and 'whenever possible'. It would be truly praiseworthy if the main centres of ecclesiastical life, cathedral chapters, published their proper heritage in an appended volume to be called *Complementaries*; adding those pieces that – in spite of their precious texts and musical forms – fell into disuse after the Tridentine reforms. These would nurture in their users strong sentiments of piety and affection towards the more ancient aspects of their own tradition, and through it, obtain a far greater adherence to the liturgical patrimony of the Church in general.

[32] First Sunday of Advent:
Matins: Responsorium 1 Aspiciens a longe; R2: Aspiciebam in visu; R3 Missus est Gabriel; R4 Ave Maria; R5 Salvatorem exspectamus; R6 Obsecro domine; R7 Ecce virgo concipiet; R8 Audite verbum domini; R9 Laetentur. // *Lauds antiphons*: 1 In illa die; 2 Jucundare filia; 3 Ecce dominus noster veniet; 4 Omnes sitientes; 5 Ecce veniet propheta // *Antiphons*: 1 Spiritus sanctus in te; 2 Ne timeas Maria invenisti // *Versicles* 1 Egredietur virga; 2 Emitte agnum; 3 Ex Sion species; 4 Vox clamantis // *Short Responsories and Versicles* to the Little Hours: R) Veni ad liberandum; V) Timebunt gentes; R) Ostende nobis; V) Memento nostri; R) Super te Jerusalem; Domine deus virtutum.
Responsory at second Vespers: Tu exsurgens Domine.
Versicle: Rorate caeli desuper.
Antiphons: 1 Missus est Gabriel; 2 Super te Jerusalem; 3 Jerusalem respice; 4 Gaude et laetare filia; 5 Ecce rex venit; 6 Vox clamantis; 7 Ego vox clamantis; 8 Omnis vallis; 9 De Sion exibit; 10 Ecce mitto angelum; 11 Exspectabo dominum; 12 Sion renovaberis; 13 Ecce veniet deus et homo; 14 Ex Aegypto vocavit.
Second Sunday of Advent: Matins: Responsory 1 Jerusalem cito, etc.
[33] See, for example, in the Ordinary Book of the Eger (Hungary) cathedral (Dobszay 2000: Nrs 433, 446, 465, 478, 491, 492, 499, 506, etc.). 'Historia' in the old terminology means the full cycle of the proper pieces of an Office (e.g. Historia Sancti Augustini) or a thematic unit (e.g. Historia de Sapientia, that is all responsories taken from the Books of Wisdom).

IV. Other Parts of the Office

The fundamental elements of the classical Roman Office are disclosed through the structure of the Hours, the principles of the distribution of the Psalmody, and the stock material of the Antiphonary. Other collections also have their own place in this system, even if their content could be considered as less stable components of the rite, mainly because they lived in local variants. Let us consider these.

The Hymnal

The Office of the Roman basilicas did not know or use hymns for a long time.[34] The hymn became a part of the Office through the Rule of St Benedict, and it remained a feature peculiar to the Benedictines for an extended period of time (at least within the Roman Rite). The place of the hymn in the Hours is fixed by St Benedict;[35] this place remained the same (disregarding inessential differences) right up to the publication of the *Liturgy of the Hours*, which finally disturbed the ancient system.

St Benedict's hymnal was probably very small, consisting mostly in the poems of St Ambrose, or others that originated at the same time, in the same environment, and with similar style. With the addition of a few new Ambrosian hymns a 'collection' was put together, which is usually named the 'First Hymnarium' in scholarly literature. (Such pieces as the *Veni Redemptor gentium*, *Hic est dies verus Dei*, *En tempus acceptabile*, *Mysterium Ecclesiae*, belong to this collection, together with others)[36].

In the period between the seventh and the ninth centuries a group of new hymns written by authors originating in the monasteries and ecclesiastical centres north of the Alps nearly supplanted the first hymnal entirely, and this 'Second Hymnarium' became the 'vulgate' collection of the churches of Europe. Quite famous items like *Conditor alme siderum*, *Ave maris stella*, *Veni Creator Spiritus*, *Vexilla Regis prodeunt* belong to this stratum.

This was the time when the secular dioceses started to admit hymns into their Office, though not in every Hour. For these secular churches the 'Second Hymnarium' became the basis of their hymnal, but they added – differently according to region – more hymns, partly selected from the old collection, partly composed entirely anew. The items in the Hymnal therefore never really became 'canonical' through this process.[37] The classical Roman Rite may boast a huge poetical repertoire, but the actual hymnals were made up of proper compositions for local or specific Uses.

---

[34] The hymn is unknown even for the twelfth- to thirteenth-century Old Roman antiphonaries; see Bonifacio Giacomo Baroffio and Soo Jung Kim (1995), *Biblitoeca Apotolica Vaticana Archivio S. Pietro B 79, Antfionario della Basilica di S. Pietro (Sec. XII)*, vol. 2. Cf. Theodor Klauser (1969), *A Short History of the Western Liturgy*, p. 83.

[35] St Benedict (1980), *The Rule of St. Benedict*, chapters IX, XII, XIII, XVII.

[36] Helmut Gneuss (2004), 'Zur Geschichte des Hymnars', pp. 63–86. For the texts mentioned see Clemens Blume (1908), *Der Cursus S. Benedicti Nursini und die liturgischen Hymnen des 6.–9. Jahrhunderts*, vol. 1, pp. 10, 11; vol. 2, pp. 55, 229.

[37] Gneuss (2004), 'Zur Geschichte des Hymnars', p. 76. Janka Szendrei (2000), *A himnusz*, p. 13.

The hymn is a genre that continued to proliferate until the late Middle Ages, developing in style, and standing always at the periphery of the liturgy. After the Tridentine Council a hymnal was fixed, which was later (in the early seventeenth century) cruelly rephrased in an attempt to achieve 'better Latinity'.[38] These rephrased hymns were published in the nineteenth- and twentieth-century liturgical books and included in the *Liber Usualis*, while the monastic orders preserved the older texts of these hymns.[39]

Sacrosanctum Concilium made provision for the restitution of the old texts.[40] The *Consilium*, however, decided to 'correct' the authentic texts all over again.[41] They multiplied the number of hymns,[42] added a lot of new poems written by the president of the subcommittee dealing with the hymnal, and repositioned the hymn in three Hours (Lauds, Vespers, Compline), thus upsetting the structure, psychological dynamism, and dramaturgy of these Hours.[43] I dealt with all these questions in the first chapter of my *Bugnini-Liturgy*.[44]

What would a 'renovation of the Rite' really mean with respect to the Hymnal?

(a) The number of the hymns in the new Hymnal has grown needlessly great. The reasonable increase that took place in the Middle Ages to between 70 and 80 individual hymns need be augmented with no more than 20 or 30 additional items.[45]

(b) The authentic texts should be properly restored, eliminating from them all recent and baroque alterations. In this regard the *Antiphonale Monasticum* may well be the best point of departure, which could be compared with the *Analecta Hymnica* and other modern scholarly works.[46]

(c) As it was in the pre-Tridentine centuries, local traditions could be granted more freedom in the compilation of their hymnals, always at the same time being required to preserve the classical Roman stock material.

[38] Bäumer (1895), *Geschichte des Breviers*, pp. 507–10. Cf. Reid (2005), *The Organic Development of the Liturgy*, p. 47. Hymni, quantum expedire videtur, ad pristinam formam restituantur, iis demptis vel mutatis quae mythologiam sapient aut christianae pietati minus congruent. Recipiantur quoque, pro opportunitate, alii qui in hymnorum thesauro inveniuntur.
[39] Compare, for example, the hymn *Jesu nostra redemptio* for Ascension in *Antiphonale Monasticum . . .*, p. 506 – cf. Blume (1908), *Der Cursus S. Benedicti Nursini und die liturgischen Hymnen des 6.–9. Jahrhunderts*, vol. 2, p. 136 – and in *Liber Usualis Missae et Officii*, p. 852 (with the incipit *Salutis humanae Sator*).
[40] *Sacrosanctum Concilium* (1963), §93: 'To whatever extent may seem desirable, the hymns are to be restored to their original form, and whatever smacks of mythology or ill accords with Christian piety is to be removed or changed. Also, as occasion may arise, let other selections from the treasury of hymns be incorporated'.
[41] Nearly all of the hymns for Lent, moreover: *Ad cenam Agni providi, Hic est dies verus Dei, Christe qui lux es et dies*, etc.
[42] The number of hymns in the *Liturgia Horarum* is 354.
[43] Cf. *Liber Hymnarius*. Also Offices without a hymn from the earliest times up to now have been given a hymn (Triduum Sacrum, The Office for the Dead).
[44] Dobszay (2003), *The Bugnini-Liturgy and the Reform of the Reform*, pp. 14–19.
[45] The number of hymns in the late medieval Esztergom Office is (the young additions included) is 94.
[46] Text edition of hymns: *Analecta Hymnica medii aevi*, vols. 2, 4, 11, 12, 14, 16, 19, 22, 23, 27, 43, 48, 50–52.

(d) The 'Second Hymnarium' could be augmented from the 'First Hymnarium' with a few pieces that are of great spiritual value that really should not be allowed to sink into oblivion.[47]

(e) Most of the medieval churches sang no hymn at Matins (the length of the Invitatory meant any hymn was quite unnecessary). This practice could be returned as a possible option, for decision in the *Customaries* of local Uses.

A common stock material of hymns for the Roman Rite could be defined as follows:

- the daily hymns by St Ambrose (*Aeterne Rerum, Deus Creator omnium, Splendor paternae gloriae*)
- the hymns for Lauds, Vespers, those of the Little Hours from the Second Hymnarium, completed with the *Christe qui lux es et dies* for Compline
- Advent: *Christi caterva, Conditor alme, Verbum supernum, Vox clara*
- Christmas: *Veni Redemptor, A solis ortus, Christe Redemptor*
- Epiphany: *A Patre Unigenitus, Hostis Herodes*
- Lent: *En tempus acceptabile, Audi benigne, Iam Christe sol, Ex more docti mystico*
- Passiontide: *Vexilla Regis, Pange lingua . . . lauream*
- Easter: *Hic est dies verus Dei, Aurora lucis, Ad cenam Agni, Iesu nostra redemptio*
- Ascension: *Optatus votis omnium*
- Pentecost: *Beata nobis, Veni Creator*
- Corpus Christi: *Pange lingua . . . corporis, Sacris solemniis, Verbum supernum*
- Dedication: *Urbs beata Jerusalem*
- Common of Saints: *Exsultet caelum, Aeterna Christi munera, Martyr Dei, Deus tuorum militum, Rex gloriose martyrum, Sanctorum meritis, Iste Confessor, Virginis proles, Iesu corona virginum*
- the Blessed Virgin: *Mysterium ecclesiae, Ave maris, O gloriosa Domina*
- other Saints: *Stephano primo martyri, Amore Christi nobilis, Salvete flores martyrum, Ut queant laxis, Apostolorum passio, Aurea luce, Apostolorum supparem, Christe Redemptor omnium, Iesu salvator saeculi.*

This makes about seventy hymns altogether, comprised almost exclusively of pieces in general use in the Roman Church, completed with 12 items from the First Hymnarium.

---

[47] Such as *Christi caterva clamitet, Illuminans Altissimus En tempus acceptabile, Optatus votis omnium, Mediae noctis tempus est, Deus qui caeli lumen es, Aeterne lucis conditor* (Blume (1908), *Der Cursus S. Benedicti Nursini*, vol. 1, p. 10, vol. 2, pp. 2, 40, 55, 395, 397, 399; *Analecta hymnica*, vol. 51, Nr 87) and of course the most important hymns of Ambrose. The reason for their restitution is that the ancient hymns summarized the mysteries of the various liturgical seasons, while the newer hymns emphasize only one or other aspect of the whole content of the doctrinal complex. Additionally, the old hymns transmit far more powerfully the theology of the patristic age.

The collection could be supplemented by local churches with (a) pieces taken from their more ancient tradition; (b) those ornamenting local feasts; and (c) a dozen or so poems restored from ancient Christian poetry.

The melody and the text were not always strictly linked together in earlier times. Though it is good if the Roman Hymnal generally draws abundantly on its musical tradition, it could quite appropriately be permitted for communities of modest capabilities to sing several texts of common meter on a common tone or melody.

The Lectionary

The Rule of St Benedict reflects the customs of the first centuries: he says that the Office readings should be taken from the Bible and the writings of the 'orthodox Fathers'.[48] He leaves it to the abbot to assign the texts to be read. Some instability remained in the lectionary until the end of the Middle Ages, or – if the breviaries of the religious orders are also taken into account – even all the way up to 1970. Two principles, however, were definitively settled in the seventh and eighth centuries: (a) the readings are taken from the Bible in the First Nocturn, from the sermons of the Fathers (or from the *Life* of the saint celebrated on the given day) in the Second Nocturn, and from homilies on the Gospel for Mass in the Third Nocturn; and (b) the books of the Bible were read continuously but in selected excerpts, while their distribution over the year was carefully fixed.[49]

The *Liturgy of the Hours* reduced the number of readings to two. These are longer texts, without interruptions by responsories (which separated the sections and kept attention alive). The biblical books succeed each other with jumps, and in alternation over shorter periods. A merit that this book possesses over what it succeeded is that the selection from ecclesiastical authors is more abundant and includes many quite beautiful pieces.

I am not competent to discuss in detail the method for selecting the readings, nor, therefore, do I intend to make specific proposals for how it should be done. Some principles, however, can be laid down:

(a) The ancient threefold rhythm to the structure of the readings in each Nocturn was a good arrangement which should be brought back (three readings on weekdays, three × three readings on feasts). Formerly on weekdays all three readings were often biblical. Now that the *Liturgy of the Hours* has established a different pattern, perhaps one solution would be to restore the original structure of the biblical readings, combining the original three into two longer passages, so that the third could become a non-biblical reading, retaining many of the attractive and appropriate passages introduced into

---

[48] St. Benedict (1980), *The Rule of St. Benedict*, chapter 9.
[49] Advent: Isaiah; after Epiphany: Epistles of St Paul; from Septuagesima: Books of Moses, from Passion Sunday: Jeremiah; in Eastertide: Acts of the Apostles, Revelation and the so-called Catholic Letters; after Trinity Sunday: Book of Kings; in August: Books of Wisdom; in September: Job, Tobit, Judith, Esther; in October: Maccabees; in November: Ezekiel, Daniel and the lesser prophets.

the *cursus* from the new lectionary. This is made possible by the fact that in the *Liturgy of the Hours* the second, non-biblical, reading does not seem in any way related to the first, biblical, passage.

(b) It is reasonable to restore the Gospel-homily in the Third Nocturn, perhaps with additional or better texts than in the preconciliar breviaries.

(c) Concerning the length of the readings: it is good to keep them moderate. If a longer text is preferred, it could be distributed over two Nocturns.

(d) The order of reading the biblical books has to be restored, all the more so, since in Ordinary Time the set of responsories corresponds to the Scripture passages.[50] The continuity of the classical Roman Rite does not exclude a reform of the selection of readings, and – within specified limits – local tradition, or the local superior, may decide on an excerpt taken from a given book. Perhaps the selections need not be fixed to particular days, since a feast day may often interrupt the continuous reading of a biblical book or passage from the Fathers. If a simple list of readings (in a *Companion*) were given for each biblical book, people could take up again the course of the readings in continuity on the day after breaking off for celebration of a feast.

Chapters and Collects

The Chapter (*Capitulum*) is not a short reading (*Lectio brevis*) but a singular sentence of admonition from the Bible, to be recited or sung by the celebrant. In the solemn Office its position is stressed also by symbolic actions and forms (the presence of lights and their bearers either side of the book, and, on more solemn occasions, assistants in copes). It stands at the centre of the cardinal hours; at this point the psalmody gives way to a series of chants of praise (hymn, canticle). In the Little Hours it opens the last of the three sections (hymn – psalmody – conclusion).

With respect to the tradition: the Chapter does not belong to the category of fixed components. Some churches divided up the daily Epistle from the Mass, repeating it in sections across the Hours; other Uses selected scriptural texts for the Hour of a longer period (for instance, at Lauds across the whole of Advent). Some of these systems have very felicitous selections arising from a textual profound meditation (such is the Praemonstratensian system). In the most ancient state of the Roman Office probably there was no Chapter at all (it is missing from the archaic structure of the Triduum Sacrum and the Easter Octave). St Benedict, however, regularly mentions it. There is no documentary evidence for this early period, but it is quite likely that it was freely selected from the various biblical books (except the Gospels and the Psalms), with due regard to the liturgical season.

Practically, it is good if the Office book contains texts for the Chapter, but

---

[50] This was, probably, a secondary development (of perhaps the seventh or eighth century). Originally the collection of Psalm Responsories might have been sung over the whole course of Ordinary Time. This could therefore be permitted, on the basis of former practice, for less trained communities (either according to custom or according to choice).

perhaps even better if they are not specified for every single day (to allow other practices, like taking excerpts from the Mass Epistle for that day), rather than for the hours of Ordinary Time and for particular seasons. Similarly, it would be quite opportune to fix an expanded *Capitulare*, perhaps not even specifying Chapters for each Hour, but allowing Chapters to be used more freely by the celebrant. At Vespers in parish churches a longer biblical text could be read, and completed with a very short homily.[51] This would as well provide an excellent liturgical context for reading and explaining the Bible in lay communities.[52]

Originally the Office may have had no closing Collect. St Benedict speaks of a *Kyrie* and *Pater noster* (though this arrangement might have been the customary use of monastic communities). In private use of the Office now it might quite properly be permitted to close the Hour simply with the Lord's Prayer, especially if there is no Missal to hand. Otherwise the Hour is ordinarily closed by the Collect of the Mass of the day. In the books of the other Old Latin rites, however, special Collects can often be found for the Hours, together with Collects with general themes. A few examples from the *Sacramentarium Hadrianum*:

Vox nostra te, Domine, semper deprecetur, et ad aures tuae pietatis ascendat.

Ut tuam, Domine, misericordiam consequamur, fac nos tibi toto corde esse devotos.

Cunctas, Domine, semper a nobis iniquitates repelle, ut ad viam salutis aeternae secura mente curramus.

Fac nos, Domine, quaesumus, mala nostra toto corde respuere, ut bona tua capere valeamus.

Celeri nobis, quaesumus, Domine, pietate succurre, ut devotio supplicantum ad gratiarum transeat actionem.

Tuere nos, superne moderator, et fragilitatem nostram tuis defende praesidiis.

Exaudi nos, Domine, Deus noster, et ecclesiam tuam inter mundi turbines fluctuantem, clementi gubernatione moderare.[53]

---

[51] As has become customary at Vespers celebrated by Benedict XVI.
[52] Such a Vespers seems to be a better form of the liturgy of the word than that introduced after Vatican II.
[53] May our voice pray to thee, O Lord, unceasingly, rising up to thy gracious hearing.
In order to obtain your mercy, O Lord, make our hearts ever devoted to thee.
Pluck out our iniquities, O Lord, that we may run firm in mind on the path of eternal salvation.
Send out from us, we beseech thee O Lord, all the evil of our hearts, that we may receive the good you give us.
Succour us with thy hasty grace O Lord, that the devotion of those who beseech you receive the effect of your grace.
Guard us, supernal Governor, and through thy protection defend our weakness.
Hear us, O Lord, our God, and thy Church, as we are tossed in the storms of this present world, guide us by thy merciful governance.

In any renovation of the classical Roman Rite the Collects of the feasts should be retained. In the weekly Psalter, however, it is well worth adopting the general 'Collects for Hours' (as was done in the *Liturgy of the Hours*). Thus in the ferial Offices or those that are prayed privately, there is no requirement for a Missal, and people on journeys or at casual gatherings are not compelled to scrabble around for the appropriate texts. As in the case of the Chapter, a certain degree of freedom could be granted in the use of Collects, without any danger to the integrity of the rite.

The Offices of the Triduum Sacrum and of the Octave of Easter have a unique arrangement. These – as remnants of the earliest period of the Roman liturgy[54] – must be left untouched. It is characteristic that in the Triduum Sacrum the monastic office does not follow its own system either, but adopts the (secular) rite of the basilicas.[55] Probably at the time of the birth of the monastic offices there already existed a stable Roman tradition, alive and to be respected. The details of this will be discussed in the last chapter.

---

[54] Without an invitatory, hymn, Chapter, *Deus in adjutorium*, etc.
[55] Three antiphons, three responsories in the Vigils, five antiphons in the Vespers. See *Corpus Antiphonalium Officii*, vol. 2, pp. 302–19.

16

THE CALENDAR

The calendar is more than a simple technical tool. It includes traditions reaching far back in time, it reflects the order of commemorated doctrinal truths and it essentially functions as a kind of indicator concerning the rank of a feast in the common ecclesiastical appreciation; by virtue of folk customs and through more personal associations it also functions as an organic organizer of social and private life.[1]

In the past, the calendar required several reforms both in secular and ecclesiastical practice. There were changes to it after the Council of Trent, and over subsequent centuries,[2] and so the mere fact that there was further reform after Vatican II cannot in itself form the basis of any criticism. The question is whether the postconciliar reforms enacted by the *Consilium* were well considered and appropriately motivated, or whether they actually harmed what they sought to improve.[3]

The calendar not only preserves the dates of feasts, but also determines their rank. This is the first point we have to study; after that we go over to the examination of the current state of the Temporal and Sanctoral cycles more closely.

1. The Gradation of the Feasts

In the Middle Ages there was no uniform terminology to designate the different ranks of feasts; dioceses and orders used a whole range of interesting and instructive specifications. The highest solemnities were, of course, identical, and on the same rank, universally throughout the Church (though often designated using different terms); the observation of feasts of lower ranks depended on local custom. Local calendars themselves do not reflect these customs precisely; often they were taken over ready-made from other sources. The body of the Missals, Breviaries and Ordinary books is clear in assigning this particular order.

The number of feasts was radically reduced after the Council of Trent, and

---

[1] As abundantly documented in Duffy (1992).
[2] Suitbert Bäumer (1895), *Geschichte des Breviers*, pp. 442–52, 498–99, 510–13, 568–75, 590–93.
[3] Cf. Klaus Gamber (2002), *The Modern Rite*, pp. 47–49.

the categories, along with the gradation of individual feasts, were rearranged. It became clear rather soon, however, that four categories (double of the first class, double of the second class, double, simple) were insufficent to reflect the differing grades of importance, and by the addition of two other categories (major double, semidouble) a six-grade system was generated, which remained in force until only recently.

Before the Second Vatican Council the number of categories was once again cut back to four (as can be seen in the 1962 Missal).[4] According to the postconciliar reforms only the highest solemnities and the next (lower) category (feasts) are distinguished, all others became memorias. Optional Memorias are not a special grade; it means only that the observation of them is not obligatory.[5]

The weakness of this arrangement is identical to the problem that arose with the Tridentine arrangement: it is not refined enough – especially in the Sanctoral cycle – to mark differences between commemorations. Except for the feasts of the Blessed Virgin, the Apostles, and a few major saints (ranked in the category of feasts or solemnities), all other commemorations are placed on the same grade. The days of less-known saints are classified as Memorias just the same way as really outstanding personalities in the history of Church. There is therefore a serious risk of disproportionality: if the universal or the local calendar were to emphasize a feast by elevating its rank, this can be done only in the category of Feast (Festum) itself, placing the saint in question on an equal level with the Apostles. What is awaited today with respect of the 1962 and 1970 Missals is practically the same as in the post-Tridentine decades: new ranks must be introduced in order to make more subtle differentiation possible.

The particular grade of a feast is not only of symbolic meaning and technical assistance in facilitating the occurrence of feasts. In an ecclesial body that takes liturgical observation seriously, gradations also regulate some rubrics, and so the manner of celebration. The number and quality of assistants (servers), the use of vestments ('on this day the Church makes use of more solemn vestments'),[6] the number of candles, the use of incense, the selection of melodies for the ordinary texts; all this is dependent on the rank of the feast. It should be the same now, so that we might maintain a vivid, varied, yet controlled observation of the liturgical year. We should not forget that the observation of feasts also has an impact on social life and public celebration.

Accordingly, what I propose here divides the category of Feast into two. The second group corresponds more or less to the earlier Greater Double (*Duplex maior*), and is assigned to the outstanding saints of the Church: great doctors, founders of well-known religious orders and other persons of great influence. Two groups are to be formed also from the category of Memoria so that the

---

[4] Alcuin Reid (2005), *The Organic Development of the Liturgy*, pp. 210–14.
[5] *Mysterii Paschalis* (Apostolic letter by Paul VI), §14.
[6] Examples from the Ordinary Book of Eger: 'Et est utendum vestibus solennioribus ecclesie.' 'Festum colendum, et tabulatur domino episcopo, chorum regant domini canonici, et ecclesia utatur vestibus solemnioribus.' 'Est festum colendum, chorum regant domini canonici in rubeis, et ecclesia utatur vestibus solemnioribus' (Dobszay (2000), *Liber Ordinarius Agriensis*, Nrs 68, 546, 590).

saints of truly 'universal importance'[7] could be highlighted. Another category of a Simple commemoration could also be added (like the old 'simplex' commemorations). The device of *ad libitum* – as an option – could be adopted in the categories of both the Memoria and the Simple.

The following gradation and attached rules of celebration are not intended to represent a complete proposal, but to function rather as an illustration of possible directions in rearrangement:

- Solemnity (*Solemnitas*): Mass attendance is obligatory or explicitly recommended. A Solemn Mass or *Missa cantata* should be celebrated in parish churches. At high Mass six candles must be lit, in other Masses four. The Office is 'full' (First Vespers on the eve, three Nocturns at Matins). In parish churches the Vigil (Matins) and/or solemn Vespers are celebrated.
- First Class Feast (*Festum primae classis*): participation in the liturgy is recommended to the faithful. One sung high Mass is celebrated in parish churches (with at least two altar servers and the Propers chanted). At High Mass four candles are lit. The Office is 'full' (with First Vespers and three Nocturns at Matins), except that the Little Hours *may* be prayed with the Ordinary texts. In parish churches, wherever possible, Vespers is sung.
- Second Class Feast (*Festum secundae classis*): the date and meaning of the feast is announced ahead of time (from the pulpit or on the church billboard). One sung High Mass is celebrated in parish churches (with at least two altar servers). In the main Mass four candles are lit. There is a proper Office (without First Vespers and with three Nocturns that could be contracted according to custom into a single, longer Nocturn). The Little Hours can be taken from the Ordinary Time.
- First Class Memoria (*Memoria primae classis*): Mass of the saint; Office of the season, but with proper readings and proper Collect (of the saint). If the feast has a proper Office: three Nocturns that may be contracted as a single longer Nocturn. Lauds and Vespers may be of the saint or of the day. The antiphon at the Benedictus and Magnificat may be proper or from the Common of Saints. The Little Hours are from the Ordinary.
- Second Class Memoria (*Memoria secundae classis*): all from the feria, with three readings only at Matins. One reading at Matins is from the saint. In the Mass and at Lauds: commemoration of the saint.
- Simple (*Commemoratio*): everything from the feria, a commemoration at Mass and in Lauds of the saint.

---

[7] Vatican Council II, Dogmatic Constitution on the Sacred Liturgy, *Sacrosanctum Concilium* (1963), §111: 'Ne festa Sanctorum festis ipsa mysteria salutis recolentibus praevaleant, plura ex his particulari cuique Ecclesiae vel Nationi vel Religiosae Familiae relinquantur celebranda, iis tantum ad Ecclesiam universam extensis, quae Sanctos memorant momentum universale revera prae se ferentes.'

II. Vigils, Octaves, Ember Days

Three elements of the traditional order of celebration that disappeared should be restored: the Vigil, the Octave and Ember Days.[8]

The number of Vigils of saints' days was increased over the centuries to too great a number. Though the practice of fasting ceased in the recent decades, if the number of vigilia is high they may cause trouble in the concurrence of feasts and also in the usual course of weekdays. In this respect, a reduction in the number of Vigils could be considered reasonable. On the other hand, the few Vigils preserved in the recent reform are not Vigils at all, but consist in only a special Mass on the eve of the day (which is often mixed up with the anticipated festal Mass itself). The solution could be found by taking a middle course: a reduction in the number of the Vigils in comparison with the Tridentine Rite, but a restoration of some Vigils compared to current practice.

Vigils could also be divided into two categories (as they were historically, at least in practice). Those of a higher rank would have a proper Mass and proper readings at Matins (sometimes with proper antiphons). Such are, for example: Christmas, Epiphany, Ascension, Pentecost, John the Baptist, Ss Peter and Paul, the Assumption. If the obligation to keep a fast cannot be restored, some kind of preparation in personal piety should be recommended as a substitution.

The second-class Vigils have a Mass (proper or from the Common of Saints), and a commemoration at Lauds. Such are: St Andrew the Apostle (an old proper Mass!), St Laurence, All Saints; *ad libitum* the other Apostles (from the Common of Apostles) and the principal Patron of the local church.

The case of Octaves is similar. No doubt, the number of Octaves was high, in the old calendar, and the liturgy of the solemnity repeated during the full week, and so many further days were taken out from the ordinary course of the year.[9] Even before the Council, however, the Octaves were truncated, disappearing almost altogether afterwards. It seems that nobody gave any thought to the role they played in prolonging the observation of the solemnity for a little longer in order to deepen its meaning. The only Octave practically alive today is that of Easter (during the Christmas Octave from very ancient times most of the days are the feasts of particular saints). At least the principal Octaves ought to be considered worthy of restoration, while their observance could perhaps become more differentiated.

In an Octave of the First Class (*Octava primae classis*) the liturgy could be of

---

[8] Though *Mysterii Paschalis* §§45–47 reserved the right to specify Rogation and Ember Days to Bishops' Conferences, in practical terms these elements of the calendar have disappeared from the life of the Church.

[9] Reid (2005), *The Organic Development of the Liturgy*, p. 212: '. . . there were grave deficiencies in the concurrence, and at times collisions, of the various octaves and feasts of the calendar'. In the Middle Ages feasts of Apostles, of the Holy Virgin, all solemnities had their Octave with the repetition of the full liturgy of the day itself. Frequently also the Octaves of different feasts overlapped each other and so quite complex rules existed to ensure the correct ordering of one to the other. Such problems occurred also in the liturgy of the recent decades; for example, for how the feast of The Immaculate Conception occurs within the celebration of Advent. These kinds of anomalies can be solved by (i) reducing the number of Octaves; and (ii) making distinctions between Octaves of different rank.

the solemnity, the Office readings are further meditations on its themes; the eighth day is observed with the rank of Feast of the Second Class. These are: Epiphany, Ascension and Pentecost (with Trinity Sunday on its Octave day). Christmas would be like this as well, but such that on the feast days of the saints within the Octave some readings, the Little Hours, and Vespers are of Christmas, with a commemoration of the following (saint's) day at Vespers.

In Octaves of the Second Class (*Octava secunda classis*) there is one reading in the Office bound to the feast, and a commemoration of the feast at Lauds. On the eighth day, the Mass and Lauds of the feast are repeated (or if it coincides with another solemnity or feast, commemorated). These are: Corpus Christi, John the Baptist, Ss Peter and Paul, the Assumption and All Saints.

In the ancient Church there was also a third type of Octave in use: with no commemoration during the octave, but with one proper reading at Matins, and a commemoration at Mass and Lauds on the eighth day. The remnant of this prac- tice can be seen in the second feast of St Agnes on 28 January. Several Octaves could take this simplified from: St Stephen Proto-martyr, St John the Apostle, Holy Innocents, St Agnes (by virtue of the long-standing tradition), St Laurence and the main Patron of the local church.

The abolition of the *Ember Days* was the destruction of a very early tradition. We learn from the sermons of Leo the Great how devotedly the Roman Church kept this observance in the fifth century. 'Et traditio decrevit, et consuetudo formavit' – 'inasmuch as tradition has decreed, so custom shaped it' – said this most liturgical pope.[10] And the same sermon proceeds so: 'ideo ipsa continentiae observantia quattuor est assignata temporibus, ut in idipsum totius anni redeunte decursu, cognosceremus nos indesinenter purificationibus indigere . . .' – 'there- fore four times are assigned for the observance of temperance, so that when the course of the year brings it back, we should understand, that we are in need of ceaseless purification'.

The roots of the Ember Days stretch back to the Old Testament. Strictly speaking, they did not pertain to the liturgical year, but rather to the sanctifica- tion of civil life, and so they can be adapted to correspond explicitly even to the demands of modern times.

The difficulty with them was that they became primarily *fasting* days, which were not easy to observe in the rush of the working week. They had established texts, which have, however, only a few links to the Christian observance. This was in part because three of the four *Quattuor Temporum* (Ember Days) weeks appear as integrated into solemn liturgical seasons (Advent, Lent, Pentecost), and only in three days in September do they retain their original feature, of marking the quarters of the year.

As much as the revitalization of these days seems difficult today, with proper instruction and good practice, however, their meaning could easily be re-

---

[10] Sermon 9 of St. Leo, *de jejunio septimi mensis, Patrologia Latina*, cols 458–60: See the reading in the Vigils of the Third Sunday of September according to the *Breviarium Romanum*. See also Leo Cunibert Mohlberg, OSB (1968), *Liber Sacramentorum Romanae Aeclesiae Ordinis Anni Circuli*, p. 101 and the 'Denuntiatio ieiuniorum quarti septimi et decimi mensis' in the Gelasian Sacramentary.

established. The four times three days are, as it were, the *decima* of the 12 months of the year. Adrift among various occupations, cares, the frailties of life – and with God's grace – the Church halts the flow of time and reflects in a religious way upon all that happens with and to us.[11]

The solution would be to return to these days their semi-liturgical character. Though they have their proper texts, they should be properly related to our lives by observances *attached* to the liturgy. We cannot change the fact that their liturgical material is seasonal in Advent, Lent and Pentecost, and is unique to themselves only in September. But there could be special devotions attached to their Masses:

- On the four Ember Wednesdays a devotion of *thanksgiving* may close the day, thinking on this chant of Ember Days: '*Exultate Deo adjutori nostro*'.[12]
- On Ember Fridays, there would be *penitential* devotions for the sins of the quarter year, with the possibility of making one's confession in churches during the day; this day could also become one of optional fasting ('accepta tibi sint . . . nostri dona jejunii, quae expiando nos tua gratia dignos efficiant . . .').[13]
- The Ember Saturdays could be regarded as special days of Christian charity, of *alms-giving* ('esuriamus paululum, dilectissimi, et aliquantulum, quod juvandis possit prodesse pauperibus, nostrae consuetudini subtrahamus').[14]

If these devotions are attached to Masses in the evening, the liturgy itself would acquire a particular focus or emphasis in the life of our communities. In order for this to succeed, catechesis would be required, and it would be necessary, of course, that the sermon on the previous Sunday should explain (as those of Leo the Great did) the meaning of this observance.

III. The Feasts of the Temporal Cycle

No radical change took place in the Temporal Cycle during the last reform. There are only a few critical points in the new order that warrant consideration. Some elements have come to be omitted from the cycle of the year, in other cases the transfer of liturgical days has caused difficulties in the sequence. To discuss this, let us proceed by following the course of the year.

I have already mentioned two changes in the Advent season: the Ember Days were left out, and the Vigil day of Christmas disappeared. Because of the reasons explained above both should be restored to the calendar.

---

[11] The Motu Proprio '*Mysterii Paschalis*', §§45–47, misunderstands the character of these days when it regards them as simply the occasion of praying for our necessities.

[12] 'Rejoice to God our Helper . . .' (Psalm 80, Introit on Ember Wednesday in September).

[13] 'May the offering of our fasting, O Lord, we beseech Thee, be pleasing in Thy sight, may it atone for our sins, make us worthy of Thy favour . . .' (*Secret* for Ember Friday in September).

[14] 'Let us hunger a little, my beloved, and that little which can benefit the poor, let us remove from our customary diet.' (From the same sermon of Saint Pope Leo, *Patrologia Latina*, vol. 54, col. 460.)

Two changes caused trouble in the Christmas period. The first one seems to be only a matter of observance, but the consequences touch upon the order of the feast. The new calendar concedes that in some regions the solemnity of Epiphany may be transferred to the Sunday nearest to January 6th.[15] Epiphany is a very ancient feast, even earlier than Christmas, and held by both the Orthodox and Protestants on its proper day. The new ordering disturbs the uniformity in the practice of the Christian churches, even across different regions of the Catholic world. The liturgy of the Sunday before January 6th has become very unstable, and if Epiphany is postponed until after January 6th, it interferes with the feast of Christ's Baptism.

What was the motivation behind this decision? Seemingly it was pastoral: to protect the solemnity of the Epiphany in countries where January 6 is a regular working day. But has this not just degraded this feast in the mind of faithful? Was this disturbance not too great a price to pay for the convenience? Can the Church not require from the baptized even their sacrifice of attending an early morning or an evening Mass on only two working days of the year (Epiphany, Ascension)? If the faithful are really prevented from doing this, then they are in any case dispensed from the obligation in virtue of the general law. The date of Epiphany is beyond dispute in the classical Roman Rite, but its restoration is desired in the *Novus Ordo* as well. As we shall see, this provision may have other good consequences.

The other anomaly concerns the feast of the Holy Family. This feast, introduced barely 100 years ago, was motivated more by moral and exhortatory aims than by the mysteries of the Nativity. When it was transferred to the Sunday after Christmas, it suppressed very ancient feasts (St Stephen Proto-martyr, St John the Apostle, the Holy Innocents) and altered the quality of the Octave even more than the presence in the Octave of the feasts themselves. In the new feast it is not really the Holy Family that is actually honoured; rather the intention is primarily didactic: to impress on the minds of the faithful the importance of family life.

Given contemporary concerns for family life, I do not think, of course, that this very modern feast[16] could be abolished. One possibility would be to preserve it (or put it back) in its original place, the Sunday after Epiphany. In fact, it is difficult to understand why it was judged inappropriate to commemorate the Holy Family of Nazareth when the high days of Christmas are over.

Should this Sunday really be reserved for the most recent feast of the Baptism of the Lord? Another serious argument against this position of the feast is that the brief season of time after Epiphany should not be shortened with yet another commemorative Sunday. In fact, the First Sunday after Epiphany had its own Mass (*In excelso throno*), one of the most beautiful propers of the Missal, which was essentially ousted by the feast of the Holy Family (and again after the most recent reforms by the feast of the Baptism of the Lord).

After due consideration, a very simple solution can be found to the problem. If Epiphany is celebrated on its proper date, the Sunday between December 30th

---

[15] *Mysterii Paschalis*, §§7, 37.
[16] Introduced in 1921.

and January 5th remains free (except when the Circumcision falls on a Sunday, which suppresses the feast of the Holy Family even in the *Novus Ordo*). The Mass of this Sunday in the classical Roman Rite (*Dum medium silentium*) is perfectly suitable for the feast of the Holy Family, only the Alleluia – taken from the Christmas Mass – need be replaced by a more appropriate one. In so doing, the feast in its new disposition would keep its relationship to Christmas, while the 'Nazarene aspect' of the Holy Family is represented in the Gospel of the First Sunday after Epiphany (that of the 12-year-old Christ-child in the Temple).

The traditional date for commemorating the Baptism of the Lord is the day of Epiphany itself. '*Lavacra puri gurgitis caelestis Agnus attigit . . .*' sings the hymn of the day.[17] '*Hodie in Iordane a Ioanne Christus baptizari vouluit ut salvaret nos . . .*' says the Magnificat antiphon of the solemnity.[18] The Office of the Octave dwells on the mystery of Christ's Baptism, and the eighth day is devoted mainly to this event. If the feast of the Holy Family is kept on the Sunday before Epiphany (with the Gospel of the *flight into Egypt*), the Gospel of the Sunday within the Octave of Epiphany is that of the *12-year-old Christ-child*, the Gospel of the eighth day is that of the *Baptism*, and that of the Second Sunday after Epiphany is the gospel of the *wedding at Cana*.

One small observation: the Diocese of Rome undoubtedly anciently commemorated the Maternity of the Blessed Virgin on January 1st. Nevertheless, this tradition is not sufficient to qualify this day as a Marian feast. This day is the Lord's feast; its three-fold motivation is marked by its compound title: the Octave of Christmas, the Circumcision of the Lord, the Maternity of the Holy Virgin.

The 'proposal' then is the following:[19]

Dec. 24.	Vigil of the Nativity
Dec. 25.	The Nativity of our Lord (S)
Dec. 26.	St Stephen, First Martyr (F-1)
Dec. 27.	F. St John Apostle and Evangelist (F-1)
Dec. 28.	F. The Holy Innocents (F-1)
Dec. 29.	F. St Thomas of Cantenbury (Commemoratio, vel Memoria ad libitum)
	Sunday between Dec. 30 and Jan. 5: The Holy Family (F-1)
Dec. 31.	St Sylvester, Pope and Confessor (M-2)
Jan. 1.	Octave day of the Nativity, Circumcision of the Lord, Maternity of the Holy Virgin (F-1)
Jan. 2.	Feria, with simple commemoration of the Octave St Stephani martyris
Jan. 3.	Feria, with simple commemoration of the Ocatave St John the Apostle

---

[17] 'The heavenly Lamb in Jordan stood, to sanctify the crystal flood . . .'
[18] '. . . this day Christ willed to be baptised by John in the Jordan for our salvation . . .'
[19] The abbreviations are here and the following paragraphs: S = solemnity, F-1 = First Class Feast, F-2 = Second Class Feast, M-1 (First Class Memory), M-2 = Second Class Memory).

Jan. 4.	Feria, with simple commemoration of the Octave of the Holy Innocents
Jan. 5.	Vigil of Epiphany
Jan. 6.	The Epiphany of our Lord (S)
	First Sunday after the Epiphany, with commemoration of the solemnity
Jan. 7–13.	Octave of the Epiphany
Jan. 13.	Octave day of Epiphany, commemoration of the Baptism of our Lord (F-2)

The elimination of the Pre-Lenten season was, to say the least, ill-considered. In earlier times it is possible to find – very often – great praise regarding the pastoral wisdom and sensitivity of the Church, in carefully preparing her children for Lent.[20] It is difficult to understand why the *Novus Ordo* did not preserve the spiritual riches of this period. Those who attacked it under the supposition that it was merely the result of historical contingencies (resolving local difficulties in the City of Rome) seemed to forget that from ancient times the Eastern churches have also observed a pre-Lenten period (the Sunday of the Prodigal Son, 'Meat' and 'Cheese' Sundays). It would be good to restore this period for the universal Roman Church, and it surely needs to be preserved in the classical Roman Rite.

The name Fifth Sunday of Lent for the Passion Sunday is justified by ancient liturgical texts, but the *rubrics* of the liturgy, mainly in the Office to be applied from this day forward, manifest the proper meaning of the period this day inaugurates. The Church truly needs a week and a half to focus on the Passion before entering the Sacred Triduum. Without this, the hymns (*Vexilla regis, Pange lingua*), the responsories and short responsories and versicles of Passiontide last only for four days (the beginning of Holy Week). The name of the subsequent Sunday (Second Sunday of the Passion, Palm Sunday) does not introduce a difficulty.

What I have already said about the date of Epiphany needs also to be said of the Ascension. Indeed, in this case the real truth of the matter at hand makes it necessary to retain or restore the proper date, since it was *not* on the 44th day after the resurrection that Christ ascended into the heavens. Anybody familiar with the liturgy (first of all, with the Office) of the Octave of Ascension must surely be unhappy about the transformation of this period (which now has the character of a period inspired by expectation of the Holy Spirit).[21] This change in meaning is the consequence of the abolition of the Octave of Pentecost. What was the reason for making this change? To close Eastertide on exactly the 50th day after the resurrection? No doubt, Pentecost belongs to the Paschal mystery, but it also has a rich content of its own, which needs and, indeed, deserves a week to be expressed and celebrated. Here the followers of the classical Roman Rite could

---

[20] For example, a popular explanation: Pius Parsch (1953), *The Church's Year of Grace*, vol. 2. chapter 1. On the debate of its abolition within the *Consilium* see Pristas (2009), 'Septuagesima and the Post-Vatican II Reform of the Sacred Liturgy'.

[21] The *Liturgia Horarum* moved the hymn *Veni Creator Spiritus* to this season!

do nothing else but adhere to both the lost Octaves (Ascension and Pentecost). After the eighth day of Ascension, there is a 'free' day (more will be said about this in the next subdivision of this chapter), and then the Vigil of Pentecost.

The place of Trinity Sunday and Corpus Christi did not change (although the option to move Corpus Christi from Thursday to Sunday has now been given, which is unfortunate but, in contrast to the solemnities of Epiphany and Ascension, not disastrous biblically and liturgically). The numbering of the Sundays after Pentecost, however, did change in the new calendar. The new method of numbering the ordinary Sundays proceeds in one continuous sequence (starting from Epiphany), causing many difficulties by disturbing the proper unfolding of the liturgical sequence. The meaning of the Sundays after Epiphany is *different* from that of the Sundays after Pentecost. In the Old Roman Rite the Sundays were counted from outstanding solemnities (St Peter and Paul, Laurence, Michael, the Dedication).[22] During the Carolingian age these Sundays were arranged in a linear sequence, and there need be no reason to change this. No doubt, the Sundays at the end of the series seem a little 'illogical' ('wandering' Sundays between the Post-Epiphany and Post-Pentecost periods), but such a minor disorder in the liturgy can surely be endured.

Another point of dispute is the rearrangement of the Sunday of Christ the King. Here we are dealing with a modern commemoration[23] for which a proper place was sought in the calendar for some time; neither the feast nor its assigned date has any stable tradition. Perhaps the postconciliar solution is not the worst, and the feast is certainly suitable to close the liturgical year. It is easier to make it the last Sunday than to supersede an ordinary Sunday at the end of October.

IV. The Feasts of the Sanctoral Cycle

Except for feasts of outstanding importance, the arrangement of the Sanctoral Cycle has varied considerably according to time and place, even in the past. Since the number of celebrated saints has kept increasing, this ever-growing number has had periodically to be reduced. In ancient times there were only a few solemnities of saints observed by the universal Church.[24] They were complemented differently by the customary feasts of regions and dioceses. The great reform after the Council is not unique in history, and cannot be regarded as an attack against the continuity of tradition.[25] The question is rather whether or not this reform was successful.

The Council itself made two decisions concerning the Sanctorale. The first is: 'the feasts of the saints should [not] take precedence over the feasts which

[22] *Monumenta Monodica Medii Aevi*, vol. 2, pp. 663–76.
[23] The feast was introduced in 1925.
[24] The number of saints' feastdays in the earliest Graduals is about 70, which might, of course, be made a little higher by days celebrated with the Common of Saints. See *Antiphonale Missarum Sextuplex* (1935). In Theodor Klauser's estimation – Klauser (1969), *A Short History of the Western Liturgy*, p. 85 – about 30 feasts were introduced in Rome between AD 600 and AD 800. For the later changes see p. 125.
[25] Bäumer (1895), *Geschichte des Breviers*, pp. 498–99, 511–13, 568–73, 590–93.

commemorate the very mysteries of salvation'; the second: 'many of them should be left to be celebrated by a particular Church or nation or family of religious; only those should be extended to the universal Church which commemorate saints who are truly of universal importance'.[26] This means that the Council's provision is to reduce the number of feasts again, and to lower their rank – for the sake of protecting the Sundays and those feasts expressing some mystery of our salvation. The second intention is to reactivate the pre-Tridentine situation when Order and local churches felt much freer to add their proper feasts to truly important universal feasts according to their own tradition.

The reform produced by the *Consilium* more or less fulfilled the first point. For the realization of the second one, however, no real opportunity was provided.

The number of saints diminished in the universal calendar; but also some new saints were added. New feasts were introduced to express the universality of the Church in time and space and to include saints from all continents, as well as saints canonized in recent times.[27] This has become the 'universality' of the calendar.

The dates of many feasts were changed. One motive was to apply greater historical perspicacity in honouring a given saint on the day of his/her death, another motive was to 'free up' some parts of the year (Advent, Lent and Eastertide).

The gradation of the feasts was further simplified. Only 10 fixed festivities received the rank of Solemnity: three are solemnities of the Lord, 3 are Marian feasts, and 4 are of outstanding saints (St Joseph, St John the Baptist, Ss Peter and Paul, All Saints). The rank of Feast was given to 23 days: 3 of the Lord, 2 of the Blessed Virgin, 13 of Apostles and Evangelists, 1 of the Archangels, 3 of martyrs (St Stephen, St Laurence, the Holy Innocents), and 1 is the feast of the Dedication of the Lateran Basilica. Memorias comprise 63 days of saints, Optional Memorias, 95. The total number of universal feasts is 96; together with the optional days it makes 191.

Disregarding certain strange phenomena (like the precedence of All Souls over the Sunday!), the new ranking system would be suitable to protect the Sunday, if an adverse trend were not more and more pressing: the acceptance of 'slogan-Sundays' contrary to the spirit of the liturgy. True, the number of 'ideological feasts' has been diminished in the calendar; but these 'action'-Sundays – although unmentioned in the calendar – have heavily impacted upon liturgical celebrations in all countries of the world.

The other wish of the Council (that there be local additions to the universal calendar) was fulfilled merely by following the earlier custom: a small local calendar with the feasts of local patrons was appended at the end of the calendar with the approval of Rome. This arrangement did not change the method; it remained the same both in spirit and criteria of organization. Particular traditions were not given a more prominent role, the rate between the universal and

---

[26] *Sacrosanctum Concilium* (1963), §111: 'Ne festa Sanctorum festis ipsa mysteria salutis recolentibus praevaleant, plura ex his particulari cuique Ecclesiae vel Nationi vel Religiosae Familiae relinquantur celebranda, iis tantum ad Ecclesiam universam extensis, quae Sanctos memorant momentum universale revera prae se ferentes.'

[27] *Mysterii Paschalis*, chapter 2.

particular elements in the calendar remained nearly the same. In fact, the new calendar did not even leave space for that: of the 200 days of Ordinary Time (which would otherwise be suitable for the augmentation of the sanctorale) 191 were already reserved by the obligatory and optional commemorations.

The Holy Father in the letter that accompanied the Motu Proprio *Summorum Pontificum* explicitly mentioned *the calendar* as a field where the new liturgy may influence the 1962 Missal.[28] Those who combine their respect for the old liturgy with a rejection of any change whatsoever must surely be unhappy to hear that some may already be thinking of certain modifications to their beloved Missal or Breviary. However, the calendar of the 'Tridentine' Rite changed quite markedly every 100 years or so, and it changed in some minor details almost every decade. The 1962 calendar is 'traditional' only with regard to the really important days.

The calendar of the 1962 Missal should, of course, remain the basis for any further revision, and the principles decided by the Council should affect *this* arrangement by a reduction of the number of obligatory commemorations,[29] the revision of their ranking, the introduction of some new feasts, and the possibility of developing local or regional calendars. These desires could surely be implemented without causing any harm to the classical tradition.

Here are some aspects which could be considered during such a revision:

(a) The 'universality' of the calendar can be stressed by the reception of a few saints of the recent centuries and especially from outside of Europe. But in earlier times this kind of demand for 'representation' was not a serious concern for the Church. The basis of the calendar was a collection of biblical saints and of the saints of the Urbs (Rome).[30] Special motives of honour allowed some others to enter (for instance, St Martin of Tours). The desire for the public cult of a given saint justified the particular supplementation of the calendar. Sometimes the cult of a saint transcended the narrow borders of birthplace or activity, and became a common feast of a region or, rarely, of the universal Church. This means that neither the universal nor the particular calendar should ever allow the liturgical memory of such a great number of 'other' saints that the basic *Roman* character of the calendar be compromised. For us the Roman saints are the symbols of our adherence to Rome and of healthy 'universality'. Even the Roman saints whose names are less familiar to us express our piety and affection towards the Holy City and the Roman Church.

(b) The aim of the local calendar is not to increase the list of local and national

---

[28] *Letter of his Holiness Benedict XVI to the bishops on the occasion of the publication of the apostolic letter accompanying the Motu Proprio Summorum Pontificum:* 'For that matter, the two Forms of the usage of the Roman Rite can be mutually enriching: new Saints and some of the new Prefaces can and should be inserted in the old Missal.'

[29] Cf. Brian W. Harrison. OS (2003), 'The Postconciliar Eucharistic Liturgy', p. 186.

[30] According to Klauser (1969), *A Short History of the Western Liturgy*, p. 126: 'no less than 85 per cent of the saints provided for in the new (= Tridentine) calendar belong to the first four centuries . . . Almost 40 per cent of the feasts were of saints from the city of Rome.'

saints to an exceedingly high number, but to open public cult to those saints (of local *or* universal importance) whose special honour is recommended by the traditions or the spiritual aspirations of the local Church.

(c) The right proportions should also be kept in the local calendar. I think one Solemnity, 5 or 6 Feasts, 5 or 6 First Class Memorias, 15 to 20 Second Class Memorias and 20 Simple commemorations leave enough space for local cults without disturbing the equilibrium of the calendar as a whole. Since it is not always easy to moderate local aspirations, the proportions could perhaps be expressed with the concrete fixing of the maximum number of possible entries.

(d) The list below contains neither Simple commemorations nor the Optional Memorias. In these two groups those saints of the old and new calendars may be included, which are omitted here; along with others from the Martyrology[31] or (in small number) from local registers.

(e) This list below is merely a possible illustration of the principles above. Neither the number nor the rank of the feasts is to be taken as a real and well-considered suggestion.

The symbols for the rank of feasts are: S = Solemnity, F-1 = First Class Feast, F-2 Second Class Feast, M-1 = First Class Memoria, M-2 = Second Class Memoria.

January 1–13 according to the Temporal
17. Anthony and Paul, Hermits M-1
    20. Fabian and Sebastian M-2
21. Agnes M-1
    22. Vincent M-2
25. Conversion of St Paul F-2
    26. Timothy and Titus M-2[32]
27. John Chrysostom, M-1
29 Francis de Sales M-1
    30 John Bosco M-2

February
    1. Ignatius M-2
2 Praesentatio Domini (Purificatio BMV) F-1
    3 Blaise M-2
5 Agatha M-1
    7 Romuald M-2
22 St Peter's Chair F-2
24 Matthias ap. F-1

March

[31] Cf. John P. Parsons (2003), 'A Reform of the Reform?', p. 253.
[32] From the new calendar.

> 6. *Perpetua and Felicity M-2*
7. Thomas Aquinas M-1
12. Gregory the Great M-1
> *18. Cyril of Jerusalem Hieros. M-2*
19. Joseph F-1
25. Incarnation of our Lord S

April
11 Leo I M-1
> *Apr. 23. George M-2*
25. Mark ev. F-2
30. Catherine of Siena M-1

May
1. Philip and James, apostles F-1
2. Athanasius M-1
3. The Victory of the Holy Cross M-1[33]
> *4. Monica M-2*
> *9. Gregory Nazianzen M-2*
> *26. Philip Neri M-2*
> *28. Augustine of Canterbury M-2*

June
1. Justin M-1[34]
> *2. Peter and Marcellinus M-2*
> *3. Karl Lwanga and socii M-2[35]*
5. Boniface M-1
> *6. Norber M-2*
11. Barnabas, apostle F-2
13. Anthony of Padua M-1
14. Basil the Great M-1
> *16. Ephrem M-2*
> *21. Aloysius Gonzaga M-2*
> *22. Paulinus of Nola M-2;*
> *Johannis Fischer and Thomas More M-2[36]*
23. Vigil of the Nativity of St John
24. Nativity of St John the Baptist S
26. John and Paul, martyrs M-1[37]

---

[33] The popular feast of the Invention of the Cross could be preserved if the liturgy is celebrated as a remembrance of Good Friday in the joyful spirit of Easter (Triumph of the Holy Cross) – instead of the elements drawn from legend. Maybe, the best day for it is not the customary May 3rd, but the free day between the eighth day of the Ascension and the Vigil of Pentecost, exactly seven weeks after Good Friday.
[34] From the new calendar.
[35] From the new calendar.
[36] From the new calendar.
[37] Saints in the Roman Canon of the Mass.

28. Vigil of Ss Peter and Paul
29. Peter and Paul, apostles S
30. Commemoration of St Paul F-2

July
2. Visitation of Our Blessed Lady F-1
3. Thomas apostle F-1
    6. Octave day of St Peter and Paul M-2
7. Cyril and Methodius M-1
11. Benedict M-1 (in Europa: F-2)
    14. Bonaventure M-2
    19. Vincent de Paul M-2
22. Mary Magadalen F-2
    23. Apollinaris M-2
25. James the Greater, apostle F-1
26. Anna and Joachim M-1
    29. Martha M-2
31. Ignatius of Loyola M-1

August
4. Dominic M-1
5. Dedication of Our Lady of the Snow M-1
6. Transfiguration of our Lord F-2
9. John Vianney M-1
    9. Vigil of St Laurence M-2
10. Laurence F-2
12. Clare M-1
    14. Vigil of the Assumption M-2
15. Assumption of the Blessed Virgin Mary S
20. Bernard M-1
21. Pius X M-1
22. Octave day of Assumption M-2
24. Bartholomew, apostle F-1
28. Augustine of Hippo F-2
29. Beheading of St John Baptist F-2

September
8. Nativity of the Blessed Virgin Mary F-1
    12. Most Holy Name of Mary M-2
14. Exaltation of the Holy Cross F-2
15. Seven Sorrows of Our Blessed Lady M-1
    16. Cornelius and Cyprian M-2
21. Matthew, apostle F-1
    27. Cosmas and Damian M-2[38]

[38] Saints in the Roman Canon of the Mass.

29. Michael, Gabriel, Raphael, archangels F-1
30. Jerome M-1

October
    2. Holy Guardian Angels M-2
3. Teresa of the Child Jesus M-1
4. Francis of Assisi M-1
    6. Bruno M-2
    7. Our Lady of the Rosary M-2
    14. Callixtus M-2
15. Teresa of Avila M-1
18. Luke, evangelist F-2
28. Simon and Jude, apostles F-1

November
1. All Saints S
2. All Souls Day
4. Charles Borromeo M-1
    8. Octave day of All Saints M-2
9. Dedication of the Archbasilica of Our Saviour in Lateran F-2
10. Martin of Tours M-1
    14. Josaphat M-2
    15. Albert the Great M-2
    16. Gertrude M-2
19. Elisabeth of Hungary M-1
    21. Presentation of the Holy Virgin M-2
22. Cecilia M-1
23. Clement M-1
    23. John of the Cross M-2
    25. Catharine of Alexandria M-2
30. Andrew, apostle F-1

December
3. Francis Xavier M-1
    6. Nicholas of Myra M-2
7. Ambrose M-1
8. Immaculate Conception of the Holy Virgin F-1
13. Lucy of Syracuse M-1
25– Jan. 13: as in the Temporal Part

With two exceptions, all feasts retain their traditional date. I recommend this especially since often the commemoration of saints' days has social aspects and connections (name days, folk customs, etc.). It would not be good if the sacral aspect of these social customs disappeared because of the conflict of the two dates. The exceptions are the feast of the Triumph of the Cross on May 3rd, as mentioned in the footnotes, and the feast of St Thomas the Apostle. His feast is, in fact, an awkwardness in the last days before Christmas; keeping the feast in July goes back to an old tradition, nearly as strong as the date in December.

In the list above:

- The number of Solemnities is five (Annunciation, John the Baptist, Ss Peter and Paul, Assumption BMV, All Saints), and more, of course, from the Temporal Cycle.
- Of Feasts of the First Class there are 13 (1 is a feast of the Lord, 3 are Marian, St Joseph, the Archangels, 9 feasts of the Apostles plus the feasts of St Stephen Proto-martyr and the Holy Innocents).
- Of Feasts of the Second Class there are 13 or 14 (2 are feasts of the Lord, 1 of the Blessed Virgin, 6 second feasts of the Apostles and Evangelists, together with Barnabas; furthermore: the Dedication of the Lateran Basilica, 3 or 4 of other saints' feasts: St Laurence, Augustine, Beheading of St John the Baptist, and the fourth is in Europe: St Benedict as the main Patron of the continent).
- Of Memoria of the First Class there are 39, of Memoria of the Second Class, 42.

In sum, the proposal is for 100 major commemorations to be completed with approximately 80–100 minor ones. The number is similar to that found in the new calendar, but almost half of it is made up of Memorias of the Second Class which only affect observation of ferial days. Although arguments may be put forward on behalf of single entries, I am not so pretentious as to regard this list as a real and complete proposal. The only thing I wanted to demonstrate is that the principles I have proposed could really work in practice.

17

THE READINGS OF THE MASS

I. The Problems and Principles of the Solution

'The treasures of the Bible are to be opened up more lavishly, so that richer fare may be provided for the faithful at the table of God's word. In this way a more representative portion of the Holy Scriptures will be read to the people in the course of a prescribed number of years.' This is everything that the Liturgical Constitution *Sacrosanctum Concilium* stipulated concerning the readings.[1]

'Though the Council laid the foundation of the reform by the Liturgical Constitution, the reform itself was implemented by a committee. Therefore, the details of the reform cannot be attributed unequivocally to the Council. The Council was an open beginning, but its broad framework left space for different kinds of realization.' Joseph Cardinal Ratzinger said this in 1994.[2]

The *Consilium* interpreted §51 of the Constitution as sufficient justification to annul the traditional order of readings entirely. A completely new system of pericopes was produced. The new system's most conspicuous characteristics are: (a) the readings are distributed across three years on Sundays and two on weekdays ; (b) an Old Testament reading has been introduced before the Epistle; (c) the books of the Bible are read semi-continuously; and (d) the *Consilium* attempted to introduce parallels between the content of the Old Testament reading and the Gospel.

To (a): an ordering of that kind may have had precedents in the very early period of Christian liturgy (there are no certain documents to support the claim).[3]

---

[1] Vatican Council II, Dogmatic Constitution on the Sacred Liturgy, *Sacrosanctum Concilium* (1963), §51: 'Quo ditior mensa verbi Dei paretur fidelibus, thesauri biblici largius aperiantur, ita ut, intra praestitutum annorum spatium, praestantior pars Scripturarum Sanctarum populo legatur'. Cf. Klaus Gamber (2002), *The Modern Rite*, p. 13.

[2] Cardinal Joseph Ratzinger (1994), subchapter 1.2: 'Die Liturgiekonstitution des Konzils hat zwar die Grundlagen für die Reform gelegt; die Reform selbst wurde dann von einem nachkonziliaren Rat gestaltet und kann in ihren konkreten Details nicht einfach auf das Konzil zurückgeführt werden. Das Konzil war ein offener Anfang, dessen großer Rahmen mehrere Verwirklichungen zuließ.'

[3] The earliest document of a fixed cycle of readings is that of the Church in Jerusalem, which

To (b): in the Roman Rite the two-reading system is typical; any reading(s) before the Epistle is an exceptional device for only some days.[4]

To (c): it is an indisputable fact that more biblical sections are read than earlier.

To (d): the comparison between the Old Testament figures or antetypes and their fulfilment in the New Testament is an important and characteristic motive of Catholic doctrine, theology and iconography, and it is based on the teaching of the Fathers.

On the other hand, the new order has at least as many problems as benefits. These were studied in detail in my *Bugnini-Liturgy*.[5]

In brief:

(a) Very old arrangements of texts – often going back to Pope St Gregory – have been put aside.[6]

(b) The richness of the readings (mostly in the Gospel) is somewhat illusory; in fact, there are not enough distinct Gospel sections, with the result that the same theme is read on different days of different years from different books, and not always in the most appropriate wording.[7]

(c) The three-year system totally dissolved the association between the liturgical day (and its texts) and the periscopes assigned; this is a loss both in a liturgical and pastoral perspective, and it is doubtful whether the loss or the gain was bigger.

(d) Continuous reading of the biblical books imports only a pseudo-regularity into the reading process: the faithful cannot follow the sequence from Sunday to Sunday; the weekly sequence is interrupted by the feasts of the saints; only few people attend Mass every day. What people can observe is not the continuity of reading, but the random appearance of themes over the three-year cycle.

(e) The rejection of the ancient order of pericopes is a loss also in an ecumenical perspective, since several Protestant traditions (Lutherans and Anglicans, among others) kept it, at least as an alternative.

(f) The rejection of the old Gospels creates many difficulties in the assignation of antiphons to the Benedictus and Magnificat in the Office.

---

survived in an Armenian translation; cf. Peter Jeffery (1992), 'Jerusalem and Rome (and Constantinople)', pp. 64–65.

[4] Aimé Georges Martimort (1984), 'A propos du nombre des lectures à le messe', pp. 42–51. James McKinnon (2000a), *The Advent Project*, p. 456: 'The classic assumption . . . formulated by Louis Duchesne in his *Origines du culte chrétien* of 1899 – and subsequently embraced by liturgiologists and musicologists alike – is that the readings and chants followed a neatly symmetrical fivefold sequence: (1) Old Testament reading, (2) psalm, (3) New Testament reading, (4) psalm and (5) gospel . . . It is hardly an exaggeration to say that Duchesne's scheme collapses entirely . . . [Martimort] observes that more often than not the sources show only a single reading before the gospel . . . either from the Old Testament or more often from the New, as opposed to the purportedly obligatory readings from both.' There is, however an Old Testament first reading in the Ambrosian Rite.

[5] Dobszay (2003), *The Bugnini-Liturgy and the Reform of the Reform*, chapter 5.

[6] McKinnon (2000a), *The Advent Project*, pp. 113–18.

[7] Dobszay (2003), *The Bugnini-Liturgy and the Reform of the Reform*, pp. 125–33.

The reform *misunderstood* the role of the Mass readings. In their rudimentary state they may have had a merely didactic function. In the classical Roman Rite, however, the readings, and first of all, the Gospels, are clearly outlined images of the *mysteries*, remarkable passages that seize hold of people's attention.[8] Therefore, not all passages are equally suitable to become Sunday pericopes.[9] Biblical catechesis, personal meditation or the Office (Vigils) are more appropriate occasions on which to learn the Bible, than the Mass itself.[10]

For those who adhere to the 1962 Missal, there is no doubt that the traditional order of the pericopes should be preserved or restored. If we interpret the Liturgical Constitution as a programme for the reform of the *traditional* Roman liturgy and not an indeterminate mandate to produce a new one, then also §51 should be interpreted with respect to the 1962 Missal. Keeping the order of the 1962 Missal without any change would be, however, tantamount to a wholesale rejection of the Liturgical Constitution *Sacrosanctum Concilium*. At the same time, following the new lectionary means that we have rejected the continuity and organic development of the Roman Rite. Consequently, the only way between the two extremes is to take the 1962 Missal and examine what possible and legitimate changes can be made in the true spirit of the Council, for the genuine benefit of the Church,[11] without breaking down the centuries-old system. In other words, the question is: how can §51 be implemented in a way that leaves the tradition of the Roman Rite essentially untouched.

What are the principles that can ensure the harmonious fulfilment of the two requirements? In my opinion the classical system of pericopes should be retained in the following way:

(a) The eminent days and seasons must have *stable* readings, associated with the liturgical day or season.
(b) The Sundays and feast days must have their proper pericopes taken from distinct and important biblical sections.

---

[8] Thomas M. Kocik (2003), *The Reform of the Reform*, p. 53 quotes from Romano Amerio: 'The policy to put as much as possible of the treasures of the Bible before the people of God during worship runs into a serious difficulty, inasmuch as it frustrates the use of the memory, as an educational principle. In the traditional rite, in the course of the liturgical year the people would hear on a Sunday a single annual cycle of Gospel passages . . . Because man's knowledge comes to very little without memory, the knowledge of the Bible produced by the new lectionary is very slight, inasmuch as the same thing only recurs every third year . . .' A one-year system prevails also in the Byzantine – Adrian Fortescue (1912), *The Mass*, 4th edn 2005, p. 258 – and the Ambrosian Rite. Also Pius Parsch pinpoints the mystical character of the pericopes: 'The liturgy does not wish to teach us in the pericopes, but to present the images of mysteries: their meaning is Christ is acting this way in the Eucharist' (Pius Parsch (1935), *Meßerklärung im Geiste der liturgischen Erneuerung*, chapter 9, paragraph 5). He consequently explains in this sense the texts of Gospels throughout the year in his *The Church's Year of Grace* ('The Gospel teaches us, on one hand, and presents the mystical image of the Mass on the other' – it says at the Fourth Sunday after Pentecost).

[9] See the examples in Dobszay (2003), *The Bugnini-Liturgy and the Reform of the Reform*, p. 131.

[10] John P. Parsons (2003), 'A Reform of the Reform?', p. 242.

[11] *Sacrosanctum Concilium* (1963), §23. Cf. Kocik (2003), *The Reform of the Reform*, p. 54; Brian W. Harrison, OS (2003), 'The Postconciliar Eucharistic Liturgy', p. 1813.

(c) Smaller additions and modifications can be made in the classical order, while leaving the order as a whole in its clearly recognizable state.
(d) The somewhat 'capricious' character of the traditional order should not be replaced by pedantic, didactically motivated schemes.

On the other hand, the conciliar reforms require:

(a) An increase in the selection of readings.
(b) That the one-year period should be extended to a longer time (but, we stress, the exact way was not defined by the Council).
(c) The Old Testament readings be given more prominence.

The draft below is not a 'plan', merely an illustration for the thesis that the two sets of requirements *can* be combined. The draft keeps the order of readings essentially intact, as they are in the 1962 Missal. It will be enough now to list the additions; the traditional scheme is written out only when it is placed in a new context.

The time *from Advent to Trinity Sunday* follows a one-year system, and it leaves the traditional arrangement nearly intact. Thus it reinstates the association between the liturgical day and its readings precisely during the 'holy half-year', the most important period of the liturgical year.

In *Ordinary Time* there are two series. The first is the same as in the traditional system; the other one (to be used in every other year) contains the most 'pericope-like' texts of the new lectionary.

A *reading before the Epistle* is read only in the first half of the year, Ordinary Time need not be weighed down with additional readings. The aim of the Old Testament readings of the first half-year period is not to coordinate them with the Gospel (this method was adapted in the traditional system only on some weekdays of Lent and some feasts[12]), but to insert significant chapters of the history of salvation, those which are most fitting to the Advent–Christmas, or the Lenten–Paschal seasons.[13] Thanks to the one-year system these will become more memorable. The reading of the Old Testament is given, of course, more space in the Office and on other occasions.

There is no need to offer a full series for *weekdays* (except the traditional ones in Lent). The reiteration of the Sunday pericopes raises their dignity and importance. Moreover, the feasts that occur during the week prevent the actual reading of six pairs of readings. In the early Middle Ages certain churches assigned Epistles and Gospels to Masses on Wednesdays and Fridays.[14] Hence it seems sufficient to add two pairs of weekly readings to the lectionary, which can be read either on Wednesdays and Fridays, or – if they are impeded by a

---

[12] Fortescue (1912), *The Mass*, 2nd edn 2005), p. 262.
[13] The Old Testament reading and the Epistle are selected also in the Ambrosian Liturgy with regard for the season and not to the Gospel of the day.
[14] A good survey of them is easily accessible in Nicholas Sandon (1984), *The Use of Salisbury*. Cf. John P. Parsons (2003), 'A Reform of the Reform?', p. 245.

feast – on any other day. For Ordinary Time a *two-year series* can be given for these weekdays. The texts can be taken mainly from the new lectionary.

The readings of the Commons of Saints were always a selection and the texts could, and can, be taken from it according to the peculiarities of the saint celebrated. The sanctoral cycle contained only a few proper readings; there is no problem regarding their selection; in this respect the difference between the old and new lectionary is negligible.

II. *The Christmas Season*

In the 'proposal' the Epistles and Gospels of the four Advent Sundays are the same as in the 1962 Missal. The other traditional Gospel pericope for the First Sunday of Advent (Christ's entrance to Jerusalem, chosen because of the '*Benedictus qui venit*' acclamation!) has a profound meaning and it is present also in some Protestant traditions. It would be difficult to reintroduce it into liturgical practice; perhaps only as an alternative option, or in the context of particular traditions.

The Old Testament readings before the Epistle are powerful prophecies from Isaiah. They are taken from the new lectionary: from year A for the First and Third Sundays; from year B for the Second Sunday, and from the Wednesday of the third week for the Fourth Sunday. Two texts of the readings are identical with the prophecies of the Ember Days in the classical Missal.

The readings of the Ember Days remain as they are, together with the rubric that allows the omission – except in the main Mass – of the five Old Testament readings on Saturday.[15] In the Tridentine Missal the Gospel for Ember Saturday was the anticipation of the Fourth Sunday text; it is replaced here by the Magnificat, and so the narration becomes full on the three Ember Days.

The weekday readings can be found in the new lectionary.

The Old Testament readings on the Vigil of Christmas and in the three Masses of the Solemnity can be found in nearly all medieval Missals.[16]

The readings of the Masses on the feasts of St Stephen, St John the Apostle and the Holy Innocents are better in the 1962 Missal than the ones selected for the new lectionary, so they would remain as earlier. The Gospel of the Circumcision is a little longer in the new lectionary, but includes also the entire old text.

The Sunday between December 30th and January 5th is regarded in the following list as the date for the feast of the Holy Family. The first reading takes over the text of the new lectionary; the Epistle of this Sunday in the Old Missal is suitable also for the feast. Of the three possible Gospels of the new lectionary the best is the 'flight into Egypt': it is most fitting in the time between the Holy Innocents and Epiphany. (The text on the prophecy of Anna will be the Gospel of the Purification; that of the 12-year-old Christ-child – which would be too early

---

[15] As in the 1962 Missal.
[16] For their use in the Sarum Rite see Nicholas Sandon (1984), *The Use of Salisbury*, vol. 2, pp. 40, 43 (with a trope!), pp. 50, 54.

only a few days after Christmas – is the traditional Gospel of the First Sunday after Epiphany.)

The first reading of Epiphany is the Epistle of the old Missal; the Epistle is taken from the new lectionary. The eighth day of the Octave is a commemoration of the Baptism of the Lord. The Epistle is from the new lectionary; the narration of the event itself is more complete in St John's text than in those of the Synoptic Gospels.

The Sundays after Epiphany – as Ordinary Sundays – have only two readings. On the First and Second Sundays they are the traditional ones. Since the 'proposal' foresees a two-year system for Ordinary Sundays, there is more 'place' to include additional texts appropriate for the period (the vocation of the Apostles on the Third Sunday; so the Gospel on the 'storm at sea' shifts one week later). In year B the readings are selected from the new lectionary.

The 'proposal' (which is not really a proposal, only a suggestion illustrating the direction of the rearrangement) is therefore as follows. The asterisk means that the reading remains as it is in the 1962 Missal:

Day	First reading	Epistle	Gospel
Advent first week, Sunday	Isa. 2.2-5 *let us go up to the mountain of the Lord*	*	*
→ feria		1 Cor. 1.3-9 *waiting for the manifestation of our Lord*	Mk 1.3-9 *A voice of one crying in the desert*
→ feria		1 Thess. 3.12-4.2 *to confirm your hearts . . . at the coming of our Lord*	Lk. 3.7-18 *I indeed baptize you with water . . .*
Second week, Sunday	Isa. 40.1-5 + 9-11 *be comforted – prepare the way*	*	*
→ feria		Phil. 1.4-6 + 8-11 *who hath begun a good work in you will perfect it*	Mt. 11.11-15 *he is Elias that is to come . . .*
→ feria		2 Cor. 3.18-4:5 *we all beholding the glory of the Lord*	Mt. 11.16-18 *on the fasting of John*

(*continued*)

Day	First reading	Epistle	Gospel
Third week, Sunday	Isa. 35.1-7 *the wilderness shall rejoice*	*	*
Ember Wednesday →	Isa. 2.2-5 *let us go up to the mountain of the Lord*	*	*
Ember Friday →		Isa. 11.1-7 *the wolf shall dwell with the lamb*	*
Ember Saturday →	(* * * * *)	*	Lk. 1.45-56 *the canticle of Mary*
Fourth week, Sunday	Isa. 45.6b-8 + 8.21b-26 *Drop down dew, ye heavens from above!*	*	*
feria →		2 Pet. 3.8-14 *the day of the Lord shall come as a thief*	Jn 1.15-18 *John beareth witness of him*
Vigil of Nativity	Isa. 62.1-4 *thou shalt no more be called Forsaken*	*	*
Nativity, first Mass	Isa. 9.2 + 6-7 *a Child is born to us*	*	*
Second Mass	Isa. 61.1-3 + 62.11-12 *the spirit of the Lord is upon me*	*	*
Third Mass	Isa. 52.6-10 *I myself that spoke, behold I am here*	*	*
Stephen martyr		*	*
John the Apostle		*	*
Holy Innocents		*	*

Day	First reading	Epistle	Gospel
Sunday of the Holy Family	Eccl. 3.3-7 *he that honoureth his father . . .*	*	Mt. 2.13-15 + 19–23 *fly into Egypt*
Circumcision		*	Lk. 2.16-21 *circumcision of the Lord*
Epiphany	Isa. 60.1-6 *be enlightened, O Jerusalem*	Eph. 3.2-3a + 5-6 *the Gentiles should be fellow heirs*	*
Post Epiphany			
First Sunday		Rom. 12.1-5 * *present your bodies a living sacrifice*	Lk. 2.42-52 * *I must be about my Father's business*
The eighth day after Epiphany		Acts 10.34-38 *how God annointed him with the Holy Ghost*	Jn 1.29-34 *the Lord's baptism Baptismus Domini*
Second Sunday		*	*
Third Sunday			
→ in anno A		*	Jn 1.35-42 *the call of Peter and Andrew*
→ in anno B		1 Cor. 1.26-31 *the foolish things of the world hath God chosen*	Mt. 4.12-23 *the call of the Apostles*
Fourth Sunday			
→ A		*	= * D3
→ B		1 Cor. 2.6-10 *we speak the wisdom of God*	Lk. 4.21-30 *Jesus in the synagogue of Nazareth*
Fifth Sunday			
→ A		*	= * D4
→ B		1 Cor. 9.16-19 *woe unto me if I preach not the gospel*	Mk 1.21-28 *Jesus in the synagogue of Capernaum*

(*continued*)

Day	First reading	Epistle	Gospel
Sixth Sunday			
→ A		*	= * D5
→ B		1 Cor. 10.31-11.2 *whether you eat or drink . . . do all to the glory of God*	Mt. 13.31-5 *the grain of mustard seed*

III. The Seasons of Lent and Easter

The traditional readings on the Sundays and weekdays during these holy seasons of the highest dignity remain nearly intact. The most important change is that the Third, Fourth and Fifth Sundays of Lent get back their ancient 'catechumenal' Gospels (as it is in year A of the new lectionary). They are: on the Third Sunday: the Samaritan woman, on the Fourth Sunday: the healing of the blind man, on the Fifth Sunday: the resurrection of Lazarus.[17] The Gospel sections of these Sundays exchange their positions with the appropriate weekdays, and this leads to a change in the Epistle.[18]

In the 1962 Missal the Gospel on the Saturday of the first week was identical with the text of the second Sunday. (Most precisely: in earlier times the Sunday had no proper Mass; later the Gospel about the woman of Canaan was taken over to this day, and finally the Saturday Gospel – kept also in its original position – was used to make up for the missing text.) Therefore, this 'proposal' takes the Gospel for the Saturday from the new lectionary (Tuesday of the first week).

On Sundays the Old Testament readings before the Epistle present the great events of salvation history: the Fall, the Flood, the sacrifice of Abraham, God's appearance to Moses, the giving of Manna, the bringing forth of water, the Decalogue. On the two Passion-Sundays the prophetical words of Christ's suffering are read.

The famous long text by Isaiah was originally read on Holy Wednesday; in the new lectionary it was moved to Good Friday (which is not really a good place for it[19]). Now it is divided in two, with the first part set down for Palm Sunday,[20] and the second in its original position (Wednesday of Holy Week).

---

[17] In these three cases the optional abbreviation given in the new lectionary can be adopted.

[18] The new first reading on the third Sunday was coordinated to the Gospel at its earlier place (Friday of the third week). The Epistle (also related to this Gospel) is read on this Sunday, in year C according to the new lectionary. The Gospel of this Sunday is moved to Friday of the third week, and since the weekday Epistles are regularly taken from the Old Testament, an appropriate reading was required, taken from the new lectionary (Thursday of the third week). The Wednesday of the fourth week had traditionally two Old Testament readings. In place of the second there is a reading in harmony with this Gospel (from year C the fourth Sunday in the new lectionary). The earlier Old Testament reading on the Friday of the fourth week is transposed, along with the day's Gospel, to the fifth Sunday.

[19] Cf. Dobszay (2003), *The Bugnini-Liturgy and the Reform of the Reform*, p. 34.

[20] The prophecy by Isaiah is also the first reading on Palm Sunday in the Ambrosian Rite.

On Good Friday the traditional order is kept, but I think it would be good to transfer the Exodus text to first place, and after that to read the passage from the letter to the Hebrews, as in the new lectionary.

The 1962 Missal has four readings for the Easter Vigil as it was fixed by Pius XII. They are well selected and the number corresponds to an old and widespread tradition.[21] However, the 12-reading system of ancient Rome should also have been preserved, at least as an appendix (for cathedrals, monasteries), with special regard to the valuable Collects following them.

The Epistle of Easter Monday was transferred to Sunday as the first reading of the day (as it is in the new lectionary). Therefore the Monday was given a similar sermon from the new lectionary (year A, Second Sunday after Easter).

The first reading before the traditional Gospel pericopes of the Easter season is taken from the Acts of the Apostles, then, commencing with the third Sunday, the first reading is taken from the Book of Revelation; this arrangement closely corresponds to the new lectionary. The Gospels on these Sundays are the same as in the traditional arrangement (each of them are the Gospel accounts of the resurrection and, from the third Sunday forward, are then excerpts from the last sermon of the Lord).[22] The two pairs of ferial readings are taken from the new lectionary coordinated with the other pericopes.

Considering these points, the 'proposed' order of readings is as follows. Those days when the Tridentine readings remained unchanged are skipped over in the list. The asterisk means that the readings are identical with the one in the 1962 Missal.

Day	First reading	Epistle	Gospel
Septuagesima	Gen. 2.7-9 + 15-16 + 3.1-8: *the fall of our first parents*	*	*
Sexagesima	Gen. 6.5-8 + 7.1-4 + 17-23 *the ark in the deluge*	*	*
Quinquagesima	Gen. 22.1-18 *the sacrifice of Abraham*	*	*
Lent, First Sunday	Exod. 3.1-9a + 13-15 *God calls Moses out of the midst of the burning bush*	*	*

(continued)

---

[21] They are as in almost all medieval lectionaries: Gen. 1.1-31 + 2.1-2; Exod. 14.24-31 + 15.1; Isa. 4.1-6 (better in the 1962 Missal: 4.2-6); Deut. 31.22-30.
[22] Cf. Dobszay (2003), *The Bugnini-Liturgy and the Reform of the Reform*, pp. 127–29.

Day	First reading	Epistle	Gospel
Ember Saturday	* * * * *	*	Matt. 6.7-15 *when you are praying . . .*
Second Sunday	Exod. 16.2-7 + 13-15 *the manna*	*	*
Third Sunday	Num. 20.1-3 + 6-13 *open a fountain of living water . . .*	1 Cor. 10.1-6, 10-12 *all drank the same spiritual drink*	Jn 4.5-42 *the Samaritan woman*
Week 3, Thursday		Jer. 7.23-28 *I have sent to you all my servants the prophets*	Lk. 11.14-28 *I by the finger of God cast out devils*
Fourth Sunday	Exod. 20.1-17 *The ten commandments*	Gal. 4.22-31 *Abraham had two sons*	Jn 9.1-41 *the man blind from his birth*
Week 4, Wednesday	Ezek. 36.23-28 *I will pour upon you clean water*	Josh. 5.9a + 10-12 *they ate the corn of the land of Canaan*	Jn 6.1-15 *the miracle of bread*
Week 4, Friday		Wis 2.1a + 12-22 *let us condemn him to a most shameful death*	Jn 8.46-59 *Before Abraham was made, I am*
Fifth (Passion) Sunday	I Kgs 17.17-24 *the widow of Zarephath*	Heb. 9.11-15 *Christ high Priest of the good things to come*	Jn 11.1-45 *Christ raises Lazarus to life*
Palm Sunday	Isa. 53.1-6 *He hath borne our infirmities*	*	*
Holy Wednesday	*	Isa. 53.7-12 *He was offered because it was his own will*	*
Paschal Vigil	*	*	*
Resurrection Sunday	Acts 10.34a + 37-43 *Peter's sermon on the resurrection*	*	*

Day	First reading	Epistle	Gospel
Easter Monday		Acts 2.14 + 22-28 *Peter's sermon on the day of Pentecost*	*
First Sunday after Resurrection	Acts 2.42-47 *persevering in the doctrine of the apostles*	*	*
→ feria		Acts 4.23-31 *with one accord lifted up their voice to God*	Jn 3.7-15 *Jesus and Nicodemus*
→ feria		Acts 4.32-5 *all things were common unto them*	Jn 3.7-15 *Jesus told Nicodemus: you must be born again*
Second Sunday	Acts 3.1-10 *in the name of Jesus Christ . . . arise and walk*	*	*
→ feria		Acts 5.17-32 *Peter before the council*	Jn 10.27-30 *my sheep hear my voice*
→ feria		Acts 11.1-18 *God hath also to the Gentiles given repentance unto life*	Jn 12.44-50 *he that seeth me, seeth him that sent me*
Third Sunday	Rev. 1.9-11a + 12-13 + 17-19 *the first vision*	*	*
→ feria		Rev. 5.11-14 *the Lamb that was slain is worthy . . .'*	Jn 14.1-4 *let not your hearts be troubled*
→ feria		Rev. 7.9 + 14b-17 *I saw a great multitude*	Jn 15.12-17 *greater love than this no man hath . . .*

(*continued*)

Day	First reading	Epistle	Gospel
Fourth Sunday	Rev. 21.1-5a *I saw a new heaven and a new earth*	*	*
→ feria		Rev. 21.10-14 + 22-3 *the holy city*	Jn 15.1-8 *I am the true vine*
→ feria		Rev. 22.1-5 *and night shall be no more*	Jn 15.18-21 *the world hateth you*
Fifth Sunday	Rev. 22.12 + 16-17 *Maranatha, come!*	*	*
Rogation days		*	*
Vigil of Ascension		*	*
Ascension	Acts 1.1-11 *the Lord's ascension*	Eph. 1.17-23 *the fullness of him who is filled all in all*	*
Sixth Sunday	Acts 1.12-14 *all these were persevering with one mind in prayer*	*	*
Vigil of Pentecost		*	*
Pentecost	Acts 2.1-11 *they were all filled with the Holy Ghost*	*	*
Within the Octave		*	*
Trinity Sunday		*	*
Corpus Christi		*	*

IV. The Readings for the Sundays after Pentecost

Following the principles explained above, the Sundays after Pentecost are arranged with two readings, but years A and B each have their own series. The readings in year A are identical with the traditional system; year B takes another series drawn from the 1970 lectionary.

In the classical Roman Rite the Gospel pericopes followed each other without any mechanical or 'rational' order. They were simply a sequence of important and memorable texts. The Epistles appear – with small exceptions – in the order of

St Paul's letters, without following any strict rule. This sequence of the Epistles is missing from the first to the fourth Sundays[23] (where there are instead two parts from the first letter of St John, and two from the first letter of St Peter, but with an excerpt from St Paul's letter to the Romans in between). On the sixth to eighth Sundays sections of the letter to the Romans follow, and on the ninth to twelfth Sundays the letter to the Corinthians, on the thirteenth to twenty-fourth Sundays the letters to the Galatians, Ephesians, Philippians and Colossians (on the eighteenth Sunday this sequence is broken with a paragraph from the first letter to the Corinthians). The sections of each letter proceed sequentially from the various chapters; but there is no strict continuous reading. The sections chosen are not coordinated to the Gospel periscope or any other part of the daily liturgy, but proceed only in the order of the New Testament canon, perhaps as a remnant of a very old practice, that of the 'set-principle'.[24]

In year B the suggested readings are arranged very similarly to the old system. Gospels having the quality of a 'pericope' are taken over from the 1970 lectionary. They are selected from the synoptic books but without any forced or didactic underlying schema. Likewise, the Epistles are taken from the 1970 lectionary, and arranged in parallel with year A.

The changing number of the post-Pentecost Sundays creates a difficulty both in the classical Roman Rite and in the new calendar. The later is based on an equal number of Ordinary Sundays during each year; so the readings of some Sundays are placed either at the end of period after Epiphany, or at the beginning of the period 'after Pentecost', depending on the date of Easter. This arrangement seems to be logical but it pays no attention to the different character and meaning of the seasons before Lent and after Pentecost.[25] The point of break and resumption may occur between different Sundays each year. The old calendar simply inserted the Sundays omitted from the period after Epiphany before the last Sunday of the liturgical year, adjusted to the number of 'free Sundays'. Although as an arrangement this is not entirely rational, and perhaps not entirely satisfactory, it seems impossible to suggest anything else: as a system it does at least have the advantage of venerable longevity of use.

As I said earlier, the position of the feast of Christ the King on the last Sunday of the year is not the worst date for this commemoration. The first reading before the Epistle and Gospel (taken from the 1962 Missal) is taken from the Book of Revelation, as it is in the new lectionary.

The table below shows the parallelism of the two years:

[23] For the additional nature of these four Sundays see McKinnon (1992a), 'The Roman Post-Pentecostal Communio Series', pp. 183–85.
[24] Other relics of this method can be found in the Lenten Communions, proper chants of the post-Pentecost Masses; in the Office-responsories in the Vigils of the post-Epiphany season.
[25] Cf. Dobszay (2003), *The Bugnini-Liturgy and the Reform of the Reform*, pp. 142–43.

Sunday	Year A	Year B
Sundays post Pentecost 1	* 1 Jn 4.8-21 *	Rom. 3.21-25a, 28 Mt. 5.1-12a *the eight beatitudes*
2	* 1 Jn 3.13-18 *	Rom. 5.6-11 Mt. 5.13-16 *you are the salt of the earth*
3	* 1 Pet. 5.6-11 *	Rom. 5.12-15 Lk. 5.1-11 *from henceforth thou shalt catch men*
4	* Rom. 8.18-23 *	Rom. 8.9 and 11-13 Mt. 10.26-33 *fear ye not them that kill the body*
5	* 1 Pet. 3.8-15 *	Rom. 8.26-30 Lk. 11:1-13 *the Lord's Prayer*
6	* Rom. 6.3-11 *	Rom. 8.35, 37-39 Mt. 7.21-7. *Not every one that saith to me, Lord, Lord . . .*
7	* Rom. 6.19-23 *	Rom. 12.1-2 Lk. 16.19-31 *of the rich man and Lazarus*
8	* Rom. 8.12-17 *	Rom. 14.7-9 Mk 4.26-34 *of the grain of mustard seed*
9	* 1 Cor. 10.6-13 *	1 Cor. 1.26-31 Mk 4.35-40 *a great storm of wind on the sea*
10	* 1 Cor. 12.2-11 *	1 Cor. 2.6-10 Lk. 17.5-10 *we are unprofitable servants*
11	* 1 Cor. 15.1-10 *	1 Cor. 3.16-23 Lk. 10.38-42 *Mary and Martha*
12	* 2 Cor. 3.4-9 *	2 Cor. 1.18-22 Mk 10.17-30 *the rich young man*
13	* Gal. 3.16-22 *	2 Cor. 4.6-11 Mt. 13.44-46 *a treasure hidden in a field*
14	* Gal. 5.16-24 *	2 Cor. 5.6-10 Mt. 14.22-33 *Jesus walks upon the sea*
15	* Gal. 5.25-6; 6.1-10 *	2 Cor. 5.14-17 Mt. 23.1-12 *call none your father upon earth*
16	* Eph. 3.13-21 *	Gal. 1.1-2, 6-10 Mt. 11.25-30 *Thou hast revealed these things to the little ones*

Sunday	Year A	Year B
17	* Eph. 4.1-6 *	Gal. 2.16, 19-21 Lk. 13.22-30 *strive to enter by the narrow gate*
18	* 1 Cor. 1.4-8 *	Gal. 3.26-9 Lk. 14.1, 7-14 *sit down in the lowest place*
19	* Eph. 4.23-8 *	Gal. 5.1, 13-18 Mk 9.30-36 *if any man desire to be first, he shall be the last of all*
20	* Eph. 5.15-21 *	Eph. 1.3-14 Mk 12.38-44 *a poor widow*
21	* Eph. 6.10-17 *	Eph. 2.13-18 Mt. 21.33-43 *He will bring those evil men to an evil end*
22	* Phil. 1.6-11 *	Eph. 4.30-5:2 Lk. 12.32-48 *let your loins be girt and lamps burning in your hands*
23	* Phil. 3.17.21; 4.1-3 *	Phil. 1.20c-24, 27a Matt. 25.1-13 *the wise virgins*
24	* Col. 1.9-13 *	Col. 1.15-20 Mk 13.24-32 *the powers that are in heaven shall be moved*
Christ the King	Rev. 1.4-8 Col. 1.12-20 Mt. 25.31-46	

I have omitted making a detailed presentation of the (twice weekly) ferial Epistles and Gospels. The narration of events and sermons as formulated in the parallel Gospels are very close to each other, but one of them is often more complete than the others. For this reason there is no real profit if the same parallel event is repeatedly retold, on different days, and from the varying Gospel accounts. If these parallel narrations are excluded from the weekday cycle, the number of pairs of weekdays per week during the years A and B are quite sufficient to provide for all the excerpts from the Gospels that are not scheduled to be read on Sundays and feasts. In the case of the Epistles, it is logical to take some sections from the same biblical book over a given time, in the manner we have already observed in the arrangement of the Epistles of the Ordinary Sundays according to the classical lectionary. Since the two-reading system of Ordinary Sundays made the number of Old Testament readings less, the majority of the ferial Epistles could be taken from the Old Testament books.

As can be seen from the proposals made, the traditional order of the classical Roman Rite remains practically unchanged. The only change (in the three

Lenten Sundays) selects not only 'better' pericopes, but in fact represents the return to an earlier tradition. To summarize, the changes in comparison to the 1962 Missal are:

(a) the presence of Old Testament readings in the first half-year
(b) the addition of an alternative series for Ordinary Time (year B) and
(c) provision for proper readings on *two* weekdays of each week (also a return to a practice with an earlier history in the classical Roman tradtion).

In this way the actual will of the Council has been fulfilled, when the Council Fathers stated: 'the treasury of the Bible is opened up more lavishly'.[26] On the other hand, the original principles of the classical Roman arrangements of Scripture are preserved untouched, such that: (1) there is a stable association between the readings and the given liturgical day; (2) the readings enjoy the quality of an appropriate pericopel and furthermore (3) the order of the readings itself has been preserved: nearly all the Epistles and Gospels – the texts deepened over the centuries by numerous meditations, spiritual and ascetical commentaries – are retained on their original days. In concrete terms, of the 130 Sunday or feast day Epistles and Gospels, 119 are the same and they are read on the same day as in the 1962 Missal (91.6 per cent); 11 readings (8.4 per cent) are taken over from the new lectionary. Fifty-four readings are additions for the Ordinary Sundays of what we have now called year B, mostly taken from the 1970 lectionary.

What I have sought to show is that what should have been aimed at as the actual *conciliar* reform (through a genuinely organic development) of the classical *Roman* Rite is indeed quite able to be accomplished.

---

[26] *Sacrosanctum Concilium* (1963), §51.

18

THE PROPER CHANTS OF THE MASS

I have discussed this topic in greater depth in several articles published recently.[1] Here, I want to concentrate on the exploration of possibilities for genuine organic development.

I. The Basic Problem

The chant of the Propers is an integral part of the classical Roman liturgy: in fact, it was one of the first elements to be crystallized during its early development.[2] Its position was so stable, so 'canonized', that it hardly developed further after the eighth century, except in one single genre, the Alleluia chant. Theologically, the selection of the chant texts (mostly from psalms) was built on a traditional biblical interpretation that can be traced to the sayings of Christ and his Apostles. This interpretation was supplied with an expanded explanation in the *enarrationes* of Origen and St Augustine of Hippo. Out of this tradition of interpretation a system of associations arose between the biblical and psalmic texts together with the other parts of the liturgy.[3] To omit the chants of the Propers from any celebration of the Roman Mass – even if they are at least recited – is an inexcusable mutilation of the Roman Rite in itself.

There are traces of an earlier stage – except on the occasion of great solemnities – when the material was presented to the singers in numerically arranged series or seasonal 'sets'. In some parts of the liturgical year the Communions, Introits, and so forth, were, until quite late, indicated in merely a numerical order.[4] When the annual cycle of proper chants was forged from this material, however – probably in the seventh century – the 'sets' were distributed among the liturgical days, and so a rich and associative connection emerged between the individual chants and the proper days on which they were to be sung.[5] These connections do not arise from any didactic project, or organizing central 'thought' for the liturgical day,

---

[1] Dobszay (2003), *The Bugnini-Liturgy and the Reform of the Reform*, pp. 85–120; (2007), 'A Living Gregorian Chant'; and (2009), 'The Proper Chants of the Roman Rite'.
[2] James McKinnon (2000), *The Advent Project*, pp. 22–36, 45–53.
[3] For an example see Dobszay (2009), 'The Proper Chants of the Roman Rite'.
[4] McKinnon (2000a), *The Advent Project*, pp. 212, 237, 331–34.
[5] James McKinnon (1995b), 'Properization: The Roman Mass'.

and the interlectionary chants (for instance, the Gradual chant) do not provide a pedagogical reflection on the previous reading;[6] rather the relationship is of an artistic and psychological nature. If we were to deny the existence and importance of these connections in the understanding and reception of the classical Roman Rite we would be falsifying its history and its meaning.

The motives that urge us to reconsider the future of this repertory are even more musical than liturgical. The most ancient group of proper chants dates back probably to the tradition of the psalm-singers, as liturgical soloists. But the full repertory and its distribution over the year was the achievement of the *scholas* of the Roman basilicas.[7] These were groups of singers living in one house, with strong institutional and financial support. They were able to undertake their work in exceptionally fruitful circumstances. The highest Church authority enabled and guaranteed the conditions of their activity, the creation, re-learning, and worthy performance of an artistic repertory. The elaborate melodies they produced reflect the results of this musical foundry. The difficulty of learning and performing these pieces came not so much from their ornate style, as from the fact that in the repertory of the Mass each text possessed an individual musical form, melody and composition. A knowledge of the style in question was, of course, a great help in acquiring the repertory, yet each piece had to be learned individually. In Office genres (the antiphons, or the responsories) the 'original' part of the repertory was produced by the varied repetition of a modest number of melodic 'ideas' or models. For somebody who knew the model, it was not really difficult to learn a new variant linked to a new text.[8] In the Mass Propers, on the contrary, several hundred melodies had to be learnt, which required constant training and, consequently, salaried, professional musicians.

After the eighth century more and more churches wanted to imitate the practice of the scholas of Rome, and in order to do so guaranteed appropriate conditions of life to the singers. In the cathedral, parish and monastic schools, many hours were reserved for liturgical singing and preparation. It was, therefore, not an unreal expectation that the proper chant be sung as an obligation in all churches from the big cities down to even small villages, from the houses of religious orders to the parish churches – and essentially in the same way, across the entire territory of Latin Christianity.

These conditions radically changed at the end of the Middle Ages. The intellectual life and the emergence of the 'school' system ceased to focus on the liturgy. With the rise of Protestantism the unity of liturgical culture came to an abrupt end. Even within the Church interests diversified, and the institutional network of educating trained singers – mainly clerics – was broken. Only some

---

[6] McKinnon (2000a), *The Advent Project*, p. 46. 'An essential element of the Duchesne position . . . is that the ancient psalmody did not function as independent liturgical items but rather as responses to the readings that preceded them . . . [in spite of the supposition that] the psalm is merely a lyric response to the preceding reading . . . The psalm is an equal partner . . . in a series of readings.'

[7] James McKinnon (1995a), 'Lector Chant versus Schola Chant'.

[8] A good example of this technique from the twentieth century is the chant of the Serbian cantor described in Dimitrije Stefanovic (1992), 'The Phenomenon of Oral Tradition in Transmission of Orthodox Liturgical Chant', p. 305.

cathedrals and wealthier cities remained where a handful of musicians could be paid for singing the accumulated repertory, at least during Masses of more solemn character ('High' Masses). The number of these institutions (called a *cantoratus*)[9] gradually diminished, and the interests of the musicians diverged toward polyphony. The great majority of Masses began to be sung without the proper chants. Their textual authenticity was protected only by the priest, who prayed the texts at the altar, while the Masses that were being celebrated musically received a heterogeneous musical accompaniment (different kinds of polyphony, folk hymns). Church music and liturgical chanting of the Propers were divorced in actual practice.

The nineteenth-century Liturgical Movement, the well-known Motu Proprio *Tra Le Sollecitudini* (*Inter Sollicitudines*) of St Pius X,[10] and other subsequent ecclesiastical documents[11] impressed upon the Church the need for a renewal of liturgical music. The number of scholas singing the propers slowly increased, but there was no church where the conditions for singing the full Mass Proper at each celebration could be maintained. When a few churches – filled with the spirit of liturgical reform – wished to re-establish the singing of Gregorian chant, it was rather the Mass Ordinary and a small set of pseudo-Gregorian insertions (*Adoro te devote*, *Adoremus in aeternum*, and other similar chants), instead of the regular singing of the Propers. At nearly all Masses, if one of the faithful did not want to miss the proper chant of the Mass, he could do nothing except read the text of the chants from his hand-missal simultaneously with the priest.

What did the Second Vatican Council do in this matter? There is a sharp difference between the provision of the Liturgical Constitution *Sacrosanctum Concilium* and the postconciliar instructions. The Constitution confirmed with ornate words the principal declarations of St Pius X.[12] The protection of the tradition, the eminent place of Gregorian chant, the strict coordination of the chant to the liturgy, the regulative role of the biblical-liturgical texts: these are the themes of *Sacrosanctum Concilium*.[13] But there is no sign that the Council fully grasped the painful tension between the liturgical importance of the proper chants and the difficulties of realization entailed; and still less that the Council was ready to propose a real solution. It appears not even to have occurred to the Council Fathers that the implementation of their otherwise positive ideas necessarily collided with the requirements they made for *actuosa participatio* and their concessions to the use of the vernacular.[14] True, the Constitution itself declared

---

[9] Robert Schaal (1958), 'Kantorei'.

[10] *Tra Le Sollecitudini* (*Inter Sollicitudines*), *Acta Apostolicae Sedis*, vol. 36 (1903–04), pp. 329–31. For the direct preparation of the document see Pierre Combe, OSB (2003), *The Restoration of Gregorian Chant*, pp. 219–34; for further precedents, pp. 147–216.

[11] Pius XI, Apostolic Constitution *Divini cultus* of 20 December 1928, in *Acta Apostolicae Sedis*, vol. 21 (1929), pp. 33–41; Pius XII encyclical letter *Musicae Sacrae Disciplina* of 25 December 1955 in *Acta Apostolicae Sedis*, vol. 46 (1956), pp. 13–48.

[12] Vatican Council II, Dogmatic Constitution on the Sacred Liturgy, *Sacrosanctum Concilium* (1963), §§112–14. For an interpetation of the part of the Constitution concerning music see Cardinal Joseph Ratzinger (1983), 'Theological Problems of Church Music', pp. 221–22).

[13] *Sacrosanctum Concilium* (1963), §§116, 121.

[14] It is characteristic that Theodor Klauser, who judged the most important task of the reform to involve the faithful, blames the post-Tridentine period for the fact that the faithful 'sang hymns

nothing contrary to tradition. But neither did it say anything that offered the least hint at a way out of this predicament. It is sad to have to make this point, but the musical chapter of the Constitution has rather more the character of a spiritual exhortation than a practical programme of true reform.

There is one point that could be interpreted as a positive suggestion. At §117 we find the requirement that a collection is to be published for the use of smaller churches containing simpler Gregorian melodies. This recommendation draws attention to two important matters: this provision makes no sense at all if the Council had not wanted to preserve the proper chants, nor if it had not wanted to protect the use of the Latin language. The planned book (the *Graduale Simplex*) has indeed been published,[15] and we will return later to evaluate it.

Whatever is written in the musical instruction issued after the Council[16] and the General Introduction of the New Missal is in sharp conflict with the Constitution itself. At first sight this may be unclear. Both in fact reiterate the positive words of the Council on the importance of Gregorian chant, the use of the *Graduale Romanum* and *Graduale Simplex*, and on the function of the individual genres of chant. Taken in itself, neither the frequently repeated concern for active participation, nor the liberal introduction of the vernacular into the liturgy, made it necessary to abandon the texts of the proper chants. Of course, it would have been useful if the Instruction 'Musicam Sacram' had given some practical advice as to what the local churches could do for the renewal of singing the proper chants.

But the deadly blow to the singing of the Propers was delivered by a short conjunction, a fateful, tiny word, 'or' in the text. We are told that the Introits and Communions should either be taken from the *Graduale Romanum*, the *Graduale Simplex*, or they can be replaced by *alius cantus aptus/congruus*: any other suitable song.[17] Common ecclesiastical sentiment wished to extend *actuosa participatio* to more and more parts of the Mass (sometimes I think that it is a miracle that the consecration remained a specifically priestly act);[18] so the *scholas* of many churches were simply expelled or shut down by the clergy. The

---

in the vernacular, whose content had little or even nothing at all to do with the liturgy' (Klauser (1969), *A Short History of the Western Liturgy*, p. 120).

15 See p. 163–65 below.

16 *Musicam Sacram*, Instruction of the Sacred Congregation of Rites, 5 March 1967, in *Acta Apostolicae Sedis*, vol. 59 (1967), pp. 300–20.

17 'Institutio Generalis Missalis Romani' in *Missale Romanum*, on the Introit, §48): 'Adhiberi potest sive antiphona cum suo psalmo in Graduali romano vel in Graduali simplici exstans, *sive alius cantus, actioni sacrae, diei vel temporis indoli congruus* . . .' Similarly on the Offertory and Communion (§§ 74, 87). In the Instruction concerning chant: 'Usus legitime vigens in aliquibus locis, passim indultis 764 confirmatus, alios cantus substituendi pro cantibus ad introitum, ad offertorium et ad Communionem in Graduali exstantibus, de iudicio competentis auctoritatis territorialis, servari potest, dummodo huiusmodi cantus cum partibus Missae, cum festo vel tempore liturgico congruant. Eadem auctoritas territorialis textus horum cantuum approbare debet' – 'The custom legitimately in use in certain places and widely confirmed by indults, *of substituting other songs for the songs given in the Graduale for the Entrance, Offertory and Communion*, can be retained according to the judgment of the competent territorial authority, as long as songs of this sort are in keeping with the parts of the Mass, with the feast or with the liturgical season. It is for the same territorial authority to approve the texts of these songs' (*Musicam Sacram*, §32).

18 Laurence Paul Hemming has noted in an unpublished paper that proposition 22 of the 2005

Constitution, the Instruction 'Musicam Sacram', and higher church authorities did not impress on the faithful at large the possibility of extending the singing of the proper chants to the congregation in any way.[19] Thus there remained no motivation to create a repertory of proper chants in the vernacular that might be worthy of the ancient tradition. The simplest way of proceeding was to have recourse to that fateful *or*, and simply drop the singing of the Propers (*sensu stricto*) altogether. As a result, the actuality of the Mass was diluted everywhere in the world, with the introduction of devotional folk hymns composed in recent decades or centuries, contemporary pieces and dry 'refrains' of enthusiastic 'composers', and the tasteless rubbish of what often amounted to little more than religious pop music.

But the 'Tridentists' have no real right to reproach the 'innovators' either. What the 'any other song' was for the 'conciliarists', the reading of the Proper by the priest at the altar was for the traditionalists: an escape from the daunting task of restoring the fullness of the Sacred Liturgy. The situation was no better even if, laudibly, in some bigger churches a *schola* had been founded, and the singers performed a few proper chants on more festive occasions. Unless we find solutions for *every Mass in every church*, the historical problem remains unsolved, and the chanting of the Propers, and their place in the Mass, is not revitalized.

II. The Graduale Simplex

Some years after the Council a collection entitled *Graduale Simplex* was published, which – according to the will of the Council[20] – was destined to make it possible for scholas (or congregations) to sing the full proper from week to week. 'It is desirable that an edition be prepared containing simpler melodies, for use in small churches.' What did this wish mean for the *Graduale Simplex*?

First, it meant that the *Simplex* is constructed not around liturgical days, but seasons and so differs from the *Graduale Romanum* which presents a full set of the five proper chants at Mass (chants for the Introit, Gradual, Alleluia or Tract, Offertory, and Communion) for each week, at times each day. Depending on the length of the season, the *Graduale Simplex* contains two or three (for Ordinary Time: seven) formulas or 'sets' of chants. It does not fix which of them is to be sung on which day. In principle it is possible to sing perhaps only one Introit, and one responsorial psalm, and so forth, for the whole season of Advent. It is clearly a great simplification of the requirements of the chant, and gives hope that not only scholas, but also lay assemblies might learn the material.

Synod of Bishops *On The Holy Eucharist* proposed: 'to break up the words of the priest with acclamations from the people in between the sections of the Eucharistic prayer'.

[19] *Musicam Sacram* declared (§33): 'Expedit ut coetus fidelium, quantum fieri potest, cantus "Proprii" participet, praesertim per faciliora responsa vel alios opportunos modulos' – 'It is desirable that the assembly of the faithful should participate in the songs of the Proper as much as possible, especially through simple responses and other suitable settings.' As is clear, however, from the context, it does not refer to the inherited proper chant texts of the Roman Rite.

[20] *Sacrosanctum Concilium* (1963), §117: 'Expedit quoque ut paretur editio simpliciores modos continens, in usum minorum ecclesiarum.'

From a traditional point of view this was not an over-audacious innovation: the Ambrosian *Graduale*, for instance, has 12 formulas for the whole of Ordinary Time, which are cyclically repeated. As seen above, such a historical situation might also have been widespread in the classical Roman Rite at times[21] – and if this is correct, the numerical series discussed earlier could well be remnants of a system that existed before the cycle for the whole year reached completion.

Second, the 'simplicity' of this thrifty collection of chants means that the *Graduale Simplex* offers, instead of the prolix and melismatic tunes of the *Graduale Romanum*, short, mostly syllabic melodies (in the antiphons); the interlectionary psalms are in the form of short responsories (*responsoria brevia*). This is a remarkable initiative because the genres that this has introduced into the Mass were, in fact, originally invented for wide-range, non-professional chanting.

The initial criticism made of the *Graduale Simplex* was that it mixed adapted genres proper to the Office with the chants of the Mass. This criticism is, however, incorrect from a historical and pastoral point of view. No doubt, the various liturgical genres separated themselves out in the course of history (and this had its advantages), but in earlier times the difference was not a matter of principle, rather it was functional. One psalm was chanted as a responsory if the congregation was able to sing no more than the response, but it was sung antiphonally if the given congregation knew the psalm as a whole. The case of Communion-responsories is well known: approximately 40 of the same texts are used in the Office as responsories and in the Mass as Communion chants in such a way that the melody is practically identical note for note.[22] Scholarly literature has repeatedly analysed various syllabic Communions that originated under the influence of Office antiphons.[23] From a pastoral point of view the criticism is even less serious. The *Graduale Simplex* could be justly criticized if it had been authored to replace entirely the *Graduale Romanum* in practical use. But the collection was specifically intended for churches where the ornate tunes of the *Graduale Romanum* are not, or could not, be sung, or for parishes where ordinarily nothing is chanted (or, at least, nothing that is liturgically correct).

The problems with the *Graduale Simplex* are of a quite different nature. The main obstacle to its adoption was that the postconciliar period came to so deviate from the actual will of Council, and therefore there was no *need* of it. If the liturgy had remained basically in Latin and the singing of the Proper items mandatory, a *Graduale Simplex* would have been surely indispensable. But what use is it in an exclusively vernacular environment? In those rare occasions when the Mass was celebrated in Latin, either there was a schola competent to perform the appropriate pieces from the *Graduale Romanum*, or there was a choir that sang 'other suitable pieces'. Was there ever any real motive for a priest or cantor

[21] James McKinnon (1992a), 'The Roman Post-Pentecostal Communio Series', p. 180.
[22] Brad Maiani (2000), 'Approaching the Communion Melodies'; Dobszay (2008), 'The Responsory: Type and Modulation'.
[23] McKinnon (2000), *The Advent Project*, pp. 331–39 with further literature.

to teach the use of the *Graduale Simplex*, since everyone rests perfectly content with *alius cantus congruus*?

There is also a problem with the second characteristic of the *Graduale Simplex*. The editors insisted – and understandably so – on the literal 'authenticity' of the Gregorian chants. Since there are hardly more than two or three historical examples of texts common for the Mass Propers and the Office Antiphonary, the editors had to abandon the traditional Mass Propers and adapt those texts from the Office which are linked to simpler melodies. The musicological aspect of this undertaking was more effective than the liturgical-textual aspect. So we have Propers with simple melodies, but the historical texts of the classical Roman Rite were lost in the process.

The third difficulty is that the editors collected syllabic antiphons with regard to the texts expressing the meaning of the given liturgical season. There remained no place for another aspect, namely, whether the selected melodies form a continuum of tunes that build upon each other in the process of learning and acquiring them. In an age of oral transmission, 1,500 years ago, the ancient layer of the antiphons could live and flourish widely, because they used model-melodies.[24] If a singer knew one piece, he knew all the other pieces within the same model. The *Graduale Simplex*, as it stands before us now, is still a collection of individual pieces. In a way, the editors artificially regenerated one of the very difficulties that had hindered the more widespread use of the *Graduale Romanum*: the individual character of each of its particular items. It is a mistake to suppose that the syllabic shape of the melody, taken in itself, is easier to learn than a melismatic texture. When a melismatic piece is 'typical' and it appears repeatedly with different texts, it might actually be easier than a syllabic one, since the singer has to bother less with reading and coordinating the text to the melody. The singer stops at a syllable and links to it full, well-interiorized musical motives. In the case of a syllabic tune the singer has to read and coordinate both the text and the melody with some degree of deftness. Syllabic melodies are easier if their shape is already known to the singers, so that only the text is new. In this case the task is no more than to observe the variation of the model-melody according to the nature (structure, accents, articulation) of the text.

The *Graduale Simplex* is the history of a fiasco. Occasionally it has been used at some of the papal Masses (in the very opposite context to that for which it was intended), but otherwise it has not really been sung anywhere else. And yet it is a useful collection because it marks the presence of a legitimate need and also the proper way to answer it. The *principle of using sets* is surely indispensable if we are thinking of the simplest environments and therefore not only of a few exceptional churches. The second principle on which it was based is correct in instinct: the solution is not to simplify the tunes of the *Graduale Romanum* but to sing texts with melodies taken from particular genres that are, by their very nature, simpler. We will apply both of these principles in what follows.

---

[24] The model melodies can be studied in *Monumenta Monodica Medii Aevi*, vol. 5/1–2–3. Cf. Dobszay (2002), 'Concerning a Chronology for Chant', pp. 219–23.

III. Principles concerning the Proper Chants

Before turning to the concrete proposal I want to suggest, I wish first to establish some principles:

(a) The proper chants and their liturgical arrangement are an integral part of the classical Roman Rite; as such they should be preserved in their full extent.

(b) Accordingly, as regards the stock material, any change, omission or rearrangement should be reduced to a minimum.

(c) It is quite appropriate to think, however, about the possibilities of an organic development of this aspect of the liturgy. First, it is permitted to restore some practices and principles lost over past centuries. After a careful study of the fullest tradition of the rite (the pre-Tridentine choir books included) additions ought to be accepted to augment the stock material.

(d) The order of chant must be the same in the Missal and the choir books.

(e) Freedom should be granted with respect to the melodies: besides the 'official versions', particular and local traditions could also be consulted and restored. Also, as in centuries past, composers should be free to create new musical works for the text of the Propers, following the directions given in the documents of the Church.

(f) According to §117 of the Constitution *Sacrosanctum Concilium*, a degree of expansion of the material is necessary to make the singing of the Propers possible even in small churches. Such a collection might be called the *Graduale Parvum* in the following (to distinguish it from the *Graduale Simplex*).

(g) Since the proper chants of the Roman liturgy should, in some way, be sung at every Mass, it is necessary to make proposals for every possible method of performance in order to indicate all realistic ways in which the chants could be sung according to different conditions.

(h) Protection should be given to the singing of the Proper in Latin; but – according to the Constitution – the regulated use of the vernacular in singing the Proper is also permitted (SC 357).

(i) The category of *alius cantus congruus* or *alius cantus aptus* as substitution should be deleted from any future editions of the Roman Missal. This deletion, however, does not mean the exclusion of singing other valuable and approved chants (hymns, sequences, vernacular hymns) at determined points of the Mass. It is not enough if any approval only applies to the actual collection of songs; it must also lay down the possible functions and points of use of the approved material within the liturgy.

IV. The Restoration of the Graduale Romanum

The *Graduale Romanum* means first of all the text material. Earlier we saw how the texts of the proper chants are an organic part of the classical Roman Rite that cannot be erased from the celebration of Mass. The repertory as a whole was preserved in the postconciliar arrangement (*Ordo Cantus Missae*, one of the liturgical books of the reform),[25] while the exact location of its individual items was frequently altered (because of the introduction of the 1970 calendar, the three-year system of pericopes, etc.). In the restored Roman Rite as I have proposed it, it becomes possible to see how a genuine organic reform would quite properly render most of these changes unnecessary.

Unfortunately, the *Ordo Cantus Missae* has had very little influence on actual use. In most parish churches – if there is chant at all in their liturgy – they usually take the option of *alius cantus congruus*. The priest, when praying the text, reads the Missal of Paul VI, which is only in part identical with the *Ordo Cantus Missae*, but otherwise contains new texts entirely deprived of any melodies.[26] The old set of Graduals and Alleluias fell into almost complete disuse because of the 1970 lectionary. An important element of the necessary liturgical restoration is that the Missal and the choir books should once again overlap.

Later I will return to the question whether and how it would be possible to restore the *Graduale Romanum* to its formal position of precedence. The question we have to examine now concerns the actual state of its text material; whether there is any need for additions or modifications. It is good to know that the cycle of Mass chants – except the Alleluias – was already stabilized by the end of the seventh century, and in a rudimentary form perhaps even earlier.[27] It was then taken over the Alps to the Franks, and from them it spread to the whole continent. The full-year cycle present in the twentieth-century (preconciliar) choir books and Missals is essentially the same as what we find in the earliest manuscripts and in the Old Roman Graduals (for instance, the old choir book of the Basilica of Saint Cecilia with staff notation).[28] I think that this venerable repertory and arrangement of material must be preserved in the same unaltered form that it has had over its long tradition. Any possible expansions should leave the heritage intact; they can only be complementary additions.[29]

I cannot accept as a genuine liturgical development the introduction of the new texts of the Missal of Paul VI, which never had melodies, and were destined to remain mere prose from the outset. New proper texts were indeed created for new feasts of the nineteenth and twentiethth centuries (the Sacred Heart and

---

[25] *Ordo Cantus Missae* (1972).

[26] While the number of Introits in the *Graduale Sacrosanctae Romanae Ecclesiae de Tempore et de Sanctis . . .* (1979), is 160, there are 146 more Introit texts in the *Missale Romanum* (2002), without any appropriate melodies. The number for the Communion is: 161/202. On the other hand, the psalmic Communions of the Lenten weekdays, probably the most ancient layer of the *Antiphonarium Missae*, have been almost entirely replaced with new texts without a melody.

[27] McKinnon (2000a), *The Advent Project*, pp. 362–74.

[28] For example, the Introits for the First week of Lent: *Invocabit me, Sicut oculi, Domine refugium, Reminiscere miserationum, Confessio et Pulchritudo, De necessitatibus meis, Intret oratio* (compare with the Tridentine Missal; in the new *Graduale Sacrosanctae Romanae Ecclesiae de Tempore et de Sanctis . . .* (1979) the Introits of two days have been replaced). Cf. Max Lütolf (1987), *Das Graduale von Santa Cecilia in Trastevere (Cod. Bodmer 74)*; Dobszay (2001), *A római mise énekrendje*; (2009a), 'The Proper Chants of the Roman Rite'.

[29] A relatively small number of such additions appeared during the Middle Ages as well, for example, surplus tracts in *Graduale Strigoniense* as compared with the Old Roman Gradual (*Monumenta Monodica Medii Aevi*, vol. 2): *Absolve Domine, Audi filia, Ave Maria, Dixit Dominus mulieri, Domine non secundum peccata, Ecce vir prudens, Hodie sanctus pater, Rex regum, Tu es Petrus*.

Christ the King), but for the most part old melodies were adapted as *contrafacta* to the new words.[30] The number of these compositions is much smaller than in the 1970 Missal. It practically never happened in history that any change or addition touched upon the chants of the ancient feasts.[31] It is quite contrary to the spirit of the classical Roman Rite that the commemorations of many saints were given new 'personalized' Introits.[32] The proper place within the classical Roman Rite for the portrayal of the individual features of a saint has always been the Office and not the texts of the Mass. These kinds of additions are superfluous. Reasonable additions to the ancient material, however, would be as follows.

A. The first group of additions restores those chants that were lost in the course of the past centuries; at least as a free option, so that the full richness of the rite appears more clearly.

The *Offertory* in the present-day liturgical books is but only a very short citation of what was once a longer text. Originally it was a responsorial (and precisely *not* antiphonal) piece, with two or three very ornate, sometimes almost passionate solo verses, and with the partial recurrence of the main part (not the full text, but only its refrain, the *repetenda*). The omission of these verses beginning in the twelfth and thirteenth centuries was a great loss for the Roman liturgy.[33] The verses develop the content of the main part, which itself sometimes only becomes intelligible together with its verses. There are offertories that cannot be rightly interpreted and related to the liturgical day without knowledge of the verses. Karl Ott's *Offertoriale* (and its new edition, the *Offertoriale Triplex*)[34] is a good scholarly resource for these texts, though his transcription of the notes has been criticized by contemporary scholars. The verses of the Offertory chants could be inserted in Missals again, even if not making their recitation fully obligatory. Let me illustrate how these texts can be understood with their verses:[35]

(Adv. Sabbato in Quattuor Temporum): *Exsulta* satis filia Sion, praedica filia Jerusalem: * **Ecce Rex tuus venit tibi sanctus et salvator.** V1. Loquetur pacem gentibus, et potestas ejus a mari usque ad mare, et a flumine usque ad terminus

---

[30] For example, Introit *Benedicta sit = Invocabit me; Cogitationes Cordis ejus = Domine refugium; Dignus est Agnus = Dum sanctificatus fuero;* Communion *Quotiescumque = Factus est repetente; Unus militum = Qui biberit aquam,* etc.

[31] For example, Introits in the Missal 1970: Christmas first Mass (*ad libitum*); Palm Sunday, Trinity, Corpus Christi, John the Baptist, Peter and Paul, St Laurence; Communions: Circumcision, First, Second, Fourth, Fifth Sunday of Lent; nearly all Lenten ferias, Easter Wednesday and Friday, Third, Fourth, Sixth Sunday of Easter, Ascension, Pentecost Sunday, nearly all Ordinary Sundays, Presentation of the Lord; etc.

[32] For example, Timotheus and Titus, Cyrillus and Methodius, Cathedra Petri, Perpetua et Felicitas, Joseph, Catharina Senensis, Matthias, Justinus, Carolus Lwanga and companions, Aloisius Gonzaga, etc.

[33] Josef Andreas Jungmann, SJ (1958), *Missarum Sollemnia*, vol. 2, pp. 36–9. Fortescue (1912), *The Mass*, 2nd edn 2005, pp. 303–4. An intermediary phase can be studied in the Sarum Use (Nicholas Sandon (1984), *The Use of Salisbury*, vol. 2, p. vii: no verse is sung on Sundays, but the verses are taken alternatively on the ferias.

[34] Ott (1935), *Offertoriale sive versus offertorium,* now *Offertoriale Triplex cum versibus* (Solesmis 1985). For a good musical variant for the offertory verses see the Klosterneuburg Graduale, Graz, Universitätsbibliothek Ms. 807. (Paléogpraphie Musicale XIX).

[35] The texts of the verses: *Offertoriale Triplex cum Versiculis,* pp. 11, 15, 25, 40, 55, 92. (The text is at some points a variation of the Vulgate Bible.)

orbis terrae. * **Ecce Rex tuus venit tibi sanctus et salvator.** V2. Quia ecce venio, et habitabo in medio tui, dicit Dominus omnipotens, et confugient ad te in illa die omnes gentes, et erunt tibi in plebem. * **Ecce Rex tuus venit tibi sanctus et salvator.**[36]

(Nativitas Domini, missa in media nocte): *Laetentur* caeli, et exsultet terra * **ante faciem Domini, quoniam venit.** V1. Cantate Domino canticum novum, cantate Domino omnis terra. * **ante faciem Domini, quoniam venit.** V2. Cantate Domino, benedicite nomen ejus, bene nuntiate de die in diem salutare ejus. * **ante faciem Domini, quoniam venit.**[37]

(Dominica III post Epiphaniam): *Dextera* Domini fecit virtutem, dextera Domini exaltavit me, * **Non moriar, sed vivam, et narrabo opera Domini.** V1. In tribulatione invocavi Dominum, et exaudivit me in latitudine, quia Dominus adjutor meus est. * **Non moriar, sed vivam, et narrabo opera Domini.** V2. Impulsus versatus sum, ut caderem, et Dominus suscepit me, et factus est mihi in salutem. * **Non moriar, sed vivam, et narrabo opera Domini.**[38]

(Quadragesima, Dominica IV): *Laudate* Dominum, quia benignus est, psallite nomini ejus, quoniam suavis est: * **Omnia quaecumque voluit, fecit in caelo et in terra.** V1 Qui statis in domo Domini, in atriis domus Dei nostri, quia ego cognovi, quod magnus est Dominus et Deus noster prae omnibus diis. * **Omnia quaecumque voluit, fecit in caelo et in terra.** V2 Domine, nomen tuum in aeternum, et memoriale tuum in saecula saeculorum, judicabit Dominus populum suum, et in servis suis consolatur. * **Omnia quaecumque voluit, fecit in caelo et in terra.** V3 Qui timetis Dominum, benedicite eum, benedictus Dominus ex Sion, qui habitat in Jerusalem. * **Omnia quaecumque voluit, fecit in caelo et in terra.**[39]

(Dominica Paschae): *Terra tremuit*, et quievit, * **dum resurgeret in judicio Deus, alleluia.** V1 Notus in Judaea Deus, in Israel magnum nomen ejus, alleluia, * **dum resurgeret in judicio Deus, alleluia.** V2 Et factus est in pace locus ejus, et habitatio ejus in Sion, alleluia, * **dum resurgeret in judicio Deus, alleluia.** V3 Ibi

---

[36] Advent, Ember Saturday: Rejoice greatly, O daughter of Sion, shout for joy, O daughter of Jerusalem, * behold thy King will come to thee, the Holy One and Saviour. V/1. He shall speak peace to the Gentiles, His power shall be from sea to sea, and from the rivers even to the end of the earth. * Behold thy King will come to thee, the Holy One and Saviour. V/2. And I will dwell in the midst of thee, saith the Almighty Lord, all nations shall be joined to thee, and they shall be thy people. * Behold thy King . . .

[37] Nativity First Mass at Midnight: Let the Heavens rejoice, and let the earth be glad before the face of the Lord * because he cometh. V/1. Sing ye to the Lord a new canticle, sing to the Lord, all the earth. * Because he cometh. V/2. Sing ye to the Lord and bless his name, shew forth his salvation from day to day. * Because he cometh.

[38] Third Sunday after the Epiphany: The right hand of the Lord hath wrought strength, the right hand of the Lord hath exalted me, * I shall not die, but live, and shall declare the works of the Lord. V/1. In my trouble I called upon the Lord, and the Lord heard me, and enlarged me, the Lord is my helper. * I shall not die . . . V/2. Being pushed I was overturned that I might fall, but the Lord supported me, He is become my salvation . . . * I shall not die . . .

[39] Fourth Sunday in Lent: Praise ye the Lord, for He is good, sing ye to His Name, for He is sweet, * whatsoever He pleased, He hath done in heaven and in earth. V/1. You that stand in the house of the Lord, in the courts of the house of our God, for I have known that the Lord is great, and our God is above all gods. * Whatsoever He pleased . . . V/2. Thy name, O Lord, is for ever, Thy memorial, O Lord, unto all generations, the Lord will judge his people, and will be entreated in favour of his servants. Whatsoever He pleased . . . V/3. Bless the Lord you that fear the Lord, bless the Lord, blessed be the Lord out of Sion, who dwelleth in Jerusalem. Whatsoever He pleased . . .

confregit cornu, arcum, scutum et gladium et bellum; illuminans tu mirabiliter a montibus aeternis, alleluia, * **dum resurgeret in judicio Deus, alleluia.**[40]

(Dominica VII post Pentecosten): *Sicut in holocausto* arietum et taurorum, et sicut in milibus agnorum pinguium: sic fiat sacrificium nostrum in conspectu tuo hodie, ut placeat tibi, * **Quia non est confusio confidentibus in te Domine.** V Et nunc sequimur in toto corde, et timemus te, et quaerimus faciem tuam, Domine: ne confundas nos, sed fac nobis juxta mansuetudinem tuam, et secundum multitudinem misericordiae tuae.* **Quia non est confusio confidentibus in te Domine.**[41]

The old *Ordo Romanus I* describes the *Introit, Offertory* and *Communion* as to be completed with verses.[42] The number of these verses for the Introit and Communion was not fixed; when the celebrant made a sign, the schola finished the psalmody with the doxology and repeated the antiphon. From late medieval times forwards, the liturgical books gave only the first verse of the psalm of the Introit, and did not include the text of the psalm in the Communion. The post-concilar edition of the *Graduale Romanum*[43] provides the one (sometimes more) verse in the Introit, and refers to a selection of verses in the Communion. These verses were chosen after careful analysis, with due regard to the old traditions. A deeper understanding of the liturgy would be greatly helped if these verses were printed in full (and not only as a reference) in altar Missals, in the Missalettes of the faithful, and, of course, in the choir books themselves.

This does not mean that all verses should be sung in full on every occasion. At solemn Masses more verses are required while the actions of the Mass are fulfilled, and the antiphon can be repeated after alternate verses. At other times the chants can be sung more briefly, but the omitted verses could be read silently as a meditation in the pew or at the altar.

The single verse for the Introit given in the books of recent centuries is there as no more than an identification of the psalm to be sung. The verse is an automatic selection, taking the first verse of the psalm, without any consideration of

[40] Easter Sunday: The earth trembled and was still * when God arose in judgment, alleluia. V/1. In Judea God is known, his name is great in Israel, alleluia. * When God . . . V/2. and his place is in peace, and his abode in Sion, alleluia. * When God . . . V/3. There hath he broken the powers of bows, the shield, the sword and the battle, Thou enlightenest wonderfully from the everlasting hills, alleluia. * When God . . .
[41] Seventh Sunday after Pentecost:. As in holocausts of rams and bullocks, and as in thousands of fat lambs, so let our sacrifice be made in Thy sight this day, that it may please thee, * for there is no confusion for them that trust in thee, O Lord. V. And now we follow thee with all our heart, and we fear thee, and seek thy face, put us not to confusion, but deal with us according to thy meekness, and according to the multitude of thy mercies. * For there is no confusion . . .
[42] *Ordo Romanus I*, §§50–2, *The Introit*: 'Et respiciens ad priorem scolae annuit ei ut dicat Gloriam; et prior scolae inclinat se pontifici et inponit. Quartus vero scolae praecedit ante pontificem, ut ponat oratorium ante altare; et accedens pontifex orat super ipsum usque ad repetitionem versus. Nam diaconi surgunt quando dicit: Sicut erat, ut salutent altaris latera, prius duo et duo vicissim redeuntes ad pontificem. Et surgens pontifex osculat evangelia et altare et accedit ad sedem et stat versus ad orientem. Scola vero, finita antiphona, inponit Kyrie elesion; §85, *The Offertory*: Et pontifex, inclinans se paululum ad altare, respicit scolam et annuit ut sileant; §117, *The Communio*: Nam, mox ut pontifex coeperit in senatorio communicare, statim scola incipit antiphonam ad Communionem et psallunt usquedum communicato omni populo, annuat pontifex ut dicant Gloria patri; et tunc repetitio versu quiescunt.
[43] *Graduale Sacrosanctae Romanae Ecclesiae de Tempore et de Sanctis . . .* (1979).

its meaning. So the intention behind the use of these verses is sometimes rather obscure. The most ancient manuscripts (like the Old Roman Graduals and some of those listed in Dom Hesbert's *Antiphonale Missarum Sextuplex*)[44] appended another verse (*versus ad repetendum*) to be recited or chanted before the antiphon is sung for the last time at the end of the chant. This is the verse which points clearly to the liturgical context. This verse needs to be printed in all the liturgical books (Missal, choir books, and so forth) and could always be sung even when the longer psalmody is omitted. The recommended order is:

antiphon

first verse + *versus ad repetendum*

antiphon

doxology (*Gloria Patri . . .*)

antiphon

The length of this short form is enough to give emphasis to the item, and corresponds to the duration of the entrance procession, the recitation of the prayers at the foot of the altar, and the incensations; it does not unduly extend the beginning of Mass, and it highlights the central meaning of the chant. (Recently, an entirely improper custom has spread abroad, whereby the doxology is omitted from the singing of the Introit. This is contrary to what appears, however, as early as the original Roman Ordinals.) If desired, especially at more solemn Masses, more verses could be inserted between the first verse and the *ad repetendum*.

In the Communion chant it is always reasonable to recite two or three pairs of verses with the repetition of the antiphon after every other verse.

The repertory and arrangement of the *Graduale* of the classical Roman Rite needs no alteration, not even if the system of readings is extended (as I have suggested might be done in Ordinary Time) over two years. Any hypothesis of coordination between the reading and the psalm is quite false.[45] After the Council this theory – outdated even by the 1960s – led the architects of the reform to link a three-year cycle of psalms to the lectionary. The *Consilium* also decided (on the same basis) on a rearrangement of the chants of the *Graduale Romanum*. Since the arguments supporting this are baseless, in any future reform the ancient order of chants in the *Graduale Romanum* should remain as they always were.

On the contrary, some old two-verse alleluias might be restored. The omission of the second verse from the Alleluia chants in the Tridentine Missal often mutilated the textual and musical meaning of these chants.[46]

---

[44] *Antiphonale Missarum Sextuplex* (1935).
[45] Cf. McKinnon (2000a), *The Advent Project*, p. 46.
[46] Some of these alleluias are: Laetatus sum (V2. Stantes erant pedes nostri; in the Old Roman use also: V3. Rogate quae ad pacem); Dies sanctificatus (V2. Ortus est sicut sol salvator mundi, et descendit in uterum virginis, sicut imber super gramen); Dominus regnavit (V2. Parata sedes tua); Pascha nostrum (V2. Epulemur in azymis sinceritatis et veritatis); Angelus Domini (V2. Respondens autem angelus); Laudate pueri (V2. Sit nomen Domini); Ascendit Deus (V2. Subjecit populos); Tu es Petrus (V2. Beatus es Simon Petre quia caro et sanguis non revelabit tibi

B. A second source of supplementation is of alternative items that were added in later times to the stock material. They do not pertain to the stock material – their use spread only regionally and not universally – but they are parts of the treasury of the classical Roman Rite. Sometimes the piece itself is an addition to the basic repertory, at other times only the assignment of a piece to a particular occasion marks it out.

One part of these additions had a rather wide circulation; and what constitutes an 'alternative' set of pieces is in fact of equal rank with the Tridentine arrangement. Such is, for instance, the *Memento nostri* Introit of the Fourth Sunday in Advent. In earlier times this Sunday was a *Dominica vacat* or 'empty Sunday' with no Mass of its own because of a prolongation of the Ember Saturday on the previous day. Later chants were borrowed from other liturgical days, for example, the *Rorate* Introit from Ember Wednesday. But north of the Alps the missing Introit was made up with another attractive composition piece, the Introit *Memento nostri*. It is quite worthy of being included in the *Graduale Romanum*.[47] The alleluia *Rex noster adveniet* appears to be as early as the *Old Roman Gradual*,[48] and in many churches it became the Alleluia of the Second Sunday of Advent (instead of the Alleluia *Laetatus sum*). In this group we can rank also other items of Old Roman origin that were later superseded by new pieces.[49]

C. The pieces of the third group are of only regional or local provenance. The most important part of them is the vast set of *Alleluia* chants which, from the beginning of the early Middle Ages, supplanted the limited and repetitious set of Old Roman Alleluias. New Alleluias were born in great number even after the Carolingian period, and all through the Middle Ages. Sometimes they were known only in one area, but often they could be found in use over a large region.[50]

Besides the Alleluias, albeit rarely, new pieces were composed in other genres, mostly for the Sanctoral cycle (some of these items originated within old local

---

sed Pater meus qui est in caelis); Te decet (V2. Replebuntur in bonis); Venite exsultemus (V2. Praeoccupemus faciem); Domine refugium (V2. Priusquam fierent montes); Cantate Domino canticum novum (V2. Notum fecit); Confitemini Domino et invocate (V1. Cantate ei et psallite); In exitu Israel (V2. Facta est Judaea); Paratum cor meum (V2. Exsurge gloria mea); Nimis honorati sunt (V2. Dinumerabo eos).

[47] For the melody see *Missale Notatum Strigoniense ante 1341 in Posonio*, fol. 8. The postconciliar *Graduale Sacrosanctae Romanae Ecclesiae de Tempore et de Sanctis . . .* (1979) assigns it to the last Wednesday of Advent. *Graduale Strigonense 9, York Gradual*, fol. 3; *Graduale Pataviense, Wien 1511*, fol. 9, etc.

[48] Max Lütolf (1987), *Das Graduale von Santa Cecilia in Trastevere (Cod. Bodmer 74)*, vol. 2, fol. 4v. *Missale Notatum Strigoniense ante 1341 in Posonio* 2v. Another alleluia for the Second Sunday of Advent: *Virtutes caeli*; see *Monumenta Monodica Medii Aevi*, vol. 7, pp. 547, 652.

[49] Such are, e.g., the *Introit*: Gloria et honore (*Monumenta Monodica Medii Aevi*, vol. 2: 6); Justus non confitebitur (64); *Gradual Chant*: Pretiosa in conspectu (122); *Alleluia*: Qui confidunt (185); Qui sanat (176). These, together with others, also featured in various Gregorian sources. There are, in addition, a few impressive items in the Old Roman books that have no direct Gregorian parallels, like the *Introit* Rogamus te Domine (*Monumenta Monodica Medii Aevi*, vol. 2: 26); *Gradual Chant* Qui Lazarum (85); *Communion* Christus qui natus est (454) – all three are from the Mass of the Dead. Moreover: *Alleluia* Confitebor tibi, Quoniam confirmata (219); *Offertory*: Beatus es Simon (374); *Communion*: Domine si tu es (489); Puer Jesus proficiebat (479 – identical with the Office antiphon of the same text, used as a Communion on the Third Sunday after Epiphany), Tristitia vestra (484 – on the Sunday after Ascension).

[50] See in *Monumenta Monodica Medii Aevi*, vol. 7, and in great quantity in vol. 8.

traditions). Many of them have attractive texts and music, and are also worthy of restoration.[51]

What should be the fate of the pieces in groups B and C? The size of group B is not large; these could be reintegrated into the basic repertory with the remarks *vel* (or else) or *ad libitum*. The most beautiful chants of group C could be placed in an appendix (with a reference on their given day to their possible use). However, their true place is in future books prepared as restorations of the ancient particular Uses of the Roman Rite.

It is necessary to consider the future of a nearly forgotten genre of the rite, the *Sequence*. The Sequences do not pertain, of course, to the stock material in a strict sense, in other words the items that originated in Rome. But if the classical Roman Rite is (as it should be) taken in the wider sense of including the rich medieval developments constructed on the fertile older ground, and if the theological, poetical and musical treasures of this unique genre are duly considered, the radical purism of the post-Tridentine decision to extirpate them is really quite surprising. It is well known that the Tridentine Reform retained only four Sequences (the Sequence *Stabat mater* is a later addition from 1727), and their selection was not the result of careful deliberation. The Sequences of Easter and Pentecost were retained, but why was Christmas deprived? The Sequence of Corpus Christi outlasted the reform, while the chants for Epiphany, Ascension and Ss Peter and Paul vanished. The Sequence of the Requiem has had a formidable post-Tridentine career (even though the Mass of the Dead has no Alleluia, consequently it should not have had a Sequence either); but Advent, the Dedication, and the Marian feasts all remained without Sequences.

Even if not all of the many hundreds of Sequences of the Middle Ages[52] were of equal worth, and they were not considered part of the central repertory in those centuries either (their place was mostly in the appendices of the various *Gradual Books*), their loss was the wasting of a valuable treasury of Catholic spirituality and poetry. The judgements made of them was rather haphazard; the logic of the liturgy was left out of consideration. This self-mutilation should have been repaired after the Second Vatican Council. Instead, the reform went even further than Trent and appointed a sequence for only two (with optional Lauda Sion: three) days of the year.

In the reform of which we are speaking now, at least a representative selection of this great repertory should be restored. I am not thinking about a full restoration of the medieval richness, nor even a larger repertory imposed as obligatory. Three categories could be offered in the restoration:

(a) Some few (let us say six to eight) sequences, determined by the liturgical rank of the day. The use of these could even be made obligatory. These could be:

---

[51] For example, *Monumenta Monodica Medii Aevi*, vol. 8, pp. 22, 26, 69, 89, 133, 134, 140, 147, 148, 155, 180, etc.
[52] Sequences in *Analecta Hymnica medii aevi*, in vols 7–10, 34, 37, 39, 40, 42, 44, 53, 54, 55. The number of sequences of a pre-Tridentine Use figures about 80–100 (in the Esztergom Use 83 pieces were sung).

Laetabundus (Christmas),[53] *Festa Christi* (Epiphany),[54] *Victimae paschali* (Easter), *Rex omnipotens* (Ascension),[55] *Veni Sancte* (Pentecost), *Lauda Sion* (Corpus Christi), *Psallat Ecclesia* (Dedication),[56] *Dies irae* (All Souls and the Requiem Mass) and a short piece for Marian feasts, for instance:[57]

1.a. Gau - de vir - go, ma - ter Chri - sti, que per au - rem con - ce - pi - sti Ga-
b. Gau - de, qui - a De - o ple - na pe - pe - ri - sti si - ne poe - na cum

bri - e - le nun - ti - o. 2.a. Gau - de, qui - a tu - i Na - ti, quem do - le - bas
ho - no - re li - li - o. b. Gau - de Chri - sto as - cen - den - te, quod in cae - lum

mor - tem pa - ti, ful - get re - sur - rec - ti - o. 3.a. Gau - de, quod post i - psum
te vi - den - te mo - tu fer - tur pro - pri - o. b. U - bi fru - ctus ven - tris

scan - dis, et est ho - nor ti - bi gran - dis in cae - li pa - la - ti - o.
tu - i per te no - bis de - tur fru - i in per - en - ni gau - di - o.

(b) The pieces of the second category could be included in the appendix of the *Graduale Romanum* for optional use. Here the short sequence of the

---

[53] *Analecta Hymnica*, pp. 54–5; G. M. Dreves and C. Blume (1909), *Ein Jahrtausend Lateinischer Hymnendichtung*, vol. 2, p. 17; Benjamin Rajeczky (1982), *Melodiarium Hungariae Medii Aevi*, p. 239. *Laetabundus* was not the most important sequence for the solemnity (in this respect Notker's *Eia recolamus* would be a better selection). But the sweet melody and attractive poetry of *Laetabundus* suggest it would achieve wider popularity. It is also supported by its continued presence in the Praemonstratensian and Dominican Uses up until the twentieth century. (*Graduale Ordo Praemonstratensis*, p. 41; *Graduale Ordo Praedicatorum*, p. 33). It can also be found in the modern *English Hymnal 1933*, Nr. 22 ('Come rejoicing faithful men').

[54] *Analecta hymnica*, vol. 53, p. 50; Rajeczky (1982), *Melodiarium Hungariae Medii Aevi*, pp. 103.

[55] *Analecta hymnica*, vol. 7, pp. 83; vol. 53, p. 111; G. M. Dreves and C. Blume (1909), *Ein Jahrtausend Lateinischer Hymnendichtung*, vol. 2, p. 142; Rajeczky (1982), *Melodiarium Hungariae Medii Aevi*, p. 146. This popular but really lengthy sequence of the feast can be slightly abbreviated: strophes 10–19 can be skipped over. Another nice and easier sequence for the feast is *Christo caelos ascendente* (Dreves and Blume (1909), *Ein Jahrtausend Lateinischer Hymnendichtung*, vol. 2, p. 148) but it is rather recent, and its use was limited to the Franciscans.

[56] *Analecta hymnica*, vol. 53, p. 398; Rajeczky (1982), *Melodiarium Hungariae Medii Aevi*, p. 132.

[57] Rajeczky (1982), *Melodiarium Hungariae Medii Aevi, Supplement*, p. 76. The translation: 1. Rejoice, O Virgin, Mother of Christ, who hearing Gabriel's announcement, conceived in your womb. 2. Rejoice, for being full of God's grace, thou gavest birth without pain and with a lily's honour. 3. Rejoice, for he who was born of you and upon whose death thou hast sorrowed, is radiantly risen. 4. Rejoice upon his ascension into heaven, for he is taken above at thy very sight. 5. Rejoice, for thou wilt also ascend after him, and great honour shall be paid to thee in heaven's palace. 6. Where it will be granted to us through thee to enjoy the fruit of thy womb in everlasting delight. Amen. Alleluia.

Italian repertory could be included, for example, the following on the Holy Cross:[58]

1.a. San - ctae Cru - cis ce - le - bre - mus de - vo - ti - o - ne ve - ne - ran - da.
   b. Si - gna - cu - lum tri - um - pha - le, per quod sa - lu - tis sa - cra - men - ta.

2.a. Sum - psi - mus cul - pa qui pro - to - pa - ren - tis he - u, e - ra - mus ex - su - les
   b. Red - em - pti er - go gra - ti - as a - ga - mus, qui nos su - o san - cto / red-

fa - cti pa - tri - ae. 3.a. In Do - mi - ni cru - ci - fi - xi lau - de / con - so - na
e - mit san - gui - ne. b. / O Crux, splen - di - dis - si - ma sa - lus, per - en - ni - tas

vo - ce mel - li - flu - a con - ci - na - mus can - ti - ca. 4.a. O Crux, glo - ri - o - sa,
vi - tae vir - tu - ti - bus to - tis es re - ple — ta. b. Sal - va / prae - sen - tem

o Crux ad - o - ran - da, quae pre - ti - um mun - di fer - re tu me - ru - i - sti.
/ hu - mi - lem ple - bem, in / lau - de tu - a ho - di - e con - gre - ga - tam.

5. Quae so - la fu - i - sti por - ta - re di - gna ta - len - tum.

From a liturgical perspective, pieces for Advent, Trinity Sunday, St John the Baptist, Ss Peter and Paul, the Assumption, Holy Cross, All Saints and two or three more for use in the Common of Saints would be fitting here. Let me mention also a charming piece for use on the Sundays after Pentecost,

[58] *Analecta hymnica*, vol. 12, p. 34, Lance W. Brunner (1999), *Early Medieval Chants from Nonantola – Part IV: Sequences*, p. 30. Translation: 1a. Let us celebrate with reverent devotion 1b. the holy cross's victorious symbol, through which we 2a. received the sacrament of salvation, we who through the fault of the first born were made exiles from our fatherland. 2b. Redeemed, therefore, let us give thanks to Him who redeemed us through His holy blood. 3a. To the glory of the crucified Lord, let us sing together mellifluous songs with a consonant voice. 3b. O cross most splendid, salvation, eternity, you are filled with all of life's virtues. 4a. O glorious cross, O adorable cross, you who deserved to bear the world's prize. 4b. Save the humble people present, gathered together today in your praise. 5. You who were alone worthy to bear the weight of the world.

originating in the Hungarian tradition, which presents the theology of the Sundays with great rhetorical power.[59]

[59] *Analecta hymnica*, vol. 54, p. 268. Rajeczky (1982), *Melodiarium Hungariae Medii Aevi*, p. 178. Translation: 1a. Coming together let us celebrate, and celebrating let us honour the feast of Christ. 1b. This is the great day of the Lord, the day of the full rest: this is the Lord's day. 2a. This is when the world was created, the day when life had its beginning: this is the day. 2b. This day Christ destroyed hell, when he led his creature back on high: this is the day. 3a. This day, whilst the doors were closed, Christ gave his Peace to the Apostles as a divine gift. 3b. This day the Holy Spirit filled with grace the Fathers of the Church.

The long period of Easter could also get another sequence in addition to *Victimae paschali Laudes,* for instance *Mundi renovatio* by Adam of St Victor[60] (but also perhaps *Pangamus Creatoris*[61] explaining the Paschal mystery, or the lovely *Agni paschali,*[62] which are items that should not lightly be surrendered to oblivion).

(c) Into the third group about 15 sequences might well find their way: they would be received into the repertory on the basis of local tradition, *secundum Usum.* In earlier times the choice of sequences (their inclusion or omission) was the decision of local churches, and this state of affairs should be revived for at least part of the repertory.

Since many sequences can be rather long, tactful abbreviations or transformations could be permitted.

To illustrate what was said above, I give below a list of chants for the Advent–Christmas period. Essential additions are marked with *; these should be included in the books even if their use is made optional. Similar ones are present, of course, all the year round. The category marked with ** form a precious legacy of the old liturgy and may adorn a liturgical day or solemnity. Alternative items also belong to this group, for instance, additional Alleluias for the Sundays, which could be used when the Sunday Mass formula is repeated during the week (these items could be distinguished by different typography). Their presence indicates the sheer musical and textual richness of the classical Roman Rite, and local churches could quite easily regulate their use. Pieces marked with *** pertain to the noble tradition of *local* churches themselves. These could belong to the repertory of particular Uses, and find their place only in their proper books. The items introduced here should be regarded only as part of an illustration.

VR means: *versus ad repetendum.*

The list below contains the Advent–Christmas section in its fullness, except if the piece is identical with the one in the post-Tridentine *Graduale Romanum.* The table demonstrates the structure of the proper chants *per anni circulum.*

Advent, First Sunday

Introit	Ad te levavi. *VR: Dirige me in veritate tua.
Offertory	*V1. Dirige me. V2. Respice in me.
Sequence	**Missus Gabriel
Communion	*Ps. 84.

4a. This day, like trumpets, the Gospel was sounded and proclaimed to the people. 4b. It is the precept of the Church that today her faithful should come to celebrate this great mystery. 5a. Therefore we have to honour and celebrate with devotion this holiest of days. 5b. And while we celebrate it, we pray humbly that on the Last Day 6a. our soul may come into its inheritence and enter into eternal rest. 6b. How happy will he be, who merits to live there, sitting on Christ's right hand, sharing with him kingdom and power. Amen.

[60] *Analecta hymnica,* vol. 54, p. 224.
[61] *Analecta hymnica,* vol. 53, p. 84.
[62] *Analecta hymnica,* vol. 53, p. 89; Rajezcky (1982), *Melodiarium Hungariae Medii Aevi,* Supplement, p. 24.

Second Sunday
Introit   Populus Sion. *VR Excita potentiam

All.   Laetatus sum. *V2. Stantes erant pedes.

OR: **Rex noster adveniet

Offertory   *Deus tu convertens. V1. Benedixisti. V2. Misericordia et veritas. V3. Veritas de terra.

Communion *Ps. 147.

Third Sunday
Introit   *VR. Ostende nobis. **Et pax nostra.

Offertory   *Operuisti omnia. V2. Ostende nobis Domine.

Communion *Ps. 84.

Ember Wednesday
Introit   *VR In sole posuit.

Offertory   *V1. Tunc aperientur oculi caecorum. V2. Audite itaque domus David.

Communion *Ps. 18.

Ember Friday
Introit   *Tu mandasti.

Offertory   *ut in Dominica III

Communion *Ps. 118

Ember Saturday
Introit   *VR Excita potentiam

Offertory   *V1. Loquitur pacem. V2. Quia ecce venio.

Communion *Ps. 18.

Fourth Sunday
Introit   Rorate caeli (ut supra on Wednesday)

OR: *Memento nostri. Ps. 105. VR. Salvos nos fac.

All.   **Prophetae sancti praedicaverunt.

Offertory   *V1. Quomodo fiet in me. V2. Ideoque quod nascetur.

Communion *Ps. 18.

Vigil of Nativity
Introit   *VR Ipse super maria

Offertory	*V1. Domini est terra. V2. Ipse super maria.
Communion	*Ps. 65.

Nativity, first Mass
Introit	*VR Postula me.
All.	***Natus est nobis.
Offertory	*V1. Cantate Domino canticum novum. V2. Cantate Domino benedicite
Communion	*Ps. 109.

Nativity, second Mass
Introit	*VR Parata sedes tua.
Offertory	*V1. Dominus regnavit decorem. V2. Mirabilis in excelsis.
Communion	*Ps. 96. vel 147.

Nativity, third Mass
Introit	***tropus (Central Europe): Hodie cantandus est.
OR	***tropus (Nonantola): Hodie Salvator mundi per virginem dignatus est, gaudeamus omnes Christo Domino, qui natus est nobis, eia et eia . . .
OR	***tropus (Old Roman): De sede Patris descendit in thalamum Mariae, Christus procedens ex virgine; de quo omnes audentes dicamus: Puer natus . . . –* VR Notum fecit Dominus
All.	***V2. Ortus est sicut sol
Sequence	*Laetabundus
Sequence	**Grates nunc omnes
Sequence	**Eia recolamus
Sequence	***Ecce annuntio
Offertory	*V1. Magnus et metuendus. V2. Misericordia et veritas V3. Tu humiliasti sicut vulneratum
Communion	*Ps. 97

So far we have spoken only about the texts. Their most authentic vehicle, or perhaps their 'native musical ambiance' is their original Gregorian melodies. It is well known that these tunes originated in the Carolingian age, during a process of reform that resulted in their transformation from earlier, Mediterranean-style variants. The Old Roman manuscripts stand probably closer to the most original forms.[63] The Carolingian redaction was to become the common property of Latin Christianity. But despite this redaction, the melodies themselves became uniform only in their general outlines, and lived in variants throughout the entire Middle Ages. Remarkable is the difference between the 'diatonic' dialect sung in Italy, France, and England (for this, see the upper stave below), and the 'pentatonic' dialect of Germany, the Netherlands, Central Europe and partly Sweden (indicated on the lower stave).[64] The former is more nuanced; the latter present the melodies in a bolder format.[65]

The melodies in the *Graduale Romanum* were edited by the Benedictines of Solesmes according to the diatonic dialect, relying mostly on French manuscripts.[66] These variants became obligatory for all churches where the *Graduale Romanum* was sung. Recently some scholars have suggested small improvements but these are so inessential that it seems hardly worthwhile to disturb current practice. The only necessary addition would be the inclusion of the Offertory verses in a new *Graduale Romanum* from a reliable source, for *ad libitum* use. It should also be quite permissable to recite these verses on psalm tones with repetition from the main text (*repetenda*), as is usual with responsories.

In many churches the introduction of the *Graduale Romanum* would be smoother if the pentatonic version were made available. These variants are easier both to learn and to perform musically. The existence of varieties is accepted by the experts, and they are not seen as aesthetically inferior. There is no reason to fear a loss of uniformity: the most important items could also be included in the

---

[63] Bruno Stäblein, in *Monumenta Monodica Medii Aevi*, vol. 2, *31–*83.

[64] Peter Wagner (1926), 'Germanisches und Romanisches im frühmittelalterlichen Kirchengesang', and (1930–32), *Das Graduale der St. Thomaskirche zu Leipzig (14. Jahrhunderts)*. David Hiley (1993), *Western Plainchant – A Handbook*, p. 573 (with further literature).

[65] *Graduale Sacrosanctae Romanae Ecclesiae de Tempore et de Sanctis* . . . (1979), p. 303. *Missale Notatum Strigoniense ante 1341 in Posonio*, fol. 183v.

[66] On the preparation of the edition of the *Graduale Sacrosanctae Romanae Ecclesiae de Tempore et de Sanctis* . . . (1979) see Combe (2003), *The Restoration of Gregorian Chant*, pp. 386–413.

alternative edition in their diatonic version; the rest will certainly not be sung on a wide scale.

This means that the normative book for the chanting of the Propers remains the *Graduale Romanum*. But the existence of further settings for the same texts (as in the past) should not be rejected today. For instance, Palestrina composed polyphonic settings in five parts for all Offertories. Other composers (Heinrich Isaac, William Byrd) attained merit by composing music for full sets of Propers or selected items. One cannot exclude the possibility of monophonic compositions on the Proper texts written by a contemporary composer. All this would be quite legitimate without disturbing the priority of the Gregorian settings.

No one need be shocked if I say that the *Graduale Romanum* – in virtue of the Liturgical Constitution[67] – can also be adapted for use in the vernacular with music. This might be done employing Gregorian melodies or in their style (the debate over the various possibilities for achieving this need not detain us here), but other musical material should not be excluded either, if it is suitable to free prose and the prayerful style of the biblical texts, and if they do not impose on the texts the shackles of a style alien to their spirit. These compositions need not rival the Latin Gregorian; rather they will assist them and pave the way for their wider use.

V. *The Graduale Parvum*

As we have already seen, the intention of the *Graduale Simplex* was to help smaller churches by giving them only a few chants in each genre over a full season; in other words: it offered them *sets*. The mature form of the classical Roman Rite used this method only in the Common of Saints; before the seventh century, however, this arrangement may have been more common for other seasons and commemorations. The loss associated with this procedure (namely, that the connection between the liturgical day and its proper chants becomes looser) is compensated by the gain that liturgical singing becomes accessible for churches with lower levels of musical ability. If the sung item is followed by praying the daily Proper in any form, the benefits of the two methods could even be combined. I think that a *Graduale Parvum* built on this principle might become an important element in an organic development of the classical Roman Rite in its capacity as an alternative choir book.

The other advantage of the *Graduale Simplex* was that it offered shorter chants on much simpler tunes than those found in the *Graduale Romanum*. To sing an antiphon and short responsory did not require professional singers in earlier times any more than it need do now. The use of these genres would ease the work of a smaller schola and still more offer opportunities for a wide participation of the assembly as a whole at any liturgical event.

A great defect of the *Graduale Simplex* was that it failed to maximize the potential of a musical peculiarity of the most ancient antiphons, which are

---

[67] *Sacrosanctum Concilium* (1963), §36.

based on 'type-melodies' or 'model-melodies' and so are perfectly suitable as vehicles for a range of different texts. Here are some examples that illustrate this quality:[68]

The use of model-melodies is good not only for easier learning of the chants. We must remember that the melodies of the *Graduale Romanum* are all individual and closely linked to the text. Therefore, a change of language requires a major adaptation. In contrast, the old antiphons are not 'works' in this sense; their authenticity is not on this level. In this respect they are similar to psalmtones: their authenticity is in the stylistically correct adaptation of a text to a scheme. A new adaptation to new texts fulfils the requirement of 'authenticity' on a higher level. So the use of the older types of antiphons and the tones of the short responsory are very appropriate for the composition of a *Graduale Parvum*.

Another defect of the *Graduale Simplex* is that it is detached from the Proper texts that the Roman Rite effectively embraces. Though in each case the texts and the melodies that were taken over from the Office are in themselves authentic, their liturgical authenticity (as Mass Propers) is actually defective. The textual selection of the Roman Propers, chosen and arranged with the utmost care, was not retained. Authenticity, however, cannot be understood as merely arising from a vague genre of 'musical composition'; rather, it is secured in the employment of musical language and types that enable the actual texts of the Propers of the classical Roman Rite also to be sung to the tunes of antiphons and short responsories.

According to this proposal the *Graduale Parvum* would now adopt the authentic but simpler genres of the Office also for the actual texts of the Mass. This device is recommended not for churches where ornate melodies can perfectly well be chanted by trained scholas, but for those where, in the absence of appropriate conditions, no other liturgical singing is possible.

The longer texts of the Proper could be abbreviated by leaving the most important phrases in the antiphon and transferring the rest to the verses (see the examples below).

The psalm verses in the *Graduale Parvum* are part of the Introit, Communion, and Offertory chants in this book as much as in its bigger sister. The Gradual chant (since it is much shorter than the melismatic piece of the *Graduale Romanum*) could be expanded with one or two additional verses (responsorial psalmody), giving occasion for a better development of the meaning of the text.

This means that §117 of the Constitution *Sacrosanctum Concilium* can be implemented without abandoning the chant texts of the Roman Mass, if they are combined with the model-melodies of antiphons and short responsories. The authenticity of the text is at least as important as the philological-historical authenticity of the individual pieces. In order to separate the philological authenticity from the musical-liturgical one, the *Graduale Parvum* should be published in the form of a textbook or libretto, while the musicians receive permission to produce different settings for the same text by adapting Gregorian melodies, producing new pieces based on Gregorian motifs, or even by using their own

---

[68] *Monumenta Monodica Medii Aevi*, vol. 5, pp. 104–49.

inspiration. The situation in this respect is the same as it was after the Tridentine reforms, when the Missale and *Breviarium Romanum* were published without music, but various musical realizations of the texts appeared in Italy and France.[69] Since the *editio typica* is 'official' only with respect to the text, the Church does not have to take responsibility for the philological authenticity of the music; at least, not in the same way she did (in fact, for the first time in history) when the Gregorian melodies were published in the early twentieth century.

According to this suggestion the libretto of the *Graduale Parvum* is identical with the texts of the *Graduale Romanum,* or at least an excerpt of it. Here is one example for the new application of the Gregorian models:[70]

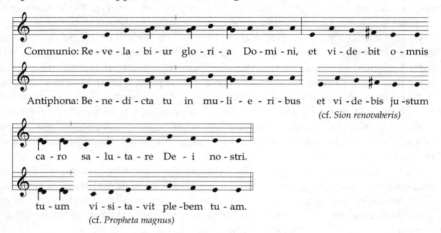

This new adaptation of the Gregorian melodies makes it possible also to sing the proper chant in the vernacular (or in Latin *and* the vernacular). The original rules governing the application of a musical model to Latin texts of different structure and articulation are helpful hints as to how their application to the vernacular texts could now be accomplished. Indubitably, this combination may somewhat modify the character of the Gregorian music, but one of the most admirable qualities of this music is its capacity for adaptation without losing its essence.[71] Alongside (and not, we hasten to assert, *instead of*) the Latin, new dialects of Gregorian chant can now be formed, linked to the phonetic pattern of different languages.[72]

---

[69] A list of Graduals in print between 1590 and 1890: Theodor Karp (2005), *An Introduction to the Post-Tridentine Mass Proper I–II,* pp. 11–78.

[70] On the lower system, examples are given for the adapted phrases from antiphons (line 1–2: from *Benedicta tu,* line 3: from *Sion renovaberis,* line 4: from *Propheta magnus*). I call attention to the fact that the tune is not a 'compilation' of different melodies, but simply the use of the variants within the sphere of approximately one hundred pieces of the type.

[71] For a more detailed explanation of the theme see Dobszay (2003), *The Bugnini-Liturgy and the Reform of the Reform,* pp. 210–13 and (2007), 'A Living Gregorian Chant'.

[72] A fine adaptation of Gregorian antiphons in English: G. H. Palmer (1926), *The Diurnal Noted from the Salisbury Use, Translated into English and Adapted to the Original Musick-Note.*

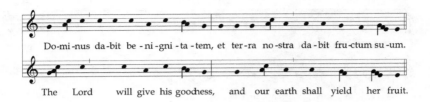

Do-mi-nus da-bit be-ni-gni-ta-tem, et ter-ra no-stra da-bit fru-ctum su-um.

The Lord will give his goodness, and our earth shall yield her fruit.

There is no reason to exclude the possibility that a composer could write new music for the vernacular translation in a Gregorian style, or using its character-istic musical idioms. Even in this case, it is desirable that not all pieces be sung on special melodies; instead, a limited number of modal structures function as vehicles for the various texts. There are many transitional forms possible between following of the Gregorian melodies and compositions 'in the spirit of' Gregorian chant.[73]

This is another argument in support of having the *Graduale Parvum* as an official *textbook*, while musicians are left free – under well-established conditions – in terms of the music. In this case the best solution is if the different linguistic regions provide their own (perhaps bilingual) editions.

I wish to give some examples of adaptations of model melodies. Once again these are only illustrations. Some pieces exemplify a method of abbreviation. First, some antiphonal pieces (Introits and Communions):

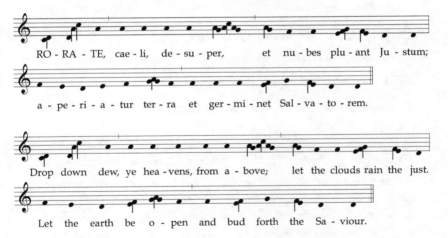

RO - RA - TE, cae-li, de-su-per, et nu-bes plu-ant Ju-stum;

a - pe - ri - a - tur ter-ra et ger-mi-net Sal-va-to-rem.

Drop down dew, ye hea-vens, from a-bove; let the clouds rain the just.

Let the earth be o-pen and bud forth the Sa-viour.

---

[73] An attempt to offer short biblical refrains to congregations has been made in the Hymnal of German Catholics (Gotteslob) and also in other similar collections. The problem is that these texts are mostly independent of the Graduale Romanum (1979), and represent only shorts 'ditties' that rarely have any genuine musical character.

ME-MEN-TO NO-STRI, Do-mi-ne, in be-ne-pla-ci-to po-pu-li tu-i; vi-si-ta nos in sa-lu-ta-ri tu-o.

V) Ad videndum in bonitate electorum tuorum + ad laetandum in laetitia gentis tuae, *
ut lauderis cum hereditate tua.

Re-mem-ber O Lord, re-mem-ber us with fa-vour un-to thy peo-ple; vi-sit us with thy sal-va-t ion!

V) That we may see the good of thy chosen + that we may rejoice in the joy of thy nation*
that thou mayst be praised with thy inheritance.

IN EX-CEL-SO THRO-NO vi-di se-de-re vi-rum quem ad-o-rat mul-ti-tu-do An-ge-lo-rum, psal-len-tes in u-num. V) Ec-ce cujus im-pe-ri-i * no-men est in ae-ter-num. IN EXCELSO.

On the throne ex-al-ted I be-held, and lo, a man sit-ting, whom a le-gion of an-gels wor-ship sing-ing to-ge-ther. V) Be-hold, his rule and go-ver-nance* endureth to all a-ges. On the throne...

Un - to thee, o Lord, I lift up my soul, for none that wait on thee

shall be con - foun - ded.

JE - RU - SA - LEM, SUR - GE et sta in ex - cel - so, vide ju - cun - di - ta - tem,

quae ve - ni - et ti - bi a De - o tu - o.

Je - ru - sa - lem, haste thee, and stand up on high, behold the joy that co - meth

to thee from your God.

GAU - DE - TE in Do - mi - no sem - per, i - te - rum di - co, gau - de - te: Do - mi - nus

e - nim pro - pe est.

Re - joice ye in the Lord, and a - gain I say, re - joice ye; the Lord

is nigh.

VI - DE - RUNT o - mnes fi - nes ter - rae sa - lu - ta - re De - i no - stri,

al - le - lu - ja.

All the ends of the earth have seen, the sal - va - tion of our God,

al - le - lu - ja.

TOL - LE PU - E - RUM, et ma - trem e - jus, et vade in ter - ram I - sra - el,

de - fun - cti sunt e - nim qui quae - re - bant a - ni - mam pu - e - ri.

Take the Child and his mo - ther, and go into the land of Is - ra - el,

for they are dead which sought the Child's life.

EC - CE AD - VE - NIT do - mi - na - tor Do - mi - nus et re - gnum in

ma - nu e - jus et pot - e - stas et im - pe - ri - um.

Be - hold, the Lord the Ru - ler is come, and the King - dom is

in His hand, and po - wer, and do - mi - ni - on.

AD-O-RA-TE DE-UM o-mnes An-ge-li e-jus, au-di-vit et lae-ta-ta

est Si-on, et ex-sul-ta-ve-runt fi-li-ae Iu-dae.

LUX FUL-GE-BIT ho-di-e su-per nos, qui-a na-tus est no-bis Do-mi-nus.

Light shall shine to-day up-on us, for un-to us the Lord is born.

NE-SCI-E-BA-TIS, qui-a in his, quae Pa-tris me-i sunt o-por-tet

me es-se? V) Fi-li quid fecisti no-bis sic? ego et pater tuus dolentes

quae-re-ba-mus te. Et quid est quod me quae-re-ba-tis? NESCIEBATIS...

How is it that ye sought me? wist ye not that I must be a-bout my

Fa-ther's bus-i-ness? V) Son, why hast thou thus dealt with us? Be-hold, thy

father and I have sought thee sor-ro-wing. And he said un-to them: How is it...

189

Now some examples for the adaptation of the short responsory. The main verse is meant to be repeated by the assembly. To the verse/verses by the solo singer the assembly answers with the *repetenda* (marked with *), or, if the sense requires it, with the full verse again. The following tune is used in Hungary throughout the whole year (like the psalm recitations for the Introits of the *English Gradual*).[74] It facilitates participation easily, while the ever-changing structure and meaning of the text always supplies new features to it.[75]

BE -NE -DI -CTUS qui venit in nomine Do -mi - ni * Deus Dominus et il - lu - xit

no -bis. V) A Domino factum est i - stud * et est mirabile in ocu -lis no -stris.

DEUS DOMINUS. BENEDICTUS....

Bles -sed is He that cometh in the Name of the Lord, God, the Lord, who hath

shone up -on us. V) This is the Lord's do -ing, and it is wonderful in our eyes.

GOD, THE LORD. BLESSED IS....

VIDERUNT omnes fi - nes ter -rae salutare De - i no -stri, jubilate Deo, o - mnis

ter - ra. V) No -tum fe - cit Do - mi -nus salutare su - um ante conspectum

gentium revelavit justiti -am su - am. JUBILATE. VIDERUNT...

[74] *The English Gradual. II: The Proper for the Liturgical Year*; David Burt (2006), *The Anglican Use Graduale.*
[75] Source: Pozsony/Bratislava Antiphonary (SQ-BRk EC Lad. 2: fol. 6v, 35r, etc).

All the ends of the earth have seen the salvation of our God, sing joyfully
to God, all the earth. V) The Lord hath made known his sal-va-tion He
revealed His justice in the sight of the Gen-tiles. MAKE... ALL THE ENDS...

SPE-CI-O-SUS for-ma prae filiis ho-mi-num* diffusa est gratia in la-bi-is
tu-is. V) E-ru-ctavit cor meum verbum bo-num + dico ego opera mea Re-gi*
* lingua mea calamus scribae velociter scri-ben-tis. DIFFUSA. SPE-CI-O-SUS.

Thou art beau-ti-ful above sons of men, grace is spread a-broad on
thy lips. V) My heart hath uttered a good word, +I speak my words
to the King, my tongue is the pen of a scrivener, that writ-eth swift-ly.
FULL OF GRACE... THOU ART...

BE-NE-DI-CTUS Dominus Deus I-sra-el, qui facit mirabilia ma-gna
so-lus. V) Sus-cipiant montes pa-cem populo su-o, et colles ju-sti-ti-am.

QUI FACIT. V)O - ri - e - tur in diebus e - jus justitia et abundanti - a

pa - cis. QUI FACIT. BENEDICTUS...

Bless - ed be the Lord, the God of I - sra - el, who alone doeth won-

der - ful things. V) Let the mountains re - ceive peace for the peo - ple,

and the hills jus - tice. WHO ALONE. V) In his days shall justice spring up;

and abun - dance of peace. WHO ALONE. BLESSED...

The melismatic nature of the *Alleluia* should be retained even in poorer singing conditions. The syllabic Alleluias (which are, in fact, Office antiphons, such as the well-known 6th-mode Alleluia-contrafact) probably cannot be fully dispensed with; the *Graduale Parvum* should contain one melody in each mode. But would it be possible for a parish community using only the *Graduale Parvum* to go beyond this level?

The answer must be in the positive. In the most ancient form of the Roman liturgy the Alleluia was sung only on Easter day. Most likely *this* Alleluia is the one that survived in the Paschal Vigil.[76] It is therefore well advised to make this Alleluia the most frequently sung piece, and, in the Easter season, perhaps even the only one. If it is sung during the full 50 days of the Easter season, the faithful would greet it with joy in the Easter Vigil of the next year, and could take it on their lips again with confident recognition.

The set of Alleluia melodies hardly developed in Rome until the eleventh and twelfth centuries. The Old Roman Gradual does not know more than four melodies (one of these is a little variable, but the other three are sung with different verses to an identical melody).[77] It seems that this was a widespread usage in the Old Latin liturgies. The Beneventan Rite knew a single Alleluia melody[78] and

[76] McKinnon (2000a), *The Advent Project*, pp. 270–72.
[77] *Monumenta Monodica Medii Aevi*, vol. 2, pp. 167–74, 178–83, 212–20, 188–99; cf. 201–06.
[78] Thomas Forest Kelly (1989), *The Beneventan Chant*, pp. 119–22.

the number of the Alleluias is no more than half a dozen in the Ambrosian chant books.[79] If the full year is filled up with only three or four alleluia melodies, these might even be quite melismatic, and the faithful would be happy to learn these beautiful pieces. A changing verse can be added, of course, by simple recitation on a psalm tone, perhaps embellished with a closing *jubilus*. Below are presented the Gregorian versions of the four old Alleluias (I, II, IV, V), completed with three pleasant pieces from the Carolingian period (III, VI, VII). Each piece of the whole reduced repertory could be assigned to one liturgical season, for example:

I. Advent:[80]

II. Christmas:[81]

III. Eastertide:[82]

---

[79] Terence Bailey (1983), *The Ambrosian Alleluias*, pp. 46–99.

[80] This tune is presented here according to the pentatonic dialect (*Missale Notatum Strigoniense*, fol. 3v); but this does not impinge upon the essence of the proposal. See the *Graduale Sacrosanctae Romanae Ecclesiae de Tempore et de Sanctis . . .* (1979) for the diatonic version: *Excita Domine* 3rd Sunday of Advent, *Graduale Sacrosanctae Romanae Ecclesiae de Tempore et de Sanctis . . .* (1979), p. 23.

[81] In the *Graduale Triplex*: Dies sanctificatus (Christmas, third Mass, *Graduale Triplex*, p. 49).

[82] The melody of the Easter Vigil Alleluia *Graduale Sacrosanctae Romanae Ecclesiae de Tempore et de Sanctis . . .* (1979), p. 191.

IV. Pentecost and Ordinary Time:[83]

Al - le - lul -ja.   V)

(jubilus ad lib.) etc.

V. Ordinary Time:[84]

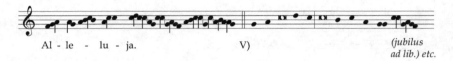

Al - le - lu - ja.   V)   *(jubilus ad lib.) etc.*

VI. Ordinary Time:[85]

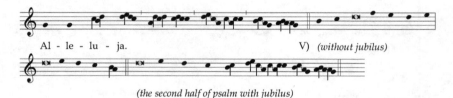

Al - le - lu - ja.   V) *(without jubilus)*

(the second half of psalm with jubilus)

VII. Ordinary Time:[86]

Al - le - lu - ja.   V)

(jubilus ad lib.) etc.

---

[83] *Missale Notatum Strigoniense ante 1341 in Posonio*, fol. 168. The pentatonic variant of the Alleluia Veni Sancte Spiritus Pentecost, cf. *Graduale Sacrosanctae Romanae Ecclesiae de Tempore et de Sanctis* . . . (1979), p. 253.

[84] *Missale Notatum Strigoniense ante 1341 in Posonio*, fol. 1. The pentatonic variant of Ostende nobis (First Sunday of Advent, cf. *Graduale* Romanum (1979), p. 16).

[85] *Missale Notatum Strigoniense ante 1341 in Posonio*, fol. 188. The pentatonic variant of Venite exsultemus 14th Sunday after Pentecost, cf. *Graduale Sacrosanctae Romanae Ecclesiae de Tempore et de Sanctis* . . . (1979), p. 324.

[86] *Missale Notatum Strigoniense ante 1341 in Posonio*, fol. 142. The pentatonic variant of Angelus Domini Easter Monday, cf. *Graduale Sacrosanctae Romanae Ecclesiae de Tempore et de Sanctis* . . . (1979), p. 201.

It would be desirable to introduce a few sequences into the *Graduale Parvum*. If they are intended for less-well-trained scholas or congregations, some special devices can be employed to make them easier. Taking into account the structure of the genre, the A-strophes can be assigned to the cantor, and an unchanging melody could be sung to the B-strophes by the choir or the congregation.

Two types of Sequences are appropriate for such a collection. The first is the short, Italian-type Sequence. For instance, the Sequence *Grates nunc reddamus* was sung in all churches during the Middle Ages (there are even vernacular variants and polyphonic settings to it).[87] It is surprising that the earliest Old Roman Gradual (of the Basilica of Saint Cecilia) has a variant of its melody with an Advent text.[88] I present here the Advent and Christmas pieces, the former with its Old Roman text, but on the vulgate European melody:[89]

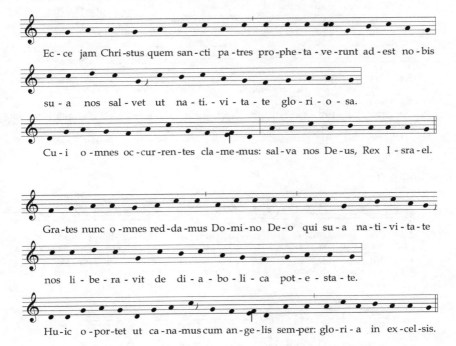

Ec - ce jam Chri - stus quem san - cti pa - tres pro - phe - ta - ve - runt ad - est no - bis

su - a nos sal - vet ut na - ti. - vi - ta - te glo - ri - o - sa.

Cu - i o - mnes oc - cur - ren - tes cla - me - mus: sal - va nos De - us, Rex I - sra - el.

Gra - tes nunc o - mnes red - da - mus Do - mi - no De - o qui su - a na - ti - vi - ta - te

nos li - be - ra - vit de di - a - bo - li - ca pot - e - sta - te.

Hu - ic o - por - tet ut ca - na - mus cum an - ge - lis sem - per: glo - ri - a in ex - cel - sis.

The other possible type is that of the strophic repertory belonging to the second period of development of Sequence poetry ('Paris style'). Since the music of the best items is sometimes rather difficult, some simplifications should be offered for the sake of bringing them back into use. In the *Dies irae*, there are

---

[87] *Analecta hymnica*, vol. 53, p. 15. Rajeczky (1982), *Melodiarium Hungariae Medii Aevi*, p. 110.

[88] *Analecta hymnica*, vol. 37, p. 14. Max Lütolf (1987), *Das Graduale von Santa Cecilia in Trastevere (Cod. Bodmer 74)*, vol. 2, fol. 1.

[89] *Missale Notatum Strigoniense ante 1341 in Posonio*, fol. 328v.

only three different melodic phrases, and all strophes repeat the musical cycle: AA-BB-CC-AA-BB-CC, etc. Similarly, melodies of two of the strophes could then be selected from a long sequence (if they share the same meter), and these two could be recycled throughout the full poem: AA-BB-AA-BB. The first member of the pairs is always sung by the cantor or precentors. For instance:[90]

Mel I.

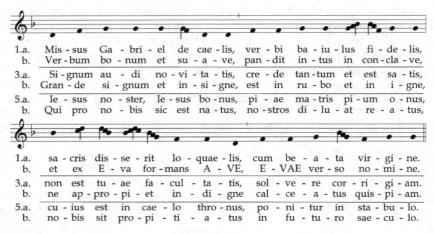

1.a. Mis - sus Ga - bri - el de cae - lis, ver - bi ba - iu - lus fi - de - lis,
  b. Ver - bum bo - num et su - a - ve, pan - dit in - tus in con - cla - ve,
3.a. Si - gnum au - di no - vi - ta - tis, cre - de tan - tum et est sa - tis,
  b. Gran - de si - gnum et in - si - gne, est in ru - bo et in i - gne,
5.a. Ie - sus no - ster, Ie - sus bo - nus, pi - ae ma - tris pi - um o - nus,
  b. Qui pro no - bis sic est na - tus, no - stros di - lu - at re - a - tus,

1.a. sa - cris dis - se - rit lo - quae - lis, cum be - a - ta vir - gi - ne.
  b. et ex E - va for - mans A - VE, E - VAE ver - so no - mi - ne.
3.a. non est tu - ae fa - cul - ta - tis, sol - ve - re cor - ri - gi - am.
  b. ne ap - pro - pi - et in - di - gne cal - ce - a - tus quis - pi - am.
5.a. cu - ius est in cae - lo thro - nus, po - ni - tur in sta - bu - lo.
  b. no - bis sit pro - pi - ti - a - tus in fu - tu - ro sae - cu - lo.

Mel II.

2.a. Con - se - quen - ter iu - xta pa - ctum, ad - est Ver - bo ca - ro fa - ctum,
  b. Pa - trem pa - ri - ens i - gno - rat, et quem ho - mo non de - flo - rat,
4.a. Vir - ga sic - ca si - ne ro - re, no - vo ri - tu no - vo mo - re,
  b. Be - ne - di - ctus il - le fru - ctus, fru - ctus gau - di - i non lu - ctus,

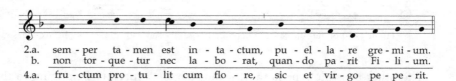

2.a. sem - per ta - men est in - ta - ctum, pu - el - la - re gre - mi - um.
  b. non tor - que - tur nec la - bo - rat, quan - do pa - rit Fi - li - um.
4.a. fru - ctum pro - tu - lit cum flo - re, sic et vir - go pe - pe - rit.
  b. e - rit A - dam se - du - ctus, si de hoc gu - sta - ve - rit.

---

[90] *Missale Notatum Strigoniense ante 1341 in Posonio*, fol. 351. Gabriel having been sent from Heaven, / this faithful bearer of the Word, / speaks with holy words / to the blessed virgin. 1b. The benign and sweet utterance / opens the very heart, / forming AVE from EVA, / reversing Eva's name. 2a. And according to the covenant, / at once the Word made flesh is present / and yet the womb of the virgin / remains undefiled. 2b. Not having known a father, she bears a son / who injureth her not, tortureth her not, / maketh her not to suffer / in her confinement. 3a. Hearken to this new sign, / believe in it, and this shall suffice: / it is beyond your faculty / to solve this mystery. 3b. Great and momentous is this sign: / it was already present in the burning bush, / and so none shall approach / this place in a manner unworthy, in sandals. 4a. The dry bough

It is more difficult to find a good musical solution for the Offertories of the *Graduale Parvum*.[91] It would be desirable if its feature were different from the Introits, Communions, and the interlectional psalmody. It is necessary to take into consideration the desire of the congregation at a parish Mass to sing something different after a long spell of Gregorian chant (for instance, a strophic hymn), or to listen to a polyphonic piece. Therefore, in parish use I could accept – exceptionally – a strophic translation of the offertory texts, with a refrain functioning as a *repetenda*.

Another possibility is a simple recitation, which leaves time enough to include some other type of music afterwards. The following tone[92] is very simple and can easily be adapted to any text. With the raising of the dominant note in the verse this piece reminds us of the more intensive quality of the melismatic, high-range verses of found in the Offertory chants.

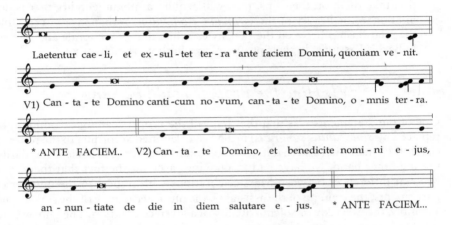

receiving no dew / bore fruit with flowers / in a new manner, according to a new rite: / this is how this Virgin too was confined. 4b. Blessed is this fruit, / the fruit of joy and not of sorrow, / and Adam will not be beguiled / if he doth taste this. 5a. Our Jesus, our goodly Jesus, / graceful offspring of the graceful mother, / whose throne is in Heaven, / is now placed in the crib. 5b. He who thus was born for us / shall wash away our sins / and show mercy to us / in the kingdom to come. Amen, alleluia.

[91] An analysis of the Offertory texts should be a theme of a separate chapter. Differently from the expectations of our day, only a few of them deal with the theme of the offertory of the Mass itself. Several Secrets speak this way: 'receive, O God, the deprecations of your Church along with the sacrifical gifts . . .' The chant is part of those 'deprecations' which accompany the process of bringing the gifts to the altar. In the *Offertóriumok Könyve* ('Book of Offertories') (Budapest, 2005) I distinguished the following main themes of the Offertory chants: 1. Offertorial themes. 2. Themes of sacrifice and intervention. 3. The expansion of the festal themes. 4. Moral themes, as offerings of our free will. 5. The sacrifice of praise. 6. Thanksgiving and deprecation for salvation.

[92] The main part is the tone of the Chapter; *Antiphonale Monasticum*, p. 1233). The tone of the verse is taken from the chant of Ambrosian psalmody (*Liber Vesperale juxta ritum Sanctae Ecclesiae Mediolensis*, p. 827). For the text of the verses: *Offertoriale Triplex*, pp. 15–16. Translation of the example: Nativity First Mass at Midnight: Let the Heavens rejoice, and let the earth be glad before the face of the Lord * because he cometh. V/1. Sing ye to the Lord a new canticle, sing to the Lord, all the earth. * Because he cometh. V/2. Sing ye to the Lord and bless his name, shew forth his salvation from day to day. * Because he cometh.

In concluding this survey I wish to remind the reader of three earlier remarks.

1. The real aim of this discussion has not been to propose concrete pieces or melodies, but to encourage others to begin thinking about viable methods.
2. Nowadays 'creativity' is not a good guide in liturgical matters. Nevertheless, the history of Gregorian chant (and the liturgy itself) enjoyed certain periods when creativity worked for the benefit of the rite, given that everything was done in concert with tradition. If the application of a certain small degree of creativity is denied to our own age, we might as well declare Gregorian chant to be dead.
3. These kinds of melodies seem to say less than the 'great' pieces in the *Graduale Romanum*, but when 200 or 300 members of a parish congregation take them on their lips, they will acquire a monumentality that is not inferior to the beauty of the *Graduale Romanum*. Perhaps we can say that the relationship between the two styles is like that of a chorale and an aria in Bach's Passions. In their proper places both work perfectly.

VI. *How the Propers could be Sung*

One of our statements was that the chant of the Propers cannot be omitted (or replaced by *alius cantus congruus*) in a Mass celebrated according to the restored classical Roman Rite, and that it needs to be sung according to ancient standards. On the other hand, we have had to take into account the fact that there may be great differences between Mass-celebrations with respect to the number of participants, the training of the assistants, the musical capacity of the singers and assembly, the everyday or solemn quality of a given celebration. The only way to satisfy all requirements is if there are several legitimate methods of *performing* the proper chants. These different possibilities should be ranked according to different levels: all methods must fit organically within the celebration. I began by describing these methods in their fullest form, and then listed the various grades all the way down to situations of necessity; all of this I will now try to formulate in a simple descriptive form.

1. All **proper chants of the day** are sung in their full form:
    1.1: In Latin from the *Graduale Romanum* (or its alternative edition according to the local tradition). To be sung:
        by the schola, or
        by the congregation led by the cantor or schola, or
        by a psalmist, a solo singer.[93]

---

[93] Instruction *Musicam Sacram* (1967), §21: 'Provision should be made for at least one or two properly trained singers, especially where there is no possibility of setting up even a small choir. The singer will present some simpler musical settings, with the people taking part, and can lead and support the faithful as far as is needed. The presence of such a singer is desirable even in

Since the priest needs to be saying his own prayers during the Introit, or is performing ritual actions during the Offertory and Communion, it is *laudable* but not obligatory for him to pray the items that are also sung. He may also pray the interlectionary chants, or he may listen to them together with the congregation.

1.2: The daily Proper is sung by a schola and/or the congregation to a simpler melody. Before or after, the choir, the schola, or the psalmist may sing the same (*ad libitum*) with its melody given in the *Graduale Romanum*.

The priest will follow the rubric above.

1.3: The daily Proper is sung in the vernacular

by the schola (psalmist, congregation) in its melismatic setting, or:

by the schola and/or congregation to a simpler melody.

Before or after, the choir, the schola, or the psalmist may sing the same (*ad libitum*) in Latin.

It is *laudable* if the priest prays in Latin all the items that are also sung in the vernacular.

1.4: The daily Proper is sung in Latin or in the vernacular, not with a Gregorian tune, however, but in a composed setting.

The priest does what is laid out above.

2. The congregation and/or the schola sing **seasonal chants** from the 'sets' of a *Graduale Parvum*. In this case the daily Proper should be prayed adopting one of the following methods:

2.1: The cantor or precentors recite the text of the daily proper as a *versus ad repetendum* before the last repetition of the 'seasonal' antiphon of the Introit, Communion and Offertory. Or:

2.2: Before the congregation commences the seasonal proper chant, the cantor (psalmist) recites or sings the text of the daily Proper.

2.3: *After* the seasonal Introit and Communion chant, and *before* the seasonal Offertory chant, the priest intones the appropriate text of the *daily* item and the congregation prays with him *recto tono* (*ad libitum*: with a very soft organ accompaniment). The psalm verse and doxology are recited by a lector, an acolyte, or altar server or in their absence by the priest himself (aloud) (turned towards the altar and not towards the assembly, since these texts are addressed to the Lord).

In case of 2.1 and 2.2 the priest reads the daily proper text; while in the case of 2.3 the priest prays along with the congregation.

3. If **neither the daily nor the seasonal proper** is sung, it should be prayed in one of the following ways:

3.1: The first words of the Introit, Offertory, and Communion are intoned aloud by the priest, then the full congregation prays with him the text (possibly, *recto tono*). The verses are recited loudly by a lector,

churches which have a choir, for those celebrations in which the choir cannot take part but which may fittingly be performed with some solemnity and therefore with singing.'

acolyte, altar server, or, in their absence, by the priest himself. The interlectionary chants are read (led) by the reader.

3.2: In Masses *sine populo* the texts are read (*elevata voce*) alternately by the priest and the altar server.

3.3: If the altar server is not capable, the priest reads alone the proper chants (facing the altar) in a way audible to those present.

Before the Introit, Offertory and Communion, or after they were read in any of the methods above, a folk hymn might be sung, which does not, however, replace the liturgical text.

By the use of these rules our aims can be fulfilled: the texts of the daily proper chant are sung (or recited), its musical and communal quality prevails, and not even the most modest conditions exempt any liturgical situation from the obligation to their performance.

19

THE SACRAMENTARY

The Sacramentary – collection of orations (the Collects, Secrets and Postcommunions) and Prefaces – is the most *Roman* component of the classical Roman Rite.[1] The readings, and the chanting of psalms, form a significant part of the liturgy in the Eastern churches as well, even though the selection and arrangement is different from the Latin church. The genre of orations, however, was born in the Latin church and received its clearest formulations in Rome. In her orations the Roman Church speaks in her own voice. She intends to *speak* of the *ineffable* Mystery, making conceivable the *inconceivable*. The orations speak of a reality beyond our experience and of mysteries inexhaustible by our minds, while, in fact, speaking in the language of the intellect. For this huge work the Church used every available intellectual art, language and rhetorical wisdom amassed by human science and ability until the age of late Antiquity. The Church employed a very precise yet expressive artistic prose to penetrate the depths of theology, a prose which always remained elegant and elevated. Outstanding scholarly works have been written about this high intellectual, theological and stylistic accomplishment.[2] It is not our task here to add anything to the manifold discussions that have extolled the qualities of the Sacramentary. What I wish to emphasize now is how great our responsibility is to preserve and communicate this treasury of faith to future generations, and how essential it is to instil these lasting qualities in the minds of the Catholic faithful through exact and beautiful translations.

---

[1] 'Nothing in the Missal is . . . so Roman as the old collects – and nothing, alas, so little Roman as the new ones' (Fortescue (1912), *The Mass*, 4th edn 2005, p. 249).

[2] I mention the articles published in Jahrbuch für Liturgiewissenschaft and the activity of the Nijmegen School (series Latinitas Christianorum Primaeva). Christine Mohrmann (1959), *Liturgical Latin: Its Origins and Character*, and (1961–77), *Études sur le latin des chrétiens I–IV.* Cf. Jean Deschusses (1982), *Le sacramentaire grégorien: Ses principales formes d'après les plus anciens manuscrits*; Mary Pierre Ellebracht (1966), *Remarks on the Vocabulary of the Ancient Orations in the Missale Romanum.* A critical approach is found in Theodor Klauser (1969), *A Short History of the Western Liturgy*, pp. 37–43.

I. The Collect, Secret (Super Oblata), and Postcommunion (Complenda)

The form of the orations took shape in the age of the great Church Fathers. They express one complex idea condensed into one complex sentence. In its most common formula, the oration begins by addressing God, and with the conjunction of *qui* (who) it calls to memory one of His important attributes or deeds. In the central part of the text the Church entreats God (with *praesta, quaesumus* or some similar phrase) for something whose significance is explained in the second half of the text; the object of the request is closely connected with what was said in the first half of God's essence or activity.[3] The theological meaning of this structure is that our deprecation is not based on our own merits, but on the essence of God himself, on the divine power and clemency we have already so often experienced.

The stock material of the Sacramentary – including the quantitatively and qualitatively most important prayers of the Roman Rite – had already reached completion by the sixth and seventh century;[4] that is, by the time that the rite of the holy city of Rome had become the liturgy of almost the entirety of Western Christianity. Supplementation of this material was necessary only when new feasts appeared, but the basic collection and its arrangement remained otherwise unchanged. The prayers produced in the Carolingian period, the high Middle Ages, or even pious thoughts developed in later periods added to and became well-beloved parts of an already established liturgy.[5] But after the mystery-theology of Christian Antiquity faded, the new compositions rarely produced the same powerful effect of the original Roman style.

The preservation and communication of this treasury is surely the binding priority of any liturgical reform. The Constitution of the Council proposes not a single word concerning any possible transformation of the Sacramentary.[6] What a shock for us then to open the 1970 Missal of Paul VI and see that no stone remained upon another in the collection of the prayers! This impression is inevitable even if we are told that a significant portion of the old orations was in fact preserved in the new Missal. Let us compare the new Sacramentary with the cycle of the classical Roman liturgy.

Starting with the temporal cycle: if the orations of the liturgical days are compared across the two missals, of the 363 items of the old Missal, no more than 46 (12.68 per cent) remained unchanged from their original position. Even if we add to this the 17 pieces (4.68 per cent with only minor, let us say, stylistic changes)

---

3 Adrian Fortescue (1912), *The Mass*, 4th edn 2005, pp. 249–51. Josef Andreas Jungmann, SJ (1958), *Missarum Sollemnia*, vol. 1. pp. 478–87.
4 On the oldest extant Roman sacramentaries: Walter Howard Frere (1930), *Studies in Early Roman Liturgy – I: The Kalendar*, pp. 29–68; Louis Duchesne (1903), *Christian Worship: Its Origin and Evolution*; 2nd edn 1927, pp. 120–50; Jungmann (1958), *Missarum Sollemnia*, vol. 1, pp. 77–82.
5 Fortescue (1912), *The Mass*, 4th edn 2005, pp. 251–52.
6 'The Council Fathers did not authorise . . . any change to the very ancient Sunday Collects; yet . . . these changes were made' (John P. Parsons (2003), 'A Reform of the Reform?', p. 229).

and the 23 (6.34 per cent) that endured substantial rephrasing which touched upon their actual content, we are still astonished to find that in 277 places (76.3 per cent), completely different orations are to be found in the new Missal.[7] A portion of the 'new' orations is, in fact, taken over from the old collection, but in each case transferred to another place. Only a very few of these transpositions can be justified with any serious justification. The impression remains that the editors wilfully subverted the order of the orations over the cycle of the year. It seems that their intention was nothing other than to make an arrangement that *does not* allow for any recognition of the old Missal in the new one. It might be claimed, of course, that it does not really matter on which Ordinary Sunday the Church should pray a given oration. If this is true, we may as well reply: if it does not matter, what exactly then is the genuine spiritual benefit for the Church in this rearrangement? Let us recall the express will of the Council: 'There must be no innovations unless the good of the Church genuinely and certainly requires them'.[8] Since in this upset no such 'genuine and certain' good of the Church can be identified, we are forced to conclude that the committee acted illegitimately by compelling the priests and the faithful to follow a standard contrary to what was in fact the higher law of the Second Vatican Council itself.

Surely, no genuine and certain good came from the rearrangement, only damage and confusion. The continuity of our liturgy has been broken. The hundreds of Missals produced during the last 1,300 years recorded the orations of the temporal cycle almost identically in every case and in the same order. While local Uses enjoyed a degree of freedom in *other* genres, by this amazing unanimity they testified to their conviction that the Sacramentary is a strict and obligatory standard of the classical Roman Rite. This unanimity was totally ignored by the architects of the reform.

I have already mentioned that in some orations small stylistic modifications were made in the new Missal. If we study these changes, we find that this transcription brought neither benefit nor harm. Sometimes the only thing changed was the order of words.[9] At other times a word was replaced by a synonym; or

---

[7] With a reference to Anthony Cekada (1991), *The Problems with the Prayers of the Modern Mass*, Thomas Kocik (2003), *The Reform of the Reform*, p. 49, writes: 'The 1962 Missal contains 1182 orations . . . about 760 of which were dropped entirely. Of the approximately 36% that remained, over half were altered before being introduced into the Missal of 1970. Thus, only some 17% of the traditional orations made it untouched into the 1970 Missal.' Cf. Brian W. Harrison, OS (2003), 'The Postconciliar Eucharistic Liturgy', p. 189.

[8] 'Innovationes, demum, ne fiant nisi vera et certa utilitas ecclesiae id exigat . . .', *Sacrosanctum Concilium* (1963), §23.

[9] Examples:
'Placare, Domine, quaesumus' – 'Placare, quaesumus, Domine' (2nd Sunday of Advent, Secret);
'Excita quaesumus, Domine . . . indulgentia tua propitiationis acceleret.' – 'Excita . . . gratia tuae propitiationis acceleret' (4th Sunday of Advent, Collect; 1970: Tuesday of the 1st week of Advent);
'Indignos nos . . . Filii tui adventu laetifica.' – 'Indignos nos . . . adventu salutari laetifica' (Saturday of the 3rd week of Advent, Collect; 1970: for Thursday of the 3rd week);
'Imploramus, Domine, clementiam tuam . . .' – 'Tuam, Domine, clementiam imploramus' (3rd Sunday of Advent, Postcommunio; 1970: Saturdays of the 1st to 3rd weeks of Advent).

an additional word was inserted.[10] The beginning of the old Postcommunion of the Saturday of the second week in Lent reads like this: 'Sacramenti tui Domine, divina libatio penetralia nostri cordis infundat'.[11] The new Missal replaced *libatio* (tasting) with *perceptio* (receiving). There is no essential difference between the two, but 'libatio' is a characteristic term of ancient cultic Latinity, which refers explicitly to a sacrificial meal. In the Collect of the Wednesday of the fifth week in Lent we read: 'et quibus devotionis praestas affectum', in the new Missal: 'quibus praestas devotionis affectum'.[12] The Collect gained nothing by the transposition of the two words, but lost its attractive rhythmic and stylistic structure. The Postcommunion on the Tuesday of the fifth week in Lent was: 'quae divina sunt jugiter *exequentes*' (we may always strive after divine things); in the new Missal: 'jugiter *ambientes*' (always walk in the wish of divine things) – which word was rarely employed in liturgical Latin before.[13] The situation is the same with all 17 orations mentioned earlier.

Modifications may, in fact, generate a change of the actual meaning. Many times one detects ideological considerations behind these changes;[14] at other times

---

[10] 'Deus qui salutis aeternae . . . per quem meruimus auctorem vitae suscipere' – 'per quem meruimus Filium tuum auctorem vitae suscipere' (Feast of the Circumcision, Collect);
'Suscipe, Domine, sacrificium, cujus te voluisti dignanter immolatione placari, praesta quaesumus, ut . . .' – 'Suscipe, quaesumus, Domine, sacrificium placationis et laudis et praesta, ut . . .' (Saturday after Ash Wednesday, Secret);
'Respice, Domine . . . quae se carnis maceratione castigat' – '. . . quae se corporalium moderatione castigat' (Tuesday of the 1st week of Lent, Collect for ; 1970: Wednesday of the 1st week of Lent);
'Sanctificationem tuam . . . quae nos et a terrenis purget vitiis' – '. . . nos et a vitiis terrenis emundat' (Tuesday of the 2nd week of Lent, Secreta for 1970: Tuesday of the 2nd week of Lent);
'Hostias, Domine . . . propitius respice' – '. . . propitius intuere' (Wednesday of the 2nd week of Lent, Secreta);
'Da, quaesumus . . . ut qui in tot adversis ex nostra infirmitate deficimus . . .' – '. . . ut qui ex nostra infirmitate deficimus . . .' (Monday in Holy Week, Collect);
'Sanctifica, quaesumus . . . hujus oblationis hostiam . . .' – '. . . haec munera nostrae servitutis' (Trinity Sunday, Secret).
[11] 'The divine taste of Thy Sacrament, O Lord, penetrate in the interior of our heart . . .' Cf. P. Bruylants, OSB (1952), *Les Oraisons du Missel Romain – Text and Histoire*, vol. 2, Nr. 996, *Corpus Orationum* (1992), vol. 8, §5152.
[12] '. . . and to those whom Thou give the affects of self-dedication', Collect '*Sanctificato/Sanctificata hoc jejunio* . . .', in the *Missale Romanum* (2002); cf: 'Sanctificata per paenitentiam . . .' (Bruylants (1952), *Les Oraisons du Missel Romain*, vol. 2, p. 1046; *Corpus Orationum*, vol. 8, §5387b).
[13] Postcommunio *Da quaesumus omnipotens Deus* . . . Da quaesumus . . . ut quae divina sunt jugiter ambientes' (Bruylants (1952), *Les Oraisons du Missel Romain*, vol. 2. p. 188; *Corpus Orationum*, vol. 2, §1023a–b).
[14] '. . . there has been such a drastic reduction or mutilation of the traditional prayers mentioning such themes as human weakness, guilt and repentance on the part of sinners, the wrath of God, hell, the souls in Purgatory, the Church's need for protection from their spiritual and temporal enemies, and other topics that were evidently considered too "negative" for the needs of "modern man", that in effect the whole spirit of the eucharistic liturgy has been seriously altered' (Harrison (2003), 'The Postconciliar Eucharistic Liturgy', pp. 189–90). The author quotes here the reformist Matias Augé, who confessed openly that just this theological change was the reason 'for getting rid ot these traditional prayers'. Cf. '. . . many of these venerable prayers were abolished or expurgated because they expressed ideas unpopular with liberal Catholics' (Kocik (2003), *The Reform of the Reform*, p. 69). About a shift in theological meaning concerning the feast of Dedication: Laurence Paul Hemming (2009), '*I Saw the New Jerusalem* – On Time in the Sacred Liturgy'.

the old content is exchanged by more contemporary expressions. Sometimes fragments of the old prayers were built into the new ones (so-called 'centoniza-tion'). I present some examples (the words from the old Missal are marked by + and from the new one by *).[15]

[15] + 'ut hujus participatione mysterii, doceas nos terrena despicere et amare caelestia'; – * '... doces nos terrena sapienter perpendere et caelestibus inhaerere' – + 'that by our partaking of this Mystery, Thou wouldst teach us to despise the things of earth, and to love those of Heaven'; – * teach us to treat wisely the things of earth and adhere to those of Heaven' (Postcommunio, Advent Second Sunday).
+ 'Sacrificium quadragesimalis ... ut cum epularum restrictione carnalium a noxiis quoque voluptatibus temperemus'; – * '... ut per paenitentiae caritatisque labores a noxiis voluptatibus temperemur, et a peccatis mundati ad celebrandam Filii tui passionem mereamur esse devoti' – 'We solemnly offer to Thee, O Lord, the Sacrifice of the Lent ... that while we curtail our eating of meat, we may abstain also from harmful pleasures'; – * 'that while we by the works of penitence and charity moderate the harmful desires, cleansed from sins we may devotedly celebrate the Passion of your Son' (Secret, First Sunday in Lent; in the 1970 Missal: Ash Wednesday).
+ 'Inchoata jejunia, quaesumus, Domine, benigno favore prosequere'; – * 'Inchoata paenitentiae opera ...' – + ' Further with Thy gracious favour, we beseech Thee, O Lord, the fasts which we have begun ...'; * '... 'the works of penitence which we have begun ...' (Collect, Friday after Ash Wednesday).
+ 'Converte nos, Deus, salutaris noster, et, ut nobis jejunium quadragesimale proficiat ...'; – * 'Converte ... et, ut nobis opus quadragesimale proficiat' – + 'Convert us, O God, our Saviour, and that this fast of Lent may profit us ...'; – * '... and that the works of the Lent may profit us ..' (Collect, Monday in the first week of the Lent).
+ 'Praesenti sacrificio, nomini tuo nos, Domine, jejunia dicata sanctifient, ut quod observantia nostra profitetur exterius ...'; – * 'Praesenti sacrificio ... observantiam nostram sanctifica, ut quod quadragesimalis exercitatio profitetur exterius ...' – + 'May the fasts that we dedicate to Thy name, O Lord, hallow us, that what we show outwardly in this Lenten observance ...'; – 'By the present sacrifice ... hallow our observance, that what the Lenten practice manifest outwardly ...' (Secret, Thursday in the second week of Lent).
+ 'Da, quaesumus ... ut sacro nos purificante jejunio ...'; – * '... ut sacro nos purificante paenitentiae studio' – + 'We beseech Thee ... give a healing effect to our fasts ...'; – '... that while the holy endeavour of penitence purify us' (Collect, Friday in the second week of Lent).
+ '... ut qui propriis oramus absolvi delictis, non gravemur externis'; – * 'ut qui propriis oramus absolvi delictis, fraterna dimittere studeamus' – + '... that we who pray to be loosed from our own sins, may not be burdened with the external things ...'; – * 'that we who pray to be loosed from the sins, endeavour to give forgiveness to the offences of our brethren' (Secret, Saturday in the second week of Lent; in the 1970 Missal: Third Sunday of Lent).
+ 'Praesta nobis, quaesumus, Domine, ut salutaribus jejuniis eruditi, a noxiis quoque vitiis absti-nentes, propitiationem tuam facilius impetremus'; – * '... ut per quadragesimalem observantiam eruditi et tuo verbo nutriti, sancta continentia tibi simus toto corde devoti, et in oratione tua semper efficiamur concordes' – + 'We beseech Thee, O Lord, grant us that taught by wholesome fasting, and abstaining from harmful vices, we may the more easily obtain Thy pardon'; * '... that taught by the Lenten observance, and fed by your word, we may be devoted to you by the holy continence and be always unanimous in the prayer' (Collect, Wednesday in the third week of Lent).
+ 'Deus, qui hodierna die per Unigenitum tuum aeternitatis nobis aditum, devicta morte, reserasti, vota nostra, quae praeveniendo aspiras, etiam adjuvando prosequere'; – * 'Deus, qui hodierna die ... ut qui resurrectionis dominicae sollemnia colimus, per innovationem tui Spiritus in lumine vitae resurgamus' – + 'O God, who on this day through Thine only-begotten Son, hast conquered death, and thrown open to us the gate of everlasting life, give effect by thine aid to our desires, which Thou dost anticipate and inspire' ; * 'O God, who on this day ... that we who celebrate the solemnity of the Lord's resurrection, regenerated by your Spirit may rise in the light of life' (Collect, Easter Sunday)
+ 'Deus, qui solemnitate paschali, mundo remedia contulisti ... ut perfectam libertatem consequi mereatur, et ad vitam proficiat sempiternam'; – * 'Deus, qui paschalia nobis remedia contulisti ... ut perfectam libertatem assecutus, in caelis gaudeat, unde nunc in terris exsultat' (Monday within the Eastern Octave, Collect; 1970: on Tuesday) + 'O God, who in the Paschal Solemnity

In 277 places we find new texts in the new Missal. From where were they taken? A portion of them existed already in the old Missal, but on different days. Another group of items is taken from the precedents of mature Roman Sacramentaries: the *Gelasian* and *Leonine* collections, and the *Hadrianum*. This means that they reinstate good and authentic Roman texts. (It is beyond our interest to identify the extent to which these texts were also modified.) Finally, there is a rather large number of entirely new formulations, sometimes stylistically in sharp conflict with liturgical tradition.

Let us now turn our attention to the sanctoral cycle. Of the 324 liturgical occasions only in 23 cases do we find the orations of the classical Roman Missal (7.1 per cent). The number of orations adopted with small 'stylistic' changes is 13 (4.01 per cent), of those heavily rephrased there are 37 (11.43 per cent). In 251 places the oration is completely different to the comparable place in the old Missal (up until 1962).

Here there are even more cases of discontinuity than in the Temporal cycle. Even without a detailed analysis we have every reason to suppose that the case here is not of simple transpositions, but of brand new compositions. The basis of this supposition is disclosed by the style of the orations: most of them have a direct allusion to the life, deeds, character and significance of the given saint, which is exceptional in the original texts. The change is rooted *theologically*, in a different approach to the Eucharistic celebration of the saints. The honour of the saints is theocentric in the Roman Mass. For the classical Roman Mass the saint is God's work (*Mirabilis Deus in sanctis suis – God is wonderful in His Saints*); they are not contemplated in their individuality. Each of them is a *typos* of the Church itself. The Church is primordially an apostle, martyr, virgin and confessor. For the Church living among the many vicissitudes of earthly existence a feast is a good occasion to see herself in a way already fulfilled in the saint – according to his or her 'category' – as a Bride decorated for her Bridegroom. The orations of the Roman Mass harken to this typology and attach to this practice of contemplation a petition for divine favour and intervention.

Contrarily, the new orations focus on the human (anthropocentric) dimension. There is also a place in the classical Roman Rite for the contemplation of the life, heroic virtues, deeds (in other words, the individuality) of a given saint. The proper place for this is, however, not the Mass but the Office. The new Missal intends to propose to the faithful – frequently in a rather didactic fashion – the given saint's exemplary and unique character. A few quotations suffice to illustrate the difference.[16]

---

didst give Thy saving remedies to the world . . . that thereby they may deserve to attain to perfect liberty and arrive at life everlasting'; * 'O God, who gave us your Paschal remedies . . . that grant your people to rejoice in Heaven in those things they now exult in the earth.'

[16] + 'Omnipotens, sempiterne Deus . . . concede propitius, ut qui beatae Agnetis Virginis et martyris tuae solemnia colimus, ejus apud te patrocinia sentiamus' – * 'ut qui beatae Agnetis martyris tuae natalicia celebramus, ejus in fide constantiam subsequamur'; – + 'Almighty and everlasting God . . . mercifully grant that we who keep the solemn feast of blessed Agnes, Thy Virgin and Martyr, may experience her advocacy with Thee'; * '. . . that we who celebrate the nativity of your Martyr, the blessed Agnes, may follow her perseverance in faith' (Collect, St Agnes).
+ 'Deus, qui universum mundum . . . ut qui ejus hodie Conversionem colimus, per ejus ad

In the examples given in note 15 above, the style of the new compositions is strikingly different from the traditional one. The trend affects the oration all the more if it is not a rephrased text, but an entirely new production. These texts proceed still further in a direction that has characterized the composition of new orations in the most recent centuries.

Concerning the proportions of redistribution, the difference between the Temporal and Sanctoral cycles is not great. If the two sections are taken together, about three-quarters of the orations are different in the two Missals; in about one-tenth of the cases the oration is the same, in a slightly larger proportion it is the same but either with smaller (stylistic) or greater (substantial) revisions.

The 1970 Missal omitted the ancient 'prayers over the people' (*Oratio super populum*) of the Lenten season;[17] but assigned many of these orations to other places in the weekdays of Advent and Eastertide.

From all this we can easily anticipate a description of the essential task for an eventual renovation. In the Masses celebrated under the recent Motu Proprio *Summorum Pontificum* the orations of the classical Roman Sacramentary should be prayed, keeping not only the texts, but also the assignations. This programme does not mean, however, that no development could be permitted. The future redactors will, however, need to consider two things:

1. The full repertory must be surveyed and modest, indeed almost imperceptible corrections can be made wherever a more abundant knowledge of sources identifies defects in the texts, or – very rarely – a nuanced improvement could be for the real benefit of the Church. Since I am not an expert in this field, I cannot judge in exactly how many cases such a revision would be justified, but I do not reckon it would attain to more than one-twentieth.

2. It is a fortunate development to survey the ancient Sacramentaries in order to restore their most beautiful texts. The richness of the old liturgies had already captured the attention and imagination of the eminent liturgist and founder of Solemes, Prosper Guéranger, 150 years ago. Yet these texts should not

---

te exempla gradiamur' – * '. . . per ejus ad te exempla gradientes, tuae simus mundo testes veritatis'; – + 'O God, who hast taught the whole world . . . that we who this day celebrate his Conversion, may through his example draw nearer to Thee'; * '. . . that drawing through his example nearer to you, may we become the witnesses of truth in the world' (Collect, The Conversion of St Paul).

+ 'Deus, qui beato Irenaeo martyre . . . ut et veritate doctrinae expugnaret haereses et pacem Ecclesiae feliciter confirmaret, da quaesumus plebi tuae in sancta religione constantiam, et pacem tuam nostris concede temporibus' – * 'ut veritatem doctrinae pacemque Ecclesiae feliciter confirmaret . . . ut nos fide et caritate renovati ad unitatem concordiamque fovendam semper simus intenti'; – + 'O God, who didst enable blessed Irenaeus . . . to overcome heresies by the truth of doctrine and happily to establish peace in the Church, we beseech Thee, give to Thy people constancy in holy religion, and grant us Thy peace in our time'; * '. . . to confirm successfully the doctrine of truth and the peace of the Church . . . that renovated in faith and love we may strive always to secure unity and concord' (Collect, St Irenaeus).

+ 'Da nobis . . . ut ejus semper et patrociniis sublevemur, et fidem congrua devotione sectemur' * '. . . ut ejus semper et patrociniis sublevemur, et vitam credentes habeamus in nomine ejus quem ipse Dominum agnovit' ; + 'Give us . . . that we may be uplifted by his patronage and follow him with fitting devotion in faith'; – * '. . . that we may be uplifted by his patronage, and by our belief have life in the Name of the one whom he confessed as Lord' (Collect, St Thomas Apostle).

[17] These have been restored for *ad libitum* use in the 2002 Missal.

be used as substitutions for the traditional texts. Perhaps the high number of weekday orations can appear too excessive in the new Missal, and the repetition of the Sunday orations is really useful from a pastoral perspective. But it would not be against the classical Roman Rite if a good collection of texts were introduced into the Missal, first of all, for the weekdays of Advent, Eastertide and the Ordinary season (even as an *ad libitum* option). The 80–100 'new' orations from the early Roman Sacramentaries might find an appropriate place in a collection of this kind.

Any completely new compositions should be limited to entirely new feasts (in particular, commemorations of those saints who really merit proper orations), as occurred routinely in the course of liturgical history.

II. *The Prefaces*

In the 1962 Missal there are nine older Prefaces (Christmas, Epiphany, Lent, Passion, Easter, Ascension, Pentecost, Blessed Virgin, Apostles); one Preface was added to these in the time of the Franks (Trinity) and four in the period after Trent (St Joseph, Sacred Heart, Christ the King, Preface of the Dead). Finally, the 'Common Preface' of the Roman Canon is a special case to be discussed later.

In the (Ambrosian) Rite of Milan, on the other hand, almost every Mass has its own Preface that pertains to the daily Proper just as much as to the orations. The number of Prefaces was also rather high in the earlier ('pre-Gregorian') Sacramentaries.[18] For instance, the Gelasian Sacramentary has a total of 47 Prefaces, several for solemnities, one for each day of the Easter Octave, one Proper Preface for each Sunday in Eastertide, and additional ones for the feast of Ss Peter and Paul, St Lawrence, St Andrew, Dedication, and even for ordination and wedding Masses, among others.[19]

This number, however, was radically reduced in the mature Roman Rite, and only the basic nine Prefaces (together with the Common Preface) were in use by about the end of the first millennium; only sporadic manuscripts add one or two additional items as relics of an earlier time.

The new Missal abounds in Prefaces, having in total 78.[20] Of the older pieces only those of Christmas, Easter and the Holy Virgin remained at their proper place, while among the more recent ones only three (Trinity, St Joseph, of the dead) were left untouched. Two of the older Prefaces were slightly modified (Epiphany, Apostles). The Lenten Preface is transferred to become the fourth of

[18] In the *Sacramentarium Leonianum* the number of Prefaces is 267, practically all Masses have their proper text (Fortescue (1912), *The Mass*, 4th edn 2005, p. 318).
[19] Leo Cunibert Mohlberg, OSB (1968), *Liber Sacramentorum Romanae Aeclesiae Ordinis Anni Circuli*, pp. 145, 151, 165, 111–13, 119–20, 209.
[20] Advent: 2, Christmas: 3, Lent: 4, Passion: 2, Easter: 5, Ascension: 2, Pentecost, Trinity, Sacred Heart, Christ the King 1–1, Ordinary Time: 8, of the Eucharist: 2, Blessed Virgin and Common of Saints: 11, of the Dead: 5, weekday Masses: 6. Moreover 18 liturgical days have their own Prefaces (including all the Sundays of Lent), and there are several Prefaces for the votive and ritual Masses.

several; that for the Ascension to the second place within a set. The old Preface for Passiontide (*de Cruce*) has been transferred to the feast of the Exaltation of the Cross, the Pentecost Preface has been relegated to those for the votive Masses. The Preface of the Sacred Heart has disappeared altogether, replaced by a new composition.

What was the cause of reduction of the number of Prefaces in the classical Roman Missal in comparison with the pre-Gregorian Sacramentaries? It was not some kind of decadence or neglect, but a deliberate decision. The orations of the Mass, and first of all the Collects, concern themselves with the mysteries celebrated on a given liturgical day. The Preface, however, as the introduction to the Eucharistic Prayer (the Canon), pertains to the central action of the Mass.[21] The first and third sections of every Preface are formulas; here textual stability was required not only for stylistic reasons, but because these two sentences actually form the essence of the text. In the first formula we give thanks to God through His Son, Jesus Christ. Through Him the earthly liturgy is united to the heavenly liturgy, together with the angels and the Church glorified in the saints. This is expressed in the last formula. This transition from the earthly liturgy to the heavenly is then expressed in the *Sanctus*, which is a chant *beyond* earthly time (since the Cherubs and Seraphs have been singing it from the beginning of Creation) and also an eschatological chant (as described in the use of the *Sanctus* in the Book of Revelation). This principal content of the Preface does not depend on the progress of the liturgical year, and could even be – with a few exceptions – an unchanged (ordinary) part of the Mass, together with the Canon. The changing section in the Preface is only a reference to a special motive of thanksgiving on a given commemoration or particular liturgical season.

All liturgical days have their proper Secret prayer ('super oblata'), said over the gifts immediately prior to their consecration. However, in the classical Roman Mass there is only one consecratory prayer, the Canon, identical at all Masses (and with only one or at most two variable shorter paragraphs, which change on only the most important liturgical days of the year). Between these two stands the Preface, in an intermediate position between the most changeable and the most stable parts of the Mass. As I see it, the Roman Church in the process of approaching the most holy action did not want to disrupt the focus of attention with the complexity of a multiplicity of intentions, but instead presented the central theme in an ever-increasingly fixed textual trajectory. Thus the *number* of Prefaces is a transition between the *many* Secret prayers and the *one* Canon.

Two structures stand before our eyes: the classical Roman Mass with very few Prefaces – stable in this form for a long while – and the *Novus Ordo* with a large and frequently changing set of Prefaces. Neither of them can be considered incorrect or opposed to the tradition, even though the classical arrangement corresponds better to the historical spirit and organic development of the Roman

---

[21] In Christian antiquity, as also in the Eastern liturgies where the Preface text never changes, the Prefaces were regarded as part of the Canon (Anaphora) itself (Fortescue (1912), *The Mass*, 4th edn 2005, pp. 317–18).

liturgy. When we are examining the renovation of the Roman Rite, surely the best foundation is always the arrangement that was transmitted historically from Rome to the rest of Europe, resulting in the form it takes in the 1962 Missal. There is also a pastoral reason that favours preserving this foundation: in multiform Prefaces the faithful are confronted with multiple thoughts in frequent succession. *Fewer* Prefaces – familiar for a longer time and frequently repeated – surely leave a deeper impression on the minds of those participating. An arrangement like this has the power progressively to direct the attention of the faithful toward the central intention of the Mass.

The addition of new Prefaces in itself does not break the continuity of the Roman Rite. In the letter attached to the Motu Proprio *Summorum Pontificum*, the Holy Father wrote: '. . . the two forms of the usage of the Roman Rite can be mutually enriching: new Saints and *some of the new Prefaces can and should be inserted in the old Missal*'. A few Prefaces were added to the collection even in the nineteenth and twentieth centuries. In the German Schott-Meßbuch four new Prefaces were published before the Council (Advent, the Holy Eucharist, Dedication, Saints).[22] Nor can we ignore the witness of the Pre-Gregorian Sacramentaries.

But some anomalies in the old Missal also justify the inclusion of new Prefaces. In the Missal of 1962 the Preface of the Trinity is recited throughout the Advent season. We have a Preface for St Joseph, but none for the feasts of other important saints of the Roman Church.

We should surely not oppose an increase in the number of Prefaces, within moderation and without disturbing the natural balance of the structure of the Roman Mass, Advent, the feast of Dedication, Corpus Christi,[23] one each for the feasts of martyrs, virgins and confessors (but used only on days of higher rank), and the Angels could be added to the collection of the 1962 Missal. The set could even be extended further, perhaps with Prefaces for the feast of St John the Baptist, Ss Peter and Paul, and the Assumption. This would add a further seven, and over that an additonal three.

The Ordinary Sundays also could benefit from additional Prefaces, but in a way that leaves intact the pre-eminence of the Preface of the Trinity. A positive arrangement might be to take the Preface of the Trinity during the Ordinary seasons on the first Sunday of each month, with three more Prefaces for the second, third and fourth Sundays.[24] The result would be a modest variety with a good degree of stability.

The Common Preface is, in fact, really a 'frame'; a formula that, ordinarily speaking, suggests the need of a variable section in its middle. The 1970 Missal

---

[22] *Schott römisches Meßbuch* (1962), pp. 490a–490c. See also the 'Gallican Prefaces' (Advent, Dedication, the Most Blessed Sacrament, St John the Baptist, All Saints) in the *The Daily Missal and Liturgical Manual*, (2007), pp. 875–78.

[23] Laurence Paul Hemming has noted: 'This was in fact changed in 1962, which was surely a retrograde step – St Thomas Aquinas' whole theology of transubstantiation is based on the intimate connection between the Incarnation and the Holy Eucharist, which is underlined in a particular way by the use of the Christmas Preface'.

[24] Although the *month* does not count as a liturgical unit in the liturgy of the Mass, the Roman Office has, however, traditionally organized the readings and responsories of Ordinary Time or the season 'After Pentecost' in this way.

clearly omitted it because of this characteristic. Precisely because of the lack of this variable 'middle section' the Common Preface permits clear expression of the essential content within the formula. Nothing more is proclaimed here than the thanksgiving (*eucharistia*) and the joining of the earthly to the heavenly liturgy through Jesus Christ. And so what at first appears only as an introduction and cadence is given real weight; attention is focused perfectly to the principal theme. Consequently, it is not only the thousand-year-old continuity of the Roman liturgy that favours the retention of the Common Preface, but also a powerful liturgical rationale. It could be reserved to the weekdays of Ordinary Time. Its brevity is proportionate to the character of a ferial celebration, but at the same time its clarity allows the most important content to be understood.

III. The Canon

According to the traditional and nearly general interpretation, the word 'Canon' means measure, standard, law ... The primary meaning of the word refers to the severe regularity, the immobile legitimacy of the principal prayer of the Eucharistic mystery; a text which is universally known and received, that is almost entirely stable and cannot be changed.

These are the words with which László Mezey began his standard treatise on the Roman Mass Canon.[25] Although the word itself has – as he reveals later[26] – a richer meaning, it is still historically justified to say that the Canon is the most respected, obligatory and definitive element of the Roman tradition.[27] There is no evidence whatsover that any other than this one Canon was ever used within the Roman liturgy. The only changing parts are the two sentences, inserted in some great solemnities in prayers known as the *Communicantes* and *Hanc igitur*. The Ambrosian Mass also has only one Canon, which is identical with the Roman Canon almost word for word.[28] In the literature of the very first centuries of Christianity there are unclear references to the 'improvisation' of the Canon. 'Improvisation' at that time meant something quite different from what we understand by the term today. This reference, and the so-called 'Canon of Hyppolitus' (which was perhaps only a guideline), pertain only to the *pre*-history of the Roman Rite.

---

[25] László Mezey (1996), 'A római misekánon', p. 277.
[26] Mezey (1996), 'A római misekánon', pp. 278–79.
[27] Fortescue (1912), *The Mass*, 4th edn 2005, p. 324: '... it is the lawful manner, the firm rule according to which we must consecrate ... the one invariable form, instead of the alternative prayers used before'.
[28] The list of saints is longer, and the words of institution are included in a slightly larger frame: 'Mandans quoque, et dicens ad eos: Haec quotiescumque feceritis, in meam commemorationem facietis: mortem meam praedicabitis, resurrectionem meam annuntiabitis, adventum meum sperabitis, donec iterum de caelis veniam ad vos.' I presume that the editors of the *Novus Ordo* had in mind this priestly sentence when they worded the words of acclamation from the congregation for inclusion at this point.

There is extensive literature on the theological, liturgical, structural, textual and artistic perfection of the Roman Canon.[29] The text has been analysed by many scholars of liturgical history, Christian literature and patrology down to the smallest detail. Various spiritual authors have written laudatory essays on this venerable prayer. While a survey of these is outside our current task, there is only one observation which seems to be useful to recall, namely the beauty of its *symmetric* structure. In the exact centre stand the words of consecration, the very words with which Christ instituted this Sacrament. The prayers immediately surrounding this focal point speak about the offering of the sacrifice. Further out from the centre we find the priest's prayers of commemoration: prior to the consecration the Church remembers the pope, the bishop, all the living (Christians) present and far off, and the saints; after the consecration come the dead, the priest himself and his assistants (*Nobis quoque peccatoribus famulis tuis*) and a second group of saints. The outer frame is the beginning of the Canon where the Church turns to the Father through Christ with deprecation (*Te igitur, clementissime Pater, per Jesum Christum Filium tuum, Dominum nostrum supplices rogamus ac petimus*), and its end: praise of the divine omnipotence (*Per ipsum . . . et tibi Patri omnipotenti . . . omnis honor et gloria*).

This structure with its multiple framing of the consecration is remarkable, not only in relation to its aesthetic or dramatic values, but also in its profound liturgical theology. We could ask, why are the commemorations divided in two? Would it not be more logical if all the prayers were said after the consecration, in the real presence of the Lord? The reason for the actual arrangement is that the Church in her wisdom developed the liturgy not according to the rules of any dry rationalism, and she has always regarded the Canon as a cohesive *unit*. The Canon in its integrity contains the manifold aspects of thanksgiving, commemoration, propitiation, offering of sacrifice and consecration. This is why its themes are arranged symmetrically, even though at first sight the modern mind may look to group them in one compound.

The *Novus Ordo* abrogated the unchangeable quality of the Canon. If only minor changes were made in the Roman Canon itself, nevertheless this ancient and unique formulary was supplemented with three other novel compilations. The Roman Canon is printed in the first place, but – for many reasons – it is given no opportunity to predominate. I do not want to praise or find fault with the texts of the new Eucharistic prayers. In the most frequently used second and third Eucharistic prayers the consecration follows (after only a few words of transition) directly after the *Sanctus*; and so the symmetric arrangement – with the consecration encased in the texture of different prayers – has been disregarded.[30]

---

[29] For sharp criticism of the Roman Canon ('patchwork character of the text'): Theodor Klauser (1969), *A Short History of the Western Liturgy*, pp. 43–44.

[30] Admittedly, this new arrangement has some analogies in the Byzantine Rite, but its structure is quite different; from the *Cherubicon* a long process precedes and leads up to the Preface and even the Creed, all pertaining to the preparation for the consecration. This means that the consecration is actually embedded in an even longer cycle in the liturgy of St John Chrysostom than in the Roman Canon. (The order of prayers: Great Entrance – Cherubicon – silent prayers of the celebrants for the acceptance of the sacrifice – Intercessions – Creed – Preface.)

The real problem with the Canon is not this. When the uniqueness and unchangeable nature of the Roman Canon ended, many interpreted it as an implicit invitation to create new Eucharistic prayers. If there is only *one* Canon, it is a privileged text, as holy as the Lord's Prayer. If there are four Eucharistic prayers, there could yet be 7 or 77! Some of these additional prayers found their way into the Missal as the outcome of official initiatives.[31] But some local dioceses at one point started to fabricate new Eucharistic prayers, and the officials of the Curia approved them, either because they did not want to offend the petitioners, or because the texts concorded with their own reformist intentions. These new Eucharistic prayers were of an ever more mediocre (at times, simply miserable) quality, totally removed from the spirit of the Roman Rite.

For those who have long waited for, and greeted with joy, the restoration of the classical Roman Rite, this is not a question: if there is anything that should be preserved in continuity with the tradition, it is the Roman Canon. The Canon should be prayed as found in the Roman Missals from the earliest documents up to 1970, without any variation, always in the same way.[32]

One thing is evident for those preferring the classical form of the Mass: the Canon is that part of the Mass where the primacy of the Latin language must be preserved. Therefore, the faithful who wish to follow this most sacred act deserve and should be given a perfect translation of the Roman Canon.

---

[31] *Missale Romanum* (2002) contains three 'Eucharistic Prayers for Masses with Children' (pp. 1270–88), and nothing more.

[32] This standpoint does not exclude, however, a discussion about possible slight improvements (e.g. the retention of the acclamation 'Mysterium fidei – Mortem tuam', the chanted version of the 'Per ipsum . . .'). Perhaps one (and no more than one) alternative Canon, for use only on weekdays, could be taken into consideration.

20

THE ORDER OF THE MASS

For many people, even those interested in liturgical matters, the postconciliar reform means – besides the questions of language and orientation – primarily the changes in the order of the Mass itself. The most conspicuous alterations are: the 'prayers of the faithful'; the introduction of new offertory prayers; the reductions in number of the priest's (and assistants') genuflections; the omission of some repetitions; the distribution of Holy Communion in the hand; and reception of Communion while standing. Some of these (like the customs surrounding Holy Communion) are neither based on decisions of the Council, nor on the new rubrics; they originated rather in the climate that is often called 'conciliar'. The mutations of the order of the Mass are, in fact, largely inessential when compared to those changes that were made in other aspects and areas of the liturgy and are not more significant than in some earlier historical periods of the Roman Rite. What we have to consider now is whether there was or is any change necessary in the order of the Mass in light of the *actual* conciliar decrees. Is some kind of an 'organic development' desirable, or is it sufficient to return at all points to the practices of the 1962 Missal, or even to still earlier forms? What is the meaning – in terms of the order of the Mass – of the sentence within the Constitution *Sacrosanctum Concilium*: 'sound tradition may be retained, and yet the way remains open to legitimate progress'?[1]

Three elements of the arrangement of the order of the Mass are to be distinguished. The first is the *structure* of the Mass; the second is the set of invariable *texts*; and the third is the *ars celebrandi* (the rubrics referring to movement, gestures, signs and postures). First, a few words about the third element, and then we shall survey the Mass part by part with respect to the first and second aspects.

Every single cult, from the most ancient to the most recent, draws upon the activity of our physical bodies in its celebration. Every cult contains regulations for posture, gestures, the touching of holy objects, and so forth. This is all characteristic of the spirituality, psychological makeup and even theology of any given cult or religion. It is especially true for the rich ceremonial legacy of

---

[1] Cf. Vatican Council II, Dogmatic Constitution on the Sacred Liturgy, *Sacrosanctum Concilium* (1963), §23. 'Ut sana traditio retineatur et tamen via legitimae progressioni aperiatur . . .'.

the Roman Rite. The gestures represent a style, and express the meaning of the words or actions to which they are attached.[2]

The traditional gestures transmitted to us through the classical Roman Rite have a special role, even in our days: they are able to give shape to the priest's mind in the liturgy. The majority of these motions are not addressed to the congregation. They make sense only if the priest believes that he is performing a service before God, which is principally of a spiritual nature even if, with regard to outward appearance, it seems rather something of a physical labour. The priest who follows the rubrics and goes through these motions, gestures and hand positions attentively is compelled in his mind 'to stay within the sanctuary'.

It is very instructive what Adrian Fortescue, the outstanding expert of ceremonies, once said:

> Probably the first impression which these descriptions of ceremonies would produce on a stranger is that of enormous complication. Really this is much less than it seems. In general, actions are far less conspicuous when done than when described in words. Most Catholics hardly notice these things when they go to church. The ministers and servers who do them constantly become so used to them by long habit that they too do them almost without thought. If one had to write out in detail all the ceremonies of getting up in the morning or of eating one's dinner, these would seem exceedingly elaborate rites . . . It is worth noticing that, the more exact details of direction are, the less complicated their performance becomes. When each person knows exactly what to do, when they all agree and do their parts confidently and silently, the effect of the ceremony is immeasurably more tranquil than when there is doubt, confusion or discussion.[3]

This view provides the underlying rationale for preserving (or restoring) the accepted ceremonies of the Roman Rite.

There is also another statement of Adrian Fortescue that is worth considering:

> Yet it may perhaps be admitted that some measure of simplification is desirable. Now that liturgical reform is so much in the air, we may hope for reform in this direction too. The chief note of the Roman rite has always been its austere simplicity. That is still its essential note, compared with the florid Eastern rites.[4]

---

[2] *Sacramentum Caritatis* (2007), §§38–40. Cardinal Joseph Ratzinger (2000), *The Spirit of the Liturgy*, pp. 171–207; Peter J. Elliot (2003), 'A Question of Ceremonial'. For a survey of the problem and its literature: David Torevell (2004), *Losing the Sacred*, pp. 149–69. See also James Hitchcock (2006), 'Liturgy and Ritual'; Helmut Hoping (2008), 'Danksagende Anbetung. Die heilige Liturgie und die Einheit der römischen Messe'; and R. Michael Schmitz (2009), 'Detail and Ritual'.

[3] Adrian Fortescue (1917), *The Ceremonies of the Roman Rite Described*, 2nd edn 1932, p. xxii.

[4] Fortescue (1917), *The Ceremonies of the Roman Rite Described*, 2nd edn 1932, p. xxiii. Cf. also *Sacrosanctum Concilium* (1963), §34. 'The rites should be distinguished by a noble simplicity

The cases mentioned by him are, in fact, inessential small changes like some reductions of the 'solita oscula' (ritual kisses) or some of the ceremonies in the Pontifical Mass; he does not question the customs of making the sign of the Cross, of hand positions, or closing the fingers after the consecration and so forth. The matter of possible or desirable simplifications, however, is outside the field of my competence, and I have no proposals to suggest here.

I. The Prayers at the Foot of the Altar

As I explained earlier,[5] these are private prayers of the priest, and an addition in the Roman Mass. Really, they form the conclusion of a series of personal preparations, beginning with the lavabo and the vesting prayers in the sacristy, and then continuing with the entrance into the sanctuary and the arrival at the altar.[6]

Today any preparatory prayers in the sacristy are neglected by most priests. Their original intention was to put the priest in a calm and meditative mind, and make a transition both in a physical and spiritual sense – from the street to the church. They are to empty his mind of worldly cares and thoughts, and direct him fully to God and His holy service. In this respect, it hardly really matters *what* the prayers actually say; they must leave time enough for this conversion in the mental state of the priest.

If these prayers were always directed towards the formation of the priest's spiritual state, all the more would they have a really medicinal effect today. If the task of the priest were no more than to speak to the people, a short supplication for a successful performance would be enough. But if the priest prepares himself for objectively effective service, he has to 'tune up' his whole existence to this. These prayers allow the priest to understand – not only on the intellectual level, but with the involvement of his full personality – that now he is about to stand in front of God, he is to perform a service in the name of the Church, on behalf of the people of God: *'pro omnibus cirumstantibus et pro omnibus fidelibus christianis vivis atque defunctis, ut mihi et illis proficiat ad salutem in vitam aeternam'* (for all here present as also for all faithful Christians both living and dead that it may be of avail for salvation both to me and to them unto life everlasting) as the old Offertory prayer says. The formal 'Preparation for Mass' found in the traditional books could prevent a generation of priests from misconceiving their vocation.

The prayers at the foot of the altar form the last section of this preparation that could be said in the sacristy,[7] and that could even be completed by other

---

. . .; they should be short, clear, and unencumbered by useless repetitions; they should be within the people's powers of comprehension, and normally should not require much explanation.' (Ritus nobili simplicitate fulgeant, sint brevitate perspicui et repetitiones inutiles evitent, sint fidelium captui accommodati, neque generatim multis indigeant explanationibus.)

5 See above. pp. 33–34.
6 Josef Andreas Jungmann, SJ (1958), *Missarum Sollemnia*, vol. 1, pp. 377–402; Fortescue (2005), *The Mass*, 4th edn 2005, pp. 225–8.
7 Cf. Jungmann (1958), *Missarum Sollemnia*, vol. 1, pp. 381–82.

similar texts.[8] In reality, these prayers were not fixed in the earlier phase of the Roman Mass.

Even so, they in a certain sense belonged to the most original form of the Roman Mass. The *Ordo Romanus* describes how, when the pope arrives at the altar, he should pray personally,[9] and when he is ready, signal for the Introit to conclude so that he can begin the Mass with the Collect. This ancient form can be seen in the Good Friday liturgy when the priest and the assistants prostrate themselves in front of the altar, and after standing up, the celebrant immediately prays the Collect. The substantial matter is not whether Psalm 42 is (or is not) a suitable start to the Mass. The priest after his arrival at the foot, and before ascending to the heights of the altar, needs to spend some time in prayer so as to recollect himself properly. In this prayer the priest seeks forgiveness of his sins, and makes supplication so that he can enter the Holy of Holies with a pure mind and heart.

Psalm 42 was taken up in this series only with regard to the antiphonal verse (*Introibo*). The text of the *Confiteor* was not totally fixed even in the high Middle Ages,[10] and was introduced by various verses of psalms, differing across the various Uses. Among these we can find: (while walking to the altar) '*Vias tuas Domine demonstra mihi, et semitas tuas edoce me. Emitte Spiritum tuum et creabuntur, et renovabis faciem terrae*'; (before the *Confiteor*) '*Confitemini Domino quoniam bonus, quoniam in saeculum misericordia ejus*'; (after the *Confiteor*) '*Peccavimus cum patribus nostris, injuste egimus iniquitatem fecimus. Sacerdotes tui induantur justitiam, et sancti tui exsultent*'; (one of the preces) '*Praesta, quaesumus, omnipotens Deus, ut reatus nostri confessio indulgentiam percipere valeat delictorum.*' The '*Aufer a nobis . . .*' (Take away from us) and the '*Oramus te, Domine, ut per merita . . .*' (We beseech Thee, O Lord, by the merits) said by the priest in the Tridentine Mass while ascending to the altar also belong in this series.[11]

Prayer at the foot of altar is necessary, and the *Confiteor* should be preserved. Nor is it right that in the form of the *Confiteor* that was redacted for the *Novus Ordo* the mention of the saints has been omitted in the first part. If I make a confession 'to you my brothers and sisters', this is made above all in the presence of the saints: first of all, before the Blessed Virgin, the very 'refuge of sinners',

---

[8] Jungmann (1958), *Missarum Sollemnia*, vol. 1, pp. 384–85. In Sarum Use Psalm 42 closes the prayers before the Mass, and the prayer at the foot of altar starts directly with 'Confitemini' and '*Confiteor*'. After the *Confiteor* a long series of psalm versicles follow. Cf. Nicholas Sandon (1984), *The Use of Salisbury*, vol. 1. pp. 6–11.

[9] *Ordo Romanus Primus*. §49–50. Jungmann (1958), *Missarum Sollemnia*, vol. 1, pp. 9–92, 416–17.

[10] Jungmann (1958), *Missarum Sollemnia*, vol. 1, pp. 387–95.

[11] The translation of the prayers above: *Before the Confiteor*: V. Shew, O Lord, Thy ways to me, and teach me Thy paths. V. Send forth Thy Spirit, and they shall be created. And Thou shalt renew the face of the earth. V. Make confession to the Lord, for he is good. For his mercy endureth for ever. *After the Confiteor*: V. We have sinned with our fathers. We have acted unjustly, we have wrought iniquity. Grant us, we beseech Thee, almighty God, that the confession of our sins can bring indulgence to our transgressions.
The versicles are documented in many sources, we took them from the Esztergom Missale (*Missale Notatum Strigoniense ante 1341 in Posonio*), fol. 130v–31.

before St Michael, the Archangel of Judgement, St John the Baptist, himself the 'preacher of penitence' and St Peter, the keeper of keys. The inclusion of the words 'and omission' in the *Novus Ordo* version, goes back to an ancient tradition and is a worthy addition. Besides keeping the prayer at the foot of the altar in its Tridentine form, perhaps an alternative form could also be recommended to priests, taken from selected 'preces' or responses modelled after the medieval sources, that could be said before the *Confiteor*.

These texts properly belong to the priest (and his assistants), while the faithful participate in the singing of the the Introit. While Paul VI insisted on keeping some sign of penitence in the Mass, this priestly prayer was transferred to a public penitential act.[12] There were those who, misunderstanding the meaning of the admonition that was added before the *Confiteor* itself, wanted to augment this penitential section with an actual examination of conscience.

However, if the *Confiteor* is kept as the priest's private prayer, what serves as a form of *common* penitence? I will discuss this question in the following subsection.

II. The Asperges and Penitential Act

We have identified a clear distinction in the actions of the Mass:[13] the prayers at the foot of the altar are not an integral part of the order of the Mass, even if the reform developed it into a public penitential act. These prayers express the desire of the priest and his assistants for the spiritual purity necessary to perform their holy service worthily. What is then the actual and public penitential part of the Mass? Though the spirit of penitence imbues the whole Mass and is stressed in individual texts and orations, we may say that there really is *no such part in the Mass*. The penitential act should take place *before* the Mass, and the community starts the Mass itself with their souls already purified. 'Gather in the day of the Lord, break the bread and give thanks. *Before*, make confession, that your sacrifice could be pure.'[14]

That this is so is indicated in the *Novus Ordo*, by omitting any penitential act when another celebration precedes the Mass. Does this mean that in this case the congregation is not in need of purification? And why, therefore, does the liturgy of Good Friday begin directly with the Collect? How is it that the act of penitence can be omitted on this particular day?

The faithful should rather be taught to seek forgiveness of their sins when they prepare themselves for the liturgy before Mass, at home, and on entering the church with the blessing of holy water at the stoup, and further when they pray silently before Mass begins or when they find themselves in need of sacramental confession. When the priest prays during the Mass to obtain pardon and says

[12] Sven Conrad, FSSP (2009), 'Die innere Logik eines Ritus als Maßstab liturgischer Entwicklung', is critical of this development.
[13] John P. Parsons (2003), 'A Reform of the Reform?', p. 236, speaks of 'First/Second Order Elements' of the Mass.
[14] Didache; chapter XIV. Cf. Parsons (2003), 'A Reform of the Reform?', p. 241.

the penitential prayers, he partly nurtures the spirit of purity required especially of the celebrant,[15] and partly makes supplication that the fruits of the Mass as a *propitiatory* sacrifice may be applied to himself and to the faithful.

This fact does not mean that the act of purification before the Mass cannot be some kind of a public celebration – not replacing, of course, personal penitence.[16] Its liturgical form is the *Asperges*, the sprinkling of the assembly with holy water, while Psalm 50 is sung in whole or part. The visible sign of holy water, – similarly to the washing of the priest's hands in the sacristy – is a *ritual* washing that refers to the bathing of the priests before their entrance for ceremonial work in the Jerusalem Temple.[17] By virtue of an outside ritual the Asperges makes the liturgical character of the penitential prayer more impressive, and alludes to the link between baptism and repentance; sometimes called the 'baptism of tears'. This liturgical action really precedes the Mass: the priest does it in a cope and not a chasuble. The liturgical books ordinarily recorded this little rite not included in the Order of Mass, but in a separate place. In the Middle Ages it was separated from the Mass by the processions that regularly took place on Sundays.

The *Novus Ordo* placed the Asperges (as an optional form of the penitential rite) after the Introit into the Mass, producing a very strange construction. Let us think, for example, of the Christmas Mass: during the solemn entrance, we sing the Introit *Puer natus*, and after that, we begin the penitential psalm!

The proper place of the Asperges would be retained before the Mass; it can be introduced by a call to the faithful and separated from the Mass by an appropriate prayer.[18]

---

[15] 'Sacerdotes Domini incensum et panem offerunt Deo, et ideo sancti erunt Deo suo, et non polluent nomen ejus' – 'The priests of the Lord offer incense and loaves to God, and therefore they shall be holy to their God, and shall not defile His Name' (from the Offertory for the feast of Corpus Christi).

[16] 'The penitential celebration . . . should be more clearly separated from the celebration of the Mass, to which, strictly speaking, it does not belong.' (Klaus Gamber (2002), *The Modern Rite*, p. 13).

[17] I owe thanks to Laurence Paul Hemming for drawing my attention to this detail.

[18] The 'In nomine Patris . . .' and 'Agnoscamus . . .' could function as an introduction. For the closing prayer I suggest the use of a pre-Tridentine text (instead of the one for blessing of houses): 'Praesta nobis, quaesumus, Domine, per hanc sanctificatae aquae aspersionem sanitatem mentis, integritatem corporis, tutelam salutis, securitatem spei, corroborationem fidei, fructum caritatis hic et in aeterna saecula saeculorum. Amen.' – 'Grant, we beseech Thee, O Lord, through the aspersion of this holy water, the health of our mind, the integrity of body, defence of health, firmity of hope, strength of faith and fruits of love, here and in the world without end. Amen.' (*Missale Strigonensis*, sine fol.; cf. *Processionale ad usum . . . ordinis Praemonstratensis*, p. 3.) For Eastertide: 'Deus qui ad aeternam vitam in Christi resurrectione nos reparas, imple pietatis tuae ineffabile sacramentum, ut cum in majestate sua Salvator noster advenerit, quos fecisti baptismo regenerari, facias beata immortalitate vestiri. Per eumdem Dominum' . . . – 'O God, who in Christ's resurrection redeemed us into an eternal life, make perfect the ineffable sacrament of your piety, that those regenerated by thee in Baptism, may be vested with joyful immortality, when our Saviour comes again in his majesty' (*Missale Strigonensis*, fol. 150v. *Processionale ad usum . . . ordinis Praemonstratensis*, p. 5): 'Concede, quaesumus, omnipotens Deus, ut qui festa paschalia (vel: Domini nostri Jesu Christi ascensionis sollemnia; vel: sollemnitatem doni Sancti Spiritus) colimus, caelestibus desideriis accensi, fontem vitae sitiamus, Jesum Christum Dominum nostrum, qui vivit et regnat in saecula saeculorum. Amen.' – 'Grant, we beseech Thee, almighty God, that we who now celebrate the Paschal feasts (or: the solemnity of the ascension of our Lord Jesus Christ; or: the solemn feast of the gift of Holy Ghost) inflamed with heavenly desires should thirst for the source of life: Jesus Christ our Lord, who liveth . . .'

But what could be done in less solemn Masses? It would be more appropriate to the preparatory character of the penitential rite if, before the entrance of the priest, the faithful, led by a deacon, a server or a cantor (or if there are none available, by the priest without a chasuble), prayed the *Confiteor* together. Attention must be paid, of course, to the fact that leading a 'pre-oration' is not a priestly function. After greeting the people, the one leading this pre-oration could briefly announce the liturgical day, give technical information (e.g. for the use of the prayer book or hymnal), and then start the *Confiteor*, which is closed by the prayer *Misereatur*, also recited by the faithful themselves (this being a request and not an absolution.) The server could even leave right after intoning the prayer, since he will say the full *Confiteor* with the priest alternately. After this a hymn might follow, and then the entrance begins with the Introit.

III. *The Introit, Kyrie, Gloria and Collect*

During the entrance and the prayers at the foot of the altar the Introit is sung by the congregation and/or the choir or cantors, as discussed in Chapter 18. If they are not skilled to do that, a folk hymn is to be sung, or the organ plays, but in this case the priest after his silent prayer should recite aloud the text of the Introit together with the faithful (or at the very least with the servers).

After his private prayers are finished, the priest ascends to the altar, kisses and incenses it, and then he may pray the Introit at the epistle side. (If the Introit was not sung, this is the place for its recitation in a raised voice, otherwise he prays it in a low voice.)

The Kyrie and Gloria are linked directly to the Introit. Local churches may well add tropes to the Kyrie taken from their ancient traditions.[19] If the Gloria is sung in Latin, the priest may join the congregation; if sung in the vernacular, the priest prays it simultaneously in Latin. The text distributed among the people should include indications of the customary bows of the head and concluding sign of the Cross so that they can make these along with the priest.

The priest recites the Collect in Latin, turning eastwards. A precise translation should be available to the faithful. The congregation listens to the Collect standing, or on fixed days kneeling.[20] The acclamation *Flectamus genua – Levate* is perhaps better sung or said in the vernacular so that the congregation can understand directly its proper meaning and follow more easily.

Concerning the number of Collects I suggest a moderate middle-way. The numerous seasonal or votive orations were already deleted before the Council,[21] and their restitution is not warranted. But the inclusion of one single commemoration (with a *short conclusion*) is desirable for keeping the memory of a superseded feast or a saint's day of minor rank. If there is no occurring feast, the

---

[19] Good examples with music notation in Sandon (1984), *The Use of Salisbury*, vol. 1. pp. 40–50.
[20] The commendable ancient custom of kneeling during the Collect in Lent time should probably be restored.
[21] Decree of the Sacred Congregation of Rites *Cum nostra* (1955).

priest may recite one single oration for a 'votive' intention. This short addition would hardly overshadow the principle oration of the day.

IV. The Readings and the Homily

The general order of the Roman Rite requires one reading (Epistle) before the Gospel.[22] According to my earlier proposal, from Advent until Pentecost there would be an Old Testament (in Eastertide: New Testament) reading before the Epistle.[23]

Concerning the readings, the classical Roman rubrics for the Solemn, Sung and Low forms of the Mass should be followed. The Latin readings are recited by a subdeacon (in his absence, a lector or the priest) facing the altar: the vernacular readings facing the assembly. The lectern should not be a fixed piece of furniture; it need only be placed there for the occasion of the reading.[24] Bilingual recitation of readings would be in the High Mass a reasonable method: first by the sub-deacon (or priest) in Latin facing the altar, then by the lector in the vernacular facing the people.[25] If the first reading or Epistle is read by the subdeacon or lector, the priest should listen from the *sedile*.

The Gradual is sung by the choir or schola, or by the psalmist from a lectern. When the formula of the responsorial psalm is selected, a cantor sings the verses from the rail of the sanctuary, so that he can lead the singing of the congregation. If there is only one reading before the Gospel, the Alleluia should be linked to the Graduale or Responsorial Psalm.

On festivities and during solemn seasons the singing of Sequences is permitted *ad libitum* at every Mass. In selecting the appropriate Sequence, the singers follow either universal or local editions (cf. Chapter 12 and 18 (pp. 173–177, 195–196)). A variety of different methods of singing the Sequence can be employed. If the strophes are to be sung alternately, suggestions for methods of alternation are:

- one cantor/choir (or assembly)
- two half-choirs
- adults/children; or: adults/children together with adults
- small choir/full choir
- cantor/congregation
- two solo singers

The priest sits while the interlectionary chant is sung. At the repetition of the Alleluia, or during the last pair of strophes of the sequence, he stands up and goes

---

[22] Cf. above, pp. 145–154.
[23] See Chapter 17.
[24] In the Middle Ages the Epistle was recited from the rood-loft on Sundays and major feasts, and from the quire-step on other days. Cf. Sandon (1984), *The Use of Salisbury*, vol. 1, p. 16.
[25] In the Middle Ages it was customary (in some Eastern churches this is done even now) to translate the reading sentence by sentence. It would be worthwhile, at least, experimenting with this in a parish setting over a period of time.

to the place where the Gospel is read. The *Munda cor* and *Dominus sit* are private supplications to be prayed silently. It is psychologically appropriate to reserve some silent prayers to the priest or deacon; these repeatedly confirm his proper attitude; in such cases he is speaking to God and not teaching the people.

A shorter homily can often be more powerful, more memorable and even more effective than a longer one.[26] Too often in recent years homilies have failed to be in keeping with the elevated style of the liturgy, or descended to the level of colourful stories, anecdotes, and long-winded verbal illustrations for the sake of popularity. The sermon should never be trivial, and needs to avoid a flowery or feigned style. The example of the Church Fathers clearly demonstrates that a moderate rhetorical quality is highly fitting for the occasion. Their sermons, or the homilies of the great spiritual writers, are truly excellent examples as to how one can steer clear of everything that is alien from this genre. The message based on the word of God must be well composed, and prepared well in advance, in order to avoid digressions and prolixity.

V. The Problems with the 'Prayers of the Faithful'

The direction of the Council is that

> . . . especially on Sundays and feasts of obligation there is to be restored, after the Gospel and the homily, the *common prayer* or *prayer of the faithful*. By this prayer, in which the people are to take part, intercession will be made for holy Church, for the civil authorities, for those oppressed by various needs, for all mankind, and for the salvation of the entire world.

On this, cf. 1 Tim. 2.1-2.[27]

One could find in some early sources of the classical Roman Rite but obscure hints to the existence of such a prayer in this form. In early non-Roman documents, however, there are references and citations concerning supplications that were attached to the dismissal of the catechumens.[28] The liturgy of the Eastern churches is woven through and through with such *ektenias*, and a trace of it also survives in the Ambrosian Lenten Masses. Thus it is safe to say that its lack corresponds to the specifically *Roman* character of our liturgy, yet its introduction would not be contrary to ancient *Christian* liturgical custom.

The trouble has not been the introduction of the 'common prayer', but the fact that it was so misunderstood and tampered with. The meaning of the expression 'oratio *fidelium*' means that after the cathecumens were dismissed, only the

---

[26] Cf. *Sacramentum Caritatis* (2007), §46.

[27] *Sacrosanctum Concilium* (1963), §53: '"Oratio communis" seu "fidelium", post Evangelium et homiliam, praesertim diebus dominicis et festis de praecepto, restituatur, ut, populo eam participante, obsecrationes fiant pro sancta Ecclesia, pro iis qui nos in potestate regunt, pro iis qui variis premuntur necessitatibus, ac pro omnibus hominibus totiusque mundi salute.'

[28] Fortescue (1912), 4th edn 2005, pp. 293–96; Jungmann (1958), *Missarum Sollemnia*, vol. 2, pp. 606–27.

baptized faithful might be present at this supplication and they participated in it by litany-style acclamations. Many people in the Church, however, interpreted the 'for' in the sense that the people must have a formative role in it. Since the Church only provided a few patterns, and left the decision about their wording to local churches, this has become the most a-liturgical part of the Mass in the last decades. Two styles of this prayer have become widespread. Priests engaged in pastoral activity fabricated verbose texts, full of didactic intentions, far removed from the original aim of this facility. These included everything that came to the minds of the authors from the daily Gospel – or even about themes yet further from it. Trivial ideas, social concerns, moral exhortations reworked into prayer, repetition of the ideas of the homily, detailed accounts of workday realities, all these can be heard here in a style very far from the liturgy itself. The other method is to prod members of the congregation to formulate their own wishes, and the congregation is forced to approve them with their acclamations. Priests feel that their pastoral success is measured by their ability to goad a grandmother, a worker, a professor, a kindergarten pupil, a divorcee or a teenager into coming out of the pews, and marching into a liturgical event. They suppose that this is the only way for the *ektenia* to become the real 'prayer of the faithful'. So the traditional litany consisting of *strict* formulas and sung by the deacon has nowhere been introduced.

Needless to say that for the supporters of the classical Roman Rite all this is a scandal; the falsification of the Council's will, a clear sign and daily vehicle of a decadence of liturgical spirit. It is no wonder that those who rejoice in the permission of the Motu Proprio will not even countenance the possibility of allowing such things in the Roman Mass.

But it would be unfair to forget that the conciliar documents gave directions not for the creation of such things, but for the preservation, enrichment and development of this classical Roman Mass. Strictly speaking: the conciliar bishops retained the 1962 Missal and envisaged the minor changes (the 'Prayers of the Faithful' included) *in this* liturgical book. Given this, we have to think about whether there is a place in the classical Roman Mass for the ancient *ektenia*, without demolishing the structure of the Mass or harming its genuine spirit. Since here we speak not of an innovation but of the restoration of an old Christian cultic practice, the voice of this old tradition should be attended to before we propose any response.

An interrogation of the circumstances in which this addition could make an (optional) positive contribution might assist us if we ask 'When, who, where, what?' I think, if good answers to these questions can be found, a litany in the style of the *ektenia* could enter the Roman Mass, and may, in fact, prove to be a gain.

When? The Constitution says: 'especially on Sundays and feasts of obligation'.[29] If one were to rest content with these liturgical occasions, celebrated with great gatherings, the litany would appear as an addition *to* (and not as an essential part *of*) the Mass.

---

[29] *Sacrosanctum Concilium* (1963), §53: '. . . praesertim diebus dominicis et festis de praecepto'.

When exactly during the Mass? The Constitution says: after the Gospel and the homily.[30] I am not sure that here the Council Fathers wished to establish precisely the order between the litany and the Creed in the sense that the litany *must* follow the Creed, as it is arranged in the 1970 Missal. I think, in fact, this is not the best place for it. We will see later that the exchange of the two could throw new light upon the Creed. Both the Gospel and the Creed are strictly fixed elements of the Mass. This stability is somehow relaxed in the homily. It would be quite natural to attach the litany (which is also a less fixed element) to the homily, and to return to the real structural parts of the Mass with the singing of the Creed. (Parenthetically, there is evidence from the age of St Augustine that the homily was closed with a prayer.)[31] The litany would then appear as much less of an interruption in the orderly progress of the Mass, placed right after the Homily.

Who? Just as in the Eastern liturgy: it is best recited by the deacon,[32] or if there is no deacon, by the priest or by a lector.

Here it is necessary to digress briefly and discuss in some detail the liturgical role that can be taken over by lay people. The faithful exercise a right received at their baptism when they follow the Mass with understanding, when they sing or recite the parts pertaining to them as an assembly, and mainly, when they offer themselves as a living sacrifice in unity with Christ's self-oblation. The guideline: 'who has an office to perform, should do all of, but only, those parts which pertain to his office by the nature of the rite and the principles of liturgy'.[33] This refers as much to the faithful as it does to the ordained. It is useful and appropriate in the present day if, in addition to this, some lay people are also prepared for liturgical offices, and from time to time practice them.[34] But in doing so, they enter into another realm: they become the servants of the altar, working on the periphery of what is properly and by *formal* right done by the ordained clergy. Now temporarily they belong not to the nave but to the sanctuary, or to the space between sanctuary and nave. This fact is symbolized when lay singers, lectors and sacristans wear appropriate liturgical dress. It is not compatible with the trepidation that pertains to treading on the most sacred ground, if some individuals (or in Western countries, whole groups – which is a yet worse abuse) invade the sanctuary and begin 'performing' there.

Briefly: the beginning and the conclusion of the litany is the task of the celebrant; the invocations, on the other hand, pertain to the servants of the altar. The supplications worded in recent times seem to have a didactic purpose aimed at the faithful in the guise of prayer. In fact, this supplication is addressed to

---

[30] *Sacrosanctum Concilium* (1963), §53: '. . . post Evangelium et homiliam . . .'

[31] Uwe Michael Lang (2004), *Turning Towards the Lord*, pp. 51–52.

[32] Jungman speaks about this prayer as the diaconal litanies ('Litaneien des Diakons'), see Jungmann (1958), *Missarum Sollemnia*, vol. 1. p. 617. Cf. Theodor Klauser (1969), *A Short History of the Western Liturgy*, p. 49.

[33] *Sacrosanctum Concilium* (1963), §28: 'In celebrationibus liturgicis quisque, sive minister sive fidelis, munere suo fungens, solum et totum id agat, quod ad ipsum ex rei natura et normis liturgicis pertinet.' Cf. *Redemptionis Sacramentum* (2004), §§36–42.

[34] *Redemptionis Sacramentum* (2004), §§43–46.

God.[35] This suggests that the deacon, the priest (or any other assistant), and the congregation must all turn towards the altar during the litany. The dramatic role of the three actors is nicely symbolized if the priest stands in front of the altar, the deacon at the Communion rail or on the 'holy peninsula' nearer to the nave (classically called the Choir), with the congregation in the nave, and all turned in the same direction, towards the virtual east of the church.

What? We have to return to the simplest wording of the litany. There is no need of intellectual 'gymnastics' to reinterpret the ideas of the other parts of the Mass, or to repeat the teaching of the sermon, or to create inventive thoughts for the prayer. The Council determined clearly what we are to pray for. The evidence we have from late Antiquity really does not transgress those points. In other words: it is necessary to give up the 'freely worded' and 'modern' character of these common prayers, as well as the fickle impulse for variety. The best solution is if the Missal contains a few formulas,[36] with the provision that at the most *one* actual or local intention could be attached to them. In the Ambrosian Rite there are no more than two formulas.[37]

---

[35] In the form used on Good Friday an introductory exhortation calls the faithful to pray for an intention; then the text turns to God and precisely formulates the particular petition.

[36] Joseph Cardinal Ratzinger proposed in a letter to Heinz-Lothar Barth that among the possible changes in the classical Roman Mass an '*oratio fidelium*', i.e. a fixed litany of intercessions following the *Oremus* before the offertory, could be included where (at least it is thought by some) such a litany took place earlier. According to Klauser (1969), *A Short History of the Western Liturgy*, p. 48): 'In Rome the form of this prayer was invariable', but later (p. 53) he says: 'one should beware of prescribing a fixed form for this prayer . . .'

[37] As an example I quote the two Ambrosian formulas of the Litany (*Antiphonale Missarum juxta ritum . . . Mediolanensis*, pp. 105, 116):

Formula I
INTRODUCTION: Having been given with God's peace and indulgence, let us cry with all our heart and all our mind: R. Lord, have mercy.
INVOCATIONS: For Thy holy Catholic Church, spread here and over the whole world – we ask Thee: R. * For our Pope, N. and bishop N., for the whole clergy, all the priests and ecclesiastical servants – we ask Thee: R. * For the peace of the churches, for the vocation of Gentiles, for the quiet state of nations – we ask Thee. R. * For this city and for all its inhabitants – we ask Thee: R. * For the good temperature of the air, for the abundant fruits of the soil – we ask Thee: R. * For the virgins, widows, orphans, captives and penitents – we ask Thee: R. * For those sailing, the wanderers, prisoners and exiled – we ask Thee: R. * For those suffering in their various frailties – we ask Thee: R.
CONCLUSION: Hear us, O Lord, in all our prayers and deprecations. R.

Formula II
INTRODUCTION: Let us all say: R. Lord have mercy.
INVOCATIONS: For the Catholic Church that you deign to conserve it, O Lord. R. * For our Pope N., bishop N., and for our priests. R. * For all the bishops, priests and laity. R. * For this city and for all its inhabitants. R. * For the good temperature of the air and the fertility of the soil. R. * CONCLUSION: Save us, O Lord, with a powerful hand and an extended arm. R. Awake, O Lord, help us and liberate us because of Thine name. R.
Here is a part from the GREAT EKTENIA of the liturgy of St John Chrysostom; it is prayed *after the Gospel*:
INTRODUCTION: Let us say with all our soul and with all our mind, let us say: R. Lord, have mercy. * O Lord Almighty, the God of our Fathers, we beseech Thee, hear us and have mercy. R. * Have mercy upon us, O God, according to Thy great goodness, we beseech Thee, hear us and have mercy. R.
INVOCATIONS: Furthermore we pray for this country, its ruler, *(title and name of the ruler)*, its people, civil authorities and armed forces. R. * Furthermore we pray for our Most Reverend

VI. *The Peace, According to the Wish of the Holy Father*

The ceremony of Peace will be discussed here because of a consultation the Holy Father initiated about transferring the sign of peace to directly before the Offertory.[38]

> Taking into account ancient and venerable customs and the wishes expressed by the Synod Fathers, I have asked the competent curial offices to study the possibility of moving the sign of peace to another place, such as before the presentation of the gifts at the altar. To do so would also serve as a significant reminder of the Lord's insistence that we be reconciled with others before offering our gifts to God.[39]

Though the place for the kiss of peace in the Roman Rite was always after the Agnus Dei, there are serious reasons for considering its transfer. One is mentioned by the Holy Father: to place us in harmony with the words of the Lord himself: '*before offering your gifts on the altar*, go and reconcile with your brother'.[40]

The kiss of peace among the clergy fits harmonically into the structure of the Mass; but when the full congregation joins in, it causes some commotion between the embolism (the prayer inserted between the end of the Lord's Prayer and its doxology) and the fraction.[41]

Bishop *(name of the diocesan bishop, or, if he be an archbishop or metropolitan, mention his rank and name)*, and for all the Orthodox bishops. R. * Furthermore we pray for our brethren: priests, deacons, monks and all other clergy, and for all our brethren in Christ. R * Furthermore we pray for the blessed ever-memorable and most holy Orthodox patriarchs, for devout kings and right-believing queens, for the blessed founders of this holy church and for all our Orthodox fathers, brethren and sisters departed from this life before us, and who rest in peace here and everywhere. R. * Furthermore we pray for mercy, life, peace, health, salvation, visitation, forgiveness and remission of the sins of the servants of God: benefactors, trustees, members and supporters of this holy church. R. * Furthermore we pray for those who bring offerings and do good works in this holy and all-venerable church; for those who labor in its service, for the singers and for the people here present, who await from Thee great and abundant mercy. R. CONCLUSION: O Lord our God, accept this fervent supplication from Thy servants, and have mercy upon us according to the multitude of Thy mercies; and send forth Thy compassion upon us and upon all Thy people, who await the rich mercy that cometh from Thee. For Thou art a merciful God and lovest mankind, and unto Thee we ascribe glory to the Father, and to the Son, and to the Holy Spirit, now and ever, and unto ages of ages.
After that they pray for the catechumens and the priest continues: All ye catechumens, depart! Depart, ye catechumens! All ye that are catechumens, depart! Let no catechumens remain! But let us who are of the faithful, again and again, in peace pray to the Lord.
Then follows the prayer for peace, and the liturgy of the Eucharist starts with the Great Entrance.

[38] In an interview in L'Osservatore Romano of 24 November 2008 Cardinal Arinze, then Prefect of the Congregation of Divine Worship refered to this consultation: 'To create a climate that is more recollected while one prepares for Communion, consideration has been given to transferring the exchange of peace to the offertory. The pope has asked for a consultation from the entire episcopate. Then he'll decide.'

[39] *Sacramentum Caritatis* (2007), Note 50: Cf. *Proposition 23.*

[40] Mt 5.23ff.

[41] '. . . in the Synod of Bishops there was discussion about the appropriateness of greater restraint in this gesture, which can be exaggerated and cause a certain distraction in the assembly just before the reception of Communion' (*Sacramentum Caritatis* (2007), §49).

The succession: Homily – Prayer of the Faithful – sign of peace represents a smooth progression, and it would correspond, if not to the Roman, at least to a wider Christian tradition. In the Ambrosian Mass after the *Antiphona Post Evangelium* the priest says: 'Pacem habete' (Have peace) and the answer to this is: 'Ad te, Domine' (In your presence, O Lord). Then the *Oratio Super Sindonem* follows, and the ritual of the Offertory.[42] In the Eastern liturgies there is no explicit ceremony of the peace; but after the litany, deprecations for peace follow: 'For the heavenly peace and the salvation of our soul, let us pray to the Lord. – For the peace of the whole world, for the well-being of the Church and for the unity of all, let us pray to the Lord.' Then the Cherubicon and the ceremony of the Offertory follow. (For the place of the Creed see the following paragraph.)

If a rite of peace were transferred here, as the pope has suggested, the 'insertions' might make a bridge between the Gospel and the Creed. I speak here, of course, only of the sign of peace by the faithful, while the kiss of peace among the priests and assistants should remain where it is, preserving the tradition of the classical Roman Rite. The meaning of these two actions (one among the faithful, one imparted from the altar, within the sanctuary) is not quite the same. The separation of these two poses no theological or practical difficulty. The text of the Mass also hints at such a separation with respect to the sacrifice: 'that my Sacrifice and yours . . .' or: 'that it may be of avail for salvation both to me and to them'.[43] The faithful of the classical Roman Mass surely did not long for the introduction of the sign of handshaking (which in recent times in any case has been much criticized).[44] In order to express the spiritual intention of the exchange of peace, the faithful could employ a short formula found in older Missals, for example: 'V) *Have the bond of peace, that be fit for the holiest mysteries. Offer the peace to each other. R. Peace to you and to Christ's Church.*'[45] The answer could be accompanied with a bow of the head towards those sitting near.[46] This way, this new element, introduced after the Council, could be retained, but in a modest and stylized way that does no harm to the tradition.

---

[42] *Messalino Festivo Ambrosiano*, p. 25. In the Sarum Use the celebrant, after the prayer at the foot of altar is finished, kissed the principal deacon and subdeacon saying: 'Habete osculum pacis et dilectionis, ut apti siti sacrosancto altari ad perficiendum officia divina' (Sandon (1984), *The Use of Salisbury*, vol. 1. p. 11).

[43] 'Orate fratres ut meum ac vestrum sacrificium . . .', 'Suscipe sancte Pater . . . ut mihi et illis . . .' in the Roman Offertory texts.

[44] The admonition 'Offerte vobis . . .' was surely imported into the *Novus Ordo* from the Ambrosian Rite.

[45] In the Esztergom Missale (*Missale Notatum Strigoniense ante 1341 in Posonio*), fol. 138): 'Habete vinculum pacis et caritatis, ut apti sitis sacrosanctis mysteriis. Amen.' The 'Habete . . .' formula is recorded in almost all medieval Missals, while the response 'Pax tibi et ecclesiae Christi' I found in a Pontifical-Missal from St Gallen (Sankt Gallen, Stiftsbibliothek, Cod. Sang. 357, p. 245).

[46] *Sacramentum Caritatis* (2007), §49 'It should be kept in mind that nothing is lost when the sign of peace is marked by a sobriety which preserves the proper spirit of the celebration, as, for example, when it is restricted to one's immediate neighbours.'

VII. The Creed

We now need to discuss the Creed, and there are strong reasons for exchanging its place with that of the Prayer of the Faithful.

The Creed was inserted into the Mass – according to scholars[47] as late as 1014, in response to a request of the Emperor Henry II. It can be found, however, in other rites in both the East and the West, although instead of its 'Roman' position, attached to the Canon, as a preparatory action. In the Byzantine Liturgy it is sung *after* the offertory (Great Entrance), and before the Preface, during which the priest lifts the syndon over the bread and wine offered. It belongs to the 'secret' part of the Mass, which is closed to the unbaptized. In the East the recitation of the Creed is preceded by an acclamation: 'The doors, the doors, let us be attentive!'

The order of these moments in the Ambrosian Mass is the following: Gospel – Antiphona Post Evangelium – the Peace among the Faithful – the Oratio Supra Sindonem – the offertory rites – Creed – the Preface and the Canon.

This suggests the need to think about the function of the Creed in the context of the rite. According to the customary explanations the Creed is the response to the essentially didactic (first) part of the Mass, and so it is the last item of the 'liturgy of the Word'. But if this is so, the catechumens would be permitted to be present during the Creed, whereas they were, in fact, dismissed before the Offertory ('depart, all ye catechumens!'), at the point when they are still sent away in the rites of the East. Both the place of the Creed and the acclamation before it testify that the Creed is regarded as a direct preparation for the holiest actions of the liturgy, and belongs firmly to the Eucharistic part of the Mass. It is the gateway to, or threshold of, the sacramental mystery.

This need not be a pretext for altering its position in the Roman Mass. But if the homily and the Prayers of the Faithful conclude the first part of the Mass, then the sign of peace among the faithful and the Creed should be seen as a transition to the second.

Accordingly, the order might be the following: After the Gospel the priest walks to the pulpit. After the homily he returns to stand before the altar (or altar steps), facing the altar, where he begins the Prayer of the Faithful (if it is to be said at all). The deacon or a lector reads or sings the invocation, and the priest concludes it. Then, ascending to the altar, the priest turns to the congregation and begins the dialogue of the Peace of the Faithful. Turning back to the altar, he intones the Creed, and then commences the action of the Offertory.

In this approach the Creed is not a mere statement of faith for those present, but, more importantly, it is also a *prayer* by which they enter into the mystery. Hence it is preferable to sing it. The most appropriate melody for the Creed, as with the Preface and the Lord's Prayer, is a simple, archaic recitation. For this purpose the most suitable is the Ambrosian Creed as it is taken up in the Roman

---

[47] Jungmann (1958), *Missarum Sollemnia*, vol. 1, pp. 600–02.

'Missa Mundi',[48] but Credo I as found in the *Liber Usualis* also suffices.[49] I would not suppress Credo III, even though I am mystified by its wide popularity. On the other hand, I do think a polyphonic (or worse still, an orchestral) setting for the Creed is alien to the logic of the rite. This means that there is no need for the priest to go to the sedile. He may sing the Creed together with the assembly if it is in Latin; if the faithful sing or say it in the vernacular he should simultaneously read and pray the Latin text.

VIII. *The Offertory*

After the Creed, the priest turns towards the nave, greets the people and says no more than *Oremus*. The architects of the *Novus Ordo* regarded this moment in the classical Roman Rite as a relic of something already obsolete and eliminated. The Ambrosian Mass shows that it is, in fact, a remnant of the *Oratio Super Sindonem*, an oration prayer to be said while the gifts are still covered. An example of one of these prayers, taken from the Ambrosian Missal (for the feast of Ascension) says: 'Look down, O God our Creator, upon the exaltation of the substance of our human being, that purified by your merciful activity we may be adapted to the sacraments of your great piety.'[50] In its fragmentary state we may understand this greeting as the priest's warning to the faithful (after the lengthy insertion of the homily and the *oratio fidelium*) – to recollect themselves and follow with devotion the Eucharistic action that is about to follow. At the same time the celebrant asks the congregation to support his priestly service with their prayers.

If the Offertory chant is sung in the vernacular, the priest now prays it in Latin (preferably with its verses).[51] If only a folk hymn, or a motet or (as in a Low Mass) nothing is sung, the priest and the congregation (at least the servers) recite or read the text of the chant aloud.

The Offertory is an *action* of great importance.[52] The gifts are separated from the profanity of the world, so that they are elevated and placed on the corporal, and then incensed. The accompanying texts are – as I have already indicated – private prayers of the priest.[53] These actions are performed by the priest carefully and without haste. The custom of bringing the paten, chalice, bread and wine to the altar in a procession of the faithful became rather widespread after the Council.[54] Where the community wishes to keep this custom, the veiled chalice

---

[48] *Kyriale Simplex* (1965).

[49] *Liber Usualis Missae et Officii . . .* (1954), p. 64.

[50] 'Exaltationem condititionis humanae substantiae Conditor respice, Deus, ut tua dignatione mundati, sacramentis magnae pietatis aptemur' (*Messalino Festivo Ambrosiano* 1956, p. 316).

[51] See the discussion of this on pp. 168–170, 199 above. The Ambrosian Missal supplies these verses on most days as obligatory; for example, *Messalino Festivo Ambrosianum* (1956), pp. 106, 112, 119, 126, 149, 161, *et passim*.

[52] Jungmann (1958), *Missarum Sollemnia*, vol. 2, p. 52.

[53] Cf. Jungmann (1958), *Missarum Sollemnia*, vol. 2, pp. 53–55. However, the deacon is to pray at least some of them with the priest, or attend to the priest while he prays them, which suggests that at least some of them are part of the ritual action of the Mass.

[54] It is, however, against the spirit of the Roman liturgy if lay people or little children touch the

should be brought by the deacon (or at the very least a server in proper choir dress) to the altar, if necessary accompanied by some chosen representatives of the congregation. The local custom of collecting money and bringing it to the altar is, of course, quite traditional.

In the last few years there has been a lively debate about the private prayers of the priest. These have been replaced in the *Novus Ordo*. As I said earlier, in my opinion the theological arguments against the new texts are weak: the Mass as a sacrifice is presented in the Secret and the Canon more clearly and more properly than in the old Offertory prayers. It is undoubtedly true, however, that the reform laid waste to a noble cycle of prayers. If not theological considerations, tradition surely supports them. With the renovation of the Roman Rite the old prayers should automatically be restored. But my personal opinion is that it would not be an assault on the Roman Rite if the priest could choose between one of two alternative series.[55]

Unlike these private prayers, the Secret is an official prayer of the Roman liturgy, and in fact, one of its most precious texts. It is in these ancient prayers that the Eucharistic theology of the Church is expressed in the richest way. Personally, I see no reason why this prayer should be read silently in the classical Roman Rite.[56] If the Collect and the Postcommunion are solemn prayers recited aloud, the Secret, as the third member within this series, should also be sung or said out loud. It surely belongs among the public parts of the Mass. If it is recited or read aloud, the awkward custom disappears whereby the priest begins the Preface by singing (in the ears of the people) the non-functional conclusion (*Per omnia saecula . . .*) The Secret gives expression to the most specific and deepest message of the Roman Church; thus it could remain in Latin, while its translation – which is a hard but inescapable task – is distributed to the assembly.

The Secret is introduced by a dialogue between the priest and the altar servers. This dialogue never had a tone – which indicates that it is not public. There is no need to involve the full assembly. The arrangement can be interpreted as if the *Oremus* at the beginning of the Offertory were now continued – after the prescribed actions are completed – with the real oration of the Secret.

---

paten and the chalice in a liturgical context. At one point it was forbidden for anyone below the level of an ordained subdeacon to touch the sacred vessels.

[55] I offer only one example for the medieval diversities. In Salisbury the bread and chalice were offered in a single action accompanied by a variant of '*Suscipe sancta Trinitas*'. Immediately after the offering of the gifts the choir was censed. The prayer during the washing of hands began thus: '*Munda me Domine ab omni iniquinamento cordis*' (Purify me, O Lord, from all my iniquities), then followed the '*In spiritu humilitatis*', the dialogue with the members of the choir '*Orate fratres*' (the response was, however: '*Spiritus sancti gratia illuminet cor tuum . . .*' – 'Let the grace of the Holy Ghost illuminate your heart . . .'), and the Secreta was linked directly to the dialogue. See Sandon (1984), *The Use of Salisbury*, vol. 1, pp. 20–22. Cf. Jungmann (1958), *Missarum Sollemnia*, vol. 2, pp. 57–88.

[56] The term Secret, from which their name derives is originally taken from the verb 'to separate', and means the same as the 'Super Oblata': an oration to be said over the gifts that, in the course of being placed onto the altar has been separated from the world and its everyday use. Perhaps the mistaken translation of the word ('secret') led to the tendency to turn it into a silent prayer.

IX. *The Preface, the Canon, the Lords Prayer and After*

We have now arrived at the *Sancta Sanctorum*, the most 'priestly' part of the Mass. The priest – as the *Ordo Romanus* had formulated – alone enters the Canon.[57] Its rite as it stands in the 1962 Missal is identical almost word for word with the most ancient documents of the Roman tradition. So it seems to be appropriate that the classical form of the Roman Mass preserves itself in every respect in this tradition.

The texts of the Prefaces and of the Canon have been discussed earlier. According to the rules of the classical Mass the priest recites (or sings) the Preface, but says the words of the Canon silently, moving only his lips. I think it would not disturb its 'closed' or secret character, however, if the priest were to pray it in a 'middle' voice (to some extent indicating that he does not stand mute at the altar) or raising his voice as starting each new prayer (as he does at the Nobis quoque peccatoribus).[58]

Most commentators regard the Lord's Prayer as an introduction to the rite of Communion.[59] They rightly refer to the Church Fathers, who related the phrase *Panem nostrum quotidianum* as much to the bread of the Eucharist as to the bread of human sustenance, and focused on the theme of mutual reconciliation (*sicut et nos dimittimus*) as worthiness for the reception of holy Communion. The *Ordo Romanus I* has no mention of the *Pater noster* but refers to the *embolismus* (the prayer attached to it) as said 'after the Canon'.[60] Pope Gregory the Great fixed it to its present-day position with the argument that it is not appropriate to celebrate the sacrifice by praying the Canon composed by scholarly hand when the Lord's Prayer is not said.[61]

All throughout the known history of the Roman Rite the *Pater noster* was prayed by the priest alone. Of course, this is not really acceptable to those who espouse the (mawkishly sentimental) view of the Lord's Prayer as the dining prayer of God's children, and so in the *Novus Ordo* the entire assembly joins in. The Rule of St Benedict shows that on occasion the communal character of the Lord's Prayer can be indicated very effectively if this sacred text is solemnly pronounced only by the superior or liturgical representative of the community.[62] If we were to be persuaded by the arguments for common recitation by the whole assembly, the last remnant of a noble and ancient custom that shows how one may do something 'on behalf of the many' disappears.

The Embolism is a very ancient text of the Roman Mass; we know that it existed even before the time of St Gregory the Great, since it was this pope who

---

[57] (*Ordo Romanus Primus*, §88): '. . . surgit pontifex solus et intrat in canonem; episcopi vero, diaconi, subdiaconi et presbiteri in presbiterio permanent inclinati'.

[58] It may also help those following the Canon from their Missalettes. Concerning the acclamation 'Mortem tuam' and the sung performance of the 'Per ipsum', see above on page 213 (footnote 31).

[59] Fortescue (1912), *The Mass*, 4th edn 2005, pp. 361–64.

[60] *Ordo Romanus Primus*, §§93–94.

[61] Gregory the Great, *Epistola* IX. 12 (cf. *Patrologia Latina*, vol. 77, col. 956). Cf. Jungmann (1958), *Missarum Sollemnia*, vol. 2. p. 345.

[62] St. Benedict (1980), *The Rule of St. Benedict*: chapter XIII, p. 207.

added the name of St Andrew to it. In the text rearranged by the *Novus Ordo* the names of the saints were omitted, yet it was lengthened by inclusion of an eschatological phrase, and closed with the doxological formula *quia tuum est regnum* which is customary in the Eastern church. The reformers supposedly wanted to adopt this conclusion because it is also used by Protestants, although, differently from them, without appending it directly to the Lord's Prayer. Such a solemn addition to the prayer is not in disharmony with the Roman tradition. This measure of influence, a borrowing – justified by historical analogies – does not result in a mixture of different rites.[63]

In this 'proposal' the sign of Peace of the Faithful is transferred to a place before the Creed; the prayer for peace (with the exchange of the kiss of peace for the clergy) is restored to its place within the series of silent preparatory prayers before the priest's Communion. This would be beneficial, since the liturgy becomes a little rambling at this point in the *Novus Ordo*.

The set of preparatory prayers and supplications could perhaps be completed by some very apt texts in use before the Tridentine reform, at the choice of the priest.[64]

X. Communion and Conclusion

During the distribution of Communion, the Communion chant is sung with its psalm, and there is no reason why folk hymns or motets cannot also be inserted. In the case of the Communion chant the same things are observed as for the other proper chants: if it is to be sung in the vernacular, the priest needs to pray it in Latin; if nothing is chanted, the priest recites it after holy Communion along with the assembly, or at least a server. The observance of some minutes for thanksgiving suggested in the *Novus Ordo* is a positive addition, and could also be inserted here in the classical Roman Mass.

The Postcommunion, and in Lent, the Prayer over the People (*Oratio Super Populum*), follows the order of the 1962 Missal, together with the conclusion

---

[63] The relationship of the Fraction to the Embolism, however, requires further investigation.

[64] For example, the priest holds the sacred Host with his right hand over the paten and says: 'Panem caelestem . . . Domine non sum dignus . . . Ave in aeternum sanctissima Caro, in perpetuum mihi summa dulcedo. Ecce Jesu benignissime, quod desideravi jam video, quod cupivi jam teneo, hic tibi, quaeso jungar in caelis' (Jungmann, (1958), *Missarum Sollemnia*, vol. 2 pp. 437–38), cited here from *Missale Notatum Strigoniense*, fol. 138v. (I will take the Bread of heaven . . . Lord, I am not worthy . . . Hail for ever, O holiest Body, always the full of sweetness to me. O most benign Jesus, what I have desired now I see; what I wished to have, I already hold in my hand: let it lead me to join you in heaven.) When taking the chalice: 'Quid retribuam . . . Calicem salutaris . . . Ave in aeternum caelesis potus, mihi ante omnia et super omnia dulcis. Sanguis Domini nostri Jesu Christi quem vere confiteor de latere ejus profluxisse mundet omnes maculas conscientiae meae et sit mihi remissio omnium peccatorum meorum. Sanguis Domini nostri . . .' (What shall I render . . . I will take the chalice . . . Hail for ever, O heavenly drink, sweet for me before and above all things. The Blood of our Lord Jesus Christ, that I confess to have poured out of His side, cleanse all faults of my conscience and let it be for the forgiveness of my sins. The Blood of our Lord . . .) The prayers in the Sarum Use are: 'Domine sancte . . . da mihi hoc sacrosanctum corpus et sanguinem . . .', 'Deus pater fons et origo', 'Domine Jesu Christe Fili Dei vivi . . .', 'Corpus et sanguinis tui Domine . . . not sit mihi judicio . . .', 'Ave in aeternum sanctissima caro . . .', 'Ave in aeternum caelestis potus . . .' (Sandon (1984), *The Use of Salisbury*, vol. 1. pp. 34–35).

of the Mass. The solemn three-fold blessings that were added as an optional possibility in the *Novus Ordo* can and, in fact, should be incorporated in the classical Roman Missal after the dismissal. In the Middle Ages these were episcopal blessings, and they communicate very effectively the meaning of the ancient liturgical theology of Rome.

Although the 'last Gospel' is an important and majestic text, it is a late medieval addition with reasons that were not liturgical at all. But it makes no disturbance if the priest reads it to himself after the blessing or on his way back to the Sacristy.[65]

Finally, it is really worthwhile to examine the Mass with regard to the use of language. As I have said before, the obligation to celebrate the Mass entirely in the Latin language should be retained for the most festive or solemn occasions, as well as being more widely preserved in certain churches, at least in the principal Mass. According to the will of the Council, at other Masses the vernacular (even combined with the Latin) could be accepted, in the readings, in the chant (both in the Propers and the Ordinary), while in this case the priest reads the Latin texts at the altar, silently in Latin. The typically priestly texts (the three main orations, the Canon, and all the private prayers of the priest) would always remain in Latin. Of course, in the use of the vernacular various degrees of balance between Latin and the common tongue could be permitted. On the two opposite ends of the spectrum stand, on the one hand, the Mass fully in Latin, and on the other hand, the maximal use of the vernacular, as suggested in the following arrangement:[66]

Latin	Latin and/or vernacular
Prayers at the foot of the altar	Introit, Kyrie, Gloria
Collect	Readings and interlectionary chants
	Homily, Prayer of the Faithful, Peace of the Faithful
	Creed
Prayers during the Offertory	Offertory chant
Secret	Preface, Sanctus
Canon	Lord's Prayer, Embolism
Preparatory prayers	Agnus Dei, Communion
Postcommunion, *Ite missa est*	
Placeat, Blessing	

[65] According to the Sarum Use the priest bows toward the altar, then while departing, says the beginning of St John's Gospel (Sandon (1984), *The Use of Salisbury*, vol. 1, p. 38).

[66] Brian Harrison's proposal (Harrison (2003), 'The Postconciliar Eucharistic Liturgy', pp. 183–85) is: 'Latin could be retained for all those parts that are recited in a low voice by the priest – that is, the whole of the Offertory and the Canon – and also for most of the unchanging (or relatively unchanging) parts of the Mass. This would leave for translation into the vernacular those publicly audible parts of the Mass that, because they change every day, would be most unfamiliar and unintellgible to the faithful if they remained in Latin.'

21

HOLY WEEK

The liturgy of Holy Week, as the most outstanding period of the liturgical year, was always uniquely protected from undue alteration in the tradition.[1] It preserved many ancient liturgical usages that were changed on other liturgical days, and in consequence the liturgy of these most holy days was left much less modified over ensuing centuries.

Nevertheless some elements of the rich ritual traditions of the great Roman basilicas were omitted after the Council of Trent, and the celebration became somewhat simplified. The reform of the Holy Week rites under Pope Pius XII made alterations (1955) while trying to maintain the tradition in its principal lines. Some of these alterations assisted the revitalization of a more widespread observance of Holy Week, whereas others proved to be disadvantageous (like the adoption of the unfortunate *Psalterium Pianum* into the texts of the Missal; the new function given to the Exsultet, and the cutting of the Litany of the Saints at the Easter Vigil in two).[2] The 1962 Missal codified these changes. In 1970, the Missal of Paul VI brought about a final devastation in the Holy Week liturgy; it was one of the worst products of the reform (as was also confessed – if the rumours are true – by some of its very architects).

Individual elements of the repeated reforms could be defended or attacked separately,[3] but they are common in one respect. While the point of departure for all the pre-Tridentine books was the usage of the great cathedrals – and they supposed (more or less) that the order they described would be implemented in parish churches and religious communities, too – after the Council of Trent this supposition became a fiction; a simplification of the ritual began, following local decisions and with the benevolent toleration of ecclesiastical authorities.

Given that the task at hand is the restoration of the classical Roman Rite, we are confronted with two basic difficulties concerning the order of Holy Week. The first problem we characterize in the following ways: the contrast (a) between the medieval traditions and the Tridentine Rite; (b) between the Tridentine Rite and

---

[1] Cf. Anton Baumstark (1927), 'Das Gesetz der Erhaltung des Alten in liturgisch hochwertiger Zeit'.
[2] Alcuin Reid (2005), *The Organic Development of the Liturgy*, pp. 172–81 and 219–34.
[3] Cf. Dobszay (2003), *The Bugnini-Liturgy and the Reform of the Reform*, chapter 2.

the reform of Pope Pius XII; and (c) between the reform of Pope Pius XII and the *Novus Ordo*. We must survey both the forms of long-standing tradition and any demands manifested in the conciliar reforms.

The other problem is: how to resolve the conflict between the full cathedral form of these rites and their implementation in parish churches. If the authentic cathedral forms are prescribed universally, there is a real danger that the majority of churches will adapt it as they wish (or best can), which may produce very unfortunate results – as has happened in past decades and centuries. On the other hand, if we take as the standard the practice of the parish churches with average competence, the full form in its exalted liturgical and artistic character will disappear from the life of the Church. The Roman ritual books themselves need to provide the range of possibilities for necessary adaptation in order to avoid abandoning the ritual of these most holy days to local emendation. This means that the official books themselves need to contain the Holy Week rites in two forms. The first is valid in principal and cathedral churches, which can and should, where possible, be used in other churches (larger parishes, religious houses) where the conditions (clergy, servers, singers) are comparable to the cathedrals. The other form is celebrated in parochial and small churches. The two forms of the celebration must clearly be in all essentials the same, differing only (a) in size and fullness; (b) in musical forms; and (c) in the rules for assistants. Certain options can be given within both forms, and these can be left for local decision.

Keeping these principles in mind, we now need to analyse each of the liturgies of Holy Week.

I. The Palm Sunday Procession

Earlier, I provided a critique of the *Novus Ordo* rites of Holy Week, which I do not repeat here.[4]

In the Tridentine Missals (and also in some medieval local Uses) the blessing of the palms was constructed after the model of a Mass. The similarity was such that even a Preface and Sanctus were to be chanted ('missa sicca'). The originating form of this rite, the celebration by the church in Jerusalem, was a solemn procession to the Holy City in remembrance of Christ's entrance.[5] The blessing of palms was originally only preparatory to this, but in the Frankish liturgy this element became highly emphasized. The reform of Pius XII reduced the ritual to a simple prayer and a reading from the Gospel of Christ's entrance into Jerusalem.[6] This change is surely acceptable from both a liturgical and practical perspective. During the distribution of the palms some antiphons are sung, and after the Gospel the procession begins.

---

4   Dobszay (2003), *The Bugnini-Liturgy and the Reform of the Reform*, pp. 26–28.
5   John Wilkinson (trans. and ed.), *Egeria's Travels to the Holy Land*, 31.1, pp. 132–33.
6   Antiphona: Hosanna Filio David; Oratio. Benedic, quaesumus, Domine, hos palmarum ramos;. Antiphonae; Gospel (Mt. 21.1-9); Procedamus in pace.

In the Missal of Pius V (as also in the 1962 Missal) there are no special actions during the procession,[7] which itself is accompanied by chants that are fixed. In the Middle Ages, however, a more vivid form was customary in many churches, and children played an eminent role in the procession, as is quite fitting for the day. The procession was punctuated by stations at which the children laid down first their palms, then some of their clothing (capes, specially put on for the purpose), always accompanied by an appropriate antiphon.[8] Another station took place when the procession arrived before the church, and then finally the Lord entering the holy City – symbolically in the form of the processional Cross – was adored inside the church. The procession halted in the nave, and after an appropriate antiphon the closing prayer followed; then the clergy and assistants re-entered the choir of the church, and the Mass of the Sunday commenced.[9]

The restoration of the stations in the procession is commendable, at least *ad libitum*. They give the procession far greater dramatic form, ritually visualizing the actual historical event, enhance the pastoral effect and create an opportunity for the direct participation of the children. Where the procession cannot leave the church (as is the case in many places), and the space inside is enough only for the movement of the priest, servers, singers and children, then the stations would provide an occasion for the faithful in the pews to enter the biblical scenes in spirit.

During the procession a series of monumental antiphons were sung in the Middle Ages, which recalled and commented on the scenes, unfolding each event in course.[10] Many of these pieces were omitted as early as in the Missal of St Pius V, and in the 1962 form very few of them were retained. Undoubtedly, such long antiphons suggest long processions and good singers, but mere brevity

---

[7] Except a solemn opening of the gates of church, accompanied by the hymn *Gloria laus*.

[8] For three stations, but in different arrangement in the Sarum Use, see Nicholas Sandon (1984), *The Use of Salisbury*, vol. 4, pp. 9–17.

[9] A spectacular description of the procession can be found in the *Ordinary Book of Eger* (Hungary): 'Chorators (= cantors): in the procession four canons in red copes but in the Mass only two in surplice. Four deacons: two canons and two priests, i.e. an altar priest and a chaplain in red dalmatics. And there is a procession to St Stephen . . . When it is done, the bishop starts blessing the flowers and branches at the arranged place as it is in the missal . . . After the flowers have been distributed and the antiphons finished, a single Collect is said as in the missal. After saying "Amen", the procession returns to the main church progressing slowly towards the portal of the cathedral while the succentor sings the antiphon *Cum appropinquaret Iesus Ierosolimam* . . . two children sing the antiphon *Pueri Hebraeorum tollentes* in the portico of the church in front of the crucifix arranged by the custos, and the choir continues singing: *Obviaverunt Domino* during which the children throw branches before the crucifix. Then two other children vested in copes sing the other (antiphon) *Pueri Hebraeorum vestimenta* and the choir continues: *Et clamabant dicentes* while the children throw their outer clothing before the crucifix. Having finished it, all the canons according to their rank and the whole clergy prostrate themselves in front of the crucifix, saluting and kissing it . . . After the cross has been saluted, the collect *Auge fidem* is said. Having done it, the procession enters the church singing the responsory *Ingrediente Domino* without Gloria Patri. Divided into two parts, the procession halts in front of the Holy Cross altar . . . the bishop says the prayer *Deus qui miro ordine*. Finishing the collect with "Amen", the succentor starts the antiphon *Turba multa* . . . And the procession goes thus into the choir . . . the bishop says . . . *Oremus* in front of the main altar, which is continued by the collect *Adiuva nos Deus* as it is in the missal. At the conclusion of the procession, Mass is started in its proper order' (László Dobszay (2000), *Liber Ordinarius Agriensis*, Nr. 212).

[10] They can be studied in Sandon (1984), *The Use of Salisbury*, vol. 4, pp. 6–18 and the *Sarum Processional*.

is not a legitimate pretext for letting them vanish. Another, entirely practicable, solution is as follows.

The *Graduale Romanum* and the Missal should contain the full cycle of the medieval antiphons. In cathedrals and larger churches the singers may choose from this set according to their capacity and the duration of the procession. In parish churches this series could be replaced by an ancient hymn, which – just like the great antiphons – records in a poetic form all the Palm Sunday events. Since this precious composition is not generally known, I provide the full text here. It could be sung on the melody of any appropriate Ambrosian hymn, or even to that of one of the better folk hymns.[11]

1. Magnum salutis gaudium,
laetetur omne saeculum!
Jesus, redemptor gentium
sanavit orbem languidum.

1. Let age to age Hosannas sing,
Glad shout of health and praise,
Now Jesus comes, Salvation's King,
Th' expiring world to raise.

2. Sex ante Paschae ferias
advenit in Bethaniam,
ubi pie post triduum
resuscitavit Lazarum.

2. Six days the Paschal night before
At Bethany He arrived,
Where, in His love, now four days o'er,
He Lazarus revived.

3. Nardi Maria pistici
sumpsit libram mox optimi,
unxit beatos Domini
pedes rigando lacrimis.

3. There Mary took of spikenard sweet
The precious pound and good,
Embalmed her Master's Blessed Feet,
And with her tears bedew'd.

4. Post haec jugalis asinae
Jesus, supernus arbiter,
pullo sedebat, inclitam
pergebat Hierosolymam.

4. Then Jesus, Judge of Heaven Supreme,
On asses colt He sate,
And on to proud Jerusalem
Advanced in solemn state.

5. O quam stupenda pietas,
mira Dei clementia!
sessor aselli fieri
dignatur auctor saeculi.

5. His tender love how marvellous,
More wondrous meekness yet!
That earth's Creator deigneth thus
On asses colt to sit.

6. Olim propheta praescius
praedixit almo spiritu:
'Exsulta', dicens, 'filia
Sion, satis et jubila!'

6. 'Twas He the Seer's clear spirit eyed,
And thrilling voice foretold,
'When Daughter, rise and shout' he cried,
'Shout, Sion, and behold!'

---

[11] *Analecta hymnica medii aevi*, vol. 51, p. 73; G. M. Dreves and C. Blume (1909), *Ein Jahrtausend Lateinischer Hymnendichtung*, vol. 2, p. 58. Translation by William John Copeland (1848), *Hymns for the week and hymns for the season*, p. 177.

7. 'Rex, ecce, tuus humilis, noli timere, veniet, pullo jugalis residens, tibi benignus patiens.'	7. 'Thy King doth come, yon lowly One, Fear not, Behold the sign, On foal of ass He rideth on, Meek, patient and benign.'
8. Ramos virentes sumpserat palma recisos tenera turba, processit obviam Regi perenni plurima.	8. From tender palm the gathering throng The new-cut branches bring, With olives green they haste along To meet th' Immortal King;
9. Coetus sequens et praevius sanctoque plenus spiritu clamabat: 'in altissimis Hosanna David filio'.	9. Before, behind, in concourse run, And in the Spirit's might, 'Hosanna' cry, 'to David's Son Hosanna in the height!'
10. Quidam solutis propriis viam tegebant vestibus, pluresque flores candidum iter parabant Domino.	10. Some strip them of their garments gay To deck the royal road, Some with bright flowers bestrew the way As less unmeet for God.
11. Ad cujus omnis civitas commot(a) ingressum tremuit, Hebraea proles aurea laudes ferebat debitas.	11. At His approach with thrill intense The trembling city rang; But Judah's golden innocence His worthiest praises sang.
12. Nos ergo tanto Judici curramus omnes obviam, palmas gerentes gloriae mente canamus sobria.	12. O let us thus run forth to greet Th' Almighty Judge and King, And bearing palms of glory meet With childlike spirit sing.

The stations, with their own antiphons, can be inserted at the proper dramatic points in both forms. The procession and its chant halts, the children sing the antiphon (or intone it, continued by the congregation) and perform the appropriate action (laying down of palms and clothing in front of the processional Cross), while the antiphon is repeated by all.

The main chant of the procession, the hymn *Gloria laus et honor*, is here associated with the veneration of the Cross (the fourth station).

I consider it important to preserve the closing prayers (in order to separate the procession from the Mass). For this purpose I quote a text found in the older Missals, which could be revived as an alternative to the one printed in the 1962 Missal:

'Adjuva nos, Deus, salutaris noster, et ad beneficia recolenda, quibus nos instaurare dignatus es, tribue venire gaudentes. Per Christum Dominum nostrum.'[12]

The order of the procession is shown in the following table:

Palm Sunday	1962	In cathedral churches	In parish churches
To the place of blessing	ant. Hosanna filio David	A. Collegerunt	Hy. Magnum salutis 1–5
Blessing	Benedic quaesumus	**Statio I** Benedic quaesumus *Deus qui miro*	**Statio I** Benedic quaesumus *Deus qui miro*
Distribution of palms	a. Pueri . . . portantes + Ps. 23 – a. Pueri . . . vestimenta + Ps. 46	Hosanna Filio (+ Ps. 23)	Hosanna Filio (+ Ps. 23)
Gospel	Cum appropinquasset	Cum appropinquasset	Cum appropinquasset
Monition	Procedamus in pace	Procedamus in pace	Procedamus in pace
Procession	Occurrunt turbae Cum angelis et pueris Turba multa Ceperunt omnes Hy. Gloria laus	Cum appropinquaret Cum audisset populus Ante sex dies Occurrunt turbae	Magnum salutis 6–8. **(Statio II) see below**
Procession	Omnes collaudant + p.147 Fulgentibus palmis Ave Rex noster (Christus vincit)	Cum angelis et pueris Turba multa Ceperunt omnes Omnes collaudant Fulgentibus palmis Ave Rex noster	Magnum salutis 9–10 **(Statio III) see below**
Branches are laid down		**Statio II** a. Pueri . . . portantes	**Statio II** a. Pueri . . . portantes

(*continued*)

[12] 'Help us, O God, our Saviour, and let us arrive in joy to the celebration of the gifts you have restored us with. Through Christ our Lord' (*Missale Strigonensis*, fol. 83v).

Palm Sunday 1962		In cathedral churches	In parish churches
Vestments are laid down		Statio III a. Pueri . . . vestimenta	Statio III a. Pueri . . . vestimenta
Before the Holy Cross		**Statio IV** Hy. Gloria laus et honor	**Statio IV** Hy. Gloria laus et honor
Entering the choir	R. Ingrediente Domino	R. Ingrediente Domino	Magnum salutis 11–12
Closing prayer	Domine Jesu Christe Rex	Domine Jesu . . . *vel:* Adjuva nos Deus	Domine Jesu . . . *vel:* Adjuva nos Deus

In the Mass the order and the general rubrics need no modification from the 1962 Missal (including the abbreviation of the Passion). The *Graduale Parvum* would provide for the replacement of the Introit and Communion with the standard chants for the whole of Passiontide (*Nos autem gloriari*; *Hoc corpus*).[13]

II. Tenebrae

A noble lesson for a true liturgical reform would have been the integration of the Office of the Sacred Triduum into the series of Holy Week celebrations – even on the level of parish churches. Earlier the combination of Matins and Lauds (widely known as Tenebrae) was an organic part of the celebration; frequently Tenebrae were published in single books that contained all the principal rites of Holy Week.[14] The Office of the Triduum has some unusual features. These are mostly remnants of the original state of the Roman Office (for instance, the omissions of the verse *Deus in adjutorium*, the Invitatory, the Hymn, the Chapter), left intact out of respect for its antiquity, and later interpreted as having been preserved in this simplified form as an expression of the solemn affectivity of a mourning Church. The Office as a whole was strikingly uniform over the centuries until the publication of the 1970 *Liturgia Horarum*.[15] A few pre-Council modifications are, however, worthy of note: for example, the order of the psalms at Lauds was edited to bring it into accord with the Breviary-reform of St Pius X, and the introduction of the *Psalterium Pianum* (by Pope Pius XII) in 1955. After the Council a completely new Office was created for these three days (with Invitatory, hymn, etc.).

[13] Proposed to Passiontide in the *Graduale Parvum*.
[14] An appropriate example of this – symbolically and practically – is to be found in the *Officium Majoris Hebdomadae Sacrae* 1923 (Regensburg).
[15] The Roman secular course is adapted in this case also in the monastic offices. See footnote 53 in Chapter 15.

Here the restoration of the Roman Rite means, first of all, a return to the form *prior to St Pius X*: the restitution of the traditional order of psalmody[16] and of the Vulgate texts. A question emerges concerning the readings of the Second Nocturn. No objection can, of course, be raised against the *Enarrationes* of St Augustine (as found in the Tridentine Breviary); but there are other, perhaps better choices, in closer connection with the full message of the given days. I find much more convincing the series of readings that are, for instance, provided in the Dominican Breviary with the sermon of St John Chrysostom on the Last Supper, and the majestic sermons of the 'most liturgical pope', St Leo the Great on Good Friday and Holy Saturday.[17] The inclusion of all three of these readings would be a real advantage for the classical Roman Rite, without introducing any substantial change.

Another gain would be the restoration of the conclusion of Lauds in its pre-Tridentine form. This ritual called *Kyrie puerorum*, also attractive in its sheer dramatic power, has a profound impression on the participants, as demonstrated by the example of some churches where it has already been reintroduced.[18]

On the great triangular stand containing a candle for each of the psalms sung at Tenebrae, each candle is extinguished after its corresponding psalm has concluded. During the repetition of the antiphon to the Benedictus, the acolyte, accompanied by other servers, takes the last candle, brings it to the main altar and hides it. Children kneel at the steps of the altar; the lectors (or other male singers) stand at the entrance to the sanctuary; the cantors kneel in their places. Then the *Kyrie puerorum* begins:[19]

---

[16] The third psalm at Lauds is (on all of these three days): 62 + 66; the fifth psalm: 148 + 149 + 150.

[17] *Breviarium juxta ritum S. Ordinis Praedicatorum*, vol. 1, pp. 661 or 665, 687, 711.

[18] Used also in Dominican, Premonstratension, etc. liturgies (*Antiphonarium Sacris Ordinis Praedicatorum*, p. 471, *Graduale ad usum Canonici Praemonstratensis Ordinis*, p. 241). There were some slight variants between dioceses in terms of the exact order of elements. In some places it was also extended with yet further additions. What I present here is simply a proposal, following the most frequent arrangement.

[19] *Breviarium Notatum Strigoniense*, fol. 158. Cf. Janka Szendrei (1999), *The Istanbul Antiphonal about 1306*, fol. 87v. The text of the Litany in English translation: I. Jesus Christ, who came to suffer for us: O Lord, have mercy on us . . . Christ became obedient till the death. II. Who promised by prophetic word: I will be, O Death, for your death . . . III. Who extending your arms on the Cross attracted everyone to You . . . Even death on the cross.

Cantors: Chri-stus Do-mi-nus fa-ctus est o-be-di-ens us-que ad mor-tem.
II. Children: Kyrie...

Readers: Qui pro-phe-ti-ce prom-psi-sti: E-ro mors tu-a o, mors:
People: Domine miserere nobis.
Cantors: Christus Dominus...
III. Children: Kyrie...

Readers: Qui ex-pan-sis in cru-ce ma-ni-bus tra-xi-sti o-mni-a ad te sae-cu-la.
People: Domine miserere nobis.
Cantors: Christus Dominus factus est obediens usque ad mortem.
Priest (on low voice): Mortem autem crucis.

They pray silently for a while, then the priest gives a sign, and the acolyte, accompanied by the children, brings back the candle. The priest reads the closing Collect (without *Oremus*) at its light: 'Respice quaesumus, Domine, super hanc familiam . . .' (and silently:) 'Qui tecum . . .' The acolyte puts the candle back on the hearse and everybody leaves in silence.[20]

In the Tridentine Office this ritual was replaced by the Gradual *Christus factus est* and the repetition of Psalm 50; the ceremony is concluded with the same Collect as above. This is a modest form which seems a little protracted because of the second recitation of Psalm 50 already prayed at Lauds. But it can be traced back to an old Italian tradition, and should be preserved as a legitimate alternative to the practice described above.

The full Office including Matins (with its three Nocturns and their musically rich responsories) and Lauds takes a long time and demands several well-trained singers. However, the return of Tenebrae is to be restored as a part of parish worship, and so an abbreviated form 'for parochial and smaller churches' is also necessary. The parish-form could contract Matins into a single Nocturn, and its completion would be a conclusion created from the most important components of Lauds. The responsories can be recited in simpler tones, or replaced by a strophic paraphrase.[21]

The use of the hearse surely belongs to the full drama of this Office. The 15 candles burning on it correspond precisely to the nine + five + one psalms of the full Tenebrae. Since the number of psalms in the parish Office need be only

[20] In cathedrals and major churches it was followed by a procession where the hymns Rex Christe factor omnium, Hymnum dicamus Domino, Laus tibi Christus qui pateris were sung. Their popularity is shown by their use in some countries as folk hymns; they found their way also into the liturgical practice of the German Lutherans.
[21] This form is already in use in several churches in Hungary. Cf. *Népzsolozsmák* (Folk Offices), pp. 155–77.

three + one + one, the rubrics must be adapted. The proposal adaptation allows the candles to be extinguished *in pairs*, and not only at the end of the psalms, but also during the responsories. So the number of extinguished candles is twice times three + three + one; that is, two times seven, the last candle being taken away after the Benedictus.

The Office of the Triduum Sacrum in its parish form looks like this:

	Feria 5	Feria 6	Sabbato S.
Psalmody	A single antiphon: *Zelus domus* Ps. 68 in three divisions	A single antiphon: *Diviserunt* Ps. 21 in three divisiones	A single antiphon: *Domine abstraxsti* Ps. 4, 23, 29
Reading first responsory	Lamentation R. *In monte Oliveti*	Lamentation R. *Omnes amici*	Oratio Jeremiae R. *Plange quasi virgo*
Reading second responsory	John Chrysostom's Sermon I R. *Tristis est anima*	Pope Leo's Sermon I R. *Velum templi*	Pope Leo's Sermon. I R. *Jerusalem surge*
Reading third responsory	John Chrysostom's Sermon II R. *Ecce vidimus*	Pope Leo's Sermon II R. *Vinea mea*	Pope Leo's Sermon II R. *Sepulto Domino*
'Pro laudibus' (on place of the Lauds)	a. *Oblatus est* Ps. 50+ a versicle	a. *Proprio Filio* Ps. 50+ a versicle	a. *O mors* Ps. 50+ a versicle
Cantile	a. *Traditor autem.* Benedictus	a. *Posuerunt* Benedictus	a. *Mulieres sedentes* Benedictus
Close	*Kyrie puerorum oratio*	*Kyrie puerorum oratio*	*Kyrie puerorum oratio*

The Little Hours were abbreviated for these three days: only the divisions of Psalm 118 were recited (sung *recto tono*, without any antiphon), which is completed in the Tridentine Rite again with *Christus factus est*, Psalm 50 and the Collect. In some rites (e.g. in that of the Praemonstratensians) one of the responsories from Matins, most fitting to the given moment of the day, is inserted (only said); followed only by a versicle and the Collect. The sparse character of the Hours is fitting to the nature of these days and assigns prayers across the whole day, which are not burdensome for either clergy or singers, who are heavily engaged in the preparation for the great evening celebrations.

	Feria 5	Feria 6	Sabbato S.
Tierce	Ps. 118 i–iii R. Tristis est anima V) Insurrexerunt in me Coll. Respice	Ps. 118 x–xii R. Caligaverunt oculi V) Diviserunt sibi Coll. Respice	Ps. 118 xix–xxi R. Jerusalem surge/luge V) In pace in idipsum Coll. Respice
Sext	Ps. 118 iv–vi R. Unus ex discipulis V) Deus meus eripe me Coll. Respice	Ps. 118 xiii–xv R. Tamquam ad latronem V) Insurrexerunt in me Coll. Respice	Ps. 118 xxii, i–ii R. Plane quasi virgo V) Tu autem Domine Coll. Respice
None	Ps. 118 vii–ix R. Seniores populi V) Homo pacis meae Respice	Ps. 118 xvi–xviii R. Velum templi V) Dederunt in escam Coll. Respice	Ps. 118 iii–v R. Recessit pastor V) Collocaverunt me Coll. Respice

Vespers also took a simpler form on Maundy Thursday and Good Friday.[22] Consisting of five psalms with antiphons, the Magnificat, and concluding with *Christus factus est*, Psalm 50 and the Collect. This simple form can be retained for those who cannot be present at the evening celebrations. The new regulation could also be offered to those who follow the classical Roman Rite, that is, that participants of the evening liturgies are not obliged to pray Vespers.

III. Maundy Thursday

The matter of the Maundy Thursday Chrism-Mass falls outside the field of my expertise. The reform of Pope Pius XII, while moving the Mass to the evening, otherwise left it essentially intact in its earlier form, so no comment is necessary. A new element of this form is the transposition of the *Mandatum* (or foot-washing ceremony) to a place within the Mass. For many churches this is surely the best arrangement.

We have to speak, however, about other elements of the celebration *after* the Mass (including the so-called *Mandatum*, which gave the day its name in English of Maundy Thursday) and about the place of the footwashing within this context. In this respect a return to the pre-Tridentine order (kept by some religious orders![23]) would represent real progress that may develop the pastoral

---

[22] In the Middle Ages Maundy Thursday Vespers was prayed at the end of Mass between the Communion chant and the Postcommunion prayer. On Holy Saturday a still more reduced form of Vespers (rather than Lauds, as it became after 1955) was sung at the end of the Vigil Mass.

[23] In the Dominican rite: 'Ad altaria abluenda', 'Ad Mandatum peragendum', 'Ad Sermonem Dominicum', see *Ecclesiasticum Officium juxta ritum Sacri Ordinis Praedicatorum . . . Triduo*

impact of the liturgy. First, let us examine the historical patterns, and then the lessons we may learn from them.

The old books of dioceses and religious orders described these ceremonies in accordance with their proper traditions but essentially in the same way. For instance, the rubrics of the *Liber Ordinarius Agriensis* (the diocese of Eger in Hungary) presents a typical arrangement:

Item: for the ceremony Mandatum the bells toll for a longer time . . . the great bell tolls a second time . . . later there is rattling in the tower. After that the bells remain silent until Saturday up to the point when the *Gloria in excelsis* is sung. Meanwhile the bishop and the canons and the whole clergy assemble at church to perform the Mandatum. After the bishop has vested his red cope with mitre and crosier, (furthermore) two deacons and two subdeacons, the chorators (that is) four canons, the acolytes and the ceroferarius from school move in procession from the sacristy to the table prepared. While doing so, the succentor and the choir sing the hymn *Tellus ac ethra jubilent*. At the end of the hymn the Epistle without title in lesson tone is *Convenientibus vobis in unum*. Then comes the Gospel *Ante diem festum Paschae*, also without title, in solemn (Gospel) tone. And when they sing *Surgit a cena*, the bishop puts a cloth before him. And at the end of the Gospel oratio as in the Missal, then he starts washing the feet beginning on the provost side. During that time the succentor and his companions sing the responsory *Accessit ad pedes Jesu*. At the end of the responsory the bishop distributes supper saying *Mandatum novum do vobis*. On concluding it the succentor starts the antiphon *Ante diem festum* with the subsequent antiphons as it is in the book. Having finished the antiphons, one of the canons assigned for it starts singing the MANDATUM in lesson tone: *Amen amen dico vobis*. Once ended, there is a sermon to the clergy, at the end of which the bishop gives blessing. Then they go over to the choir to WASH the altars singing the antiphon *Diviserunt sibi vestimenta mea* and the psalm *Deus Deus meus respice* without Gloria Patri. And after each verse they repeat the antiphon *Diviserunt sibi*. After the high altar and the others have been washed, the canons step one by one to the high altar and the bishop anoints their forehead according to custom, likewise the whole clergy approaches it. At the end of the psalm *Deus Deus meus respice* the Compline is started in the choir . . .[24]

ante Pascha, pp. 82–130. Cf. *Processionale ad usum . . . ordinis Praemonstratensis*, pp. 67–78; for the Sarum Rite see Sandon (1984), *The Use of Salisbury*, vol. 4, pp. 75–88.
[24] Dobszay (2000), *Liber Ordinarius Agriensis*, Nrs 223–24: 'Ad faciendum MANDATUM . . . fit longus pulsus . . . alter pulsus cum magna campana, et postea fit clapernatio in turri et deinde usque sabbatum diem silent campanae usque cantatur Gloria in excelsis. Interim dominus episcopus ac domini canonici et totus clerus conveniant ad ecclesiam ad peragendum mandatum. Ipso domino episcopo rubea cappa induto cum mitra et baculi pastorali, duo diaconi et duo subdiaconi, choratores quattuor canonici; accolyti et ceroferarii de scholis exeant processionaliter de sacrastia ad mensam preparatam. Interim succentor cum choro cantat hymnum Tellus ac ethra iubilent. Finito hymno dicitur epistola sine titulo ad tonum lectionis Convenientibus vobis in unum. Deinde evangelium Ante diem festum Pasche similiter sine titulo ad tonum festivalem. Et cum cantatur "Surgit a cena", dominus episcopus precingitur manutergio. Et finito evangelio

Here the footwashing ceremony is separated from the Mass.[25] The celebrant assumes a red cope (not the white of the Mass, but the colour of the Passion). From what is written later (of the entrance to the choir), it seems that the celebration takes place somewhere in the nave or narthex; according to other sources this was in the chapter house. First comes the footwashing; after that the bishop – somewhat probably as a remnant of an earlier *agape* – 'distributes the supper' (supposedly in a symbolic form).[26] The second element is the reading of the Lord's farewell discourse,[27] followed by a sermon. (Other sources place the sermon after the footwashing.) Afterwards they make a procession to the choir of the church,[28] coming to a stop before the altar, where the washing of the altars begins. The text, in a way similar to that found in other pre-Tridentine books, speaks of the washing (and not only of the stripping) of the altars. There is an essential difference between the liturgical meaning of the two. 'Stripping' places the accent on the deprivation or seizure of ornaments (according to the glosses on the text, commemorating the stripping of Christ's body). The altar-washing, on the other hand, is a positive gesture: a homage to the altar on the evening when Christ – having established the Eucharist – changed the meaning of the symbolism of an altar *vis-à-vis* the pagan rites and the Jewish temple. The celebration closes with Compline. Thus the ceremony combines three independent elements (Footwashing, Farewell Discourse, Washing of the Altars), we should not be surprised at historical variations in the order of these events.

This ceremony represents the most special feature of the liturgy of Maundy Thursday. To leave the church empty after the evening Mass would be a sign of impiety. This is the motivation for the different devotions diversely organized on this night, proving that the faithful actively seek out quasi-liturgical occasions

---

dicitur oratio, ut in missali. Deinde incipit lavare pedes ordinatim, primo a parte prepositi incipiendo. Interim succentor cum suis canit responsorium Accessit ad pedes Iesu. Finito responsorio dominus episcopus dividit cenam dicendo Mandatum novum do vobis. Quibus finitis succentor incipit antiphonas, videlicet Ante diem festum cum sequentibus antiphonis, ut in libro habentur. Finitis antiphonis unus ex dominis ad hoc tabulatus cantat MANDATUM in tono lectionis, videlicet Amen Amen dico vobis. Quo finito fit sermo ad clerum. Finito sermone dabit dominus episcopus benedictionem. Deinde transeunt ad chorum ad LOTIONEM altarium cantando antiphonam Diviserunt sibi vestimenta mea. Psalmus: Deus Deus meus respice, sine Gloria. Et post quemlibet versum repetitur antiphona Diviserunt sibi. Loto altari magno cum vino domini secundum seriem accedant ad altare maius. Et dominus episcopus liniat vertices eorum more solito. Similiter et totus clerus accedat. Finito psalmo Deus Deus meus respice incipitur in choro completorium . . .'

[25] The beginning of the celebration is signalled by the ringing of bells and immediately following by the use of rattles thereafter; that is, the bells are muted at this moment and not, therefore, used during the Mass.

[26] In the Sarum Use the first event is the Washing of Altars: 'They begin with the high altar, pouring wine and water onto the crosses at both horns of the altar, while the responsory . . . is sung . . . After the responsory the senior priest recites in a quiet speaking voice the versicle and collect of the saint to whom the altar is dedicated . . . Afterwards the altar is kissed by the priest and the other participants. All the altars in the church are washed in the same way . . .' Then follows the Maundy Ceremony (footwashing) and a 'loving-cup is shared'. The ceremony is closed by reading the Last Discourse of St John's Gospel (see note 27 below). For the details see Sandon (1984), *The Use of Salisbury*, vol. 4, pp. 73–88.

[27] Jn 13.21 (or from 13.34) through to the end of chapter 17.

[28] Other sources have them process to the choir or church upon arriving at these words of Christ: 'Surgite, eamus hinc' (Arise, let us go hence).

after the Mass has concluded. Wherever the footwashing is better located within the Mass, it can be separated from these other ceremonies. It may actually be more convenient in some places if the stripping and washing of the altars were to follow the Mass directly. In this case the reading of Christ's farewell discourse becomes an independent ceremony. In other places perhaps the discourse could also be read outside the church, linked to an *agape*. Therefore, it is useful to discuss the three elements of the cycle separately.

If the footwashing is done as a separate rite, it is best introduced by the ancient hymn *Tellus ac aethra*,[29] followed by the Gospel and a short sermon.[30] Unfortunately, the main chant of the footwashing fell into disuse as early as the period of the Tridentine reforms. In most of the medieval Uses this was the first chant, and the celebrant performed the prescribed actions as they were being mentioned by the chant. The restoration of this chant is very desirable, as can be witnessed by the version here:[31]

After further chants (like *In hoc cognoscent, Maneant in vobis, Ubi caritas et amor*) and a closing Collect, the reading of the Farewell Discourse is introduced

[29] *Analecta hymnica*, vol. 51, p. 77.
[30] The Tridentine books already omitted the Epistle.
[31] *Graduale Strigonensis*, fol. 123v: 'Before the festival day of the Pasch, Jesus knowing that His hour was come, that He should pass from this world to the Father, when the supper was done, He riseth having taken a towel, girded Himself, He putteth water into a basin and began to wash the feet of the disciples. He cometh to Peter. And Peter saith to Him: Thou shalt never wash my feet. Jesus answered him: If I wash thee not, thou shalt have no part with Me. Lord, not only my feet, but also my hands and my head.' See also Sandon (1984), *The Use of Salisbury*, vol. 4, p. 86.

by the antiphon *Mandatum novum*. The discourse itself is sung on the Gospel tone until the words 'Surgite eamus hinc'[32] after which it is only read, without a melody. After the discourse – if there is no other ceremony, or if Compline does not follow – an appropriate hymn may bring the ceremony to a close.

Greater honour is rendered to the altars of the church if their stripping is followed by a ceremonial washing. In this case the priest pours water onto the four corners of the altars and spreads it carefully (using the branches from Palm Sunday or some other implement). Then the priest dries the altars with a cloth and pours some wine on the middle in the shape of a cross. In the meanwhile Psalm 21 is sung with the frequent refrain of the antiphon *Diviserunt*.[33] In churches and the houses of religious orders where side altars were also stripped and washed, the psalm was interrupted at each altar, and a responsory was sung with the proper Collect of the saint to whom the altar is dedicated. This custom has also a pastoral meaning: it is a reminder of the altar's Patron. Since singing a responsory might prolong the action unnecessarily, it would be enough to interrupt the psalmody with a short invocation, for instance: 'Intercessione beati N. adjuti percipiamus, Domine, quam plenius in his diebus gratiam beatae passionis et resurrectionis Jesu Christi. Amen.'[34]

IV. Good Friday

The postconciliar reforms touched upon the liturgy of Good Friday at two essential points: the first is the changes to the readings (together with their subsequent chants); the second is the rewording of the solemn prayers. Earlier, during the reform of Pius XII: (a) a Collect was placed before the first reading; (b) the *oratio pro Judaeis* was altered; (c) instead of the hymn *Vexilla regis* three antiphons were linked to the procession with the Host to the altar; (d) the possibility of receiving holy Communion was extended to the faithful; (e) the rite of Communion became rearranged and the whole congregation should on this very day, pray the Lord's Prayer together with the priest; and (f) the celebration was assigned a different conclusion with three beautiful Collects.

In fact, the Tridentine reform did not follow in every respect the ritual traditions of the earlier period either. The order of chants while the Cross was being brought into the sanctuary and then during its veneration was somewhat different to that of earlier practice (see below).

As things stand, it would be problematic to say that a simple return to the 1962 (or earlier) Missal would solve all the problems raised by the desire for a genuine restoration of the liturgy of this day. Each of the reforms that resulted in the 1962 rite contained elements worthy of remark.

---

[32] Jn 14.31.
[33] 'Diviserunt sibi vestimenta mea, et super vestam meam miserunt sortem' – 'They parted my garments amongst them, and upon my vesture they cast lots.'
[34] 'Helped by the intervention of saint N. grant us to know, O Lord, at the fullest during these days the grace of the blessed Passion and Resurrection of Jesus Christ. Amen.'

Up to the Vatican II reforms, a prophecy of Hosea (6.1-6) was read after the magnificent opening Collect, completed by the Tract, in a text taken from Habakkuk. The *Novus Ordo* altered this to become an extended text from Isaiah, a prophecy on the suffering Messiah. The subsequent canticle was also changed. Originally the second reading was the narration on the sacrifice of the Paschal Lamb (Exod. 12.1-11). The new reading is from the Letter to the Hebrews. The tract from Psalm 139 was also replaced.

In the reform that I am proposing to the 1962 form of Good Friday, the two original readings with their concomitant chants could, of course, be retained. It cannot be denied, however, that the text from Hosea has only a distant relation to the theme of the liturgical day (one reference: *in die tertia suscitabit nos*); while adopting the passage from the Letter to the Hebrews proved to be a real benefit. For reasons I have already explained,[35] I would suggest transferring the reading of the respected and important chapter of Isaiah to a different position in this liturgy. Therefore, it would be reasonable to transfer the reading concerning the sacrifice of the Paschal Lamb to the first place, and leave the reading from the Letter to the Hebrews currently found in the *Novus Ordo* as the second reading. The first tract (*Domine audivi*) is one of the most remarkable texts of our liturgy, which express the astonished devotion of the Church when contemplating a great deed of God;[36] so it must be preserved. For the second reading, however, the *Christus factus est* (in the form of a tract) would be perfectly suitable, instead of the *Eripe* (which in turn was only a substitute for the old Roman text that began *Qui habitat*[37]). Since the prophecy from Isaiah and the tract *Eripe* are exceptionally long, the new arrangement should make the section before the Passion a little more concise.

In the solemn prayers most changes found in the *Novus Ordo* are really superfluous, and they appear somewhat alien when compared to the old text. The rephrased orations for the unity of the Church and for the Jewish people, on the other hand, are tactfully worded and speak in a non-offensive tone about the same themes without any change in meaning.[38]

One more improvement, at least as an option, could be proposed for the solemn prayers. The celebrant calls the congregation to pray *for* (*Oremus pro . . .*), then the deacon admonishes them to kneel down (*Flectamus genua*), and after a short silence the subdeacon adds: *Levate* (Stand up).[39] Experience shows that as the prayer proceeds, the duration of kneeling gets shorter and shorter, and the movements follow each other too quickly. This incited the *Consilium* reformers

---

[35] See Chapter 17 (subsection III).

[36] It is also sung in the Christmas Office (verse of the responsories *Benedicta et venerabilis* or *Beata es et venerabilis; Ave Maria*); also in the responsory about the Fall of Adam, *Dum deambularet Dominus*. In the Old Beneventan office the tract was sung during Paschal Vigil after the reading of the Creation (Paléographie Musicale XIV, pp. 340–41)! It is also remarkable that in the Roman Office the full text of the canticle is sung from ancient times on in the Lauds of every Friday.

[37] *Monumenta Monodica Medii Aevi*, vol. 2, p. 646.

[38] In the meanwhile the text of the oration *pro Judaeis* of the 1962 Missal has been altered by the Holy Father Pope Benedict XVI himself.

[39] This role was denied to the subdeacon after the 1955 revisions, being transferred to the deacon: it should be restored to the subdeacon.

to make this old custom only optional. According to the rubrics of some medieval manuscripts, the subdeacon's *Levate* is sung only after the oration (or before its conclusion), and so the kneeling is a posture not only for silent prayer, but also of listening to the oration. (*Oremus pro . . . – Flectamus genua – oratio – Levate.*[40]) This is in harmony with the old rubric that normally the faithful should listen to the Collects standing, whereas during Lent they should kneel. With this new regulation the paragraphs of the texts and the bodily postures would follow each other in a more even and fitting sequence. The celebrant priest or bishop would, of course, stand (alone) for the orations.

In most medieval churches the order of bringing the Cross into the sanctuary was exactly like, or followed closely, what we find in the *Liber Ordinarius Agriensis* of Eger.

> After the prayers the clergy with the bishop and the deacons in his retinue descend to the Holy Cross altar. In the meantime two canons putting on red vestments for the Mass (chasuble) bring from the sacristy the cross covered with red chasuble with a *pacificale* on the chest and one of them sings slowly *Popule meus* while two young men (procedentes) putting on red dalmatics on top of the bare surplice walk in front of them with lighted candles; and these young men sing after each verse of *Popule meus: Agios o Theos*. The choir repeats after them: *Sanctus Deus, Sanctus fortis*. Walking slowly with the cross, they proceed to the bishop at the Holy cross altar. After having finished *Popule meus* with all of its verses the bishop and two canons raise the cross[41] and he sings in a lamentable voice: *Ecce lignum crucis*. The choir continues with *In quo salus mundi*. While doing so, they slightly remove the chasuble from the cross. The bishop sings *Ecce lignum crucis* a second time, raising his voice a bit higher and unveiling the cross even more. The bishop sings *Ecce lignum crucis* a third time in a similar way, raising his voice sorrowfully and unveiling also the front of cross completely. The choir continues with *In quo salus mundi* together with the verse *Beati immaculati*. And the bishop salutes and kisses the cross while the choir sings *Dum fabricator mundi*. And the canons also salute and kiss the cross in the order of age. Likewise the whole clergy while the children sing: *Crux fidelis*.[42]

---

[40] For example, Oremus et pro beatissimo papa nostro . . . – Oremus. Flectamus genua. – Omnipotens sempiterne Deus . . . augeatur. – Levate. – Per Dominum nostrum. (*Missale Notatum Strigoniense ante 1341 in Posonio*, fol. 110; also in other medieval Missals).

[41] They do not sing, merely assist the bishop in raising the Cross.

[42] Dobszay (2000), *Liber Ordinarius Agriensis*, Nr. 226): 'Finitis orationibus descendat clerus ante altare Sancte Crucis episcopo cum astantibus ipsos sequente. Interim duo canonici rubeis casulis induti de sacrastia exportant crucifixum coopertum casula rubea et habentem in pectore pacificale unum, cantantes lenta voce Popule meus. Et duo procedentes super suprapellicium solum dalmaticis rubeis induti ipsos cum lucernis ardentibus precedunt, et post singulum versum Popule meus ipsi procedentes cantent: "Ayos o Theos" choro post ipsos repetente: "Sanctus Deus, sanctus fortis". Interim cum crucifixo lente venientes ducunt ad altare Sancte Crucis ad episcopum. Finito Popule meus cum suis versibus tandem episcopus cum illis duobus canonicis primum levando crucifixum cantent Ecce lignum crucis flebili voce choro prosequente In quo salus mundi. Interim parum levent casulam super crucifixo. Secunda vice iterum episcopus cantet

In the Tridentine Rite the Cross is brought in without any chant, and the chant *Popule meus* is sung during the adoration of the Cross.[43] Earlier I analysed the inconveniences of this arrangement.[44] If making appeal once again to pre-Tridentine practices, the ceremony could proceed today in the following way.[45]

The Cross (dressed, as in the Middle Ages in a red chasuble, signifying sacrifice, or as today, covered by a veil) is brought in by the deacon (accompanied behind by two singers, if the deacon cannot sing). The two acolytes are younger men able to sing (or if they are not able, then are accompanied by two younger singers or children). During the procession they halt three times. At each station the deacon sings one section of the *Improperia* (the first *Popule meus* in the *Liber Usualis*). The acolytes answer with the *Hagios*, the choir and congregation with the *Sanctus*. The Trisagion can also be sung by two half choirs. The most fitting for the liturgical habits of our day would be, however, if the three acclamations were alternatively sung between the two acolytes or the two half choirs in Greek and Latin, and then repeated by the congregation in the vernacular (*Hagios* / *Sanctus* / Holy). A simple recitative form of the whole piece is needed for parochial and smaller churches.

After the third station the procession arrives before the celebrant, who takes up the Cross, and unveils it with the three-fold intonation of *Ecce lignum crucis*. In many churches the celebrant cannot sing the intonation correctly, especially the phrase 'in quo salus . . .' (In the Middle Ages at this point the choir joined in.) Since the intonation is not a privileged priestly function (the rubrics assign the singing to the celebrant only because of the dignity of the chant), this difficulty is easily overcome if two good singers stand in front of the Cross, six to nine feet to the right and left, who sing the antiphon while perhaps extending their arms towards the Cross. The assembly join with the refrain (as in the *Improperia*).

In many medieval churches the cycle of chants during the adoration was initiated with the monumental antiphon, *Dum fabricator*, which would be a felicitous reintroduction into the rite in cathedrals and major churches. The text is as follows.

> Dum fabricator mundi mortis supplicium pateretur in cruce, clamans voce magna tradidit Spiritum. Et ecce velum templi divisum est, monumenta aperta sunt, terraemotus enim factus est magnus; quia mortem Filii Dei clamat mundus se sustinere non posse. Aperto ergo lancea militis latere crucifixi Domini exivit sanguis et aqua in redemptionem salutis nostrae.

Ecce lignum crucis parum altius levando vocem et ipsum crucifixum similiter melius aperiendo. Tercia vice similiter episcopus cantet Ecce lignum crucis flebiliter, altius levando vocem, et crucifixum abante totaliter discooperiatur choro repetente In quo salus mundi cum versu Beati immaculati. Et episcopus salutet et osculetur crucifixum. Interim chorus cantet Dum fabricator mundi. Et domini secundum senium salutent et osculentur crucifixum. Similiter et totus clerus cantantibus pueris Crux fidelis.'

[43] This is probably the original, simpler rite of Rome, as can be seen in the Old Roman antiphonary of St Cecilia. Max Lütolf (1987), *Das Graduale von Santa Cecilia in Trastevere (Cod. Bodmer 74),* fol. 76r.

[44] Dobszay (2003), *The Bugnini-Liturgy and the Reform of the Reform*, pp. 35–36.

[45] Cf. also Sandon (1984), *The Use of Salisbury*, vol. 4, pp. 97–99.

V) O admirablile pretium, cujus pondere captivitas redempta est mundi, tartarea confracta sunt claustra inferni, aperta est nobis janua regni!'[46]

The series of chants during the long procession for the adoration of the Cross could be extended by the hymn *Vexilla Crucis*, the antiphon *Nos autem gloriari*, or a section of the sequence *Laudes Crucis attollamus*.[47] In the postconciliar period many quite inappropriate hymns have been employed at this point by virtue of local decisions; it would be very useful if a list of hymns and motets were made available in dioceses from which any choice can be made.

According to the 1962 Missal, the Hosts for holy Communion are brought to the altar while the hymn *Vexilla Crucis* is sung. Today this is done in silence. Before the Tridentine reform a hymn was sung in many churches, which explained the inseparable relationship between the sacrifice of the Cross and the Eucharist. It began:[48]

Lau-des o-mni-pot-ens fe-ri-mus ti-bi do-na co-len-tes cor-po-ris im-men-si san-gui-nis at - que tu-i. Laudes. Pan-gi-mus ec-ce tu-am rec-tor san-ctis-si-me men-sam, tu, li-cet in-di-gnis pro-pi-ti-a - re tu-is. Laudes. Etc.

In many local churches the celebrant while elevating the Host intoned the Communion 'Hoc corpus quod pro vobis tradetur . . .', which was followed by the choir.[49]

---

[46] 'When the Creator of the world suffered, condemned to death on the cross, crying with a loud voice, he yielded up his spirit. And behold the veil of the temple was rent, the graves were opened, there was a great earthquake, for the world exclaimed that it could not bear the death of God's son. And as the soldier pierced the side of the crucified Lord, forthwith came there out blood and water for our salvation. V. O miraculous ransom, whose weight redeemed the world from capitivity, the locks of hell burst asunder, and the gate of heaven opened up to us.' For the melody see Sandon (1984), *The Use of Salisbury*, vol. 4, pp. 103–04, *Sarum Processional*, fol. 63r, *Missale Notatum Strigoniense ante 1341 in Posonio*, fol. 111.

[47] For the text see: Dreves and Blume (1909), *Ein Jahrtausend Lateinischer Hymnendichtung*, pp. 262–3; for the melody (which is identical with that of the Lauda Sion) see Benjamin Rajeczky (1982), *Melodiarium Hungariae Medii Aevi; Sequenzen*, vol. 2, p. 52.

[48] *Missale Notatum Strigoniense*, fol. 112v: 'We offer thee praise, Almighty God, celebrating the immense gifts of thy body and blood. Now we sing, O King, at thy most holy Table, though we are unworthy, have mercy on us.'

[49] 'The archdeacon extends a corporale onto the bare altar. The bishop ascends and kisses the

In every other respect, the order of 1962 Missal could be regarded as definitive.

Accordingly, here is the 'proposed' scheme of the full celebration:

	In cathedral churches	In parish churches
Prayer	Deus qui peccati	Deus qui peccati
Reading	Hos. 6.1-6 vel: Exod. 12.1-11	Hos. 6.1-6 vel: Exod. 12.1-11
Tract	Domine audivi	Domine audivi
Prayer	Reminiscere	Reminiscere
Reading	Exod. 12.1-11 vel: Heb. 4.14-5.10	Exod. 12.1-11 vel: Heb. 4.14-5.10
Tract	Eripe me	Eripe me vel: Tract. Christus factus
Passion	Jn 18.1-40; 19.1-42	Jn 18.1-40; 19.1-42
The great intercessions	ut in missali	ut in missali
Exhibition of the Holy Cross	**Forma A:** Popule meus I Ecce lignum **Forma B:** Ecce lignum Popule meus I	**Forma A:** Popule meus I Ecce lignum **Forma B:** Ecce lignum Popule meus I
Adoration of the Cross	A. Dum fabricator mundi A. Crucem tuam + Ps. 66 Hy. Crux fidelis Popule meus II a. Crucem tuam + Ps. 66 Hy. Crux fidelis a. Cum Rex gloriae Sequ. Laudes Crucis Hy. Vexilla Regis a. Adoramus te Christe) a. Per lignum servi a. Salvator mundi salva nos	a. Crucem tuam + Ps. 66 Hy. Crux fidelis a. Adoramus te Christe Sequ. Laudes Crucis attollamus Hy. Vexilla Regis a. Nos autem gloriari aliae antiphonae, cantiones et mutetae
Communion procession:	Laudes omnipotens vel alius hymnus	sub silentio

(continued)

altar, saying the words of the common confession, then taking the Host from the hands of the archdeacon sings: This is the Body given for you . . .' (*Missale Notatum Strigoniense*, fol. 112v).

	In cathedral churches	In parish churches
Communion	Hoc est corpus, cantiones	Hoc est corpus, cantiones
Postcommunion prayers	Super populum tuum Omnipotens . . . qui Christi Reminiscere miserationum	Super populum tuum Omnipotens . . . qui Christi Reminiscere miserationum

V. The Paschal Vigil

The most miserable result of the 1970 reform is the upset visited on the most Holy Night of the liturgical year.[50] Already the earlier reforms of Pope Pius XII – besides introducing a number of beneficial changes – caused some disturbance to this most venerable of liturgical celebrations.[51] The reform of Pope Pius XII abrogated the proper function of the Exsultet and cut the Litany in two.

Consequently, even if it is reasonable to regard the 1962 Missal as the standard, it would be salutary to make some modifications, or more correctly: restorations. There are a few points where new elements could be proposed to provide a degree of choice.

Such is, for instance, the restoration (at least *ad libitum*) of the beautiful hymn by Prudentius (*Inventor rutili dux bone*), which was used to open the celebration in many medieval churches,[52] but was abolished in the Tridentine reform. The first verse is a refrain, appropriate for congregational singing either in Latin or in the vernacular (even in darkness); three strophes follow the procession to the fire, and the verse *Tu lux vera* together with the refrain is suitable for the period after the procession but before the Exsultet, while the assistants take their positions in the sanctuary.[53]

In -ven -tor ru - ti -li dux bo -ne lu -mi -nis qui cer -tis vi -ci -bus tem -po -ra

di - vi -dis mer -so so -le cha -os in -gru -it hor -ri -dum, lu -men red -de tu -is

Chri -ste fi - de - li - bus. Inventor...

---

[50] Cf. Dobszay (2003), *The Bugnini-Liturgy and the Reform of the Reform*, pp. 37–43.

[51] Klaus Gamber (2002), *The Modern Rite*, pp. 80–2; Reid (2005), *The Organic Development of the Liturgy*, pp. 219–34.

[52] Or: to accompany the solemn entering the Church after the fire was blessed. See Sandon (1984), *The Use of Salisbury*, vol. 4, pp. 109–11.

[53] The variant is taken from the Gradual of Ferenc Futaki, p. 1463 (now in Istanbul, Topkapi Sreail Library).

V/1. Quamvis innumero sidere regiam, / lunarique polum lampade pinxeris, incussu silicis lumina nos tamen / monstras saxigeno semine quaerere. Inventor...

V/2. Ne nesciret homo spem sibi luminis / in Christi solido corpore conditam, qui dici stabilem se voluit petram, / nostris igniculis unde genus venit. Inventor...

V/3. Tu lux ver(a) oculis, lux quoque sensibus, / intus tu speculum, tu speculum foris, lumen, quod famulans offero, suscipe, / tinctum paciferi chrismatis unguine. Inventor...

In addition to the two Collects in the 1962 Missal for the blessing of the fire and incense, I now include a third one from medieval use, which makes an admirable opening for the holy night:

Omnipotens sempiterne Deus, mundi Conditor, luminis siderumque fabricator, per cujus ineffabilem potentiam omnis claritas sumpsit exordium, te in tuis operibus invocamus, aperi nobis, quaesumus, labia nostra ad confitendum nomini tuo, et ad laudem gloriae tuae, ut digne celebrare mereamur sacrum officium tuum, quia in hac sacratissima noctis vigilia de donis tuis Cereum tuae suppliciter offerimus majestati. Per Dominum . . .[54]

The difference in comparison to the 1962 Missal is that the phrase *Christus heri* . . . would be shifted from here to the Exsultet, and the flame would be brought in the church on the three-forked candle (trident). After the three *Lumen Christi* acclamations the third strophe of the hymn *Inventor* could be sung while the *Exsultet* is prepared.

The Exsultet is not simply a Praeconium or hymn of praise, but also an actual consecration of the taper.[55] Theological, liturgical and pastoral arguments support the restoration of this function. The actions interrupting the long text are useful even to maintain people's attention. The words introduced by the reform of Pope Pius XII (*Christus heri* . . .) can be inserted in the Exsultet before the words *In huius igitur* (similarly to the insertion of *Haec nobis praecepta* in the Preface for the blessing of the Font).

The ordinary singer of the Exsultet is the deacon, but in cases of necessity it is better to appoint a good singer for this function if the alternative is merely to read the text. If the singer is not ordained in the proper grade, the Prologue would carry an adaptation that excludes the reference to the order of Levites

---

[54] *Missale Notatum Strigoniense*, fol. 113v: 'Almighty, everlasting God, the Creator of the world, maker of light and the stars, whose unspeakable power is the origin of all splendour, we invoke thy name upon these creatures of thine; we beseech thee to open our lips to confess thee, to give praise to thy glory, that we may worthily celebrate this sacred office; when we offer to thy majesty in this most holy night Vigil this Candle taken from what have received from thee.'

[55] Dobszay (2003), *The Bugnini-Liturgy and the Reform of the Reform*, pp. 39–40.

(deacons); and the Preface-dialogue would be led by the celebrant, who would take over the blessing and lighting of the Candle.

The reforms of Pope Piux XII reduced the number of readings to four, a judicious number in accordance with an existing tradition.[56] If the tract *Jubilate* were taken over from the *Novus Ordo* (after the reading of the Creation account) then all the four readings would be accompanied by a canticle. However, in order to preserve the ancient 12-reading arrangement (together with its marvellous Collects) from being lost entirely, this larger cycle should also be included in the liturgical books, with an indication that their use in cathedral and larger churches would be preferable.[57]

There is a difficulty with the framing of the Baptismal ceremony. At one time it began very appropriately with the tract *Sicut cervus*. In the reform of Pope Pius XII, the second part of the Litany is sung *after* the blessing while the clergy are in procession to the sanctuary, which is illogical. A yet worse arrangement was invented by the architects of the *Novus Ordo*, who transposed the consecration of the Font to after the Gospel of the Mass.[58] In the pre-Tridentine rite the Litany of the Saints was sung after the tract, and the procession returned to the sanctuary during another Litany, with a Kyrie at the end, which also marked the beginning of the Mass. This is surely the correct arrangement, for in it the quality and sacred function of the two Litanies are clearly distinguished. The Litany of the Saints as sung within the Vigil was shorter in the Middle Ages: the list of saints was shorter, with the focus of the third part on the sanctification of the Font. This is very proportionate and appropriate to the length of the rite. After the blessing of the Font a strophic Litany was used in the Middle Ages, which was clearly related to the sacrament of Baptism (see verses 5–8):

R. Rex sanctorum angelorum totum mundum adjuva!

V/1. Ora primum tu pro nobis virgo mater germinis, et ministri Patris summi ordines angelici. R.

. . .

V/6. Mitte sanctam nunc amborum Spiritum Paraclitum in hanc plebem, quam recentem fons baptismi parturit. R.

V/7. Fac in terra fontis hujus sacratum mysterium, qui profluxit cum cruore sacro Christi corpore. R.

V/8. Et laetetur mater sancta tota nunc Ecclesia ex profectu renascentis tantae multitudinis. R.

---

[56] This was the most usual number also in the Middle Ages. *Missale Notatum Strigoniense*, fol. 116v–118v; Sandon (1984), *The Use of Salisbury*, vol. 4, pp. 119–25, and many other sources.
[57] The seven-reading system of the *Novus Ordo* is without roots or antecedent in the tradition.
[58] Dobszay (2003), *The Bugnini-Liturgy and the Reform of the Reform*, pp. 41–42.

V/9. Praesta Patris atque Nati compar Sancte Spiritus, ut te solum semper omni diligamus tempore. R.[59]

The chanting of the Kyrie that follows this makes a transition into the Mass itself.

It can never be emphasized enough that the ceremony of the Vigil is not a part of the Mass (the architects of the *Novus Ordo* clearly failed to see this), but a ceremony in its own right.[60]

The Vigil liturgy is a series of events endowed with its own logic and progressing with dramatic dynamism; after it is concluded the assembly celebrates the Eucharist together with the newly baptized. There are visible signs that indicate this dramatic drift. The altar stands bare until the Mass. The priest celebrates in a cope or even simply in an alb; the colour is red or violet; the deacon dons a white dalmatic for the singing of the Exsultet, but it is laid aside afterwards. Once the Baptismal ceremony is over, the altar is dressed and lit, and the priest puts on solemn Mass vestments.

The order of the Mass in the 1962 Missal is traditional and needs no change to restore it to the classical Roman tradition. There are two tropes in local traditions of the Middle Ages which would make fine additions (at least in an appendix to the rite). In many churches the celebrant was invited by the deacon or other singers to intone the Gloria with the following words: 'Sacerdos Dei excelsi, veni ante sacrum et sanctum altare, ut in laude Regis regum vocem tuam emitte. Supplices te deprecamus, et petimus dic, domne (Gloria in excelsis).'[61]

The alleluia – after its long absence – was also introduced by a trope:

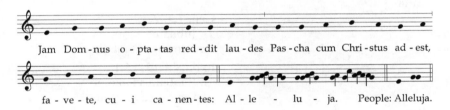

Jam Dom-nus o-pta-tas red-dit lau-des Pas-cha cum Chri-stus ad-est,

fa-ve-te, cu-i ca-nen-tes: Al-le - lu - ja.   People: Alleluja.

---

[59] 'O King of the holy angels, help to the whole world. V) Pray for us, first of all, Thou, the virgin mother of the Son, and also the ministers of the Father, the high orders of Angels. R . . . V) Send now your Holy Ghost the Paraclete upon this people who are born by this baptismal font. R. V) Open the holy mystery of this font in the earth (the water) that was poured out with blood from Christ's holy Body. R. V) Let now the whole Church rejoice as mother of the great multitude of her newly born children. R. V) Grant, O Father and Son, and equal to them, O Holy Ghost, that at all times we may ever love only you. R.' *Missale Notatum Strigoniense*, fol. 122. It was regularly sung also in the Sarum Use; see the full text with melody in Sandon (1984), *The Use of Salisbury*, vol. 4, pp. 133–5.

[60] Dobszay (2003), *The Bugnini-Liturgy and the Reform of the Reform*, pp. 41–42.

[61] 'O priest of the most high God, come to the holy and sacred altar, and raise there your voice in the praise of the King of kings. We humbly pray and beseech you, proclaim it loudly (Gloria in excelsis).' Cf. Thomas F. Kelly (1984), 'Introducing the Gloria in Excelsis', pp. 479–506.

During the Communion an abbreviated Vespers was sung (Alleluia, Psalm 116, the antiphon *Vespere autem* with the Magnificat). Unfortunately, this is omitted in the *Novus Ordo*. Given that the celebration of the Vigil has (since 1951 and 1955) been moved to the night, this Vesperal act has been replaced by an equally shortened Lauds (Alleluia, Psalm 150, antiphon *Valde mane* with the Benedictus), a solution that is quite fitting.

In some countries a procession followed, outside the church. Now the Vigil has been transferred to the night, this is no longer really fitting. In those countries where this tradition is still remembered the Vigil Mass could be concluded by solemnly returning the Blessed Sacrament to the tabernacle, and then singing the *Te Deum*. On the other hand, it would be praiseworthy to restore the great procession before the Sunday High Mass (along with the *Ludus Paschalis*),[62] as was customary in the Middle Ages.

The difference between larger and smaller churches should not be more than that of simplifying the tunes for the chants, and permitting the parish churches to celebrate the Vigil in the vernacular up until the offertory.

Blessing of the fire	(Hy. Inventor rutili) or. Omnipotens . . . mundi or. Deus qui per Filium or. Veniat . . . super hoc
Procession	Lumen Christi (ter) (Hy. Inventor rutili)
Blessing of the Candle	Exsultet (+Christus heri)
Readings[63]	or. Gen. 1.1–2.3 Tr. Jubilate or. Deus qui mirabiliter
	Exod. 14.15–15.1 Tr. Cantemus Domino or. Deus cujus antiqua
	Isa. 4.2-6 or 5.1-7 Tr. Vinea facta est or. Deus qui in omnibus
	Deut. 31.22-30 Tr. Attende caelum or. Deus, celsitudo
Procession to the Font	Tr. Sicut cervus Litania

[62] A collection of different settings is Walther Lipphardt (1975–81), *Lateinische Osterfeiern und Osterspiele. I–VI.*

[63] In cathedral churches 12 readings *ad libitum*.

Blessing of Font	or. Omnipotens . . . adesto praefatio (baptismus) renovatio promissionum
Procession to the altar	(Hy. Rex sanctorum) Kyrie
Gloria	(trope: Sacerdos Dei excelsi)
Prayer	Deus qui hanc
Epistle	Col. 3.1-4
Allelluia	(trope: Jam domnus optatas) Confitemini
Tract	Laudate
Gospel	Mt. 28.1-7
Offertory	–
Secret	Suscipe quaesumus
Agnus	–
For the Lauds	a. All. + Ps. 150 a. Et valde mane + Bndcs
Postcommunion prayer	Spiritum nobis

VI. The 'Gloriosum Officium'

In the pre-Tridentine period, the celebration of Easter Day was closed by a joyful 'Baptismal Vespers' repeated over each day of the whole Easter Octave. Amalarius, the renowned liturgist, most appropriately referred to this Office with the words *Gloriosum Officium*.[64] The birthplace of this rite was the 'Mother of all Churches', the Lateran basilica and Cathedral of the Pope,[65] where, following an abbreviated Vespers, the newly baptized were led into the Baptistery. After honouring the Font, they were led to the chapel of the Holy Cross, the place where they had received the sacrament of Confirmation on the night of the Vigil. After procession returned to the basilica, the pope made a gift of excellent wines to those who had diligently assisted in the rites of Holy Week.[66]

This rite spread from the 'Mother and Head' of all basilicas to the cathedrals and parish churches of the continent, with the only difference that, in the absence of a separate building for the rite, the procession went to the Font instead of any

---

[64] *Monumenta Monodica Medii Aevi*, vol, 2, pp. *119, *149.
[65] *Monumenta Monodica Medii Aevi*, vol. 2, pp. *84–*118.
[66] 'Deinde descendunt primates ecclesiae ad accubita, invitante notario sive vicedomini, et bibunt ter: de graeco (vino) primo, de pactisi secundo, de procovia tertio. *Monumenta Monodica Medii Aevi*, vol. 2, pp. *118, cf. *87.

Baptistery, and a station was held before the Great Crucifix that hung from the rood or triumphal Sanctuary Arc, commemorating the station at the chapel of the Holy Cross. These Baptismal Vespers were celebrated everywhere[67] except in those monastic churches and the chapel(s) of the papal court-officials (following the *Ritus Curiae*) where there was no baptismal Font. Under the influence of the curial rite, one of the most beautiful moments of the Roman liturgy was abandoned in the Tridentine reform. It would have been fitting to the genuine spirit of Vatican II – and so could be said to be an obligation for a true reform in its name – to restore this Vespers, adapted to the conditions of our day.

In the order of the Baptismal Vespers there are some conspicuous character-istics. Some of these are enduring archaisms (the omission of the versicle *Deus in adjutorium*, the Chapter/*Capitulum* and the Hymn; and also the inclusion of a Kyrie at the beginning). Other features relate to the degree of solemnity of the day (the inclusion of the Gradual and Alleluia chants from the Mass); again other items are particular to the baptismal procession. Since this ceremony is unknown even for many of those who are interested in the liturgy, I have suggested below a form in which it could be restored.[68]

Vespers starts with a solemn Kyrie instead of the customary versicle.[69] Then Psalms 109–11 are sung according to the Vespers of Sunday, followed by the Gradual and Alleluia taken from the Proper of the Mass of Easter Day. This abbreviated celebration of Vespers is closed by the choir singing the Magnificat and the Collect for the day. The procession then forms: a crucifer leads servers bearing the consecrated oils from the Mass of the Chrism, the Paschal Candle (which is taken down and brought into the procession), incense thurifer, and banners. The procession lines up while the antiphon *Vidi aquam* is sung.[70] During the procession to the baptismal Font, Psalms 112–13 are sung.[71] At the Font an appropriate chant (for instance, the Alleluia *Nonne cor nostrum*) can be sung, while the priest censes the Font and the holy oils. Taking into account modern conditions and expectations, the celebration at this point could be extended with a short admonition (perhaps with a fixed text), calling the faithful to honour the

---

[67] It was also integrated in the Office of some religious orders that were based on a priestly environ-ment, like Praemonstratensians (*Breviarium Ordo Praemonstratensis. Pars Verna*, pp. 451–66), Augustinians (*Klosterneuburg Antiphonary* 1010, fol. 147r–v), etc.

[68] From 1969 on this Office has been restored in several churches in Hungary. Cf. *Népzsolozsmák* (Folk Offices), pp. 55–63.

[69] 'In secundis vesperis non dicitur Deus in adjutorium, sed canitur Kyrie eleison nonies' – 'At second Vespers, Deus in adjutorium is not said, but Kyrie is sung nine times' (from the *Eger Ordinary*: Dobszay (2000), *Liber Ordinarius Agriensis*, Nr. 241).

[70] 'Praeparent se ad fontem cum vexillis, crismate, oleo, tangendo in organo vel cantando *Vidi aquam*' – 'They prepare themselves for the procession to the font with banners, the chrism, oil, while *Vidi aquam* is played on an organ or is sung' (Dobszay (2000), *Liber Ordinarius Agriensis*, Nr. 241).

[71] In the restored form in Hungary (1968) verses 1-8 of Psalms 113 are sung with a simple Alleluia-antiphon.

holy water and the oils.[72] After a versicle and oration[73] the procession returns to the sanctuary singing the Great Antiphon *Christus resurgens* (or other appropriate Easter chant), but stops for a station in the nave, turning towards the Cross. Here again a versicle and oration[74] are recited, and upon entering the choir and sanctuary the celebration ends with the Easter tone of the versicle *Benedicamus domino*.

The scheme is as follows:

	In cathedral churches	In parish churches
Psalmody	a. Angelus autem Ps. 109 a. Et ecce terraemotus Ps. 110 a. Erat autem aspectu Ps. 111	ant. sola: Alleluia Ps. 109–11
Instead of the chapter etc.	Gr. Haec dies. V. Confitemini All. V. Pascha nostrum. V2. Epulemur	*in tono simplici:* Haec dies. V. Confitemini All. V. Pascha nostrum. V2. Epulemur
Antiphon to the Magnificat	a. Et respicientes + Mgt.	a. Alleluia Resurrexit Dominus + Mgt.

(*continued*)

---

[72] In the restored form in Hungary the celebrant says: 'Recordamini, fratres sacramenti nostri baptismi, idest aquae hujus fontis. Recordamini, quod haec est aqua quae lavit scelera peccatorum vestrorum, et virtute Spiritus vos regeneravit in puritatem filiorum Dei per Dominum nostrum Jesum Christum Redemptorem et Judicem hujus saeculi. Clamemus ergo cum reverentia: Ave fons baptismatis!' Populus: **'Ave fons baptismatis!'** ('Remember, O brethren the sacrament of our baptism, that is, of the water of this font. Remember, that this is the water that washed away the dirt of your sins, and regenerated you in the purity of the children of God, through our Lord Jesus Christ, our Redeemer and the Judge of this world. Therefore let us cry with reverence: Hail, O Baptismal Font. Faithful: Hail, O Baptismal Font!')
'Similiter honoremus, carissimi, etiam adventum olei et chrismatis nuper consecrati, gratias Deo agentes, qui hanc creaturam virtute Spiritus Sancti redemptionis suae instrumentum reddidit. Recordamini, quod postquam ex aqua et Spiritu renati estis, hoc oleum sanctum recepistis velut signum sanationis vestrae, et accepistis etiam sanctum chrisma id est unctionem sacerdotum, regum ac prophetarum velut signum christianae dignitatis. Clamemus ergo cum reverentia: Ave sacrum oleum!' Populus: **'Ave sacrum oleum!'** ('In like manner let us honour, my beloved brethren, the advent of the oil and chrism consecrated in these days. Let us give thanks to God, who through the virtue of the Holy Ghost made these creatures the instrument of our redemption. Remember, that after you were reborn from water and Spirit, you received this oil, as a sign of your healing, and received also the holy chrism, the unction of kings and prophets, as a sign of your Christian dignity. Therefore let us cry with reverence: Hail, O Holy Oil! R.: Hail, O Holy Oil!')

[73] 'Deus, qui credentes in te populos gratiae tuae largitate multiplicas, respice propitius ad electionem tuam, ut qui sacramento baptismatis sunt renati, regni caelestis mereantur introitum' – 'O God, who by the grace of Thy generosity multiplies the number of people who believe in Thee, look down with loving-kindness upon Thy election, that those who have been reborn in the sacrament of baptism, may deserve to enter in the heavenly reign' (*Breviarium Ordo Praemonstratensis. Pars Verna*, p. 451).

[74] 'Deus qui nos fecisti hodierna dei paschalia festa celebrare, fac, nos, quaesumus, in caelesti regno gaudere' – 'God, who gave us to celebrate the Paschal solemnity on this day, let us, we beseech Thee, rejoice in the heavenly reign' (*Breviarium Ordo Praemonstratensis. Pars Verna*. p. 452). Both orations change daily during the Octave and this set is a fine source of baptismal theology.

	In cathedral churches	In parish churches
Prayer	Deus qui hodierna die	Deus qui hodierna die
Chant before the procession	a. Vidi aquam	a. Vidi aquam
Procession to the Font	a. Prae timore Ps. 112. a. Respondens autem PS. 113	a. Alleluia Ps. 113.1-8
At the Font	(All. Nonne cor nostrum) monitio V) Quoniam apud te est Or. Deus quo omnes in Christo	(All. Nonne cor nostrum) monitio V) Quoniam apud te est Or. Deus quo omnes in Christo
Return and statio	A. Christus resurgens V) Dicite in nationibus Or. Deus qui nos fecisti Benedicamus	A. Christus resurgens *vel hymnus de resurrectione* V) Dicite in nationibus Or. Deus qui nos fecisti Benedicamus

SUMMARY

I have reached the end of what I wanted to say. And now I beg the patience of my reader, once again, to return to the first pages of this book and, having become familiar with the details of my various proposals, to read those early pages again.

Many particular matters required discussion, which has not only been strenuous but has also made it difficult to keep the whole picture in perspective. Allow me, therefore, to make a summary of all the main guiding principles.

The Roman Rite preserved its identity over a period of 1,500 years, yet all this time it developed continuously and organically. The will of the Second Vatican Council was to reform *this* living Roman Rite, and not therefore to create a new liturgy.[1] Contrary to this intention, the *Consilium*, under Archbishop Bugnini, manufactured a new liturgy that broke the ancient continuity of the classical Roman Rite. The solution can only be to return to the situation of the rite in 1962, not in order to stop there, but to implement the intended conciliar reform in small, genuinely organic, steps. These steps will take the way that was already foreseen, even before the Council, and in the manner actually intended by the Council itself. The only sure points of orientation are the latest editions of the preconciliar liturgical books. But to exclude in principle the possibility of introducing certain minor reforms would not only be a categorical renunciation of the Council, but would also be tantamount to immuring the Roman Rite in a ghetto, restricted to the limited group of its staunchest supporters. In the course of a true reform one has to consider attentively not only the expectations of the Second Vatican Council, but also the pre-1962 and pre-Tridentine elements of the classical Roman Rite, and without an ideological aversion to including elements of the *Novus Ordo*, aspects of this too could be integrated inasmuch as they represent genuine historical developments. This book is not intended as a proposal for an exact itinerary, but seeks to show that such a reform, a real 'organic development', *can* be accomplished without ruining or abandoning the classical Roman Rite in the style of the Bugnini-led *Consilium*. In this I have taken the 1962 liturgical books as a point of departure, and here I mention only the suggested alterations in the summary below.

---

[1] Klaus Gamber (2002), *The Modern Rite*, pp. 77–82.

1. The *Office* returns in terms of its structure and distribution of psalms to the ancient Roman system, as it was before the 1911 breviary reform. The continuous course of the psalmody of Matins (and optionally also the Vespers), *can,* however, be distributed over a period longer than one week.

    The content of the liturgy is the full Roman Office, but its course may be said according to the schemes of 'Full Form', 'Common Form' or 'Brief Form' following the regulations or specific legislation of a given ecclesiastical body.

    The antiphonary is made available in two forms. The first is a reduced (basic) repertory that makes the singing easier by optional rubrics (singing the psalms under a single antiphon, the principle of sets and so forth). The other form draws as richly as possible upon the repertory of antiphons and responsories developed and composed in the course of long centuries.

2. In the *calendar*, for the sake of properly differentiating the observation of commemorations, the hierarchy of a six-degree system – in use before the twentieth-century rearrangement – is restored.

    In the Temporal Cycle the 1962 disposition is valid, but two modern feasts (Holy Family, Christ the King) receive a more appropriate location.

    In the Sanctoral Cycle the number of commemorations observed universally and mandatorily is reduced, while that of *ad libitum* commemorations drawn from local calendars increases.

3. The *readings of the Mass* follow the age-old system of pericopes as found in the 1962 Missal, except the Epistles and Gospels of the Third, Fourth and Fifth Sundays of Lent, which are replaced by more suitable and more traditional texts.

    In obedience to §51 of the Liturgical Constitution *Sacrosanctum Concilium*, the number of biblical texts available in the Lectionary increases, namely:

    (a) Before the Epistle, a first reading is given for the half-year from Advent to Pentecost.

    (b) The lectionary offers two pairs of readings to be used on two free weekdays during the week, throughout the year.

    (c) In *Ordinary Time*, besides the traditional series of pericopes, an alternative series is composed for a year B.

4. The *proper chants of the Mass* are as they stand in the classical *Graduale Romanum* with the following additions:

    (a) The second verse of the Introits, the second verse of some older double Alleluias, the Offertory verses, and a selection of psalm verses for Communion chants are included in the liturgical books for use *ad libitum.*

    (b) Some valuable older chants of the pre-Tridentine books are reintroduced into the *Graduale Romanum* as alternative items.

    (c) The *Graduale Romanum* is amplified with more Sequences (partly for use *ad libitum).*

    (d) For smaller churches a *Graduale Parvum* is suggested, compiled from texts taken over from the *Gradale Romanum*, but (i) with an arrangement of some items for use over a longer season rather than a single day;

(ii) with freedom to adapt simpler melodies (for instance, antiphons); (iii) some items are abbreviated in a way that the omitted phrases are transferred from the given antiphon into its verses; and (iv) the Gradual chant is presented in the form of a sung responsorial psalm.

5. The *Sacramentarium Gregorianum* is restored essentially in its traditional form.

The series of Collects, Secrets, and Postcommunions is augmented by texts taken from the ancient Sacramentaries for *ad libitum* use on weekdays.

The 1962 repertory of the Prefaces is raised to around 25 (with additions for Advent, Dedication, Corpus Christi, solemnities of saints, ordinary Sundays, etc.).

The Roman Canon regains its privileged position as the stable principal form.

6. The *Order of Mass* as given in the 1962 Missal does not suffer any essential change in its ceremony, structure and texts.

The penitential act (as a public rite: *Asperges* or *Confiteor*) if it is to take place, comes *before* Mass begins.

A small alteration is made between the Gospel and the Offertory; the Gospel is followed by the homily, the Prayer of the Faithful (from set texts) *ad libitum*, the Peace of the Faithful, and the Creed.

A few alternative texts can be added to the private prayers of the priest (at the foot of the altar, at the offertory, before Communion).

Contrary to the previous (and 1962) rubrics, the Secret or 'Prayer over the Gifts', the doxology at the end of the Canon and the Embolism are sung or said aloud.

7. The Liturgy of Holy Week remains in its essentials the same as in the 1962 Missal, but it is presented in two variants: one for larger and another for smaller churches. The aim of this double-arrangement is to assist smaller churches in ensuring worthy celebrations, while the cathedral traditions of greater churches are duly preserved.

The order of celebration follows – except in the use of the *Psalterium Pianum* – the reform of Pope Pius XII, but some elements of the pre-Tridentine rites (as inherited from Christian Antiquity or the medieval churches) can be revived *ad libitum*, namely:

(a) The three *stations* of the Palm Sunday procession.

(b) The Litany at the end of the Office of the Triduum Sacrum (*Kyrie puerorum*), both in the cathedral and parish form.

(c) The *Mandatum*, as a cycle of celebrations (footwashing, Last Sermon, stripping and washing of the altars) which could be performed separately or continuously, after the Mass, within it (the washing of the feet), or linked to it (stripping and washing of the altars).

(d) The readings of Good Friday are changed; the pre-Tridentine form of bringing in and adoring the Cross is introduced as an optional (alternative) rite.

(e) In the Paschal Vigil the *Exsultet* regains its original function (as a consecration of the taper), the Litany of the Saints is recited without interruption prior to the baptismal rite. The celebration of Easter is completed by the *Gloriosum Officium* (baptismal Vespers) in an elaborate form (in cathedrals and large churches) or simple form (in parish churches).

8. For the *use of languages* the direction of the Liturgical Constitution is mandatory. This means that the primacy of Latin must be preserved; this should be guaranteed by clear rules so that the Latin would be present not only in the books, but also in the living practice of churches. On the other hand, the vernacular can be used within specified parameters, namely:

   (a) The Office celebrated with the faithful can be prayed in the vernacular (in part or entirely); when the priests pray the Office privately, they should attain proficiency in the Latin tongue (except in the patristic readings) by the fifth year of their ordination.

   (b) The administration of the sacraments and sacramentals can be in the vernacular, but for specific actions (exorcisms, the words of the sacramental form) the Latin is advised.

   (c) In the Mass:

      (i) The readings and admonitions can be read in the vernacular, and the priest is not obliged to say them simultaneously in Latin.

      (ii) The chants of the Ordinary and Proper of the Mass *can* be sung in the vernacular by the congregation, but if so, the priest should also pray them in Latin.

      (iii) In some Low Masses or those of ferial or less festal days the Preface with the Sanctus and the Lord's Prayer with the Embolism can be said in the vernacular.

      In the classical Roman Mass the following parts always remain in Latin: (i) the three main orations (Collect, Secret, Postcommunion), (ii) the Canon, and (iii) the private prayers of the priest.

      For all the parts that remain in Latin, precise translations should be prepared and made widely available to the faithful.

9. The *orientation of the celebration* does not depend on the rite. The spiritual orientation of the celebration, however, is an important requirement: all the parts, except when the priest directly addresses the congregation, should be performed in a 'spiritual' direction towards God.

   When celebration is *versus populum*, the arrangement of the altar should make it manifest that in these parts the priest addresses not the congregation but God; the majority of the words and actions in the Mass are directed towards God. Only at moments of teaching, admonitions, the distribution of the sacraments and the imparting of blessings does the liturgy address the people directly. At these points, the priest – if he celebrates *versus orientem* – turns to the assembly.

   This fact is, of course, more clearly expressed if the priest presents the prayers of the Church to God and offers the holy sacrifice by facing the same direction as the people; that is, he celebrates the Mass before the altar *versus absidem*. Visually this corresponds better to the nature of the words and actions; furthermore, it is highly formative of the spirituality and attitude of the priest. This way it will be made more clearly perceptible not only for those standing in the nave, but also for the celebrant that he is a *priest* 'taken from among men, ordained for men in the things that appertain to God, that he may offer up gifts and sacrifices for sins' (Heb. 5.1). He stands before God, presenting sacred offerings to Him on behalf of the people.

The words and actions of the Mass make it clear that the major part of the liturgy is addressed in the first place to God: praising Him, rendering Him the sacrifice of thanksgiving, in adoration, propitiation and impetration. *'Sacrificium laudis honorificabit me'* (a sacrifice of praise shall glorify me) – 'thus says the Lord' (Psalm 49). The liturgy serves the good of men, first of all, with the graces that it imparts. In the acts of teaching, admonishing, administering the sacraments and imparting abundant blessings, the liturgy addresses the people, and thus the priest turns to them in a visible manner. Yet the liturgy also teaches people when it instructs the priest to celebrate the liturgy *before* God. This is so because this *sacrificium laudis* is at the same time the means by which God shows people the way to salvation: *'illic iter quo ostendam illi salutare Dei'* (Ps. 49.23).

BIBLIOGRAPHY

Ameit, Robert (1999), *La veillée pascale dans l'Église Latine: I Le rite romain* (Paris: Éditions du CERF).

Amerio, Romano (1997), *Stat Veritas. Séguito a Iota unum* (Milano, Napoli: Riccardo Ricciardi Editore).

—— (1999), *Iota Unum: A Study of Changes in the Catholic Church in the XXth Century* (Kansas City, MO: Sarto House).

Analecta hymnica medii aevi (= *AH*), ed. Guido Maria Dreves, Clemens Blume and Henry Marriott Mannister, 55 vols (Leipzig, 1886–1922); Register (1978), ed. Max Lütolf, 3 vols (Berne).

Antiphonale Missarum juxta ritum Sanctae Ecclesiae Mediolanensis (1935), (Rome: Desclée).

Antiphonale Missarum Sextuplex, (1935), ed. René-Jean Hesbert (Rome: Herder).

Antiphonale Monasticum . . . (1934), (Solesmis).

Antiphonarium Sacris Ordinis Praedicatorum (= AntOP) (1932), (Rome).

Athanasius, St (1939), *De incarnatione*, ed. F. L. Cross (London: SPCK).

Bailey, Terence (1983), *The Ambrosian Alleluias* (Surrey: The Plainsong and Mediaeval Music Society).

—— (1994), *Antiphon and Psalm in the Ambrosian Office* (Ottawa, Canada: The Institute of Mediaeval Music).

Baroffio, Bonifacio Giacomo and Soo Jung Kim (1995), *Biblitoeca Apotolica Vaticana Archivio S. Pietro B 79, Antfionario della Basilica di S. Pietro (Sec. XII)*, Musica Italiae Liturgia (Rome: Torre d'Orfeo), vols 1–2.

Baumstark, Anton (1927), 'Das Gesetz der Erhaltung des Alten in liturgisch hochwertiger Zeit', *Jahrbuch für Liturgiewissenschaft* 7: 1–23.

Bäumer, Suitbert (1895), *Geschichte des Breviers* (Freiburg im Breisgau: Herder).

Benedict XVI (2007), Motu Proprio of July 2007, *Summorum Pontificum*, in *Acta Apostolicae Sedis* (Vatican: Libreria Editrice Vaticana), vol. 99, pp. 777–81.

—— (2007), Apostolic Exhortation (*Caritatis Sacramentum*) *Acta Apostolicae Sedis*, vol. 99, pp. 105–80.

Benedict, St (1980), *The Rule of St. Benedict* (Collegeville, MN: Liturgical Press).

Blume, Clemens (1908), *Der Cursus S. Benedicti Nursini und die liturgischen Hymnen des 6.–9. Jahrhunderts* (Leipzig: Resiland), vols 1–2.

Bonneterre, Didier (2002), *The Liturgical Movement: Guéranger to Beauduin to Bugnini* (Kansas City, MO: Angelus Press).

Bouyer, Louis (1967), *Liturgy and Architecture* (South Bend, IN: University of Notre Dame Press).

Braga, Carlo and Annibale Bugnini (2000), *Documenta ad Instaurationem Liturgiam Spectantia (1903–1965)* (Rome: Centro Liturgico Vincenziano).

Breviarium juxta ritum S. Ordinis Praedicatorum (1930), (Rome).

BIBLIOGRAPHY

Breviarium Notatum Strigoniense (s. XIII), Musicalia Danubiana 18 (= BNS), (1998), ed. J. Szendrei (Budapest: MTA Zenetudományi Intézet).
Breviarium Premonstratense (1930), (Mecheliniae: Dessain).
Brunner, Lance W. (1999), *Early Medieval Chants from Nonantola – Part IV: Sequences* (Madison, WI: A-R Editions).
Bruylants, P., OSB (1952), *Les Oraisons du Missel Romain – Text and Histoire* (Louvain: Abbey du Mont César).
Bugnini, Annibale (1990), *The Reform of the Liturgy 1948–1975*, trans. Matthew J. O'Connell (Collegeville, MN: Liturgical Press).
Burt, David (2006), *The Anglican Use Graduale* (Mansfield, MA: Partridge Hill).
CANTUS (online database), http://bach.music.uwo.ca/cantus/.
Casel, Odo, OSB (1922), *Die Liturgie als Mysterienfeier* (Freiburg im Breisgau: Herder).
—— (1932), *Das christliche Kult-Mysterium* (Freiburg im Breisgau: Herder).
—— (1941), *Das christliche Festmysterium* (Paderborn: Bonifacius-Druckerei).
Cekada, Anthony (1991), *The Problems with the Prayers of the Modern Mass* (Rockford, IL: TAN Books).
Combe, Pierre, OSB (2003), *The Restoration of Gregorian Chant – Solesmes and the Vatican Edition*, trans. Theodore N. Marier and William Skinner (Washington, DC: The Catholic University of America Press).
Conrad, Sven, FSSP (2009), 'Die innere Logik eines Ritus als Maßstab liturgischer Entwicklung', in *Pope Benedict XVI and the Holy Liturgy* (forthcoming).
Copeland, William John (1848), *Hymns for the week and hymns for the season* (London: W. J. Cleaver).
Corpus Antiphonalium Officii, Volumes 1–4 (1965–79), ed. René-Jean Hesbert (Herder: Rome).
Corpus Antiphonalium Officii Ecclesiarum Centralis Europae (ed. CAO-ECE), ed. L. Dobszay (Budapest: Zenetudományi Intézet) 1988– 2008 (vol. I: Preliminary Report; II/A: Salzburg Temporale; III/A: Bamberg Temporale; IV/A: Aquileia Temporale; IV/A–B. Praha: Temporale–Sanctorale; V/A–B: Esztergom/Strigonium: Temporale–Sanctorale; VI/A–B: Kalocsa–Zagreb: Temporale–Sanctorale).
Corpus Christianorum Series Latina – Corpus Orationum, (1999), ed. Eugenio Moeller, Ioanne Maria Clément and Bertrandus Coppieters't Wallant (Tournhout: Brepols).
The Daily Missal and Liturgical Manual . . . (2004), (London: Baronius Press; 2nd edn 2007).
Davies, Michael (1976), *Liturgical Revolution – Volume I: Cranmer's Godly Order – The Destruction of Catholicism through Liturgical Change* (Dickinson, TX: The Angelus Press).
—— (1980), *Liturgical Revolution – Volume III: Pope Paul's New Mass* (Dickinson, TX: The Angelus Press).
—— (1991), *Mass Facing the People: A Critique* (Long Prairie, MN: Neumann Press).
—— (1992), *Liturgical Time Bombs in Vatican II: Destruction of the Faith through Changes in Catholic Worship* (Rockford, IL: TAN Books and Publishers).
—— (1997), *Sanctuary and the Second Vatican Council* (Rockford, IL: TAN Books and Publishers).
de Certeau, H., SJ, (1987), *La fable mystique* (Paris: Gallimard; 1st edn 1982).
de Lubac, Cardinal Henri, SJ (1949), *Corpus mysticum: l'Eucharistie et l'Église au moyen age* (Paris: Aubier; 1st edn 1944); English translation by C. J. G. Simmonds, R. Price, R. and C. Stephens (2006), (ed. L. P. Hemming and S. F. Parsons) as *Corpus Mysticum: The Eucharist and the Church in the Middle Ages* (London: SCM Press).
—— (1953), *Méditations sur L'Église* (Paris, Aubier); English translation by M. Mason (1956), *The Splendour of the Church* (London: Sheed & Ward).
—— (1965), *Le mystère du surnaturel*, in *Théologie 64: Études publiées sous la direction*

de la Faculté de Théologie S. J. de Lyon-Fourvière (Paris, Aubier); trans. Rosemary
Sheed (1998), *The Mystery of the Supernatural* (New York: Crossroads).

Deschusses, Jean (1982), *Le sacramentaire grégorien: Ses principales formes d'après les
plus anciens manuscrits*, I–III (Fribourg: Éditions Universitaires, 1971–82) (Spicilegium
Friburgense 16, 24, 28).

Discourse to the Roman Curia, 22 December 2005, *Acta Apostolicae Sedis*, Vatican,
vol. 98 (2006).

Divino afflatu, St Pius X, motu proprio, 1 November 1911, *Acta Apostolicæ Sedis*,
Vatican, vol. 3, pp. 633–37; 636 (English translation in Vincent Yzermans (ed.), *All
Things in Christ* (Maryland: Westminster Press), pp. 251–54.

Dobszay, László (1997), 'Offizium', *Die Musik in Geschichte und Gegenwart. Sachteil Bd.
7* (Kassel and Basel, etc.: Bärenreiter esp. pp. 593–609.

—— (2000), *Liber Ordinarius Agriensis*, Musicalia Danubiana Subsidia, vol. I (Budapest:
Zenetudományi Intézet).

—— (2001), *A római mise énekrendje* [The Order of the Chants in the Roman Mass]
(Budapest: Liszt Ferenc Zeneművészeti Egyetem).

—— (2002), 'Concerning a Chronology for Chant', in *Western Plainchant in the First
Millenium: Studies in the Medieval Liturgy and Its Music* (ed. Sean Gallagher, James
Haar, John Nádas and Timothy Striplin) (Aldershot and Burlington, VT: Ashgate),
pp. 217–29.

—— (2002), *Responsoria de Psalmista* (Budapest: Liszt Ferenc Zeneművészeti Egyetem).

—— (2003), *The Bugnini-Liturgy and the Reform of the Reform*, Musicae Sacrae
Meletemata, vol. V (Front Royal, VA: Catholic Church Music Associates).

—— (2004), 'The Liturgical Position of the Hymn in the Medieval Office', in *Der
lateinische Hymnus im Mittelalter*, edited by Andreas Haug, Christoph März and Lorenz
Welker (Kassel, Basel etc.: Bärenreiter), pp. 9–22.

—— (2007), 'A Living Gregorian Chant', *Music and Liturgy: The Journal of the Society of
Saint Gregorie*, 33.4, 24–28.

—— (2008), 'What Does the "Roman Rite" Denominate?', in *The Liturgical Subject*, ed.
James G. Leachmann, OSB (London: SCM Press), pp. 57–73.

—— (2008), 'The Responsory: Type and Modulation', *Studia Musicologica* 49, 3–33.

—— (2009), 'The Proper Chants of the Roman Rite', in *The Genius of the Roman
Liturgy*, Proceedings of the CIEL Conference, Oxford, September 2006.

—— (2009), 'Short Remarks about the Antiphons of Christmas Vespers', in *International
Musicological Society Study Group Cantus Planus, Papers Read at the Papers Read at
the 13th Meeting, Niederaltaich, Germany, 2006* (Budapest: Hungarian Academy of
Sciences Institute for Musicology).

—— (2009), 'The Perspectives of an Organic Development', in *Pope Benedict XVI and the
Holy Liturgy*.

Dreves, G. M. and C. Blume (1909), *Ein Jahrtausend Lateinischer Hymnendichtung*
(Leipzig: Resiland), 2 vols.

Duchesne, Louis (1903), *Christian Worship: Its Origin and Evolution* (London:
MacMillan, cited from the 2nd edn 1927).

Duffy, Eamon (1992), *The Stripping of the Altars: Traditional Religion in England
1400–1580* (New Haven, CT and London: Yale University Press).

*Ecclesiasticum Officium juxta ritum Sacri Ordinis Praedicatorum . . . Triduo ante Pascha
. . . (= Triduum OP)* (1949), (Rome).

Ellebrach, Mary Pierre (1966), *Remarks on the Vocabulary of the Ancient Orations in the
Missale Romanum* (Nijmegen, Utrecht: Dekker & Van de Vegt).

Elliott, Peter J. (2003), 'A Question of Ceremonial', in Kocik, pp. 257–73.

Emerson, John A. (2002), *Albi, Bibliothèque Municipale Rochegude, Manuscript 44:
A Complete Ninth-Century Gradual and Antiphoner from Southern France*, ed. Lila
Collamore (Ottawa, ON: The Institute of Mediaeval Music).

Énekes Zsolozsma az Esztergomi Breviárium alapján: Népzsolozsmák (1990), [Chanted Offices following the Esztergom Breviary: Folk Offices] (= Folk Offices) (Budapest: Szent Ágoston Liturgikus Megújulási Mozgalom – St Augustin Liturgical Renewal Movement).
Éneklő Egyház [The Singing Church] (1986), (Budapest: Szent István Társulat).
The English Gradual. II: The Proper for the Liturgical Year (= Burgess Gradual), ed. Francis Burgess (London: The Plainchant Publications Committee, n.d.).
The English Hymnal with Tunes (1933) (London: Oxford University Press and Mowbray).
Etherie Journal de Voyage (1957), ed. H. Pétré (Latin, French – in the series *Source Chrétiennes*, vol. 21) (Paris: Cerf).
Fortescue, Adrian (1912), *The Mass: A Study of the Roman Liturgy* (2005), (Fitzwilliam, NH: Loreto Publications; 4th edn).
—— (1917/1932), *The Ceremonies of the Roman Rite Described* (London: Burns, Oates and Washbourne Ltd).
Földváry Miklós István (2002), 'Istenünk tornácaiban. Az osztott templomtér jelentőségéről' [In the Courts of our God: The Importance of the Partitioned Church Space], *Magyar Egyházzene* IX (2001/02): 171–82.
—— (2003), 'A kultikus tér szerveződése a kereszténységben' [The Organization of the Cultic Space in Christianity], (2003), in Barsi Balázs and Földváry Miklós, *"Belépek Isten oltárához": Bevezetés a templom misztériumába* ['I Will Go In to the Altar of God': Introduction to the Mystery of the Church], Sümeg, Keresztény Értelmiségiek Szövetsége – Szent Ágoston Liturgikus Megújulási Mozgalom, pp. 103–69.
—— (2008), 'The Lectern in Liturgical Culture', *Sacred Music* 135.4, 14–20.
—— (2009), 'The Variants of the Roman Rite – Their Legitimacy and Revival, in *Pope Benedict XVI and the Holy Liturgy*.
Frere, Walter Howard (1930), *Studies in Early Roman Liturgy – I: The Kalendar* (London: Oxford University Press).
Gamber, Klaus (1992), *La Réforme Liturgique en Question* (Le Barroux: Sainte-Madeleine Press).
—— (2002), *The Modern Rite: Collected Essays in the Reform of The Liturgy* (Farnborough: St Michael's Abbey Press).
—— (2003), *The Reform of the Roman Liturgy: Its Problems and Background* (San Juan Capistrano, CA: Una Voce Press).
Gneuss, Helmut (2004), 'Zur Geschichte des Hymnars', in *Der lateinische Hymnus im Mittelalter. Überlieferung – Aesthetik – Ausstrahlung*, ed. Andreas Haug, Christoph März and Lorenz Welker), *Monumenta Monodica Medii Aevi*, Subsidia Volume 4 (Kassel and Basel, etc.: Bärenreiter), pp. 63–86.
Goffine, Leonard (1690) *Handpostille oder Christkatholische Unterrichtungen auf alle Sonn und Feyer-tagen des ganzen Jahrs* (Mayence/Metz).
Graduale ad usum Canonici Praemonstratensis Ordinis . . . (= GrOPraem) (1910), (Rome and Tornai: Desclée).
Graduale iuxta ritum Sacri Ordinis Praedicatorum (= GrOP) (1936), (Rome: In Conventu Sanctae Sabinae).
Graduale Pataviense, Wien 1511, (1982), Herausgegeben von Christina Väterlin, Das Erbe Deutscher Musik, Volume 87 (Kassel and Basel, etc.: Bärenreiter).
Graduale Sacrosanctae Romanae Ecclesiae de Tempore et de Sanctis . . . (= Graduale Romanum) (1979), (Desclée).
Graduale Simplex in usum minorum ecclesiarum (= Graduale Simplex) (1967), (Vatican: Libreria Editrice Vaticana).
Graduale Strigoniense (s. XV/XVI). I–II, Musicalia Danubiana 12, ed. Janka Szendrei (Budapest: MTA Zenetudományi Intézet, 1990–92).
Graduel de Klosterneuburg (= Klosterneuburg Graduale), (1974), ed. Dom Jacques Froger, Palégoraphie Musicale XIX (Berne: Herbert Lang).
Guardini, Romano (1918), *Vom Geist der Liturgie* (Freiburg am Breisgau: Herder).

—— (1922), *Von Heiligen Zeichen* (Rothenfels am Main: Deutsches Quickbornhaus).

Harrison, Brian W., OS (2003), 'The Postconciliar Eucharistic Liturgy: Planning a "Reform of the Reform"', reprinted from *Adoramus Bulletin* (November 1996–January 1997), in Kocik, pp. 151–93.

Hemming, Laurence Paul (2008), 'The Liturgical Subject – Introductory Essay', in *The Liturgical Subject: Subject, Subjectivity and the Human Person in Contemporary Liturgical Discussion and Critique*, ed. James G. Leachmann, OSB (London: SCM Press), pp. 1–16.

—— Hemming, L. P. (2008), *Worship as a Revelation* (London: Burns & Oates/ Continuum).

—— (2009), '*I Saw the New Jerusalem* – On Time in the Sacred Liturgy', in *Pope Benedict XVI and the Holy Liturgy*.

Herwegen, Ildefons, OSB (1955), *Liturgy's Inner Beauty* (Collegeville, MN: Popular Liturgical Library).

Hildebrand, Dietrich von (1943), *Liturgy and Personality* (London: Longmans, Green).

—— (1967), *Trojan Horse in the City of God: The Catholic Crisis Explained* (Manchester, NH: Sophia Institute Press, repr. 1993).

—— (1993), *The Devastated Vineyard* (Harrison, NY: Roman Catholic Books).

Hiley, David (1993), *Western Plainchant – A Handbook* (Oxford: Clarendon Press).

Hitchcock, James (1994), *The Recovery of the Sacred* (San Francisco, CA: Ignatius Press).

—— (2006), 'Liturgy and Ritual', *Adormus Bulletin* XII (December 2006–January 2007).

Hoping, Helmut (2009), 'Danksagende Anbetung. Die heilige Liturgie und die Einheit der römischen Messe', in *Pope Benedict XVI and the Holy Liturgy*.

'Institutio Generalis Missalis Romani' (= IGMR) (2002), in *Missale Romanum*, 20–86.

Jeffery, Peter (1992), 'Jerusalem and Rome (and Constantinople): The Musical Heritage of two Great Cities in the Formation of the Medieval Chant Traditions', in *International Musicological Society Study Group Cantus Planus, Papers Read at the Fourth Meeting Pécs, Hungary, 3–8 September 1990*, ed. László Dobszay, Ágnes Papp and Ferenc Sebő (Budapest: Hungarian Academy of Sciences Institute for Musicology), pp. 163–74.

Jungmann, Josef Andreas, SJ (1958), *Missarum Sollemnia. Eine Genetische Erklärung der Römischen Messe*, I–II (Freiburg: Herder).

Karp, Theodor (2005), *An Introduction to the Post-Tridentine Mass Proper I–II* (Middleton, WI: American Institute of Musicology).

Kelly, Thomas Forest (1984), 'Introducing the Gloria in Excelsis', *Journal of the American Musicological Society*, 37.3, 479–506.

—— (1989), *The Beneventan Chant* (Cambridge and New York: Cambridge University Press).

Klauser, Theodor (1969), *A Short History of the Western Liturgy – An Account and Some Reflections*, trans. John Halliburton (London, New York and Toronto: Oxford University Press).

Knauz, Nándor (1865), 'A magyar egyház részi szokásai. I: A római rítus behozatala' [The Ancient Customs of the Hungarian Church. I: The Introduction of the Roman Rite], *Magyar Sion* 3, 401–13.

Kocik, Thomas M. (2003), *The Reform of the Reform? A Liturgical Debate: Reform or Return* (San Francisco, CA: Ignatius Press).

—— (2007), 'Benedict XVI and the "Tridentine" Question', *St Austin Review* (May/June).

—— (2009), 'The Reform of the Reform in Broad Context: Re-engaging the Living Tradition', in *Pope Benedict XVI and the Holy Liturgy*.

Kyriale Simplex (1965), (Vatican: Libreria Editrice Vaticana).

Lang, Uwe Michael (2004), *Turning Towards the Lord: Orientation in Liturgical Prayer* (San Francisco, CA: Ignatius).

—— (2009), 'Once Again: Orientation in Liturgical Prayer and the Sacrificial Character of the Mass', in *Pope Benedict XVI and the Holy Liturgy*.

Le Roux, R. (1963), 'Les Répons de Psalmis pour les Matines, de l'Épiphanie à la Septuagésime', *Études Grégoriennes* VI: 39–148.

Lectionarium: Missale Romanum (1971) (Vatican: Libreria Editrice Vaticana), 3 vols.

Liber Antiphonarius pro diurnis Horis, vol. 1–2. Solesmis, 2005, 2006.

Liber Hymnarius . . . (1983), (Solesmis).

Liber Usualis Missae et Officii . . . (1954), Parisiis, Tornaci (Rome: Desclée).

Liber Vesperalis juxta ritum Sanctae Ecclesiae Mediolanensis (Rome: Desclée).

Lipphardt, Walther (1975–81), *Lateinische Osterfeiern und Osterspiele. I–VI* (Berlin and New York: Walter de Gruyter).

Liturgiam Authenticam (2001), Congregatio de Cultu Divino et Disciplina Sacramentorum de usu linguarum popularium in libris liturgiae Romanae Ecclesiae Instructio Quinta 'ad Exsecutionem Constitutionis Concilii Vaticani Secundi de Sacra Liturgia recta Ordinandam' (ad Const. art. 36), *Acta Apostolicae Sedis* 93, 685–726 (for an English translation, see *Sacred Music* 128 (Summer 2001): 4–32).

Lord, Albert B. (1964), *The Singer of Tales* (Cambridge, MA: Harvard University Press).

Lothian, James (2000), 'Novus ordo Missae: The Record after Thirty Years', *The Latin Mass – A Journal of Catholic Culture* (October), 26–31.

Lütolf, Max (ed.) (1987), *Das Graduale von Santa Cecilia in Trastvere (Cod. Bodmer 74)* (Cologny, Genève: Fondation Martin Bodmer).

Maiani, Brad (2000), 'Approaching the Communion Melodies', *Journal of the American Musicological Society* 53, 209–90.

Marmion, Columba, OSB (1924), *Christ in His Mysteries* (London: Sands).

—— (1925), *Christ the Life of the Soul* (London: Sands).

Martimort, Aimé Georges (1984), 'A propos du nombre des lectures à le messe', *Revue des sciences religieuses* 58, 42–51.

Martyrologium Romanum (2001) (Vatican: Libreria Editrice Vaticana).

McKinnon, James (1992a), 'The Roman Post-Pentecostal Communio Series', in *International Musicological Society Study Group Cantus Planus, Papers Read at the Fourth Meeting, Pécs, Hungary, 3–8 September 1990*, ed. László Dobszay, Ágnes Papp and Ferenc Sebő (Budapest: Hungarian Academy of Sciences Institute for Musicology, 1992), pp. 175–86.

—— (1992b), 'The Eighth-century Frankish-Roman Communion Cycle', *Journal of the American Musicological Society* 45, 179–227.

—— (1995a), 'Lector Chant versus Schola Chant: A Question of Historical Plausibility', in *Laborare fratres in unum: Festschrift László Dobszay zum 60. Geburtstag*, ed. Janka Szendrei and David Hiley, Bd. 7, Spolia Berolinensia (Hildesheim: Weidmann).

—— (1995b), 'Properization: The Roman Mass', in *Cantus Planus: Papers Read at the Sixth Meeting, Eger, Hungary, September 1993*, ed. László Dobszay (Budapest: Hungarian Academy of Sciences).

—— (1998), 'Vaticana Latina 5319 as a Witness to the Eighth-century Roman Proper of the Mass', in *Cantus Planus: Papers Read at their Seventh Meeting, Sopron, Hungary, September 1995*. ed. László Dobszay (Budapest: Hungarian Academy of Sciences, Institute for Musicology).

—— (2000a), *The Advent Project: The Later Seventh-Century Creation of the Roman Mass Proper* (Berkeley, LA and London: University of California Press).

—— (2000b), 'The Origins of the Western Office', in *The Divine Office in the Latin Middle Ages: Methodology and Source Studies, Regional Development, Hagiography*, ed. Margot E.Fassler and Rebecca Baltzer (Oxford and New York: Oxford University Press), pp. 63–73.

McPartlan, P. (1993), *The Eucharist Makes the Church: Henri de Lubac and John Zizioulas in Dialogue* (London: T&T Clark).

Mediator Dei (1947), Encyclical of Pope Pius XII on the Sacred Liturgy, in *Acta*

Apostolicae Sedis (Vatican, Typis Polyglottis), vol. 39; see also in A. Reid: *A Pope and a Council on the Sacred Liturgy* (2002), (Farnborough: St Michael's Abbey Press).

Messalino Festivo Ambrosiano (1956), (Milano: Paoline).

Mezey, László (1996), 'A római misekánon']The Canon of the Roman Mass], *Magyar Egyházzene* [Hungarian Church Music] III (1995/96): 277–86.

Missale Notatum Strigoniense ante 1341 in Posonio (= MNS), (1982), ed. Janka Szendrei and Richard Ríbarič, Musicalia Danubiana I (Budapest: MTA Zenetudományi Intézet).

Missale Romanum . . . auctoritate Pauli Pp. VI promulgatum . . . (2002), (Vatican: Typis Vaticanis).

Mohlberg, Leo Cunibert, OSB (1968), *Liber Sacramentorum Romanae Aeclesiae Ordinis Anni Circuli (Cod. Vat. Reg. lat. 316/Paris Bibl. Nat. 78193, 41/56)(Sacramentarium Gelasianum)*, Rerum Ecclesiasticum Documenta, Seriess Maior, Fontes IV, in *Verbindung mit Leo Eizenhöfer OSB und Petrus Siffrin OSB* (Rome: Herder).

Mohrmann, Christine (1959), *Liturgical Latin: Its Origins and Character* (London: Burns & Oates).

—— (1961–77), *Études sur le latin des chrétiens I–IV* (Rome) (Storia e Letteratura – Raccolta di Studi e Testi 65, 87, 103, 143).

Mole, John W., OMI (2001), 'Problema Idem Perduret: A Look at the Roman Rite and Its Future', *The Latin Mass – A Journal of Catholic Culture* (Spring), 17–22.

Monumenta Monodica Medii Aevi, Volume 2, *Die Gesänge des altrömishcen Graduale Vat. lat. 5319*, (1970), ed. Bruno Stäblein (Kassel and Basel, etc.: Bärenreiter).

Monumenta Monodica Medii Aevi, Volume 5/1–2–3, *Antiphonen*, (1999), ed. László Dobszay and Janka Szendrei (Kassel and Basel, etc.: Bärenreiter).

Monumenta Monodica Medii Aevi, Volume 7, *Alleluia-Melodien I. bis 1100*, (1968), Karlheinz Schlager (Kassel and Basel, etc.: Bärenreiter).

Monumenta Monodica Medii Aevi, volume 8, *Alleluia-Melodien II. ab 1100*, (1987), Karlheinz Schlager (Kassel and Basel, etc.: Bärenreiter).

Mysterii Paschalis, 'Litterae Apostolicae Motu Proprio Datae Normae Universales de Anno Liturgico . . .' (2002), *Missale Romanum*, 89–103.

Nichols, Aidan (1996), *Looking at the Liturgy: A Critical View of Its Contemporary Form* (San Francisco, CA: Ignatius Press).

—— (2000), 'A Tale of Two Documents: Sacrosanctum Concilium and Mediator Dei', *Antiphon – A Journal for Liturgical Renewal*, V.1, 23–31.

—— (2003), 'Salutary Dissatisfaction: An English view of Reforming the Reform', in Kocik (2003), pp. 195–210.

Nowacki, Edward Charles (1980), *Studies on the Office Antiphons of the Old Roman Manuscripts* (Brandeis University PhD).

—— (1990), 'The Performance of Office Antiphons in Twelfth-century Rome', in *Cantus Planus, Papers read at the Third Meeting Tihany, Hungary, 1924 September 1988* (Budapest,: Institute for Musicology), pp. 79–91.

Offertoriale Triplex cum Verisculis (Solesmis, 1985) (the new edition, with added neumes, of Karl Ott's *Offertoriale* (1935), (Paris, Tournai and Rome: Desclée).

Offertóriumok Könyve [The Book of Offertories] (2005), Gödöllő (A Premontrei Rend Gödöllői Kanóniája és a Szent Ágoston Liturgikus Megújulási Mozgalom).

Ordo Cantus Missae (1972), Editio Typica (Typis Polyglottis Vaticanis).

Ordo Romanus I, (1931–61) published in Andrieu, Michel: *Les Ordines Romani du haut moyen âge*, Spicilegium sacrum Lovaniense, 11, 23–4, 28–9 (Louvain).

Ottaviani, A. and A. Bacci (1992), *A Short Critical Study of the New Order of Mass* (Rockford, IL: TAN Books and Publishers).

Overath, Johannes (1983), 'The Liturgical and Musical Innovations of the Second Vatican Council', in Skeris, pp. 169–83.

Oxford Bodleian Library Ms. Lat. liturg. b. 5 (= York Gradual) (1995), ed. David Hiley (Ottawa, Canada: The Institute of Mediaeval Music).

Paléographie Musicale XIV, *Le Codex 10 673 de la Bibliothèque Vaticane Fonds Latin (XIᵉ siècle) Graduale Bénéventain* (1931) (Tournai: Desclée).

Paléographie Musicale, Deuxième Série I, *Antiphonaire de Hartker, Manuscrits de Saint-Gall* (1992), 390–391 (Solesmes).

Palmer, G. H. (1926), *The Diurnal Noted from the Salisbury Use, Translated into English and Adapted to the Original Musick-Note* (Wantage: St Mary's Press).

Parsch, Pius (1935), *Meßerklärung im Geiste der liturgischen Erneuerung* (Klosterneuburg: Volksliturgisches Apostolat).

—— (1953), *The Church's Year of Grace* (Collegeville, MN: Liturgical Press, 1953).

Parsons, John P. (2003), 'A Reform of the Reform?', reprinted from the *Catholic World Report* in Kocik, pp. 211–56.

Pieper, Josef (1991), *In Search of the Sacred: Contributions to an Answer* (San Francisco, CA: Ignatius Press).

Pius X, Pope St (1904), Motu Proprio of 22 November 1903, *Tra le Sollecitudini*, in *Acta Sanctæ Sedis* vol. 36, Vatican.

Pope Benedict XVI and the Holy Liturgy (Proceedings of the International Conference, Budapest, 21–24 August 2008, forthcoming).

Pristas, Lauren (2002), 'Missale Romanum 1962 and 1970: A Comparative Study of Two Collects', *Antiphon* 7.3 (2002), 29–33.

—— (2003a), 'The Orations of the Vatican II Missal: Policies for Revision', *Communio: An International Catholic Review*, 30.4 (Winter), 621–53.

—— (2003b), 'Theological Principles that Guided the Redaction of the Roman Missal (1970)', *The Thomist* 67 (April 2003): 157–95.

—— (2005), 'The Collects at Sunday Mass: An Examination of the Revisions of Vatican II', *Nova et Vetera*, 3:1 (Winter), 5–38.

—— (2007), 'Post Vatican II Revision of the Lenten Collects', in *Ever Directed to the Lord*, ed. Uwe Michael Lang (London: T&T Clark), pp. 62–89.

—— (2009), 'Septuagesima and the Post-Vatican II Reform of the Sacred Liturgy', in *Pope Benedict XVI and the Holy Liturgy*.

Processionale ad Usum Sarum 1502 (= Sarum Processional), (1980), compiled by Richard Pyson (Clifden, Ireland: Boethius Press).

Processionale ad usum . . . ordinis Praemonstratensis (= Processionale OPraem) (1932), (Parisiis etc.).

Quam singulari (1910), Decree of Pope Pius X, in *Acta Apostolicae Sedis* (Rome: Vatican).

Rajeczky, Benjamin (1982), *Melodiarium Hungariae Medii Aevi: I. Hymni et Sequentiae*; 1st edn 1956; 2nd edn (with a supplementum) (Budapest: Zeneműkiadó).

Ratzinger, Cardinal Joseph (1983), 'Theological Problems of Church Music', in Skeris, pp. 214–22.

—— (1992), *Preface* to K. Gamber, *La Réforme Liturgique en question* (Le Barroux: St Madeleine Press).

—— (1994), 'In der Spannung zwischen Regensburger Tradition und nachkonziliarer Reform', *Musica sacra* 114.5, 379–89 (reprint: 1995, *Ein neues Lied für den Herrn*) (Freiburg im Breisgau: Herder).

—— (1998), *Milestones; Memoirs 1927–77*, (San Francisco, CA: Ignatius Press).

—— (2000), *The Spirit of the Liturgy*, trans John Saward (San Francisco, CA: Ignatius Press).

—— (2005), Preface to Reid.

Redemptionis Sacramentum (2004), Instruction of the Congregation for Divine Worship and the Discipline of the Sacraments, Instruction Redemptionis Sacramentum of 25 March), in *Acta Apostolicae Sedis* (Vatican: Libreria Editrice Vaticana), vol. 96, pp. 555–7.

Reid, Alcuin (2005), *The Organic Development of the Liturgy* (San Francisco, CA: Ignatius Press).

275

—— (2006), 'Looking Again at the Liturgical Reform: Some General and Monastic Considerations' (English Benedictine Congregation Liturgy Commission Symposium on 'Liturgical Renewal: A Reform of the Reform?', Downside Abbey, Bath); published at: www.benedictines.org.uk/ theology/2006/reid.pdf.

—— (2009), 'The Liturgical Reform of Pope Benedict XVI', in *Pope Benedict XVI and the Holy Liturgy*.

Sacramentum Caritatis (2007), Post-Synodal Apostolic exhortation of Pope Benedict XVI of 22 February 2007, in *Acta Apostolicae Sedis* (Vatican: Libreria Editrice Vaticana), vol. 99, pp. 105–80.

Sacrosanctum Œcumenicum Concilium Vaticanum II: Constitutiones; Decreta; Declarationes (1966) (Vatican: Libreria Editrice Vaticana); translated by Norman Tanner, in Decrees of the Ecumenical Councils, 2 vols (London: Sheed & Ward, 1990), vol. 2.

Sandon, Nicholas (1984), *The Use of Salisbury – 1: The Ordinary of the Mass; 3: The Holy Week* (North Harton: Antico Edition).

Sacra Tridentina Synodus (1905), decree of Pope Pius X, in *Acta Apostolicae Sedis* (Rome: Vatican).

Sacrosanctum Concilium (1963), Constitution on the Sacred Liturgy Solemnly Promulgated by His Holiness Pope Paul VI on 4 December 1963, (2004), in *Acta Apostolicae Sedis* (Vatican: Libreria Editrice Vaticana), vol. 56, pp. 97–138.

Schaal, Robert, 'Kantorei', in *Die Musik in Geschichte und Gegenwart*. (Herausgegeben von Friedrich Blume), Volume 7 (Kassel and Bassel, etc.: Bärenreiter); esp. pp. 635–47.

Schmitz, R. Michael (2009), 'Detail and Ritual: Human Communication with the Divine', in *Pope Benedict XVI and the Holy Liturgy*.

Schott, Anselm, OSB (1962/2006), *Das vollständige Römische Meßbuch* . . . (Freiburg im Breisgau: Herder, 1962; Nachdruck: 2006).

Skeris, Robert A. (1983), *Crux et Cithara: Selected Essays on Liturgy and Sacred Music* . . . (Altötting: Alfred Coppenraht).

—— (1994), 'Ideology and Liturgy', *Faith and Reason* (Spring), 5–12.

—— (2009), 'On the Theology of Worship and of its Music: From Joseph Ratzinger to John Paul II to Benedict XVI', in *Pope Benedict XVI and the Holy Liturgy*.

Stefanovic, Dimitrije (1992), 'The Phenomenon of Oral Tradition in Transmission of Orthodox Liturgical Chant', in *International Musicological Society Study Group Cantus Planus PLANUS, Papers Read at the Fourth Meeting Pécs, Hungary, 3–8 September 1990*, ed. Dobszay, Ágnes Papp and Ferenc Sebő (Budapest: Hungarian Academy of Sciences Institute for Musicology), pp. 303–10.

Stickler, Cardinal Alfons (1999), 'Recollections of a Vatican II Peritus', *The Latin Mass – A Journal of Catholic Culture* (Winter).

Szendrei, Janka (1999), *The Istanbul Antiphonal about 1306*, Musicalia Danubiana vol. 18 (Budapest: Akadémiai Kiadó).

—— (2000), *A himnusz* (The Hymn) (Budapest: Liszt Ferenc Zeneművészeti Egyetem).

Taft, Robert F., SJ (1986), *The Liturgy of the Hours in East and West: The Origins of the Divine Office and Its Meaning for Today* (Collegeville, MN: St John's Abbey).

Tanner, N., SJ (1990), *Decrees of the Ecumenical Councils* (London: Sheed & Ward) 2 vols.

Torevell, David (2004), *Losing the Sacred: Ritual, Modernity and Liturgical Reform* (London and New York: T&T Clark; 2nd edn).

Tra le solicitudini, (1903), Motu Proprio of 22 November, in *Acta Sanctæ Sedis*, vol. 36, pp. 329–39.

Treitler, Leo (1985), 'Oral and Literate Style in the Regional Transmission of Tropes', *Studia Musicologica* XXVII, 171–83.

Vatican Council II (1963), Dogmatic Constitution on the Sacred Liturgy *Sacrosanctum Concilium*.

BIBLIOGRAPHY

Wagner, Peter (1926), 'Germanisches und Romanisches im frühmittelalterlichen Kirchengesang', in *Bericht über den I. musikwissenschaftlichen Kongreß der deutschen Musikgesellschaft in Leipzig vom 4. bis 8. Juni 1925* (Leipzig).

—— (1930–32), *Das Graduale der St. Thomaskirche zu Leipzig (14. Jahrhunderts)* Publikationen älterer Musik, 5–6.

Wathen, James F., SJ (1971), *The Great Sacrilege: A Critical Essay on the* Novus Ordo Missae *of Pope Paul VI with Particular Reference to its Moral Impact and Ramifications* (Rockford, IL: TAN Books and Publishers).

Wilkinson, John (trans. and ed.), *Egeria's Travels to the Holy Land* (Warminster: Ariel).

Wolter, Maurus, OSB (1891–1907), *Psallite Sapienter, 'Psalliret weise!'. Erklärung der Psalmen im Geiste des betrachtenden Gebets und der Liturgie*, vols 1–4 (Freiburg im Breisgau: Herder).

CPSIA information can be obtained
at www.ICGtesting.com
Printed in the USA
LVHW08s2134300818
588668LV00006B/96/P

9 780567 033864